Alexander Walker was the revered film critic of the London *Evening Standard* from 1960 until his death in 2003. He was born in Northern Ireland, educated there; at the Council of Europe's College d'Europe, Bruges; and at the University of Michigan, Ann Arbor, where he did postgraduate studies and lectured in government. He was three times named Critic of the Year in the annual British Press Awards (1970, 1974, 1998). He wrote and presented many radio and television pro grammes on cinema and was the author of twenty-two books on various aspects of Anglo-American and European cinema. Walker was a member of the jury at many international film festivals, including those held in Berlin (1967), Cannes (1974) and Chicago (1995). He was appointed a Chevalier de l'Ordre des Arts et des Lettres in 1981. He died in 2003.

By Alexander Walker

Icons in the Fire: The Rise and Fall of Practically Everyone in the
British Film Industry 1984–2000
The Celluloid Sacrifice: Aspects of Sex in the Movies
Stardom: The Hollywood Phenomenon
Stanley Kubrick Directs
Hollywood, England: The British Film Industry in the Sixties
Rudolph Valentino
Double Takes: Notes and Afterthoughts on the Movies 1956–76
Superstars
The Shattered Silents: How the Talkies Came to Stay
Peter Sellers: The Authorised Biography
Joan Crawford
Dietrich
No Bells on Sunday: Journals of Rachel Roberts (*edited*)
National Heroes: British Cinema in the Seventies and Eighties
Bette Davis
Robert Benayoun, Woody Allen: Beyond Words (*translated*)
Vivien: The Life of Vivien Leigh
It's Only a Movie, Ingrid: Encounters on and off screen
Elizabeth: The Life of Elizabeth Taylor
Zinnemann: An Autobiography (*jointly*)
Fatal Charm: The Life of Rex Harrison
Audrey: Her Real Story
Stanley Kubrick, Director

HOLLYWOOD, ENGLAND

The British Film Industry in the Sixties

Alexander Walker

To be an Englishman in the
film industry is to know
what it's like to be
colonised.
TONY GARNETT

ORION

An Orion paperback

First published in Great Britain in 1974
by Michael Joseph Ltd
This paperback edition published in 2005
by Orion Books Ltd,
Orion House, 5 Upper St Martin's Lane,
London WC2H 9EA

1 3 5 7 9 10 8 6 4 2

A CIP catalogue record for this book is available
from the British Library.

ISBN 0 75285 706 1

Printed and bound in Great Britain by
Clays Ltd, St Ives plc

www.orionbooks.co.uk

For 'G.W.'

Contents

Illustrations

Oliver Reed and Alan Bates in *Women in Love*
Mick Jagger, Anita Pallenberg and Michele Breton in
    Performance
Malcolm McDowell and Christine Noonan in *If . . .*

Acknowledgements

The author wishes to acknowledge his indebtedness to the writers and publishers of the following works quoted in the text:

The American Cinema, by Andrew Sarris (Dutton Paperback, New York, 1969)

Anatomy of Britain Today, by Anthony Sampson (Hodder and Stoughton, London, 1965; Harper & Row, 1965)

Anger and After, by John Russell Taylor (Methuen, London, 1962; Hill & Wang, New York, 1963)

Antonioni, by Ian Cameron and Robin Wood (Studio Vista, London, 1968)

The Beatles, by Hunter Davies (Heinemann, London, 1968; McGraw Hill, New York, 1968)

The Cinema of Joseph Losey, by James Leahy (Zwemmer, London; Barnes, New Jersey, 1967)

A Competitive Cinema, by Terence Kelly, with Graham Norton and George Perry (Institute of Economic Affairs, London, 1966)

Confessions of a Cultist: On the Cinema, 1955–69, by Andrew Sarris (Simon & Schuster, New York, 1971)

The Contemporary Cinema, by Penelope Houston (Pelican, London, 1963)

David Bailey's Box of Pin-Ups, with text by Francis Wyndham (Weidenfeld & Nicolson, London, 1965)

The Film Director as Superstar, by Joseph Gelmis (Secker and Warburg, London, 1971; Doubleday, New York, 1970)

Film World, by Ivor Montagu (Pelican, London, 1964)

Folk Devils and Moral Panics, by Stanley Cohen (MacGibbon and Kee, London, 1972)

I Lost It at the Movies, by Pauline Kael (Cape, London, 1966; Little, Brown, Boston, 1965)

The James Bond Dossier, by Kingsley Amis (Cape, London, 1965)

The Life and Times of Private Eye, edited by Richard Ingrams (Allen Lane, London, 1971)

ACKNOWLEDGEMENTS

The Life of Ian Fleming, by John Pearson (Cape, London, 1966; McGraw Hill, New York, 1967)

Lindsay Anderson, by Elizabeth Sussex (Studio Vista, London, 1969)

Losey on Losey, by Tom Milne (Secker & Warburg–British Film Institute, London, 1967; Doubleday, New York, 1967)

The Making of a Counter Culture, by Theodore Roszak (Faber, London, 1970; Doubleday, New York, 1969)

The Making of Feature Films: A Guide, by Ivan Butler (Pelican, London, 1971)

Michael Balcon Presents . . . A Lifetime of Films (Hutchinson, London, 1969)

The Neophiliacs, by Christopher Booker (Collins, London, 1969; Gambit, Boston, 1970)

The Pendulum Years, by Bernard Levin (Cape, London, 1970; Atheneum, New York, 1971)

Play Power, by Richard Neville (US edition) *Run it down the Flagpole* (Cape, London, 1970; Random House, New York, 1971)

Revolt into Style, by George Melly (Allen Lane, London, 1970; Doubleday, New York, 1970)

Television: The Ephemeral Art, by T. C. Worsley (Alan Ross, London, 1970)

Today There Are No Gentlemen, by Nik Cohn (Weidenfeld and Nicolson, London, 1971)

The Uses of Literacy, by Richard Hoggart (Chatto & Windus, London, 1957; Oxford University Press, New York, 1957)

Grateful acknowledgement is made of quotations from articles, interviews and reviews in the following publications: *Evening Standard, Daily Mail, The Times, The Financial Times, The Daily Telegraph, Morning Star, The Guardian, Evening News, Daily Express, Daily Mirror, The Observer, The Sunday Times, The Sunday Telegraph, Weekend Telegraph, The Sunday Times Magazine, The Observer Magazine, The Spectator, New Society, New Statesman, Peace News, Universities and Left Review, Isis, Harper's Queen, Sight and Sound, Movie, Monthly Film Bulletin, Films and Filming, In Focus, Films, Kinematography Weekly, Today's Cinema* (now *Cinema–TV Today*),

ACKNOWLEDGEMENTS

Screen, The New York Times, The New Yorker, The New York Magazine, Saturday Review, Time, Newsweek, Rolling Stone, Variety. Her Majesty's Stationery Office is thanked for permission to quote from the Monopolies Commission's Report on the Supply of Films for Exhibition in Cinemas and from the National Film Finance Corporation's Annual Reports and Statements of Accounts. Acknowledgement is made of quotations from the Thames Television series *Moviemen,* directed by David Wickes, and from radio interviews produced by Elizabeth Smith and Charles Lefeaux, as well as a television programme in the series *Escape to Fulfilment,* directed by David Gerrard, all of which were transmitted by the British Broadcasting Corporation.

The stills and other material used for illustrations are the copyright of the following companies or individuals: Anglo-E.M.I., British Lion, Elstree Distributors, *Evening Standard,* Metro-Goldwyn-Mayer, Paramount, Romulus, Thames Television, Tim Graham, 20th Century-Fox, United Artists, Universal, Warner, Woodfall. For help and advice in obtaining the photographs and other material for the book, thanks are due to Janet Bedwell, Charles Berman, Alistair Clark, Derek Coyte, John Fairbairn, Gerry Lewis, Edward S. Patman, Leslie Pound, Tony Richardson, John Trevelyan, John Troke, Jack Worrow.

In addition to those named in the Preface and credited elsewhere for the interviews they granted him, the author wishes to express his gratitude to the following people for the personal or professional assistance they gave him in his research: Brenda Davies and Staff of the British Film Institute Reference Library; the Staff of the National Film Archive Stills Library; the Chief Librarian and Staff of the British Museum Newspaper and Periodical Library.

And for the patience they showed, thanks is too small an acknowledgment to Sally Baker, Raleigh Trevelyan, Caroline Dawnay and Nicholas Thompson.

Preface

All that I would claim for this book – not too immodestly, I hope – is that there has been none quite like it before. Had there been, I should have had it down off the shelf to find out how it was done. For it is an attempt to illustrate the diversity of talents and motives, economic changes, historical accidents and occasional artistic achievements making up what was called the British film industry during a brief, turbulent part of its existence the sixties.

The era has left an indelible mark on many of us who experienced it. Now we can look back almost incredulously at the vast variety of events it comprised. Whether we played a part in it, or were mere spectators, many of our present-day reactions and attitudes have been formed by the period between 1959 and 1970; and the cinema that these years produced recalls the constellation of influences under which we all grew up, or grew older. This is why any book about the film industry in the sixties has also to be about the society of the time – at least in part – and show us how we became what we are. Other writers like Bernard Levin and Christopher Booker have already chronicled the social changes more comprehensively than I can and I am indebted to them for the ground they have broken. I am particularly indebted to Levin for his sense of ironic comprehensiveness which encouraged me to tackle a smaller part of human activity – the one which encapsulates, and sometimes encourages, change in the films it produces. And I am grateful to Booker for providing a *schema* that serves to show how the bizarre transformation of Britain during the sixties was accompanied and often anticipated by the movies of the era. Booker saw the sixties as a decade of trauma, in which a nation's collective energies found their release in an increasingly feverish 'vitality fantasy.' Each new trend or phenomenon that emerged – affluence, youth, satire, permissiveness – was keyed to a higher and higher pitch of sensation. The outcome, as he saw it, could only be an 'explosion into reality' which left us to begin the present decade in an aftermath of exhaustion and apprehension. Booker's view is vulnerable to the criticism that anyone risks who tries to find a pattern in the social lava, particularly before it has cooled; but his sense of a 'vitality fantasy' strikes me as a truthful and useful one to apply to the cinema, one of the chief agents of fantasy contributing to the social revolution in Britain during this past decade.

But my book has another theme that can hardly be regarded as secondary, so intrinsically is it linked with the British film industry. The very word 'British' indicates it. For to talk of the 'British' cinema in these years is to ignore the reality of what underpinned the industry – namely, American finance or the dollar economy of what, for convenience sake, we may call 'Hollywood.'

At one time in the 1960s the Americans were contributing nearly 90 per cent of the finance for the production of films in Britain; and it is no accident that they were doing this at the very same time as this country was undergoing a period of unprecedented change. The links between the two nations form a continuing part of my enquiry into how American power operated on British talent. Why was it that a national film industry, whose previous successes in penetrating the world market had been few and sporadic, should suddenly have become in these years one of the most internationally viable? Why was it a source of fascination and profit to the very country, the United States, which had for so long rebuffed the alien film-makers' attempts to gain a share in its domestic market? What did the social revolution in Britain, and the forms it took on the screen, owe to the massive American presence in our film industry?

And why did our own native efforts, apart from an unprecedented proliferation of talent, go so unsupported and unrewarded that, when the Americans withdrew at the end of the decade, we were left with practically no resources to fall back on? This book tries to suggest some of the answers.

I also want to record something of the sheer profusion of talent, irrespective of nationality, which erupted in the sixties. Most books about films dwell on their directors; by now the notion of the film director as superstar, in Joseph Gelmis's phrase, isn't easily gainsaid. I have not tried to do so: I believe the director deserves the chief acclaim. But some recent writing has been over-lavish in attributing all aspects of a film to its director, simply because the 'auteur theory' gives a convenient roundness to a product that must be far from a single man's creation, if a film is considered as an industrial process. The best directors are the ones who control the process and at the same time manage to create their own aesthetic out of the product. But as I have said elsewhere in this book – and it bears repeating – the film industry is not really a creative one: it is an imitative one in which only a few creative people are tolerated at any one time. Many of these 'creative people' are dealt with here; and not all of them are film directors. They are photographers, writers, designers, stars; and because it is the 'industry' I am considering, not just the 'cinema,' some of them are producers. The tendency to ignore the role of producers or production chiefs has to be resisted if films are to make sense as an industry that can sometimes create art.

I must admit that it is hard to see 'sense' in an organization like the film industry. The absurdities built into it may be equally revealing, however; and I hope my account of how the most significant film trends came into being will suggest the alarming incidence of sheer accident, to say nothing of short-sightedness and occasional wilful stupidity, that fought against their appearance. I have tried to let these events assert themselves – and not to impose too deliberate a pattern on them. But as such patterns are part of the politics of film-making, they are inevitably highly subjective; they tell one as much about the nature of the people who make the film as about the films themselves. This is another reason why I have tried, wherever it is possible and appropriate, to present the industrial process in its human shape – or shapes, for few other industries can surely yield such a variety of humanity in highly estimable or distinctly dubious forms.

I have used a roughly chronological structure, since events in the cinema often attract and feed on each other. One needs to sense the sequence of cannibalism. And I have been generous, rather than sparing, in the matter of dates: nothing is more frustrating for a reader than to chance on phrases like 'in the same

year,' or 'a few months later,' or even 'the next year,' which send
one searching back and forth for a handy day, month or year by
which to get one's temporal bearings. I hope I have mostly
avoided this. (All important films, at their first mention, are
followed by their year of exhibition; those dealt with at any
length are accompanied by the date of their London première.)
But I have not held rigidly to chronological sequence: there are
times when one needs to anticipate coming events. In general,
each chapter begins a little before the previous one ends and
concludes a little after it in time. An industry chronology is
included as an appendix.

In dealing with an industry where much information is
necessarily restricted, and a large amount of it personal, one has
to go warily. I have accepted the facts and figures quoted when
I have good reason to believe they come from reputable sources;
and where 'facts' differ, I have presented their differing interpretations. Not everyone sees the same road-accident, but there is no
need to assume from the various accounts that anyone is lying.

Converting sterling into dollars, and vice versa, wherever a
figure is mentioned would make for an unattractive text; so I have
left the figures in the currency that the speakers found appropriate. (For those who want to do their own conversion, the
pound sterling stood at $2.80 from 1950 until 1967, when it was
devalued to $2.40. In 1950 the equivalent sterling purchasing
power of $100 was £68; in 1967 it was £42.)

Almost every important contributor to the film industry quoted
at any length in this book was specially interviewed for it. I have
also referred to a few interviews I conducted for television or
radio programmes; and I have drawn on an acquaintanceship with
other figures in industry, not directly quoted, which has spanned
nearly twenty years. To thank all of them would be impossible
here; I hope the footnotes to their first 'entrances' into the
narrative will signify my gratitude to them for their time and
frankness. But without two of them it would have been difficult
to write several sections of the book; and I express my warmest
thanks to George H. Ornstein, production chief in Britain for
United Artists during a vital part of the decade, and to Francis

Wyndham, the critic and journalist.

Many of the events related occurred during my tenure as film critic of the London *Evening Standard*. For giving me the opportunity as well as the complete freedom to observe and comment on them over the decade I must thank Sir Max Aitken, Chairman of Beaverbrook Newspapers, and Charles Wintour, Editor of the *Evening Standard* and a man of measureless candour and encouragement.

Davos, 1971 London, 1973

Part One
LOOK AT LIFE

. . . now you are living in a
new world. Turn the page, if
you want proof that you are
living in a . . . BOOM.
Queen magazine, 1959

Chapter One: Package your own Revolution

Your demands are impossible: but how can they be less? To make a film is to create a world.

Lindsay Anderson

Lindsay Anderson helped to begin the revolution, if anyone did. He always had the makings of a good guerrilla. He could travel light, go hungry, live frugally, above all shed blood with no regret if it served the cause. The cause, one should note, not the leader. In any band of dissidents, Anderson would be the one to retain his independence, his inner freedom; so that after the revolution had succeeded and the presidential palace had a new occupant, Anderson would be the one whom the newly installed ruler would be wary of, lest he failed to meet the strict standards of his ex-lieutenant.

I first met Anderson, appropriately enough, after Bunuel's severe and humanist study of pre-revolutionary loyalties, *Cela s'appelle l'aurore*, had been screened for the Press in Cannes, in 1956; and this compact, wiry-haired terrier of a man in a red shirt – his *lucky* shirt, it was, and it accompanied him all through his career till it finally appeared along with him in his film, *O Lucky Man!* nearly twenty years later – accosted me while we were still blinking in the sunshine of the rue Alexandre III and barked, 'Well, did you like it?' It was not just a query, but a challenge to declare where one stood: first-hand evidence of the 'Stand up, stand up, for Jesus' side of Anderson's temperament that makes friends and acquaintances brace themselves for constant acts of witness. Yes, I replied, I had liked the film. 'I should think so!' he snorted.

One recognized in this the tone of a schoolmaster who acknowledges his agreement with a pupil in some classroom catechism as if he were administering a rebuke – as if one *could* be so stupid as to return any other kind of answer!

Impatience with the stupid or those who were out of sympathy with him – in his outlook the two categories often overlapped – accounts for much of Anderson's prickly self-reliance. To take offence quickly seems to him the best means of self-defence. But what probably constitutes the driving spring of his creative nature is his need to interact socially without sacrificing his individuality. By its nature, the British film industry – *any* film industry, for that matter – has never made fulfilment easy for men of this stamp: and indeed the probability is that Lindsay Anderson would not be happy if the medium he worked in were more conciliatory. He thrives on battle. He provokes discomfort. His stoicism has had an increasingly self-destructive feeling; his sense of fraternity, a tendency to anarchy. It is a commonplace of an Anglo-Saxon upbringing – no less true because of it – that a nature like his is shaped by a public-school education. Those whose ways are not set for life in conformity with public-school hierarchies, habits, taboos and restrictions conversely find that the grinding experience sharpens the cutting edge of their personalities. Such things are not sent to try them so much as harden them. In fact an English public-school education is a very good training for any indignities the film industry can inflict; it fosters guile, deviousness, a low cunning that can divert anger or avoid disaster in crises where rational resistance would be useless. On a few, of course, it confers something infinitely more dangerous than an education. Namely, a vision. Anderson is one of them.

If he wears the stigmata of his upbringing inwardly, he has learned to buckle the armour forged by it on his outside and to keep his vision of a New Jerusalem before him. No accident that when he was sent an original screen treatment in 1966, it was its title *Crusaders* that instantly gained his sympathy: but this is anticipating things.

Anderson's vision is social, not political: or, at least, not *party* political. It would be easy to call him a humanist, yet not quite correct. He is, if anything, a scourge by nature. A puritan. He has a Roundhead's love for his fellow men, but the purge is also a necessary part of his philanthropy. An American might categorize him quickly enough as being in the liberal intellectual middle-class slot. What an American might miss, paradoxically enough, is just that sense of ethnic self-reliance which is nearer the historical experience of the United States. Anderson's stock is Scottish and his lack of indebtedness to anything English was fortified by his being born in India. He thus escaped the constrictions of English class and caste, while being able to observe both at work in the society he lives and works in: both, in his view, stiffening that society's resistance to change, to his own values and vision. Work plays a large part in this: work in the sense of contributive labour. 'These are people who work,' a critic said about one of his films, 'not working-class people.' A perceptive comment. For Anderson's Scottish sense of the classless community enabled him to separate 'work,' which everyone did, from 'class' which no one presumed to possess. It is not just manual labour, but the ideal of service. Though one of the best of his non-feature films, *Every Day except Christmas* (1957), about the Covent Garden flower, fruit and vegetable market, expresses this concern for work in its very title – for what goes on every day except Christmas but work? – he nevertheless expressed a vital shade more than this in a programme note: 'I was to make people – ordinary people, not just Top People[1] – feel their dignity and importance, so that they can act from these principles. Only on such principles can confident and healthy action be based.'

Significantly, perhaps, Anderson's very first film, a 33-minute documentary called *Meet the Pioneers* (1948), was made in and about a workplace, a north of England factory manufacturing conveyor belts, one of which became the first 'dolly' he set his camera on. The 'dignity and importance' of the work people, reinforced by the family nature of the firm, took pride of place over the product. In this and other sponsored industrial shorts which he made in the late 1940s and early 1950s, his idealism reached out ever more confidently to connect with ordinary people, usually at work in a community that might be as compact as a factory floor or as widespread as a newspaper's circulation area. In *Thursday's Children* (co-directed with Guy Brenton, 1953), the community was the Royal School for the Deaf, but the theme was the same. The children's breakthrough into pathetically articulated speech brings to each a sense of individual identity at

[1] A tilt at *The Times* newspaper, then advertising itself as taken by 'Top People.'

the very moment, in the very same breath, as they discover the excitement of communicating among themselves. Anderson might feel 'connecting' is a better word than 'communicating.' It implies a mutual dependence. 'Only connect,' the epigraph E. M. Forster put on his best novel, also became Anderson's article of faith. It was the title he gave to a contribution in *Sight and Sound* (April–June 1954) in praise of the film-maker he himself then most resembled, Humphrey Jennings, director of those poetic documentaries of the war years, *Diary for Timothy* and *Fires were Started*. The 'continuous sensitivity of its human regard,' which Anderson perceived in Jennings's work, was to be his own uncompromising goal, though in his case it went with a tougher will, a less vulnerable sensitivity, than Jennings's. Anderson never needed the 'hot blast of war' to warm *him* to passion: he was born near boiling point.

'Improvisation,' in the sense of creating the opportunities to do what one wants, is a virtue found in most revolutionaries. And 'improvise' was what Anderson and his associates began to do in 1955: they started off with the desire, then invented the means; and then with the shrewdness of publicists, which some of them were soon to sense they possessed in no small measure, they allowed others to make the discovery that what they had begun was 'a movement.' The name they decided to give it was 'Free Cinema.'

NO THEORY PLEASE — WE'RE BRITISH

' "Free Cinema" was nothing more than a label of convenience,' Lindsay Anderson recalled in 1971, looking back fifteen years later to the period from which the British cinema's creative rebirth really dates.[1] 'It was never planned as anything other than a way of showing our work. It was pragmatic and opportunist.' Anderson in 1955 had been helping a young Italian, Lorenza Mazzetti, edit a film she had shot after finishing her studies at the Slade School of Art. *Together* (1956) was about a pair of deaf-

[1] Lindsay Anderson interviewed by the author, 25 February, 1971. Unless stated otherwise, all subsequent quotes from Anderson come from the same source.

mutes living in London's East End and the tensions their afflictions set up between themselves and the uncomprehending community. It was unlike anything else then to be seen on the commercial screen: the money to make it had come from the British Film Institute's Experimental Film Fund, which had also doled out a little money to allow two other newcomers, Tony Richardson and Karel Reisz, to set up their first film, *Momma don't Allow* (1956), a study of jazz enthusiasts in a metropolitan dance-hall. The fund provided the frugal means, but not the outlets for the finished films. 'We asked ourselves, what on earth can we do with them, where can we show them,' said Anderson. 'No one was interested in drawing attention to them, least of all my friends who were film critics.' It was probably Karel Reisz who got the idea of screening them at the National Film Theatre, on the south bank of the Thames, where he had been programmes officer from 1952–5; but it was Anderson who forged the slogan 'Free Cinema' so that 'the journalists' – a word he can almost manage to outlaw from polite speech by the inflection he gives it – 'would have an *idea* to write about and not just a cinema programme. Without that declamatory title, I honestly believe the Press would have paid us no attention at all . . . it was a successful piece of cultural packaging.'

Actually, he had worked the same trick earlier in an article on the American *avant garde* cinema published a few years before in the Oxford University magazine *Sequence*, which Anderson had helped to edit with Gavin Lambert and, later, with Karel Reisz and Penelope Houston. 'Free Cinema' was the title he stuck on the piece and admitted, with the engaging candour that recollection allows, that 'I re-wrote the article to make it appear more significant and I inserted the phrases "Free Cinema" in the last paragraph, *in capitals*.' Even then, he left nothing to chance.

The first 'Free Cinema' programme was screened in February 1956, and, as well as the two films already mentioned, it included Lindsay Anderson's *O Dreamland* (1953), a sardonic study of a cheap funfair that pointed up the pathetic way in which human nature lets itself be debased by a devitalized form of pop culture. As such, *O Dreamland* has the power of a sour metaphor for the committed artist's struggle and the small amount of help he can hope for from the apathetic masses. (Incidentally, the apostrophizing O, with its mock poetic undertone, survived strongly enough in Anderson's affections to be tacked on to the title of his first film in the 1970s, O Lucky Man!)

'Free Cinema' was supported by programme notes which Tony Richardson referred to in 1971 as 'basic principles of the cinema without any real revolutionary theory. Unlike André Bazin's writings, which were the theoretical basis of the French *nouvelle vague* directors, ours was a quite unpretentious statement of what we believed movies to be all about.'[1] Its key affirmation in Richardson's view and – significantly, perhaps, in view of his own development – the only one that had stuck in his mind after fifteen years was, 'Perfection is not an aim.' Some of the others were, 'The image speaks. Sound amplifies and comments. No film can be too personal. Size is irrelevant. A style means an attitude. An attitude means a style.' The sharp tone, calculated to wake up the dull boys in the class, is clearly Anderson's. The manifesto also declared, 'Implicit in our attitudes is a belief in freedom, in the importance of people and in the significance of the everyday.' It was a 'cinema' that affirmed its belief in being imaginatively in touch with the present – a reaction against what was held to be the obsolescent and class-bound attitude exhibited in the studio-made features of the time. And it was 'free' in several loose senses of the word: free in its independence of the commercial cinema; free to make intensely personal statements; free to champion the director's right to control his picture and not the production company's.[2] If it had any outstanding charac-

[1] Tony Richardson interviewed by the author, 18 February, 1971. Unless stated otherwise, all subsequent quotes from Richardson come from the same source.

[2] In one sense only was it not 'Free': people still paid to see the films – a fact so self-evident as to be hardly worth mentioning except for a story, widely believed to be apocryphal, about a British film company executive at an East European trade fair in the late 1950s who told his hosts they had got hold of the wrong end of the stick when they talked of 'free cinemas' being operated in Britain. The most appalling feature of the story is that it is true. I heard the individual concerned tell it, almost boastfully, against himself and he survived various palace revolutions in his own company to retire with profit in the 1970s.

teristic, it was the encouragement of a poetic response to a subject. 'Poetic' in what sense, though? In the sense, Anderson told Elizabeth Sussex in 1970, 'of larger implications than the surface realities may suggest . . . the most important challenge is to get beyond pure naturalism into poetry.'[1] The images in the first 'Free Cinema' programme, and in the five others that followed in the next three years, were those of actual places and ordinary people, but heightened by the way the maker's style – if he had one, that is – operated suggestively on audiences, so that they were imaginatively stimulated. At both ends of the 'Free Cinema' movement the link was *people* – the traditional humanist attitude which was characterized by a programme note with the third 'Free Cinema' series in May 1957, as 'neither exclusive and snobbish, not stereotyped and propagandist – but vital, illuminating, personal and refreshing': a category so large and generous that it practically acted as a catch-all container for anything the 'Free Cineastes' cared to bag. Such was the case. As well as the British-made short, the six programmes included early films by Franju, McLaren, Lionel Rogosin, Truffaut, Chabrol, Jan Lenica, Walerian Borowczyk and Roman Polanski. Whatever the selectors responded to was eligible. An impulse of the heart controlled 'Free Cinema,' not the hard grind of a critical faculty.

Most of the home-produced films were not statements of social consequences – though there has lately been a tendency to represent them as such – so much as romantic sympathy. 'I am very conscious,' Anderson said later, 'that the romantic attitude, which doesn't necessarily mean the sentimental one, is a self-portrait quite as much as a social comment.' Nowhere does this come out more strongly than in 'Free Cinema's' attitude to the concept of 'work.' In films like *Momma don't Allow* and Karel Reisz's *We are the Lambeth Boys* (1959), a piece of reportage on a London youth-club, work is presented as simply 'something to be done.' The service element is plugged hard, if unconsciously so. Certainly the films celebrate the escape from work and don't conceal the fact that many of the youngsters are doing dirty, dull or dead-end jobs; but there is no incitement to revolt against the

[1] *Lindsay Anderson*, by Elizabeth Sussex (Studio Vista, 1969), p. 12.

conditions or the society that enforces them – indeed hardly any resentment at all. 'The work is there, it's got to be done.' That's the attitude. It was the most strikingly dated element in the films when they were screened again in their original home, the National Film Theatre, early in the 1970s. Teenage affluence had by then erased the need to do most of the dullest jobs and it was the quietism of the kids, not in any cowed, servile sense, but simply their *acceptance* of their lot, which struck an almost nineteenth-century note.

But sometimes the work is idealized into poetic commitment, as in Anderson's *Every Day except Christmas* and invested with a sense of human communion so that the all-night labour of fruit and flower porters and long-distance truck-drivers becomes a labour of brotherly love.

It was 'Free Cinema's' highly subjective character, or at least its intimate, personal approach to the people in the films, that attracted attacks from the Left *and* the Right. For whatever 'Free Cinema' was, it had not sprung from the British documentary movement founded in the 1930s by John Grierson. This traditionalist school had, by the mid-1950s, gone stale and flat, its original impulse and vitality exhausted, and the old excitement it once kindled usurped by television documentaries. Some of its founder members were now in positions of patronage in the film units of industrial or public corporations, but as Anderson and Richardson recall, none was very helpful, and some were actively hostile. Nor was this necessarily due to artistic jealousy, or the generation gap, or the ascent into the Establishment. With the shining exceptions of Grierson and Humphrey Jennings and Paul Rotha, the later documentary directors were sociologists before they were artists. Their approach was didactic. Where 'Free Cinema' tried to see people as ends in themselves, the traditionalists saw them as social statistics. 'Free Cinema' was nearer in spirit to post-war neo-realism, even if there were class assumptions that made it hard for the British to push their roots as deeply into the proletarian sub-soil as they wanted to. The Right suspected that the emphasis on the lives of people who worked committed the 'Free Cinema' activists to taking sides in the class war. They need not have worried. The 'Free Cinema' people were politically conscious in a romantic, simplistic way, and any hopes they nourished at one time for an alliance of the artists and the activists of the New Left were quickly dashed when the radical movement degenerated into a post-war generation of politicians and theorists. 'It wasn't long before we found out that *their* interest in the arts was simply for political propaganda,' said Anderson.

Traditions are not that easily rejected. Even where the group has been rationally rejected, the shared sense of belonging to it can linger on. This has always been a poetic counterforce to Anderson's radical will. *Every Day except Christmas* has an aching undertone of envy for the shared purpose in life of the Covent Garden workers: just as the film about the rebellion at a public school, which he directed twelve years later, aches with the barely concealed nostalgia of its maker who *did* belong to one like it.

Another source of resentment against the 'Free Cinema' propagandists lay in the producers and directors of TV feature-documentaries who believed their work to be every bit as 'revolutionary' in its commitment to contemporary reality humanely observed, disliked the self-advertising claims of 'Free Cinema' and its founding sons, and themselves secretly hankered after a career in the commercial cinema – just as the 'Free Cinema' boys did, on *their* terms of course. An opposition group got going, helped by a sympathetic cell within the British Film Institute, which set up a movement called "Captive Cinema' that lauded the virtues of television films. But, of course, with such a self-defeatist title, it hardly drew its second wind. It is incontestable that the feature programmes made for television from the mid-1950s onwards opened up British society like an ice-breaker, shattering class barriers and moral taboos and forcing people to take stock of the life around them much more radically than 'Free Cinema' could ever have achieved. But then television was *the* – often uncontrolled – means for social change in this period. 'Free Cinema' was less important for its influence, which was minimal, than for its existence and the experience it gave its principal practitioners. If not absolute beginners, they were pretty well sandwich-course learners. They had to make films while they did other jobs. What sustained them, unlike the TV professionals, was scarcely much more than improvisational zeal; and what they omitted from their pictures is quite as much part of the self-portrait Anderson mentions as what they put in. It is not fair to blame them for the absence of comment on things as the 'generation gap,' which is another of the surprises of a retrospective viewing, for the teenagers at the youth-club 'bull' sessions in *We are the Lambeth Boys* are doggedly attached to their parents', and even their grandparents', opinions on social issues thrown up in a determinedly 'positivist' way by their club leader. But the film-makers show no desire, either, to *provoke* among their subjects reactions that don't correspond to accepted traditions. Class consciousness is present, but likewise muted. Socially superior types and their girl-friends go slumming in a lower-class jazz-club in *Momma don't Allow* – unscrewing their car mascot for safe-keeping before they enter – and their more prim gyrations are unsympathetically contrasted with the local youngsters' less self-conscious gyrations. But the slumming expedition does not take the film-makers very deeply into the landmined territory of class distinctions. As Raymond Durgnat points out in *A Mirror for England*, the vast majority of working-class boys and girls at this time preferred pop to jazz, and soon rock 'n' roll to everything else. The social encounter is reversed in *We are the Lambeth Boys*, when a cricket team from the youth-club in the back streets takes on a minor public school. But again the class distinctions are not rubbed in. The sequence counts for surprisingly little: what surfaces on the way back to their own South London bailiwick is not resentment, but the cocky feeling of the slumland community coming to Town. 'London notices when the boys pass through it,' says the narrator, as the truck with the team aboard crosses Westminster Bridge, 'and the boys like it that way.' Community differences are more implicit than class consciousness; local pride gets the nod, not social deprivation. There is a respect for prole-tarian traditions and no desire at all to overturn the system that maintains them. The revolution that the 'Free Cinema' group had in mind was a way of looking rather than acting. They represented themselves as a 'challenge to orthodoxy,' but as long as their films were nearer in form and spirit to personal essays than to revolutionary pamphlets, then it was not a challenge to political orthodoxy. The documentary which Anderson made in 1958 about the Easter march by the Campaign for Nuclear Disarmament on the Aldermaston atomic weapons factory does not contradict this: it was made by a film-makers' collective under his supervision, not by a 'Free Cinema' group.

ONWARD AND INWARD

'Free Cinema' was no more effective a challenge to the orthodox ways of the film industry. It proved that enthusiasts could work fruitfully, if frugally, outside the commercial set-up; but such films as they did make were excluded from the commercial circuits of cinemas. Trade-union regulations applying to the permissible ways of producing them would have kept them off the commercial screen if the exhibitors' lack of interest had not done the same thing in any case. Their screenings were mainly confined to film societies and 'art' houses, or cinemas catering for the same minority audience that patronized foreign-language films. Their biggest audience was reached on the rare occasion when some of them got screened on television: it took television to show *Every Day except Christmas* in order to overcome its rejection by the British committee selecting shorts for the 1958 Venice Film Festival, and even after it won the main prize in its section there, it got no more of a welcome back home.

Outside Britain things were rather more encouraging. Abroad, 'Free Cinema' was interpreted as the first ripple of a British 'new wave' – a cheering if premature prospect, though at this time it was of small consolation to those in the 'Free Cinema' group who had hoped it was their passport into the commercial industry. 'When I did get the opportunity to make a film,' Lindsay Anderson told Joseph Gelmis in 1969, no doubt referring to an approach from Ealing Studios for him to make a film about the casualty ward of a hospital, into which Ealing ultimately wanted an element of romance injected, 'there seemed to be a row

B

because what I wanted to do was too individual.'[1] Anderson and Richardson eventually accepted invitations to direct for the theatre, and Karel Reisz turned to sponsored documentaries and commercials for the 'independent' television network that began operations in 1955 as a counterforce to the British Broadcasting Corporation's monopoly of broadcasting in sound and vision. The note to the sixth and last 'Free Cinema' programme in March 1959, tacitly acknowledged the uncompromised, but for the moment unfulfilled, aims of the group: 'In making these films and presenting these programmes, we have tried to make a stand for independent, creative film-making in a world where the pressures of conformism and commercialism are becoming more personal every day. We will not abandon these convictions, nor the attempt to put them into action. Free Cinema is dead. Long live Free Cinema.' Such a valedictory note, a salute, a wave of the hand very much like the one Lindsay Anderson had admired so much from the student at the end of Wajda's film *A Generation*, 'defeated but unconquered,' was characteristic of the persisting isolation that the 'Free Cinema' group had felt throughout its short lifetime and the stiff upper-lips they had maintained in a tradition that they would have possibly rejected had it been suggested to them. They had not carried their beach-head into a successful invasion of the commercial cinema, though their motives here had been somewhat ambiguous: they didn't want to beat the enemy, or join him – perhaps just to convert him. The enemy went on with his heathen practices and took absolutely no notice.

No wonder the group's isolation manifests itself in subjects like jazz clubs, youth-centres, fun-fairs, flower-and-vegetable market-life, or the interdependence of deaf-mutes, which evoke a responsive sympathy for the lonely or restricted, a mutual understanding and concern about their aspirations, the brief escape and fulfilment that goes with the body's release on the dance-floor or the longer lasting benefits of the tongue's breakthrough into speech, and an implicit envy for those who can be part of a system

[1] Joseph Gelmis, *The Film Director as Superstar* (Secker and Warburg, 1970), p. 100.

and retain their individuality. Gavin Lambert in the most perceptive article about the first 'Free Cinema' screenings wrote, 'Isolation of the individual, isolation of the crowd, isolation of escape – this is what one senses behind the Free Cinema programme, is perhaps why the films most strongly complement each other. "This is the world," the makers quote Dylan Thomas, "Have faith . . ." '[1]

'Free Cinema' started and ended as an isolated phenomenon of little commercial consequence: where it fulfilled itself was on the practical, personal plane. It provided a few enthusiasts with a chance to learn the trade of making films. It channelled the urge into the act. It was a training-school and loosely constituted seminar for the artistic impulse of people not long down from the universities, at a time well before portable tape-recorders and 16 mm. cameras were added to the schoolboy's satchel. It is the relative rarity of such tools of self-expression in those days which gives a strange prediluvian feeling to the 'Free Cincma' pioneering, although in comparison with the earlier documentary-makers they were able to use new equipment to get a closer, more intimate tone into their studies from the life. They were able to handle the actual material of film; shoot, cut and screen it; gauge its effectiveness with audiences; measure their hopes against their achievement. Without such banal bench-marks there is no sense of advance; and it was a rare success to be able to realize them in the late 1950s. We should never forget that.

They were experiences that the 'Free Cinema' group carried into the commercial cinema when it was ready to admit them; and this only happened when it had a sound commercial reason for making films from the same material, sometimes from the self-same themes, as the 'Free Cinema' productions, once such material had been tested and proved to yield a profit in places other than cinemas – namely, in the lists of best-sellers and long-running plays. The commercial cinema was like a perverse parent: it refused to acknowledge its own children, but adopted other people's.

As Karel Reisz looked back on this time from the vantage

[1] 'Free Cinema,' *Sight and Sound* (Spring 1956), Vol. 25, No. 4, p. 174.

point of the 1970s, it seemed to him that 'Free Cinema' was a cinema of reaction, not revolution – 'a reaction against the Ealing tradition that films were made in a "school" and the Rank system that they were made in a factory. With the British film industry in bad straits, this kind of power structure was becoming irrelevant, so this was the moment to say, "We shall take things into our own hands and become film authors." And it did give the films we made a very different feel – directors' films, not industry films.'[1]

Reisz's sympathies, like Lindsay Anderson's, were moulded by his upbringing, which had been that of 'a middle-class Jew from Central Europe' – from Czechoslovakia, to be precise – who had been put through the classic English educational mangle of boarding-school and university. He was not drawn towards a working-class milieu by political ideology – any more than any of his 'Free Cinema' confrères. He had been a Left-winger in his teens, but the Stalinist coup in Czechoslovakia in 1947 had disenchanted him. What influenced him more than doctrine was the experience of teaching in an English secondary-modern school after graduation. 'Coming straight from university, the whole impact of that outside world was very, very strong. It was probably the first kind of wider community life I'd come across at all; for though I'd been happy at boarding-school and university, I'd felt totally encapsulated there. Teaching was my first taste of social reality: and you can't deal daily with working-class youngsters and their parents in their own habitat and retain an archaic view of the lower classes as comic relief or criminals, the roles they traditionally filled in British films. Nor could you regard them as documentary statistics: no one has a greater contempt for these, and all the denial of diversity they imply, than the man or woman whose back is to the blackboard.' Once more one sees the mixed blessings of education, their own and that of others, on the 'Free Cinema' film-makers. Jazz-club and youth-club, the milieux of Reisz's two films, were not only the rallying points of

[1] Karel Reisz interviewed by the author, 11 December, 1969. Unless stated otherwise, all subsequent quotations from Reisz come from the same source.

boys and girls after school was out: they were places where the social education of the ex-teacher was continued once he himself had quit the classroom for good.

Some of the criticism made of 'Free Cinema' turned out to be as influential on members of the group as the films they made. Richard Hoggart, in a generally welcoming review of *We are the Lambeth Boys* in 1959, questioned 'the legitimacy of the limits' that Karel Reisz imposed on his films. Addressing Reisz directly, he went on, 'It does not deal, you have said, with "the inner life," with "the deeper dissatisfactions" . . . My own inclination would be towards asking this kind of essay to become much more subjective and to encompass the inner life. For, even when we have praised its great virtues and understood your limited aim, there is something unsatisfactory about the experience presented in *We are the Lambeth Boys*. You show very well indeed some of the great primitive virtues of the group life of these young people. But the "public" life can't be separated from the personal life (or indeed virtues from vices) without a distortion . . . I think that if this sort of film-essay is to develop, it must accept the disciplines, the disinterested (not the "redressing") disciplines of art. Its makers must be prepared to be judged neither by their "objectivity" nor by their prior commitment, but by the quality of their imagination, by the depth and honesty of their insight. Think of Tchekov's short stories, which are often superficially like documentary; it's that kind of commitment, that kind of disciplined art, which is not at all a matter of aesthetic formalities, that ought to be sought . . . Free Cinema . . . will only stand out clearly and sharply committed and concerned in the right way when it faces better the more demanding (and exciting) problems of the imagination."[1]

When Karel Reis made his public reply to this exacting piece of encouragement, he didn't do so in writing – but in the film *Saturday Night and Sunday Morning* which he directed and Tony Richardson produced a year later.

'Yes,' Reisz wrote considerably later still, in reply to an en-

[1] 'We are the Lambeth Boys,' *Sight and Sound* (Summer–Autumn 1965), Vol. 28, Nos. 3–4, p. 165.

quiry, 'in a sense *Saturday Night and Sunday Morning* is an answer to Richard's strictures. The hero of the picture is, if you like, one of the Lambeth Boys. An attempt is made to make a movie about the sentimental and social education of *one specific* boy: thus the 'inner' things which the *Lambeth Boys* type of picture simply cannot apprehend (it is not possible or desirable to make non-professionals' close-ups convey specific, *directed* feelings, as Richard quite rightly sensed in the Mill Hill public-school sequence) was attempted in *Saturday Night and Sunday Morning*. To put it more simply, and risking pretentiousness, the first work attempted a picture of a world, the second a portrait. This simplifies it all, of course. I think Richard is a little shaky about what you can actually *do* with non-professionals. In this sense the comparison with Tchekov (Tchekov! Jesus! Which league are we playing in?) is quite irrelevant; it is precisely the 'inwardness' which in Tchekov of course is the very substance that you *can't* and *shouldn't* attempt with documentary. Speaking personally and looking back at that whole period, I very much regret that we never had the chance, any of us, to go further with this *Every Day except Christmas–We are the Lambeth Boys* genre. We were only at the very beginning, and some of Richard's notions pointed a way forward; pointed out limitations I was very aware of. *But there simply is no money or audience for this kind of movie in the English cinema* . . . I spent two years as the full-time films officer at the Ford Motor Company, doing their advertising on condition they gave me money for the two pictures, and you simply can't spend your life like that for long periods. Besides, we never found an audience for the pictures. (The booking fee for *We are the Lambeth Boys*, in circuit houses where it played as a second feature, was £5!) I feel in retrospect that we could have gone much further. (I had a fine script and had done six months' research for an eighty-minute 'essay' on a Northern music-hall, but never raised the money.) There is a sense of freedom, of improvisation, of direct response to life which is very precious and very hard to find an equivalent for with a feature film crew and budget.'[1]

Hard, yes: but the way things were changing at the end of the 1950s, no longer impossible.

[1] Karel Reisz in a letter to the author. The italics are Reisz's.

Chapter Two: 'Top' People

The notorious reluctance of the British cinema to consider the
contemporary scene seems to be weakening.
Financial Times, 26 January, 1959
'Still, perhaps such people exist . . .'
The Times, 26 January, 1959

From Christopher Booker's *The Neophiliacs* and from Bernard
Levin's *The Pendulum Years*, and no doubt from many another
forthcoming history of contemporary Britain, one year springs
out of the calendar in the way the wind used to flutter the leaves
in an old-time Hollywood film till a date of dramatic significance
came up. This year is 1956. It has already been noted as the birth-
date of 'Free Cinema.' But 'Free Cinema' as a prognosis of change
was only a quiver on the seismic scale among the many other
violent shocks that society was undergoing. 1956 was the year of
the Suez crisis, the last grand fling at imposing a British solution
by collusive force of arms on a recalcitrant foreigner. It led
speedily to disenchantment with the lingering romanticism of
'limited warfare,' at least as far as western democracies were able
to practise it, and left a turbulently divided and self-critical
society trying to reassemble its bits and pieces into a new image.
Britain in the second half of 1956 suggested affinities with the
United States in the early 1970s, when the Vietnam war finally
rebounded on domestic sensibilities to produce bewilderment,
anger, resentment and guilt.

But where the mass media were concerned, the year 1956 was
one of immense opportunity – for some. It saw the growth of a
commercial television network financed by advertisements that
punctuated, though did not directly sponsor, the programmes.
Thus the thirty-three-year monopoly of the British Broadcasting
Corporation was ended; and the inward-turning impetus of post-
Suez society was given a boost of extraordinary force by the new
era of consumer advertising appearing directly in the home,
advocating expenditure on one's self, one's family, and soon one's
fantasies. As Christopher Booker observed; 'No breeding ground

for fantasy is so fertile as a society in a state of disintegration and flux, a society in which the basic certainties which derive from a reasonably stable social framework are themselves breaking down.'[1] Important, too, were other apparently minor events, such as the acquisition of the *Queen* magazine by Jocelyn Stevens in 1957, for this young man had the panache, perception and opportunism to turn a traditionalist old periodical into one that defined and disseminated the revolution in every branch of consumer society and made it attractive and enviable to an audience far wider and far, far less sophisticated than *Queen*'s readership in the decade ahead. The media borrow from the media, taking in each other's laundered linen and displaying it in their own way for their own clientele; and there is no doubt that the pop communicators were grateful to *Queen*, and later to the colour supplements published by the 'posh' Sunday or daily newspapers, for a picture of what was new, smart, interesting and occasionally of value. Sex came into prominence as part of this release of commercial energy concurrent with political disenchantment, and the two were to run into each other in a sensational way before very long. Popular sales of the James Bond thrillers really got going in 1956. The Wolfenden Report on prostitution and homosexuality, recommending a more tolerant legal attitude towards what was then a criminal offence punishable by hard labour, stimulated open public discussion on the subject after 1957: more and more attention was focused on the abnormalities of sex. After much hesitation, *Lolita* was finally published in Britain in 1959, the same year that a new Obscene Publications Act was passed by Parliament, relieving publishers of some of their anxiety about prosecution – well, *successful* prosecution – though not, as the trial of Penguin Books for publishing an unexpurgated edition of *Lady Chatterley's Lover* proved in 1960, about the possible ruinous cost of facing trial and winning an acquittal.

The sexual energies of working - and middle-class boys and girls, not yet welded together into a separate sub-culture called 'the teenagers,' but very near to it, was given a jolt into public prominence when the film *Rock around the Clock*, starring Bill

[1] Christopher Booker, *The Neophiliacs* (Collins, 1969), p. 80.

Hayley and his Comets, provoked the earliest outbursts of juvenile demonstration in British cinemas in 1956. Teenage consumer industries were tooling up throughout the same year, ready to accelerate into exploitive high production and provide the newly affluent young with clothes, discs, motor-scooters and a multitude of other services that fortified their increasing sense of separateness – or, in a term that was coming into current use in the 1958–9 period, their 'image.'

But it was an event on the theatrical, not the political front in 1956 that provided a rallying point for people's disaffections and uncertainties: the presentation of John Osborne's *Look Back in Anger* at the Royal Court Theatre in May of that year. The 'Court' was the headquarters of the English Stage Company, an enterprise founded to retrieve the native drama from its year-in, year-out spate of classical revivals, 'well-made' matinée plays, and West End farces, by encouraging new dramatists or established writers-turned-playwrights – anyone in fact whose view of life was contemporary and close to truth. What the 'Free Cinema' people were attempting, George Devine at the Royal Court was simultaneously achieving. Osborne's play was the breakthrough; it was directed on the stage by Tony Richardson, who had accepted Devine's invitation to join the Royal Court when, like Reisz, he felt frustrated at not being able to find a wide audience with 'Free Cinema,' nor a job in the commercial cinema. Jimmy Porter's outbursts of rage against life, class and society in May 1956 sundered 'all that stifling atmosphere of socially deferential conservatism which had settled over Britain since the early fifties. At last the young urban lower class, the 'huge unfashionable hinterlands' of London, had found articulate voice.[1] Jimmy Porter was the Identikit face of his time, with features composed of anger, impotence, isolation and resentful helplessness, and recognizable not just to intellectuals and liberals or those whose political orthodoxy was shattered by Suez or whose Left-wing sentimentality was jolted by the Russian invasion of Hungary in the same year, but in particular by the youthful products of Britain's post-war Education Act. The Act had opened up places for them

[1] Christopher Booker, *op. cit.*, p. 109.

in high-schools and universities and allowed them, like Jimmy Porter, to convert the energies that had been blocked so long in the limited aspirations and menial jobs available to working-class children into full intellectual self-assurance. But society had still denied them fulfilment. They had been educated, like Jimmy, into articulate contempt for its outworn institutions and class-bound attitudes, but saw no means of changing and replacing them. *Look Back in Anger* didn't provide the means, but it gave their rage its release.

Like the term 'Free Cinema' which Lindsay Anderson shrewdly appreciated would assist publicity, or at least avoid a more precise but probably divisive declaration of intent, there came into use the equally all-purpose label of the 'Angry Young Men' – or 'The Young Angries,' as they were soon mockingly called by the orthodox, who can scarcely have realized the extra service they were rendering the movement by placing the emphasis on 'youth.'

Like many successful social revolutions which begin with form, this one swiftly developed substance. It advanced to power from a sound commercial base. Osborne's success proved there was profit in anger, though it is to the eternal credit of the Royal Court that the reliable profit which the revivals of *Look Back in Anger* brought in was used to subsidize untried talent, regardless of its commercial prospects. But the term 'anger' was applicable to any strident rejection of the system, particularly if it had provincial origins and a working-class accent, and almost at once impresarios and publishers, journalists and critics, magazine and newspaper editors, and radio and television producers, indeed the whole reflex machine, went into action to reflect, analyse, reproduce *and market* the phenomenon they were witnessing. The fact that the world of communications was itself relatively classless – where those who worked in it were concerned, if not the sectional interests they appealed to for their living – assisted the speed with which the excitement was diffused through every level of society between 1956 and 1959. Out of these years, documented in detail by others, came dramatists and writers like Arnold Wesker, John Arden, Keith Waterhouse and Willis Hall, Alun Owen,

Shelagh Delaney, Harold Pinter, Robert Bolt, Kingsley Amis, John Braine, Alan Sillitoe, David Mercer, and many more writers who changed British theatre and literature decisively throughout the next decade. There was only one place that showed no instantaneous awareness of the ferment that was happening around it — and this was the British cinema.

SPEAKING OF SEX

It is not astonishing that there should be a considerable time-lag between the appearance of plays and novels by the new writers and their successful translation into movies. Except in wartime, the British cinema had no tradition of responding swiftly to social change. It had no tradition at all of precipitating it. At the end of the 1950s, the cinema was going through one of its recurring periods of self-delusion, believing that it could crack open the foreign market, especially the El Dorado of the American market, if its product looked passably like the Hollywood fare, and featured internationally acceptable stars. Few of these, if any, were of the home-grown stock. In any case, to bring the themes and characters of the new plays and novels to life on the screen meant approximating to contemporary reality, which required a wholly new class of indigenous actors of a type the British cinema had never recruited – the genuine working-class or lower-middle-class boys and girls. There was censorship, too, to reckon with. Just prior to 1958, film censorship in Britain had become unworkably restrictive. A new censor, appointed by the film industry but independent of it, had brought to the job the stiff rectitude of his Civil Service background instead of the expected ability to know when to resist and when to relent. Relations between the film industry and the Censorship Board were near breakdown when the former finally decided that enough was enough and picked a new man, one of the Board's examiners, to be its executive secretary. The increasingly liberal tone that this excellent choice, John Trevelyan, managed to maintain from 1958 until his retirement in 1970 helped to create the atmosphere in which a new kind of cinema could flourish in Britain, once the other fertilizing elements were applied to it.

The post-Osborne writers, challenging class traditions and sexual *mores*, did not find a cinema prepared to welcome their aggressively individualist values until these self-same values could be demonstrated not to hurt the box-office, but actually to augment it. The industry itself was one of the most fortified outposts of diehard conservatism in Britain. The only thing that breached its reluctance to change was – profit. Yet the prospect of higher profits seemed all the bleaker because of the new X. Certificate, or rating, which, it was felt, would inevitably be applied to many of the films based on works by the new wave of writers. The X. Certificate illustrates the pitfalls of trying to achieve a positive result by a negative means. It had been introduced in 1951 by the British Board of Film Censors to indicate a type of film that the Board deemed unsuitable for children under sixteen years of age. Such children were admitted to A. Certificate films at their parents' discretion, in the company of a bona fide guardian, but up to the introduction of the X. the only category of film barred to them was the H. certificate – H. standing for 'horror.' It was obvious to the censor that more and more material was getting submitted for an A. which certainly couldn't be rated as 'horrific' yet equally clearly was not suitable for showing to children under sixteen. Hence the X. Certificate. It was intended to promote the more serious treatment of non-H. topics, but it was an ill-omened designation from the beginning. Something lubricious and prurient attached itself to the letter X. and the stigma has stayed on it ever since, despite every effort to point out that X. can cover a multitude of virtues as well as sins. In the late 1950s, the X. was turned into a titillating 'come-on' by the cheaper sort of film-maker and exhibitor who displayed it prominently as a promise (seldom kept) of more than usually brazen entertainment 'for adults.' To the large chains of cinemas wholly owned by the Rank Organisation [henceforth referred to as the Rank cinemas or circuit) and the Associated British Picture Corporation (henceforth known as the A.B.C. cinemas or circuit), the X. tended to be a strong minus factor, cutting down a film's potential box-office by excluding the under-sixteens.[1] The 'family audience,' like some semi-mythical animal in a medieval bestiary, was what the cinema owners venerated, in spite of the demonstrable fact, becoming clearer and clearer with each passing year, that 'the family' no longer took its pleasures together, but on separate sides of the generation gap. However, the failure to see how the cinema must pitch its appeal to smaller and varied sections of the once huge audience of habitual film-goers was not exclusive to the British film industry: Hollywood shared the same reluctance to recognize change, and paid the same price.

Timeliness counted almost as much as talent in allowing the new social realism to reach the screen as well as the stage and the printed page, and the film that achieved the breakthrough was premièred in Britain at the beginning of 1959, though the book on which it was based had appeared nearly three years earlier. It was like a sudden new bit of testimony from an unexpected witness in a case which had long since been thought lost.

Room at the Top (22 January, 1959) was the first important *and successful* film to have as its hero a youth from the post-war working class. Its theme was not a radical one, though: indeed in many ways it was a conservative, almost a reactionary story. John Braine's plot of the poor boy who gets the rich man's daughter pregnant and becomes acceptable, through necessity, to her social class, and the heir by marriage to her father's capitalist enterprise isn't the stuff of anger or protest. Its driving force is the wish to acquire the values and possessions of the class above, not reject them, and even the note of watery-eyed remorse which Joe Lampton strikes as the limousine speeds him off from his wedding, up the hill to 'the top,' is ambiguous, directed less at his own lost integrity than at the loss of a mistress whom he would surely have regarded as one of the luxurious accessories legitimately available to him in his new-found social status. What one feels most strongly in *Room At the Top* isn't anger – but envy – the envy of a have-not for what he wants to acquire. In one

---

[1] In mid-1956, the Rank circuit numbered about 575 cinemas, the ABC circuit about 340. See John Spraos, *The Decline of the Cinema* (Allen & Unwin, 1962), for a more detailed account of the circuits.

part of the film Joe talks of escape from the prison camp where he spent part of the war as being 'an officer's privilege.' The sentiment defines him well. He is hatched out of the Other Rankers' resentful sense of being excluded, and their determination never again to be sold short by their betters. It was this feeling that swept the first post-war Labour Government to power on the Services' vote. But just as the working-class talents of the 1960s were to merge their own uninhibited attitudes with the life-styles of the affluent world they penetrated, and be made welcome for the excitement and profit they brought, so Joe Lampton was recognised by the audience that went to movies – a wider audience than the one that read books – as an up-thrusting new type of screen hero, and provincial type, into the bargain. At that date it was a rarity to hear a regional accent on the lips of a British film star, even if it did come and go occasionally, and the casting of Laurence Harvey as Joe took it beyond vocal novelty by revealing a star sinking his customary identity, partially anyhow, into a characterization. A year or so later there probably would not have been quite such a warm and astonished welcome if the role had been cast from the ranks of established film stars; but at this date, those plebeian cadets, the Finneys, Stamps, Courtenays and Caines, either had not made the scene or were not in demand for leading film roles.

Admittedly, the film plays down Joe's working-class origins – probably as much in the interest of British audiences as of American, for to most metropolitan or south of England filmgoers at that date, John Braine's 'north country' was foreign territory. Joe's return to his birthplace in a provincial slum comes late in the film and his own passionate reference to it – 'I'm working-class an' proud of it!' – comes in the middle of amateur theatricals and sounds as phoney as any line from the play in rehearsal. (Mispronunciation of 'brassière' as 'brazier' in the scene is hardly a proletarian trait that Richard Hoggart would authenticate in *The Uses of Literacy*; and in any case Joe's slip of the tongue is plainly aimed at North America, where 'brassière' is habitually pronounced 'brazier.') The fact that Joe is not out of the top drawer is continually emphasized in all his dealings with his future father-in-law, but since the latter does not come much higher up the social scale himself, it soon looks like the clash of generations rather than the class conflict. Elsewhere, the emphasis of interest is placed on Joe's sexuality, not his social origins.

The idea of a thrusting newcomer who uses sex to win social advancement was a novelty on a British screen, its heartlessness much more Gallic than Anglo-Saxon. Even less familiar was an open acknowledgment by a young English girl, played by Heather Sears, that having sex was actually pleasurable. This went dead against the grain of English screen history, where characters extracted emotion out of guilt, not pleasure. Her debutante-like breathiness – 'Oh, Joe, wasn't it super, wasn't it simply super!' – after they have copulated on the river bank was the first time British film-goers had heard the sex act referred to in one of their films in such a candid fashion. There was some complaint that casting Simone Signoret as the mature woman who gives Joe the sexual fulfilment he misses in his quest for affluence showed the opportunism of the international box-office. Yet it is not by any means false to reality. Continental-born wives are not uncommon in north-country towns, where the staple industry has strong business links with European wholesalers, and inter-marriage has assisted trade. Signoret, moreover, had an eroticism few English actresses of her age could have matched; but even more to the point was what she did not have – which was an English, i.e. a classbound accent. Alice's character has to represent in Joe's eyes a quality of worldly experience far more nourishing than his own limited sexual goals can give him: and this would have been fatally betrayed if she had been felt to represent only one more conquest by him among the English upper classes. A French accent, apart from its innate exoticism, effectively conceals Alice's own social origins from Anglo-American ears. And by contrast it emphasizes the shallow, class-bound allegiances of the girl he eventually has to marry.

Contrary to the impression that has since formed, *Room at the Top* did not receive an overwhelming welcome from British critics at the time. Without wishing to accuse anyone of insincerity, one may suspect a native puritanism among the notices, possibly reflecting what some of the reviewers felt their readers would feel. There was a moralizing note about many of the reviews, condemning the hero for his social climbing, adulterous relations, and generally over-sexed nature. Under the headline, 'Ex-Soldier with a Giant Inferiority Complex,' a critic in *Screen* wrote, 'The hero . . . never rises above the level of a D. H. Lawrence gardener (sic) . . . Sex is laid on, but mostly it is seedy and not rising to the level of honest passion.'[1] The anonymous critic of *The Times*, this time under the headline 'A Film not quite out of the Top Drawer,' took a tone of aloof condemnation: 'Joe, indeed, is more of a cad than a card. The members of the town's upper set, or whatever they call themselves, display the most deplorable manners, and Joe's private class war is, to a certain extent, justified by the behaviour of his natural enemies. Still, perhaps such people exist . . .'[2] Nina Hibbin, critic of the Communist morning paper, took a predictably partisan line which nevertheless hewed surprisingly close to *The Times*'s. 'Now it's unhappily true that some working people have corrupt social ambitions,' she wrote. 'But in a film that sets out to explore class relations and sex relations between classes, it is a trick to select an immature, oversexed, unprincipled climber as the main representative of the working class.'[3] They were not simply politically commited critics of the Left who resented a working-class lad being drawn in 'unflattering' terms. Jympson Harman in the *Evening News*, a newspaper with a wide London circulation among lower-class readers but no noticeably radical commitment, complained, 'hero or villain, the chap in the film on the way to the top failed to convince me he was anything but a sloppy messer-up of his own and other people's lives.'[4] (And much the same kind of criticism, anticipating the outrage of working-class moral righteousness, whether politically or socially based, would manifest itself as late as 1962 against Albert Finney's randy young factory worker in *Saturday Night and Sunday Morning*.)

[1] *Screen*, The Journal of the Society for Education in Film and Television, 16 June, 1959.
[2] *The Times*, 26 January, 1959.
[3] *Daily Worker*, 26 January, 1959.
[4] *Evening News*, 22 January, 1959.

Evidence of how rarely the film's most striking quality had been encountered in their native cinema came from the British critics' frequently voiced complaint about the 'not niceness' of the people in the film, and the dubious substitution of 'candour for artistic restraint' in sexual matters. C. A. Lejeune wrote, 'I wasn't much impressed by what I saw, and what remains in my mind is a series of enormous close-ups, so large that every face was magnified, with the forehead frequently cut off to make room for the nude upper torso, suggesting the suppressed ardours and satisfactions of a physical relationship.'[1] Small wonder that Paddy Whannel, in the course of a long analysis of this backlash, queried whether British film critics would recognize a 'breakthrough' on the screen if they saw one.[2] Regretfully, one has to conclude that in spite of some perceptive reviews from, among others, Dilys Powell (*The Sunday Times*) and Philip Oakes (*The Sunday Dispatch*), the majority of the British critics, to judge from their reviews, would have preferred to shut their eyes and deny the relevance to the contemporary scene of what they saw in *Room at the Top*.

The Americans, on the other hand, were far quicker on the uptake, less inhibited by feeling a need to make moral judgments that might correspond to their readers' prejudices. 'Not only do bourgeois morals take an awful drubbing here,' John McCarten wrote, 'but so does the general moral climate of our time.'[3] Arthur Knight praised the film's willingness to venture into fresh areas of post-war life and, above all, its willingness to allow the characters an identity of their own outside the moralizing, conformist stereotypes enforced at that time by the Hollywood Production Code. He said, 'There has been no attempt to "lick" John Braine's acrid book to conform to movie morality. Its characters . . . connive, commit adultery like recognizable (and not altogether unlikeable) human beings. And the effect is startling. One feels that a whole new chapter is about to be written in

[1] *The Observer*, 25 January, 1959.
[2] *Universities and Left Review* (1959), No. 6, pp. 21–4.
[3] *The New Yorker*, 11 April, 1959.

motion-picture history.'[1] In general, one can say, British critics reacted to the way the film rejected social orthodoxy, the American critics to the way it transgressed Hollywood convention: one group found it offensive, the other liberating. In any case, the American cinema, whatever other hypocrisies the Legion of Decency and the Production Code enjoined on it, did not have to suffer the rigid class stratification built into the traditional subjects and characters in British cinema. The working-class American hero from 'across the tracks' had been a familiar figure on the Hollywood screen for decades, living proof of social mobility and 'making good' in a restlessly heterogeneous society. Where Americans were concerned, Joe Lampton was not an offensive interloper rushing the crash-barriers of the upper-class enclosure: he was cut to a well-established pattern. And for every American film-goer who appreciated his specific relevance to changing Britain, many, many more were impressed by the sexual candour he displayed in his rise to riches. The unwonted frankness of the film's approach to sex was what won it large audiences, not withstanding a dubious moral rating from the Legion of Decency, and made it one of the very few British films at that date to be shown widely and profitably in the United States.

In Britain, too, it was enormously successful. It broke the X. Certificate curse by showing British distributors and exhibitors that a quality film costing £280,000 and containing material not deemed fit for 'family' viewing could nevertheless do exceptionally well – better, in fact, than many an A. Certificate movie.

Actually the objections of the censor to the script of *Room at the Top* submitted to him in advance of shooting were more extensive than has been generally thought. I must plead guilty to encouraging this view, by suggesting in an earlier book dealing with the sexual aspects of the censor's role, that his principal reservation concerned a too clinically detailed description of the car crash in which Joe's mistress is killed. In order to bring home to him the consequences of his callousness, the dialogue was littered with overheard phrases like 'scalped,' 'crawling about,' 'hanging off,' etc., which the censor felt were unnecessarily lurid.

[1] The *Saturday Review*, 11 April, 1959.

He asked for them to be reduced. After resistance, they were. But he also requested deletion of the lines, 'Damn you to hell, you stupid bitch' and 'Don't waste your lust on her.' 'Bitch' was changed to 'witch' and an alternative line, 'Don't lust after her' was reluctantly approved. Objection was also made to a scene that left one in no doubt about Joe seducing a girl he met casually in a bar: the dialogue accompanying this scene as shot for the film softened the bluntness of his approach. But the river-bank seduction gave no problems. What continued to concern the censor and his examiners in the liberalising years ahead wasn't so much the visually explicit material in a film as language which they regarded as unnecessarily coarse or blasphemous.

AUTHOR, AUTHOR

Room at the Top took two of the 1959 Academy Awards (for Simone Signoret's performance and Neil Paterson's screenplay), made Laurence Harvey into an international star, and introduced Jack Clayton to full-scale feature direction. Clayton had previously made a medium-length version of Gogol's *The Bespoke Overcoat*, costing a mere £5,000, which had caught the eye of the producer James Woolf. Woolf was a rarity in British films at the time, and would still be so if he were alive today: a man of taste and judgment who loved craftsmanship and supported a director instead of suffocating him or using him as a surrogate talent for the film he himself would have liked to direct had he dared. James Woolf and his equally successful and financially shrewder brother John, constituting Romulus Films, had also the then fairly uncommon distinction of producing British films like *The African Queen* and *The Story of Esther Costello* which, while not specifically British in cast or theme, were successfully geared to the international box-office. Outside the 'cult' tradition of the Ealing comedies, it is hard to say this of many other British film-makers in the 1950s. James Woolf had served his apprenticeship with Columbia in Hollywood and had the flair for 'production' more commonly found there than in Britain: he was an obsessional film-maker, loving the wheeling and dealing, relishing the juggling with human talents that it involved, and taking pleasure in spotting youthful protégés and promoting their careers, thereby gaining a vicarious satisfaction from their success that was lacking in his own basically lonely nature. He had bought the film rights to *Room at the Top*, thinking the parts of Joe and the rich young girl he seduces were perfect for Stewart Granger and Jean Simmons – a piece of shrewd commercial casting, more in line with Hollywood's approach to the box-office, since the two stars at that time were husband and wife. Later on he saw that these particular players could not give the story the right distribution of emotional sympathies, so Laurence Harvey and Heather Sears were cast. Simone Signoret was Clayton's suggestion: one of his fellow directors said later, somewhat unkindly, that she was also his 'signature' in the film. Her performance gave the film its personal style. And Andrew Sarris put it even more bluntly: 'The only Clayton constant is impersonality.'[1]

There is some truth in this, though it was not so evident in 1959. Then the initial excitement of seeing a new sort of film hero stalk across a fresh kind of social scene in a British film made it natural to pigeonhole Clayton as a social-realist director: which proved no kindness to him and, in the light of his later career, was a reputation that had to be lived down. He was no revolutionary: quite the reverse. Clayton was a traditionalist, as his subsequent films showed, working inside the British school of fine craftsmanship. He had a well-developed, indeed rather over-developed moral sensibility towards his material, but no apparent social or political allegiance whatsoever. The timeliness of *Room at the Top* – Clayton has an almost superstitious trust in the 'timeliness' of films where the public is concerned – encouraged us to confuse the social resentment at the core of the story with what we imagined to be the director's own committed sympathies. Not so. As Sarris wrote, with the advantage of hindsight, each of Clayton's projects dictates its own style. 'I am totally intuitive in everything about film-making,' Clayton admitted much later. 'I don't work by intelligence; I have to feel it, not think it. If I

[1] Andrew Sarris, *The American Cinema* (Dutton, 1968), p. 191.

make the illusion work for me, the feeling is the victory.'[1] Such a man, constantly referring the emotional stimulus of a project back to himself, makes it difficult to locate with any regularity the themes he will be drawn to. He is apt to work more through his performers than through his *mise en scène*; fortunately for Clayton, his touch with performers is true and subtle. The social theme of *Room at the Top* scarcely excited him: he felt the story was far from original and had been done better in Dreiser's novel *An American Tragedy*. 'But it was infinitely more truthful about relationships between people than films in that genre which had preceded it.'

Such a traditionalist approach tended to be overlooked in the gratitude, expressed by at least some influential British critics at the start of 1959, for the fact that at long last something was alive and kicking against convention in their native cinema. But anxiety should have been felt along with elation, if only on the grounds that the innovative freshness which *Room at the Top* represented in screen terms was itself derived at second-hand from literary origins. The film had certainly transferred the novel to the screen without compromise – but also without extension. Perhaps it was too early to appreciate just how much of the British 'new wave' in the cinema was going to depend on the tidal flow of the plays and novels of the '1956 generation.' Yet the same issue of *Sight and Sound* which declared, in 1959, that 'if this new movement at present so vaguely discernible is to stand for anything, it must be discovery,' published a symposium of replies from feature-filmmakers who had been asked 'what particular subject they would personally choose to film at this moment, assuming that they enjoyed a completely free hand.'[2] The answers were disquieting.

The nine replies received – itself a mournfully small number – elicited no great sense of release, no passionate desire to originate film material, as distinct from adapting plays or books. On the

[1] Jack Clayton interviewed by the author, 15 January, 1971. Unless stated otherwise, all subsequent quotations from Clayton come from the same source.

[2] 'A Free Hand,' *Sight and Sound*, Spring 1959, Vol. 28, No. 2, p. 60.

contrary, where they were able to think of specific subjects at all, the directors thought in terms of stage hits and best-selling novels or biographies. Jack Lee wanted to film the Willis Hall play *The Long and the Short and the Tall* 'because it is a powerful drama yet (sic) has something to say.' Tony Richardson planned films of Osborne's *The Entertainer*, Shelagh Delaney's *A Taste of Honey* and Colin MacInnes's novel *City of Spades*, claiming that 'none of these films is based on conventional material.'[1] Paul Rotha 'would like to direct a film about Michael Collins' based on Frank O'Connor's biography *The Big Fellow*: 'One actor only can I name for the role – Marlon Brando.' Robert Hamer declared he 'would like to make a film about Crime' and made it sound a Dostoievskian task of research – 'on what scale or in what framework this endeavour might be pursued, I hope I would not begin to know' – before concluding lamely that 'with a new Penal Reform Act promised, it may seem a little late in the day to make this essay for a film.' Seth Holt seemed the only one with a screen original ready to go, '*Gratz* . . . a story written for the screen by J. P. Donleavy,' but he confessed he found himself 'temperamentally incapable of considering the project without the market and the limitations arising from the nature of that market . . . the basic facts of life in a manic-depressive world.'

Extraordinarily timorous, woolly-minded, pessimistic, conventional except in a few instances (and all but one of these derivative), the symposium was headed by a contribution from the director of *Room at the Top* which pinpointed the dilemma with unintentional accuracy. Jack Clayton did not lack passion. 'It must be a subject that has at least some aspect one can believe in, love and actually feel. It should, even if only partially, give the opportunity of expressing some facet of man to his inner self and of that same man to the outside world. It must be valid for today: not the today of the newspaper stop-press, which is usually dead by the time it is read, but the real today, which, with different clothes, is true of yesterday and tomorrow. Finally, the subject must try above all else to prize open the doors of convention and

---

[1] Richardson at the time of writing had just directed *Look Back in Anger*. See Chapter Three.

snap through as many archaic rules as possible.' One would not dissent from a line of this. But in acknowledging that he did not expect to find all of his requirements in *one* subject, Clayton drew a revealing inference from the question put to him by the magazine editors. 'It seems to me to imply that *under one magic book cover* may be hidden all the many varied things that one feels worth saying in a film today.[1] Think of the literary graveyard of rejects one would stand in; so many containing the thread or the bones and even sometimes the flesh of something very worthwhile.'

A response that fairly rings with crusading zeal. But to what exactly is one responding? Between the passion of the film subject and the dedication of the film-maker lies the inevitable barrier of 'the book cover,' whether magic or not, singular or plural. British cinema in 1959 was taking its lead from the directions provided by others, the playwrights and novelists who had caught and defined the public mood and, in doing so, altered it and prepared it for the film-makers to follow up. One literary adaptation had already been used with enormous success to break through the commercial cinema's 'doors of convention' – but what was one now breaking through to? A real renaissance or simply a successful transplant?

[1] Italics mine.

Chapter Three: The Angry Brigade

While I was on honeymoon I took *Look Back in Anger* to Jack Warner to show him: after all, his company had financed it, so I figured he should see it. Jack and I looked at it and after about seven or eight minutes Jack said, 'What language are they talking?' 'English,' said I. 'This is America,' said Jack and got up and walked out.

Harry Saltzman

'How do I look back on *Look Back in Anger?*' (May 28, 1959) Tony Richardson said, echoing my question. 'I don't look back.' Nevertheless, he did.

The Royal Court Theatre's first season in 1956 had been remarkably successful in establishing it as a 'writer's theatre' – a theatre that George Devine insisted, should resume contact with life and living people and nurture the realistic tradition in the writing and directing of plays. A later Royal Court director, William Gaskill, characterized this as a 'non-theatrical approach, a lack of concern with abstractions and symbols, stylistically natural and non-expressionistic.' He might have been defining the film style that sprang from the same theatrical cradle. Because John Osborne's play *Look Back in Anger* had had locked into it so much of the mockery and energy of the post-war generation, now brought into hard focus by the post-Suez disenchantment, it was the season's outstanding revelation, and was included in a selection of plays which the Royal Court presented in New York in 1957. Tony Richardson went over to direct the play he had originally done in London, then returned 'to look after the shop.' Soon letters started arriving from Osborne, Devine and the others mentioning a 'marvellous character they'd met in New York who was supposedly going to conjure up a private bank of gold for the Royal Court, a kind of Anglo-American artistic subsidy, and meanwhile was giving them a wonderful time, helping them discover New York, having a ball in the 1950-ish jazz cellars . . . to believe the letters, it was as if F. Scott Fitzgerald had come back to life.' When the others returned, Richardson went to New York in order to obtain a firm offer of patronage from this cultural Midas, but soon realized there wasn't to be any: 'he didn't know anyone with resources to play the impresario on the scale he had in mind. Still, he was certainly inspiring company. When I knew the "Grand Project" would come to nothing, I said to him, "Well, I *do* want to make a film, maybe we could at least get one under way with *this*" – "this" being *Look Back in Anger*. "Oh no, no, that's impossible," he said. But I got Richard Burton interested, we formed Woodfall Films with John, and our friend and patron got Warner Brothers to back us. And we made the film.'

The 'angel' in this not untypical account of film financing was Harry Saltzman, a Quebec-born North American and a natural entrepreneur who had already left enough careers behind him to preoccupy several men. Moving from the United States to France and back again, he had worked in vaudeville, in a travelling circus, in advertising, in television, in fact in anything that was attractive to his gambler's instinct, his roving curiosity, and his genuine fascination with the mystique as well as the machinery of popular culture. He could make money work and things happen: not always to his advantage, though generally so. He could open and close deals, two talents by no means always found lurking together in the same person; and, though it wasn't at all immediately apparent in his career, the skills of the operator concealed the aspirations of a popular educator: he had served with Unesco for a period immediately after the war. His career throughout the following decade was inextricably linked with the rising fortunes of the British film industry, over some sections of which he and his working partner, 'Cubby' Broccoli, came to exercise virtually imperialist suzerainty.

In 1958, largely on the strength of *Look Back in Anger's* international reputation and Richard Burton's Hollywood one, not then too badly dented by some of the appalling pictures he had made there, Saltzman had extracted a budget of between £200,000 and £250,000 from Warners and Associated British-Pathé, a British distribution company in which the American studio owned a part interest. Burton was not by any means Saltzman's first choice. Later on, he referred to the casting as 'a monumental miscalculation. Jimmy Porter was a confused and vulnerable youth, spewing out his resentment in impotent rage, whereas Burton, who was too old anyway, looked as if he could handle himself so capably that he'd lay anyone he hated out flat.'[1] But without such a star, he admitted, he couldn't have financed the film. 'Fortunately Burton owed Warners a film on a "play him or pay him" basis. If he did *Look Back in Anger* at least they'd get a picture out of their deal: if he didn't, they'd still have to pay him $125,000. He did it – but it made nonsense of the text.' Burton's fee was the largest item in the 'above the line' cost of a budget that represented a fair sized sum for a British film in those days, particularly with a risky subject. No one else took much: Claire Bloom, the only other name in the cast with a cinema following, received about £10,000; Richardson received no fee at all for directing; and he and Osborne, apart from the sale of the film rights in the play, 'were all in for £2,500, which was to be deferred. There was no question of percentages.' Richardson recalls that he and Osborne were lent 'a couple of thousand pounds' to live on while making the film – 'and about four or five years later, we were asked to pay the loan back. "First", we said, "may we have a full accounting of how the film has done?" ' Possibly out of sympathy, they were allowed to keep the loan.

STAGE TO SCREEN

The box-office does not reflect the significance of *Look Back in Anger*. 'It didn't do much business anywhere in the world,' said Saltzman, adding ruefully, 'I never made a film that got such good reviews and was seen by so few people.' Where its importance lies is in the fact that it got made at all, in the period in which it was made, and in the appearance in the cinema of the talents who made it.

[1] Harry Saltzman interviewed by the author, 17 February, 1972. Unless stated otherwise, all subsequent quotations from Saltzman come from the same source.

Osborne was quoted at the time as saying he was so weary of his play that he could not face writing a screenplay: this was entrusted to Nigel Kneale, a practised hand at film and television scripts, whose science-fiction thriller, *The Quatermass Experiment*, had created sensational interest on BBC TV five years before. Kneale had met Richardson when both of them were working for BBC TV. As one of the Corporation's two script-editors, Kneale had adapted a Chekhov play which Richardson directed with George Devine in the lead: so the founding talents of the Royal Court Theatre knew and trusted him. Nevertheless, Kneale believes that his being brought in to script *Look Back in Anger* caused Osborne some distress, especially when he put the emphasis on opening up the play and re-locating scenes outside the Porters' flat. 'Saltzman was very keen on dispersing it,' Kneale later recalled. 'Had it been utterly claustrophobic, like Pinter's *The Caretaker*, I would have resisted the idea: but that was not the essential nature of the Osborne play. We got the financial backing on the first draft, which paid for the finished script. The jazz prologue was Richardson's idea; and so, of course, were those scenes where he utilized the resources of the locations. As we had heard so much about Jimmy Porter's market stall in the play, I felt there was no reason why we should not see it and have scenes set there. Moreover, the introduction of a coloured Indian stall-holder was a wish on my part to test Jimmy by giving him a cause to fight for.'[1] Kneale wasn't totally in sympathy with – still less in awe of – Jimmy Porter's angry rhetoric, which sounded to him like the petulant irritation of a writer with a bad case of 'block' or a pile of rejected manuscripts. At one time he did venture to give Jimmy some literary leanings, only to have Osborne object to this touch and insist on removing it from the screenplay. 'I suppose he didn't want any echo of *Epitaph for George Dillon*,' says Kneale.[2] The casting was a worry to Kneale, too. Kenneth Haigh, the stage Jimmy Porter, had struck an angry-

---

[1] Nigel Kneale interviewed by the author, 30 April, 1971. Unless stated otherwise, all subsequent quotations from Kneale come from the same source.

[2] An earlier play by Osborne about a failed writer.

young-mannish note just by the way he stood and looked; but it
was feared that the outbursts of the forceful Burton might take on
sado-masochistic overtones and make the censor apprehensive.
This didn't happen, though such words as 'Christ,' 'bitch,' and
'bastard' were deleted. And there was concern about showing
Jimmy and his wife Alison in bed together – which was then one
of the Hollywood Production Code taboos. Looking back,
Kneale admired Richardson's flair for visual composition and
recalled his frustration at having to shoot so much of the film in a
studio, where even the hospital ward, where Jimmy's patron, Ma
Tanner, lies dying, was re-created *in toto* for what Richardson
merely wanted to be an impressionistic touch. The extremely
mobile photography was Richardson's reaction to being penned
up in a sound-stage, Kneale concluded. Unable to free himself at
this early stage in his career, he freed the next best thing – his
camera.

Had it been filmed eighteen months later, much about *Look
Back in Anger* might have been different and probably better. The
new wave of working-class or lower-middle-class actors might
have conferred a more class-conscious sharpness on Jimmy
Porter: but they certainly would not have handicapped the
character with the already established image of a film star like
Richard Burton. Not that Burton's performance, in this critic's
opinion, is unintelligent or indeed unsuccessful. In spite of looking too old, too well armoured within and without to be vulnerable to the *mal de siècle*, he renders the character's essence powerfully, especially his Hamlet-like misogyny, his self-reproach, his
impotence to change the world, his incapacity to love his wife
Alison, played by Mary Ure, the only survivor from the stage
production, who perfectly complements Jimmy's tormented
energy with the drained face of a long-suffering partner. But since
screen tradition understands patient Grizeldas less well than
budding Jezebels, it is Claire Bloom, as the cold bitch Helena,
who emerges as the hardest thing in the film. The screen also
changed the emphasis that a stage production must give to Cliff,
the lodger-friend played by Gary Raymond. More plainly than
in the play, he is Alison's silent comforter; less plainly, since the

camera often keeps him literally out of the picture, he is the
disturbing and ambiguous third member of an ill-assorted
ménage in which a husband is more at ease horsing around with his
male pal than reaching an understanding with his wife.

But the changes wrought in the dramatic relationships are
meagre compared with the revisions made in the play to widen its
appeal on the screen. Nigel Kneale's adaption doesn't cool off
Jimmy's anger, but it does tune it down to a more bearable
volume and absorbs the impact of his monologues into the
shapely, taut sense of sequence he given the three-act play. By
ranging widely outside the attic digs, it pits his rage against a
picture of the real world and, once he is involved so personally in
a world he has reviled in the vacuum of his own loathing, he is to
some extent forced to eat his words – a hefty meal. The coloured
market stall-holder, as much an outcast in provincial England as
he was an untouchable in India, finds a champion in Jimmy
Porter – so there *are* some good, brave causes left. The film
deepens his humanity as it lessens his spleen by sparking off a
warm-hearted response to the old lady who set him up in business
as she lies dying. Above all, the film subtly internationalises Jimmy
Porter. It divorces him from his specifically English background
as a 'child of the times' and sets him against three themes that
meant most in international cinema in the 1950s – the generation
gap, race prejudice, and jazz music.

The crucial differences of class are still active in the film: as
Time's critic remarked, Jimmy behaves towards his wife as if he
had captured her from the upper class and was torn between
despising her antecedents and desiring her personally. But now it
is extended into a resentment of the smothering family or the
intolerant elders, those barriers to communication which had
become a staple theme of the American cinema in the mid-1950s.
As David Robinson said, 'The inability of (Alison's) Daddy and
Cliff to meet and talk on equal terms, even though each is impelled by complete honesty and good will, becomes much more
apparent when it is seen on the screen.'[1] It is also much more
obviously a difference of age than class. The Indian stall-holder
signifies the presence of immigrant faces on the British scene – a

few months later came the film *Sapphire*, whose murder riddle was solved by a racial clue – and the colour prejudice he suffers causes Jimmy to look *forward* in anger to social intolerance, thus linking him, however tenuously, with a viewpoint already familiar to American liberals and film-goers. And his competence on the trumpet accompanying the Chris Barber Band in the credits sequence – was this a memory of Saltzman's tour of the New York night-spots? – permits him to speak with the international voice of jazz.

In spite of the three-year delay between the play and the film – or, perhaps, because of it – Jimmy Porter evoked reactions from a number of film critics which matched those of the theatre critics on the first night. The *New York Times*'s critic liked the film but hated Jimmy Porter – 'a consistent weakling, a mature cry-baby, who can't quite cope with the problems of a tough environment and vents his spleen in nasty words.'[2] John Mc-Carten likewise found him detestable: 'He inveighs against his surroundings, his spouse, her middle-class relatives and a civilisation that has made him an outsider. It is hard to imagine any civilisation that would make him an insider.'[3] Yet it also seemed that the delay in filming the play had affected it in a more debilitating way than any understandable desire to make it explicable to the widest number of film-goers might have done. Time has overtaken the Jimmy of 1956. 'What makes it seem diluted,' Isabel Quigly wrote, 'is that Jimmy Porter no longer turns up as a surprise. At the tail end of the fashion he once set, he now comes with a manner, a voice, opinions and grudges we know all too well: already we know the reactions he set up, the sacred cows he (only too effectively) helped to demolish; indeed the angry young man, cosseted till his anger looks like petulance, has become a stock figure of our society.'[4]

True enough. And yet the film *as a film* remains enormously fresh and invigorating in feeling – and precisely in those aspects of it that had nothing to do with the play, but everything to do

[1] *Sight and Sound*, Summer–Autumn 1959, Vol. 28, Nos 3 and 4, p. 123.
[2] *The New York Times*, 30 September, 1959.
[3] *The New Yorker*, 3 October, 1959.
[4] *The Spectator*, 5 June, 1959.

with its director. The purposeful camera, the scuffed, well-worn look of life that it records – it was hard to say where locations ended and studio sets began, though the latter predominated – creates a world of Jimmy Porter that the stage never could. Ma Tanner dies in a ward with streetcars rattling and sparking past outside and becomes just part of the cemetery clay. Alison waits for news of her pregnancy in a dark and squalid G.P.'s surgery such as the screen had rarely showed, up to then. The church belfry booms pompously above the hideous back-to-back houses. People beat stiffly up the street against wind and rain to the service, the Sunday papers with their ration of sex and violence left reluctantly behind . . . The film moved around far more freely than *Room at the Top* in the kind of industrial town recognisable everywhere at the time – except on the cinema screen. And occasionally it used the environment as a poetic extension of harsh reality very much in the manner of 'Free Cinema.' Such is the sequence where Jimmy's outburst against a conventional guts-and-glory war film is continued outside the cinema as his bitter humour contrasts the world's self-seekers with its sufferers: the camera, picking up the dead eyes of old men on park benches, finally crowns his gibes with its own stealthy irony and comes to rest on the statue of some obscure local worthy above whose complacent brow the figure of Fame poises the laurel crown.

A MAN FOR ALL WEATHERS

It was to escape from 'perfection' that Tony Richardson sought escape from the film studio. 'Perfection is not an end,' the 'Free Cinema' founders had proclaimed. So what was? *Look Back in Anger* suggested at least one answer in the rough-cast texture he tried to create whenever location realism collaborated with him – or even when it did not, and so forced him into intuitive improvisation. In this and later films, Richardson sometimes made things deliberately difficult for himself so as to get a realistic atmosphere. From the very first he had hated working inside a studio, as Kneale has stated. He had learnt from his television experience that it cramped him creatively and kept him at a distance from his material. But it also cramped him physically, and this made a significant contribution to the feel of Richardson's films. The powerful 'physicality' they have comes partly from a talent for positioning actors in relation to their environment, but it is also the response of a man whose own lanky, oddly disjointed and restless body, with the scornful, dismissive gestures characteristic of him in the early days, made him continuously sensitive to his surroundings. Anderson and Reisz can both plan in their heads: Richardson prefers to start functioning when he gets himself to the scene of the action. Anything that irons out the natural truth of what he responds to is anathema to him. Of Tom Courtenay, whom he cast in *The Loneliness of the Long Distance Runner* three years later, he once remarked, 'He has a very interesting face with a good set of broken teeth. He could have a great future, I feel, provided he doesn't get his teeth fixed, as some fools are already trying to get him to do.'[1] Yes, even in others, perfection was not an end.

Better than any other English director, except perhaps Peter Brook, Richardson can cast his films physically so that a historical period or a life-style is summed up in a character's posture or build: it is not accidental that his greatest success with actors has come with parts where their body movements are built into a tradition, like the English music-hall of *The Entertainer*, or are associated with a peculiarly English type of satirical caricature as represented by *Tom Jones* and *The Charge of the Light Brigade*. Richardson's need to respond to reality would sometimes become a source of danger in later films, imposing a naturalism where the dramatic essence of the subject resisted it; but it served him well and gave him the vigour of an innovator by instinct when he set out to break down the four-wall look of the studio set-up. Thus the stage-plays that set the drama in the English provinces found the most timely kind of interpreter in someone with a compulsion to take the camera there, too; and their themes of protest against social smugness or a dead-end environment seemed sharpened by

[1] Tony Richardson, interviewed by Thomas Wiseman, *Evening Standard*, 7 April, 1961.

the reality, not to say the discomfort, of location shooting. Both morally and physically, the Puritan was served!

The high value which Richardson put on imperfection, the freshness of the sketch compared with the worked-over deadness of the finished painting, also changed the nature of the acting he demanded and, before long, the kind of actors he cast to achieve it. One observer, Derek Prouse, wrote, 'I have seen him on location, with his actors ready and word-perfect, suddenly assume a look of deep concentration and say flatly, "This is awful, isn't it? Why don't we change it all?" And there and then, text, moves, even mood would be changed, and always for the better. It is a technique to which young, agile actors can respond with creative enthusiasm, but older ones, with a traditional approach to work, often find unnerving.'[1] Richardson's own comments at the time of *A Taste of Honey*, his third film, bear this out. 'The way we are shooting the film we are at the mercy of real life. If it's raining we don't wait for the sun to come out, we just play the scene in the rain. If there's a wind blowing which gets the leading actress's hair untidy, we shoot her looking untidy. Of course if we had a big female star in the film we couldn't do this . . . we haven't the time or the inclination to bother about obtaining the most flattering shots.'[2] Considering the conditions that are taken for granted in filming today, remarks like this now sound like something out of the pre-history of the cinema: but it is vital to remember how unorthodox they were at the time, almost heretical coming from someone working inside the industry's studio-centred traditions of England or Hollywood. They again show the timeliness of Richardson's entry into film-making. The new sort of players demanded by the realism of the roles found a man temperamentally and, pretty soon, *technically* equipped to integrate them naturalistically with the action – and so extend them beyond the narrow range of the 'trad' film stars.

Escaping from the studio shaped Richardson in another important way: it gave him the discretionary power of a field commander. And again his nature equipped him to use it to the

[1] *The Sunday Times*, 13 February, 1968.
[2] Thomas Wiseman, *op. cit.*, 7 July, 1961.

C

full. It wasn't simply that he didn't have a producer in an office along the corridor from the sound-stage where he was shooting who only needed to twitch a short rein to remind him who was boss. Richardson soon learned that it was not enough to enjoy the right creative atmosphere: there was another sort of power that went with it, the power a producer wields, a political sense rather than a creative skill. Sheer physical distance from those who would control him helped to establish this kind of independence. 'I am much more of a politician than John Osborne,' he remarked early in his career. 'John is a writer and he, basically, has only to have a relationship with a sheet of paper in his typewriter. I have to deal with people, with actors and artists and financiers . . . I have to be more of a diplomat.'[1] A stubborn diplomat, it must be added. Richardson's north-country bluntness has sometimes more wilfulness in it than will-power. He, John Osborne and Lindsay Anderson have in common a predilection for the impromptu or ill-considered act or utterance which they stick to through thick and thin, however embarrassing or even harmful the public reaction is. In less resilient natures, this could be fatal: but in a producer-director, such as Richardson and Anderson soon became in deed if not in title, it is a source of strength to be drawn on in the testing time of mutual bluff which they have often had to endure while setting up a film with the financiers.

There was one final aspect of Richardson's nature that had a bearing on the kind of director he became: it was one he shared with Jimmy Porter. Call it a sort of shame. Richardson in those early days felt himself, like Jimmy, eternally damned for being simply lower-middle-class, the son of a Yorkshire chemist, whereas he would have liked to boast of coming from right the other side of the barricades, from the working class. He didn't even have Jimmy Porter's masochistic consolation of going to a 'red brick' – i.e. provincial – university. A scholarship had taken Richardson to Oxford, where his leftishness was sharpened in that politically abrasive generation which included so many of those, as Christopher Booker has noted, who were destined to take over and reshape the mass media in the 1960s. Being one of the privi-

[1] Ibid.

leged fortified Richardson's 'secret shame,' as he ironically referred to it, that in getting this far he had availed himself of the school system which he despised on ideological grounds and accused of stifling individuality, of choking off passion, and of creating people who were 'too intelligent.' A reaction based on class guilt was transformed into a temperamental characteristic which in turn showed itself in his film-making. For in compensation – perhaps in expiation – he put a high price on the display of passion, on not hiding one's emotions but, rather, flaunting them. A sense of 'I feel, therefore I am' pervades his earliest utterances. 'What is so disheartening about the British cinema,' he wrote, just after finishing *Look Back in Anger*, 'is that few of the producers have any sort of convictions at all, not even determinedly commercial ones. Behind all their actions and decisions is a timidity which leads to a falling between every stool, so that their products are totally without vitality . . . This is a permanent revolution that we all have to fight. This is why it is so important to any director to have around him a crew who would always go to the barricades over every detail.'[1]

In passion lay risk, but also reassurance. And the notion of a man who set out totally to expose his feelings in his films was a novelty in a cinema where, traditionally, feelings were not things one owned up to, if one possessed them, or tried to cultivate if one did not, lest it be held to be bad form.

[1] 'A Free Hand,' *Sight and Sound* (Spring 1959), Vol. 28, No. 2, p. 64.

Chapter Four: What about the Workers?

> A British film nowadays, if it is to be taken seriously, must set its scene among the more or less rebellious young people of the industrial North or Midlands; it must be tough, realistic, iconoclastic (possibly nihilistic, too) and thoroughly working class.
>
> *The Manchester Guardian*, 25 September, 1962

'Independence' was of necessity in the air in 1959. Eighteen months earlier the British film industry had plunged into one of its periodic crises, though at first this one looked more disastrous than most. The box-office suffered a horrendous slump in 1957, admissions barely reaching the 900,000,000 mark: the decline was more than double the rate in 1955 and 1956, and in the latter year the film industry still paid an entertainments tax of precisely half the net box-office receipts. An All-Industry Tax Committee had presented a prayer to the Chancellor of the Exchequer on 8 February, 1958, pointing out that until this tax was cut 'the film industry has no funds available for improvement and development and it is virtually impossible to inject new capital into the industry in the present conditions.' The cost of a first-feature film had been around £100,000 in 1953; by 1958 it was £180,000 and still rising – and Wardour Street, where the film Establishment had its offices, regarded anything over £200,000 as 'very risky' and needing international stars and guaranteed distribution to attract the backing. Britain's biggest studio was Pinewood, lying at the end of a rhododendron-flanked drive and a gate-lodge with a sign like that of a quiet country inn. Owned by the Rank Organization, it had had to declare 300 workers redundant at the start of 1958, owing to the postponement of four films with a total budget of £1 million. Things were black on the labour front at other studios: almost 1,000 film workers had lost their jobs since January, 1958. With more money needed to make films and less opportunity to recoup it in Britain, the result had been an energetic drive to widen the foreign markets. At the end of the 1950s, the main production groups were moulding the character of their films for specific foreign markets, co-starring artists well known in Germany, France, Greece or even Japan, resorting more frequently to foreign locations – in short becoming more akin to exporters than producers. The specifically 'British' character of a film had been growing more and more nebulous. Columbia, 20th Century-Fox and Warners, as well as other Hollywood companies with British production outfits, took care to ensure that many of the films they made in Britain or on location in Europe – nominally 'British' production – were sometimes indistinguishable in look and tone from the product turned out by the home studios in California.

Times were particularly hard for the so-called 'independent' British producers: those who weren't 'tied' to American companies in Britain or the two British production-distribution-and-exhibition groups, Rank and A.B.C. Their work had become infinitely more hazardous since the 1957 credit squeeze and the unprecedented drop in admissions. Many of them expected to get a significant proportion of their budgets from the National Film Finance Corporation – the portion known as the 'risk' capital – and if business was bad the N.F.F.C. might lose the whole of its investment, as it was the last to be paid from the profits. Independent producers also relied on funds drawn from a levy on box-office receipts. As might be expected, it wasn't in good shape. The Cinematographic Film Act of 1957 had anticipated that the levy would total £3,750,000 in its first year, to be apportioned among the makers of British films according to their success at the box-office. On the figures available, it seemed unlikely that the Eady Levy, as it was called after its originator, would exceed £2,500,000 – and the All-Industry Tax Committee calculated that, in order to cover losses and provide a decent prospect of profit, a production fund of twice that amount was essential.

Yet if there is any constant factor at work determining the rise or fall of a film industry's economic or artistic fortunes, it is that revolutions are not launched in periods of abundance, but paradoxically when things look their blackest. The slump in the film industry at the end of the 1950s promoted two beneficial effects: rootlessness and restlessness. And out of these flowed new amalgams of talent, fresh combinations of finance, and a much swifter recognition of any new trend that bucked the adds and found favour where it counted most – at the box-office. One cannot insist too strongly throughout this study on one unchanging aspect of the film industry – any film industry, but especially the Anglo-American one. It is not basically a creative industry. It is, on the contrary, an overwhelmingly imitative one in which only a few genuinely creative people are tolerated at any given time. A handful of such people – Anderson, Reisz, Richardson, Clayton, the Woodfall Films group – who were artistically innovative and, in the case of *Room at the Top*, financially successful as well, have already been examined. One now has to see how such breakthroughs as they made were integrated into the changing pattern of the industry.

One man who found himself in 1958 without the firm anchorage of past success was Sir Michael Balcon. In 1955 his cramped but creative old domicile, Ealing Studios, so long the fertile source of the quixotic Ealing comedies, had been sold reluctantly for a little over £300,000 to BBC TV. Balcon had been under the impression that 'we would then move to Pinewood Studios where a special "household" would be set up, allowing us to retain our "team" and the Ealing "image."'[1] Ealing had close links with the Rank Organization, whose distribution wing, General Film Distributors, handled their films, and as Rank then had a substantial holding in the Hollywood company, Universal, this was an invaluable entrée into the American market. But, for reasons he was still reluctant to go into fifteen years later, Balcon's expectations of being able to preserve his independence at Pinewood proved deceptive. He had to look elsewhere – and quickly – and found ready assistance from Arthur Loew, an old friend and the new president of M.G.M. and early in 1956 he re-established Ealing Films, as it was now called, at M.G.M.'s British studios, at Borehamwood, intending to make six films which would be available for distribution by M.G.M. in the United States.

[1] Sir Michael Balcon, interviewed by the author, 14 January, 1972. Unless stated otherwise, all subsequent quotations from Balcon come from the same source.

Although the loss of Ealing – one almost writes 'Eden' – left Balcon with a heavy heart, he hoped 'it was people that counted, not buildings.' But he later confessed in his autobiography that 'this was not strictly honest, as over the years there had developed at Ealing a spirit which had seeped into the very fabric of the place.'[1] During his three-year stay at M.G.M. he produced six films, among them *The Man in the Sky* (1956), *Barnacle Bill* (1958), *The Shiralee* (1956), and *Dunkirk* (1958): but seen against the less amiable, more sceptical pattern of life emerging in Britain at the end of the 1950s, the calculated humour, whimsy and heroism of unpretentious or eccentric people such as those in the films only induced a feeling of dated irrelevance. Even the *Dunkirk* epic, coming in the masochistic aftermath of the Suez débâcle, only served to remind folk of the days when a military setback was not so much a defeat as a retrieval of unity and will. Ealing Films, in short, was now somewhat out of joint with the times. And Balcon himself was soon out of touch with the M.G.M. management; for, very shortly after his team had moved in at Borehamwood, Arthur Loew had left the parent company in Hollywood and in the interregnum Balcon found himself unable to establish even the most fleeting contact with the contending powers at Culver City, California.

He had an even more personal anxiety on the home front, where British film exhibitors were strenuously endeavouring to keep old movies off the television screens. Although this was ultimately self-defeating and a dire distraction from what should have been their primary task of keeping audiences in the cinemas by good management and prompt response to changing habits, it made Balcon fear that film-makers like himself would be black-listed on future movies if they sold their old ones direct to television. A boycott of one producer had already been attempted. So he agreed readily enough when the Associated British Picture Corporation approached him in 1957 with an offer for all the Ealing company assets. A.B.P.C. owned A.B.C. TV, the fourth largest commercial television company in Britain, and thus had

[1] Michael Balcon, *Michael Balcon Presents . . . A Lifetime of Films* (Hutchinson, 1969), p. 187.

an entrée for the screening of old movies on the box without risking a film-trade embargo. Thus the film industry paid lip-service to the embargo while continuing to feed the monster that was gobbling up its audiences. Balcon believed he had a verbal agreement with A.B.P.C. to continue joint production at their Elstree studios just across the road from M.G.M. This never materialised. He completed one of his M.G.M. films, *The Siege of Pinchgut* (1959), at Elstree and then faced the fact that for the first time in several decades he would have to make films as an individual minus the old team. The buildings had gone – now the people followed.

But the 'team spirit' is deeply ingrained in Balcon. And the fact that more and more independents such as he were finding it harder and harder in the 1959 slump to get distribution guarantees – i.e. the lion's share of the budget advanced by the companies who distribute the finished films on which the makers can then raise the completion or 'end' money from the N.F.F.C. – added the spur of necessity to temperamental inclination. He reacted favourably when another independent producer, Maxwell Setton, proposed the formation of a film-makers' co-operative, a group of producers or producer-directors whose collective reputation – and credit-worthiness – would give them easier access to distribution guarantees – even to fresh sources of finance. The result was Bryanston Films, launched in April 1959, with Balcon as part-time chairman (by this time he was producing his film version of *The Long and the Short and the Tall:* 1960), and Max Setton as managing director.

'Getting Balcon was the easiest step in setting up Bryanston,' Setton recalled later.[1] 'I looked round for someone who was well-heeled, interested in the creative urge, with experience, a successful industry personality – and turned to him. Then it was a matter of going to producers and directors, or teams of the two, and persuading them to join; about sixteen creative people all told, who came in by stages.' Among the more prominent

---

[1] Maxwell Setton interviewed by the author, 12 August, 1971. Unless stated otherwise, all subsequent quotations from Setton come from the same source.

names were old Ealing talents like Michael Relph, Basil Dearden
and Charles Frend; Norman Priggen (later Joseph Losey's close
associate and producer); Ronald Neame (photographer turned
producer – *Great Expectations*, etc., and director – *The Horse's
Mouth*, etc.); John Bryan (production designer turned producer –
The Card, etc.); Monja Danischewsky (producer – *Whisky Galore*);
Albert Fennell; and Julian Wintle and Leslie Parkyn (independent
producers who released films through the Rank Organization).
'The Shipman brothers, Gerald and Kenneth, were very helpful
since they owned Twickenham Studios,' said Setton, 'and the
studios and processing laboratories could put up finance in the
form of credit facilities. Each of the active members contributed
£5,000 – the Shipmans put in £20,000 – and Lloyd's Bank gave
us three-to-one revolving fund.' This meant that the bank recovered its loan first from the proceeds of the film, and the sum
available continued 'revolving.' British Lion, the independent
distribution company, was to handle the films, half-a-dozen a
year, it was hoped, for which they contributed an advance
guarantee, charged a fee of 25 per cent and took 17 per cent of the
distributor's gross. British Lion's studios at Shepperton were also
to be used for some of the films. The capital available was about
£1 million. 'We set up a small sub-committee of producer-
directors who would vet the projects,' said Setton. 'It rotated and
they acted as the creative advisers of a financial undertaking,
examining the scripts in turn. Then I synthesized the views
expressed on them and we thrashed it out at a board meeting.'
Obvious risks lay in passing judgment on projects cherished by
other members of the co-operative. 'The voting arrangements at
Bryanston for the approval of a project called for a clear majority
of two, but there had to be a quorum of seven members,' Balcon
recalled, adding with characteristic cautiousness: 'to put it
another way, if only seven directors were at a meeting, five
favourable votes would be needed for approval.'[1] Setton declared
that budgets were to be kept, where possible, between £150,000
and £180,000, and Balcon stated flatly that there were to be no
'blockbusters.' It wasn't just that funds didn't run to 'spectacles' –

[1] Sir Michael Balcon in a letter to the author, 15 February, 1972.

'Beyond £250,000 we really had to pause and think hard,' said Setton – but Balcon still instinctively shyed away from the fatal English urge to emulate Hollywood's international success by inflating the compact English product, sacrificing its native character and forcing up costs in the process. The 'Little England' image of Ealing was slow to fade away. Lastly, Bryanston members were not bound to make films for it exclusively; and outsiders would be welcomed if they brought along attractive propositions.

Such was the attempt to rescue independent British film production from the doldrums of the 1959 slump. It was enterprising but cautious; it had as many safeguards as opportunities built into it; it made a virtue of independence but sought to reduce its risks by consensus opinion and committee decision. All these things should be remembered in view of what subsequently developed; for in many ways the Bryanston co-operative and its company rules and aspirations were a group portrait of its members, and its character was to be of decisive moment at one of the earliest turning-points determining who should have the financial muscle in the British film industry of the 1960s – the indigenous residents or the new American settlers.

Most of the early Bryanston films were modest in proportion and intention. Comedies about keeping American progress at bay by pinning your faith to old-established English eccentricity (*The Battle of the Sexes*, 1960), about whimsical kidnapping (*The Boy who stole a Million*, 1960), about the wartime humours of a searchlight battery (*Light Up the Sky*, 1960); dramas about technological disasters (*Cone of Silence*, 1960), about delinquency in the classroom (*Spare the Rod*, 1961) – all these showed the depressing gravitational pull of traditional cosiness, understatement and easy sentiment: they were all acquiescent films, not anxious to assert an alternative to contemporary behaviour or to affront the comfortable prejudices of their likely audiences. Even the most socially conscious of them, *Spare the Rod*, had been postponed for several years because of the film censors' reluctance to see the already shaky authority of the British schoolteacher further impaired by any sensational treatment like that in the Hollywood film *Blackboard Jungle*. It finally arrived on the screen in a watered-down form made all the more antiseptic by the casting of a popular light comedian as the harassed hero. In fact, the first notably non-conformist film which Bryanston financed didn't come from among its members at all. It was brought to the consortium for approval – and cash, of course, too – by a team of outsiders, Woodfall Films.

GETHSEMANE-ON-SEA

Look Back in Anger had left Woodfall tasting the sour flavour of failure. 'In England it was a disaster,' Saltzman recalled, 'opening in a heatwave that turned London into an outdoor city for at least a fortnight – people sleeping in the parks at night – and drawing mixed reviews. In France, it fared slightly better. *Le Figaro* did something it's never done since: it took two bites at the film, advising readers to see it, saying it would help young people to understand their own frustrations and older ones to communicate with their children. What it saw in the film wasn't a class system – as the English did – but a generation gap. But it didn't do much business anywhere in the world.' The experience with Warners hadn't been happy, either, and one reason for Woodfall's going to Bryanston was to keep control of their work. The project they put up was Osborne's play *The Entertainer:* once again the repertory of the Royal Court was the most negotiable collateral they had to offer. Bryanston advanced 75 per cent of the budget; the National Film Finance Corporation came up with most of the rest; and Richardson believes 'there was a little' from Walter Reade Jr., the American distributor-exhibitor who was to handle the film in the United States. Estimates of the cost vary: some say it was £200,000, others nearer £300,000. Certainly it was high, too high for a 'risk' subject, and out of line with Bryanston's vows of financial prudence, but it was swollen by a variety of difficulties, technical, artistic and human, right from the start. Nigel Kneale was again contracted to adapt Osborne's play for the screen, with the author himself contributing additional dialogue. But the project began with a basic contradiction which the completed film never successfully resolved. Saltzman and Richardson wanted to free the play from the stage; at the same time they also wanted to re-create Laurence Olivier's *tour de force* performance as Archie Rice, the stage 'entertainer' of the title. Olivier had agreed to work in the film for a pittance, against a percentage of the net profit, and Saltzman and Richardson resisted pressure to replace him by a box-office star, figuring that he was the only person with the equipment to do the part justice and that, anyway, his name and presence in the first modern-dress role he had played in fifteen years must mean *something* in cinema terms. Kneale, on the other hand, felt constricted by the obligation to provide room in a film scenario for a star actor whose own keen recollection of the audience-response to his unforgettable stage performance to some extent dictated the way the part had to be conceived for the screen – in short, it had not got to be altered, or very little.

But the disjuncture went deeper. John Russell Taylor diagnosed what had gone wrong when he wrote, 'In *The Entertainer* . . . the influence of Brecht is very marked in a number of incidentals, though one would guess that, at that time at least, he (Osborne) had not fully grasped what the epic theatre was about. (The totally misconceived film version . . . which tries to transplant all the least realistic sections unchanged into a setting of documentary realism, would tend to support such an opinion.)'[1] Kneale had seen this trap and felt that the play should have been completely recast for the screen, even if it meant forfeiting Olivier, since this was the only means he envisaged of getting *carte blanche* for a completely naturalistic approach. But he had also promised Richardson to take the play out of doors as much as possible – on to the pier, at the beauty-queen contest, into the caravan on the sand flats where Archie seduces the teenage winner – so as to give the director all those opportunities he wanted for improvising scenes according to some felicitous accident of the location or the shooting set-up. Thus the balance of the film was tilted towards the director's naturalistic preference, but had to accommodate the star's non-naturalistic techniques.

[1] John Russell Taylor, *Anger and After* (Methuen, 1962), p. 47.

That Olivier's screen performance would almost, if not quite, conceal the jarring construction of the film is evidence of the self-corrective intuition possessed by the very greatest performers.

There were other problems of adaptation. Kneale decided that in opening up the play he would bring in some of the characters kept off-stage by Osborne, notably the boy-friend of Archie's daughter, Jean, and Archie's son Mick, whose death on the Suez expedition pierces through the old stager's self-pity like a stab of genuine pain in the middle of anaesthesia. Mick, the simpler creation, was played by Albert Finney, making a screen début that was as bright for his future as a promissory note. But, feeling that Osborne's off-stage characters tended towards caricature, Kneale attempted to re-create the 'Burlington Bertie' type – which was how *he* interpreted the text's references to Mick – as a contemporary working-class opportunist, a man on the make who despised his own social origins. When Kneale eventually parted company with the film, and Osborne took over, the character reverted to something nearer its original form.

With shooting over, the film overran its allotted running-time and had to be shortened; there was trouble, too, over the quality of the sound recorded on location – a contest, it was said, between Olivier and the Morecambe seagulls. The West End première was cancelled, the film was rejected as the official entry at the Cannes Film Festival in favour of 20th Century-Fox's British production *Sons and Lovers*, with the American star Dean Stockwell as the young D. H. Lawrence, and the atmosphere when *The Entertainer* at last opened in London on 28 July, 1960, was edgy and pessimistic.

The Entertainer shows its weakness and its director's relative inexperience by its over-insistence on being a film – and not a filmed play. Like the extremely mobile camera which Richardson used in *Look Back in Anger* as compensation for being penned up on a sound-stage, the blatant shock cuts and abrasive sound effects of *The Entertainer* seem to be trying to capture the vulgar energy of the seaside comic postcards in what Roger Manvell called a conscious revolt against British gentility. But if Richardson was ruthless in his use of music, he was effective too, and he created an uncaring climate of noise around Archie, while his camera kept cutting to his despair like a blind suddenly snapping up in the face of a man with a morning hangover. Rock 'n' roll blaring out inhumanely, crashing chords giving a hollow music-hall build-up to the hollow entertainer, and, more subtly, the traditional dance-hall rhythms percolating into the caravan where Archie has seduced the young girl and has turned a bored middle-aged eye on her gushing tribute to his residual prowess. *The Entertainer* is a film one seems to hear rather than see. The trouble is that with all this unflagging energy out to lacerate one's sensibility with an impression of Gethsemane-on-Sea, there is precious little encouragement, or even chance, for an audience to reflect on what they do hear and see. All too aptly is it titled *The Entertainer:* fear of not being entertaining enough is behind the film's overloaded feel. Happily, Olivier's performance sidesteps the danger. It is only slightly more obviously a 'performance' than it was on the distancing stage, and there is actually a gain for realism in the presence of a 'film audience' which gets over the awkward illogicality of the audience at the Royal Court, who roared their appreciation of every gag of Archie's that was supposed to 'die,' because of the way Olivier brilliantly reproduced the effect of the man's third-rateness. By not requiring Olivier to play directly to us in the cinema, as if *we* were Archie's audience, the entertainment of the performance is no longer in conflict with the flop of the entertainer. Nor is the figure which Archie cuts so wilfully degenerate, as it is on the stage. The gap in the front teeth has been narrowed, the hair glossed down, ten years have been taken off his age, though all this is done as much for the benefit of probability in his seduction scene as for his inspection by the camera in close-ups. But inside Archie, Olivier suggests the eroded soul of the man who makes a martyr of himself twice nightly. 'When Archie's sky darkens and total failure has finally to be faced,' Paul Dehn wrote, 'he faces it with the line, "I have a go, don't I, ladies? I have a go." Sir Laurence looks and speaks this like a corpse still kicking.'[1]

It is entirely due to Olivier that the film's end is genuinely

[1] *News Chronicle*, 29 July, 1960.

moving, for the extra scenes written into it, like the funeral of the son killed at Suez, are stupendous anti-climaxes. To draw a classical actor of Olivier's stature into a contemporary role was an achievement that the stage passed triumphantly on to the film. But a greater augury for the changing cinema was the presence in the film of Albert Finney, as Mick – neither a film personality with a popular reputation nor yet a name from the traditional West End theatre. Finney came from Salford, and drew on his provincial roots and repertory-company background for his independent outlook; he had a commitment to do work that would help break down the polite middle-classness of his profession. Interviewed around this time by Louis Marcourelles, the French film critic, Finney said, 'I've always felt strongly about the fact that the cinema in England has been regarded as a kind of hobby, which pays a little extra on the side, while the theatre is the place where I do my real prestige work. I want to do my prestige work in the cinema as well; and I think that feeling is growing.'[1] It was. The speed with which Finney, and others like him, were accepted by cinema audiences was one of the strongest impetuses which the new film-makers enjoyed.

THE SATURDAY NIGHT FEELING

'After the financial flop of *The Entertainer*,' said Harry Saltzman, 'I was as dead as any producer could be.' Though Saltzman personally liked the film, he had to admit that the reluctance of the exhibitors to book it was right – and as he put it, he had practically to 'blackmail' the Rank Organization to show it in their cinemas. The results bore out everything Saltzman had absorbed about show-business, virtually through his pores, since his small-town boyhood 'when a film would open on a Friday, and by mid-day Saturday you knew if the Palace had a hit or a flop. The public somehow know if they'll like it: if they don't get this feeling, nothing will make a hit out of a miss. I come from a circus and vaudeville family and I know this initial instinctual push from the

[1] 'Talking about Acting,' *Sight and Sound* (Spring 1961), Vol. 30, No. 2, p. 59.

public is what counts – their sense of acceptance is infallible.' All
of which might seem just one more show-business cliché except
that Saltzman's next production bore out the truth of it to the
letter. And the extraordinary series of hits which began with the
phenomenal Bond saga exemplifies the very real way in which he
applied his piece of 'folk wisdom,' so that 'you don't work with
the screen, you work with the audience.' The lessons of these early
reverses were being read and digested.

In their early months Woodfall Films had bought the film
rights to a novel by Alan Sillitoe which another producer,
Joseph Janni, had owned but failed to set up – largely because
none of the orthodox distributors he turned to were prepared to
finance an English film in which the working classes were portrayed as leading an active sex life, and a rather irregular one at
that.[1] The book was *Saturday Night and Sunday Morning.* His
option expiring, Janni reluctantly sold it to Woodfall for 'about
£2,000.' The only trouble was, Saltzman had no money to pay a
scriptwriter of any reputation, so he was obliged to turn to
Sillitoe, who had never written for the screen, and cajole him into
doing the adaptation. 'It was a matter of economics as much as
anything,' he recalled. This was the last and possibly the most
fruitful economy Harry Saltzman ever needed to make.

Sillitoe's relationship to the project was ambivalent. To begin
with, he had been astonished in the first place when it had been
bought for filming. To him, it didn't seem a story in any real
sense: the first chapter had really been started as a short story
which he sent to the *London Magazine* around May 1955 'and of
course it came straight back.' So he wrote another story with the
same character, a working-class factory hand called Arthur
Seaton, and a similar set of interests, and he soon had half-a-dozen
such tales. These he ploughed into a novel, giving it an episodic
character. It is fair to believe that it was this naturally episodic
structure which facilitated the structural flow of the screenplay he
eventually wrote. 'I'd been to very few films in my life,' he
recalled later. 'To me at the time, a film was likely to mean an

[1] For a fuller account of Janni's frustrated ambitions for *Saturday Night
and Sunday Morning*, see Chapter Six.

Ealing comedy.'[1] He did remember *Love on the Dole*, however – 'a very moving experience.' 'But I told myself I'd managed to write a novel without experience, so why not a film script? But it was a hard job. I had to read the novel twenty times and ended up hating it, and the script took about nine months and four or five drafts before it came down to a more or less 100-scene play.' Interestingly, Sillitoe, in speaking about his main difficulty 'which was cutting things out,' referred to Visconti's film *Rocco and his Brothers*, which he envied for having the running time to put everything in, and a curious family feeling is detectable between the two proletarian milieux, one Italian, the other English, which indicates a possible if perhaps unconscious source of inspiration.

When the script was finished – 'I had hardly the money to keep up the weekly payments,' Saltzman recalled – the problem of finding a director had to be faced. Richardson demurred. Saltzman felt 'he had been disappointed by the reception of his first two films and George Devine was telling him to come back to the Royal Court and make the stage his career instead of playing around with "this mad producer Saltzman."' So Woodfall turned to Karel Reisz, who badly wanted to make a feature film and 'this film in particular, if it could be set up.' Richardson agreed to produce; Bryanston was persuaded to put up 70 per cent of the budget; and the rest was to come from the National Film Finance Corporation and Walter Reade. The total sum involved was £100,000 and Twickenham Studios advanced a credit of £25,000 in deferred rentals. This really was a knotted shoestring budget – and at the end of the first week's shooting, Walter Reade suddenly lost faith in this movie 'about a boy in a factory' and pulled out his £25,000 share of the budget. 'We finished the picture,' Saltzman recalled colourfully, 'with arms linked in a human rescue chain.'

For Karel Reisz the film was a chance to scratch the itch set up by Richard Hoggart's article in *Sight and Sound* in 1959 in which he had advised Reisz to expand 'the legitimacy of the limits' which

---

[1] Alan Sillitoe interviewed by the author, 19 June, 1972. Unless stated otherwise, all subsequent quotations from Sillitoe come from the same source.

he and the other 'Free Cinema' directors had imposed on themselves. It represented an opportunity to bring the 'public' life of a young person into the 'personal' life – to extend the 'film essay' type of 'Free Cinema' project into the imaginative breadth and deeper artistic intentions possible in a full-length feature film. And he approached *Saturday Night and Sunday Morning* in a way that was characteristic of both his early film-making and his belief that 'the only way to get to know a place is to work there.' Accompanied by Sillitoe, he took a small film unit north to the factories and collieries around Nottingham and proceeded to shoot a dry run for his major project in the shape of a documentary film about a miners' welfare centre. The Central Office of Information paid for it and Sillitoe wrote the commentary. 'Not a very good film,' Reisz recalled, but it served the purpose of a man who is in several respects the direct opposite of Tony Richardson.

Reisz prefers working in what he calls 'a painstaking, stamp-collector's way . . . I like to have it all at my fingertips before I start. It is a form of fear, I suppose.' It is also a form of thoroughness that helps account for this film's success in tunnelling more deeply than most into a layer of human life at a particular time and place. Reisz's thoroughness doesn't stop at planting other men's seeds: he does his own soil analysis. He worked closely with Sillitoe, on the script and afterwards, for the film was shot where the latter grew up and his own mother's house was used for some scenes. As Sillitoe recalled, 'It gave me a wonderful emotional shock to see Albert Finney standing at exactly the same place at the bench in the Raleigh factory where I had worked.' Reisz's determination to avoid any suspicion of 'going slumming' helped his push-through to fundamentals of people's lives and habits, and the earlier documentary film made it possible to keep to an extremely tight schedule – the film was budgeted for six weeks' shooting: even the huge fair-scene had to be filmed in a single night – and actually imparted an impetus to the production.

But undoubtedly a major reason for its success was the decision to cast Finney as Arthur Seaton. 'He wasn't my idea of Arthur,' Sillitoe said. 'My Arthur was taller and thinner in the face and the whole film should have been rougher, more brutal, to match him.' Finney did not think that Arthur resembled himself very much, either – 'but I did understand the character's dilemma. I'd known quite a few Arthurs in my boyhood in Salford: I'd also worked ten weeks in a factory to fill in the time before drama school. I am the sort of actor who draws things from people, consciously and unconsciously picking them up. I first realized that when I was acting in grammar-school plays and from that time on I began to make mental notes of how people behave. From my short spell in the factory I knew this character's rebellious attitude towards those in authority; I felt in touch and was able to give it a popular identity. And of course Reisz is the kind of director who invites you to chip in with ideas, to contribute to the film.'[1] From the film's opening frames, the looks, attitudes and, above all, the tone struck by Finney drew an instantaneous response from audiences. The identification really was immediate. One highly recognizable kind of temperament was split open for inspection in a workbench soliloquy that localized a whole stratum of English social class: 'Nine hundred and fifty bloody five. Another few more, that's the last for a Friday. Fourteen pound three and tuppence for a thousand of these a day. No wonder I alus got a bad back, though I'll soon be done. I'll have a fag in a bit. No sense working every minute God sends. I could get through it in half the time . . . but they'd only slash me wages, so they can get stuffed. Don't let the bastards grind you down. That's one thing you learn. What I'm out for is a good time. All the rest is propaganda.' An earlier script had opened with the men clocking out of the works: the shooting-script, opening with the stream-of-consciousness soliloquy, put thoughts and words on to a British screen with a vernacular directness totally alien to the cinema's polite, middle-class traditions. With his wary eye, cocky banter, short neck and jutting chin, Finney possessed the naturalistic vitality of a working-class environment where survival bred swift responses and not too much care for

---

[1] Albert Finney interviewed by the author, 16 September, 1971. Unless stated otherwise, all subsequent quotations from Finney come from the same source.

other people's feelings. The Beatles were soon going to turn such an attitude into a stock-in-trade. But its novelty was brand new in *Saturday Night and Sunday Morning*, and to see it welded together into an anti-hero, unrepentantly sexy in a repressive community, sharper than his mates, tougher than the pub brawlers he worsts, anti-romantic in his view of a woman as providing a night's pleasure, reconciled to paying the penalty for his pleasure, but resistant to all life could do to him, as well as to the factory foreman: this was a new force, a new surprise in the cinema. 'The creation of a contemporary backyard-and-factory conscience,' was Peter John Dyer's summing-up of the achievement.

Tone, probably even more than content, set the film apart from others of the time that shared the same setting in the back-to-back rows of near-slum houses, canal banks, and steep, mean streets sloping down towards the factories like greasy pie-crust that has fallen in. The tone was not the rage of *Look Back in Anger*, or the envy of *Room at the Top*. *Saturday Night and Sunday Morning* had a truculence about it. Arthur Seaton wolfed up life like hot dinners. He was not agin' society; he was for self. 'He is a well integrated person,' Sillitoe said, somewhat cynically, 'a loudmouth, in a sense, who does nothing, not aware of being part of an oppressed class because he is too bloody comfortable as it is.' He is satisfied with his environment for the opportunities it offers him to whore, booze and fight – the attributes of a good-time-boy who believes that 'all the rest is propaganda.' The measure of the film's skill is the way Reisz, Sillitoe and Finney manage to make manifest the almost imperceptible settling down and cooling off which is Arthur's lot. The brutal beating he gets from the pals of a workmate whose wife he has got pregnant – Rachel Roberts played her, growing ever more fearful and hunted till she and her 'lover' see each other in the denuding light of male pleasure versus female pain – is far more than a film's nose-bloodying retribution to square things with the censor. Along with the experience of finding himself hitched on to a girl every bit as sharp as himself, it changes Arthur's nature, and the film ends with a dim perception of how a way of life has claimed him, as it's claimed generations before him, and will eventually tame

him into social conformity in spite of his half-hearted gesture of
chucking stones in the direction of the new housing estate whose
middle-classness beckons so temptingly to his girl-friend.

There has been controversy over the meaning of this ending.
An earlier screenplay ended with the marriage, done with a good
deal of laconic humour. 'Marriage voluntarily entered into for
life, to the exclusion of all others,' intones the minister, whereupon 'Arthur's face shows disappointment at this last clause, as if
he wants to begin bargaining about numbers.' The 'stone-
throwing' new ending is held by Sillitoe to be 'just Round One,'
and his rather bitter reference at the time we spoke in 1972, to
'the bloody Tory Government and then the Labour people'
makes one think that he saw Arthur Seaton's settling down into a
placid consumer society as only a temporary lapse from militancy
which would revive when things got economically tougher.
Karel Reisz, on the other hand, saw it as a surrender. 'In a
metaphorical way Arthur embodied what was happening in
England: he was a sad person, terribly limited in his sensibilities,
narrow in his ambitions and a bloody fool into the bargain – by
no means a standard-bearer for any ideas of mine. I never work
with spokesmen. All my education, my teaching experience
warned me off treating people as representatives of their world,
rather than giving them the dignity of individuals; and I certainly disagree strongly with the idea that Arthur Seaton embodied
my values, my outlook – I am a middle-class Jew from Central
Europe. The stone-throwing is a symptom of his impotence, a
self-conscious bit, telling the audience over the character's
shoulder what I think of him. I wanted to continually contrast
the extent to which he is an aggressor with the extent to which he
is a victim of this world. I wanted the end to have this feeling of
frustration, but I'm not too keen on it today.'

FINNEY THE GOLDEN BOY

Albert Finney's success in the part was total: he said later that he
could have gone on playing Arthur Seatons for years. Not that he
was in any sense a 'discovery.' He had already established himself

on the stage and everyone knew it was just a matter of time, and luck, before he proved himself in the cinema. The bit part in *The Entertainer* showed that the hopes were not misplaced. Saltzman had heard that Peter O'Toole was interested in the role of Arthur, but he showed shrewdness in perceiving that, although Arthur Seaton needed to be youthful, he didn't need to be attractive looking – in the way that O'Toole conspicuously was and Finney wasn't. 'There were not "pretty" boys in factories then,' Saltzman said, 'and I felt the character's fantasies were conditioned by his environment. They were crude ones: he had to sleep with his mates' wives when they were on night shift and the women provided a free lay for the young fellow as an escape from their own domestic drabness. "Charm" was not necessary, or wanted. Finney agreed to play the part for £1,000 – if I could get it.' Finney was then at Stratford-upon-Avon, playing Edgar in *King Lear* when Reisz, accompanied by Sillitoe, paid a surprise visit. Sillitoe recalls that Reisz asked him, 'What do you think?' Sillitoe reflected that '*King Lear* didn't offer much opportunity to judge his effectiveness as Arthur Seaton. "He'll be all right," I said. "An actor is an actor."'

What was astonishing was the magnitude of Finney's success. It was one of those cases, more common in the American than the British cinema, where an actor's participation in the performance is so powerful that the characteristics of the role are fed back into him so that he seems more vivid and highly charged than he would have been simply by projecting an intelligent understanding of the character through technical finesse. He was passionate. There was none of the awful English vice of well-mannered but low-voltage characterization. The films that Marlon Brando made in the 1950s had strongly influenced Finney. Like Brando, he used a role to search himself, which is why he needed a director who gave him the freedom to explore. As he has said, he has something of Brando's intuitive talent for picking what he wants out of life, the ability to mimic, refine and absorb other people's characteristics into his own concept. 'I'm not someone who works things out consciously in the mind and then does it. I go by the feel of it. It has to feel right,' he said in an early, revealing interview. 'I use everything in acting that ever happened to me. If someone had told me my best friend had dropped down dead, one part of me would be feeling the pain of it, but the actor part of me would be watching and taking notes and saying, "So that's how it feels. You can use that. You can use that in a performance." [1]

One reason why acting had attracted him was its lure for a nature that was basically non-conformist. Finney was a forerunner of the anti-stars of the mid-1960s: no sooner had he achieved success in a part than he rejected its allure and attributes and sought a new variety of experience, an extension of self, in a radically different role. This is more than simply saying that he resisted type-casting. In the interviews he gave at this early, more accessible stage in his career, what comes through with the power of a phobia is his alarm that he might be trapped, tied down, forced to give himself some ultimate definition in a role – in short, the fear of allowing other people to commit him to expressing their view of him. 'As soon as something starts to feel secure, I scratch at it,' he confided at this time: no wonder he feels an affinity with Lindsay Anderson, who has directed him on the stage (but not, so far, in films). Both are puritans at heart in a profession full of sybaritic temptations. To survive, Finney decided early on that it was necessary to pack a hair-shirt in one's luggage. He did so almost immediately after *Saturday Night and Sunday Morning* by refusing Sam Spiegel's overtures to star in *Lawrence of Arabia*, recognizing how inevitably the star concept, to say nothing of the multiple-picture contract, would tie him financially, restrict him imaginatively, consume him utterly. One couldn't carry the weight of someone else's investment in oneself – and live. It was bad enough having to commit oneself to playing a character in a film which could not be altered once the film was shot and edited. For the same reason, he tended to take short engagements in West End plays, lest constant repetition hammer him into a pattern. Wariness of this kind was altogether new among British film actors at that time. But then Albert Finney was the earliest of a new breed.

* * *

[1] *Evening Standard.* Interviewed by Thomas Wiseman, 16 September, 1961.

EXIT SALTZMAN

It was word of mouth that made *Saturday Night and Sunday Morning* such a stupendous success,' Harry Saltzman said. 'People's identification with Finney, especially young people and *working-class* young people, was total. Of course it was well directed and acted, and a very well-written film, but it was this empathy people had for the character which was more responsible than anything else for the business it did.'

Incredible though it seems now, it very nearly did not get the chance to do any business at all. When it was finished and shown to the bookers, not one would agree to show it in a cinema, much less a chain of cinemas. 'They all hated it,' Saltzman recalled, except a friend of his who owned a cinema outside the West End and agreed to book the film if he was guaranteed a house figure of £700 a week. The makers speedily discovered a Siberia-like winter closing around them, for though the budget had been barely over £100,000, it was money which Bryanston and the National Film Finance Corporation could ill afford at that bad period in film production; and only the unexpected failure of a Warner Brothers film at their West End showcase cinema, plus the advantage to the cinema of at least playing a British film and gaining quota credit before getting back to the money-making American product, gave Woodfall the chance to open *Saturday Night and Sunday Morning*, on an advertising budget that was one-third of the minimum of £5,000 then current in London's West End. It had to be supplemented, according to Saltzman, by a loan from a relative of his in North America. The first week's business was so phenomenal as to cause an instantaneous turn-round in the popularity of the film-makers *vis-à-vis* the film industry, a situation whose irony is graphically illustrated by Saltzman's recollection of having shown the film to an executive of Columbia Pictures before it opened. The executive opined that the Finney character looked tubercular, the women were most unappetizing, and the factory locations were 'some of the ugliest that had ever gotten into any feature film meant for entertainment.' Two days after the opening, the same man called Saltzman and said he would like to see Finney play Lawrence of Arabia. 'The lesson I learned was one that I have never forgotten,' Saltzman said. 'In this business, nobody knows anything for sure.'

The film's treatment by the censor also reveals how social acceptability of new themes, language and characters was advancing in line with their popularity at the box-office. The censor's principal reservations concerned language. Such words as 'whore,' 'bitch,' and 'bastard' were singled out for a 'caution' in the script submitted to him in advance of shooting for a preliminary but non-binding opinion: but they were passed in the film itself, one of John Trevelyan's staff of examiners pointing out that their utterance in the cinema would constitute 'considerable novelty' for the public. Three very strong marks of disapproval were registered for the presence of the word 'sod,' which the censor wished to keep out of films, 'bugger,' and the phrase 'knockin' up wi' a married woman.' 'Christ Almighty' was changed to 'God Almighty.' Over the abortion sequence, the wish was expressed that it shouldn't depict a casual attitude to the problem, without stressing the characters' own responsibility for the dilemma they were in. As it turned out, the married woman's abortion of her lover's child was rendered more obliquely in the film than the script had indicated; one was allowed to believe the pregnancy had been terminated, instead of being told so directly, on even shown. 'Reasonable' was to be the degree of intimacy permitted in the film's two bedroom scenes, one with Arthur in the bed of his workmate's wife, the other with him on the floor with his girl-friend.

These scenes were what brought the film into conflict with Warwickshire County Council, one of Britain's most powerful local authorities, even though it had got the censor's expected X. Certificate. The council demanded forty seconds of cuts; the distributors refused, and the film was banned, in Warwickshire, though it played to capacity audiences in Birmingham, which is within the county but had its own city-council powers to show the film.

Warwickshire's objections went deeper than the scenes' explicit sexuality. They sprang from indignation that a working-class character should be shown behaving immorally: it was the local manifestation of the more general criticism of Arthur Seaton's *enjoyment* of sex that had been made in some quarters. 'We know,' wrote Richard Hoggart in *The Uses of Literacy*, 'that the pressure to conform expresses itself in an intricate network not of ideas but of prejudices which seek to impose a rigid propriety. They gain strength from the remains of the puritanism which once so strongly affected the working classes, and which still rules fairly strictly a number of working-class lives. On most the puritanism, buttressing itself against the hard facts of working-class conditions, even now has some effect, lives to some degree among those in whom can be found the wider forms of tolerance.'[1] The Warwickshire reaction to *Saturday Night and Sunday Morning* is like the last spurt of prejudice from a dying tradition which the onward march of the consumer society and the films of the next few years successfully extinguished by bringing sex into the areas of personal, enjoyable and largely classless practice and illustrating how the 'dense and concrete' conditions of daily existence, as Hoggart called them, had depressed and distorted it.

Saturday Night and Sunday Morning made over half a million pounds' profit for the parties concerned and was certainly the foundation of Woodfall Films' fortunes and a timely infusion of cash and encouragement into the Bryanston consortium. But soon after it opened, it was announced that Harry Saltzman was leaving the board of Woodfall, by mutual agreement with Richardson and Osborne. Differences of temperament were one of the reasons. The company hadn't room for two impresarios. Saltzman had always been one; Richardson hadn't taken long 'acquiring' the talent to become one. Saltzman was by nature bearlike and gregarious; Richardson had a sharp, feline side to him. Saltzman possessed the promoter's power to 'change the atmosphere' and conjure up money for the deal; but now that Richardson was 'acceptable' to the distributors, money wasn't quite the problem it had once been. 'Richardson had energy and imagination,' Saltzman recalled, 'but what he needed and still needs is

---

[1] Richard Hoggart, *The Uses of Literacy* (Chatto & Windus, 1957), pp. 79–80.

discipline. He can't "edit" himself, he can't do everything connected with the film, though he thinks he can. Telling him was useless: no mother ever believes her own child is ugly.' According to Saltzman, matters came to a head over the filming of Shelagh Delaney's play *A Taste of Honey*. 'I felt the story was too provincial and too English,' said Saltzman. 'It really had little appeal or popular identification for people in other countries. As I saw it, the film should have been set in France, with Simone Signoret as the mother and Leslie Caron as the girl, which would have made it into an international picture. But Tony couldn't see it that way, so our partnership was dissolved.' Perhaps the truth was that Saltzman had had enough of social realism; he had tasted success, big success, with *Saturday Night and Sunday Morning*, and now itched to move on to the international circuit where the stakes were larger, the gambles more hazardous, but the rewards and the respect of the 'majors,' as the Hollywood companies were called, added up to a proportionately richer satisfaction. Perhaps he had caught an early whiff of escapism in the air, a popular hankering for more polished productions, larger adventures. Richardson and Osborne, on the other hand, quite apart from the projects they had committed themselves to filming, were more austere and dedicated to the proposition which Bishop Wilson enunciated in the late 1850s, that in England 'the number of those who need to be awakened is far greater than that of those who need comfort.' By the end of 1961, of course, they were not the only film company engaged on the missionary work of 'awakening.'

Chapter Five: Actors' Take-Over

An actor must have arrogance, conceit. He's got to believe, no matter how unsuccessful he is, that he has the makings of an Olivier. I need to believe that, although I know now that I would never have made it as an actor. But I still have that conceit. Making films is a conceit; after all, why should I assume that anybody will want to come and see my pictures?

Bryan Forbes, interviewed by Barry Norman,
Daily Mail, 24 August, 1967

In 1949 Walter Lassally, a German-born photographer in his early twenties, joined his talent to that of a budding director, Derek York, and both of them set up a company called Screencraft to make a film. The title was *Saturday Night*. 'It should not,' Lassally said ironically over twenty years later, 'be in any way confused with *Saturday Night and Sunday Morning*.'[1]

It was a film about a young man coming out of the Army, feeling lonely, in need of a girl, wandering through night-time London, holding a dialogue with a recruiting poster, finally ending up with a prostitute for company. It began as a twenty-minute film, shot mostly on location in Piccadilly and elsewhere in London's West End, and it got longer and longer . . . 'because anything over thirty minutes had a better chance of a commercial booking,' said Lassally. Production went on spasmodically over four years and it was never completed; for along with experience came the desire to go back and reshoot the earlier scenes – only the leading man was no longer available. In fact he had had to post-synch his role in a hurry in order to accompany his then wife, a screen actress called Constance Smith, to Hollywood, where the young husband hoped to continue his own film career. Neither it nor his marriage prospered and he was soon back in England, resigned to acting in film after film where his boyish looks, allied to the resolutely middle-class character of British films, confined him to the role of a constant subaltern,

[1] Walter Lassally interviewed by the author, 5 April, 1971. Unless stated otherwise, all subsequent quotations from Lassally come from the same source.

whether or not he actually wore a uniform, a hoverer behind the stars, personifying the attractive qualities of young manhood in this picture, or the game-for-anything enterprise of wartime initiative in that one, while all the time trying to infiltrate into roles that had more to them than a smooth chin and cub-like charm.

Either they did not exist or he did not get them. But this period of Bryan Forbes's life, now unregretfully relegated to the afternoon's old movie on week-end television, played its part in shaping one of the most extraordinarily successful careers of the 1960s, a decade which he began as one of the earliest actors to turn producer and ended as production chief of one of the last British studios to attempt to run itself on Hollywood lines. It is a career that has brought him controversy, antipathy and outright hostility in quite as large a measure as congratulations. It would be said that he had acquired status without achievement; that he had been opportunistic or just plain lucky; that he was a reactionary posing as a radical. But in truth the swiftness of his ascent – of anyone's ascent – in the film industry always breeds its own envious response, and this was particularly true of an actor in Britain at that date.

Whereas the break-up of the Hollywood contract system in the early 1950s gave the leading American stars the power to raise their fees to heights unparalleled since the 1920s, while their tax laws gave them the incentive to set up in production with their own companies, the British film actor had no high pay, no tax advantages, and no power of any kind in the industry. The 'one who got away,' slipping under the barbed wire of Elstree Studio or tunnelling out of the P.O.W. compound at Pinewood, as Forbes might have put it, considering the number of roles he seemed to have played 'in captivity,' might be sure of incurring resentment at his presumption or, even worse, at his success or, more unforgiveable still, at his enjoyment of it. Then, too, Forbes saw, and still sees, life from the vantage point of an actor. He not only extracts situations, characters or lines of dialogue from what reality offers him: he wouldn't be the first screenwriter to do that. He also, one suspects, sees reality as offering him a role to play.

When I interviewed him for television on one occasion, he gave a significant reply to the question, 'Why did you stop being an actor?' He replied, 'I didn't stop . . . I suppose I'm acting right now. I very much regret that I wasn't a great actor. Of all the things within this medium, I think being a great actor is possibly the most satisfying.' – 'Better than being a great director?' – 'I think so. Yes, I really do.'[1] Although it is anticipating things, such an attitude suggests why Forbes's two years as production chief at Elstree Studios may have seemed irresistible to him on his being offered the job. Being the studio boss was a 'part' which life wrote for very, very few actors: the only other one was Robert Evans, who had begun as a Hollywood actor and who at the end of the 1960s, became responsible for Paramount's production. Whatever enmities, frustrations, disappointments or apprehensions each day brought to Forbes in his executive suite at Elstree, were committed to his diaries in the evening and no doubt underwent dramatic sharpening that, without in any way falsifying experience, extracted from them the essence of the power game he was committed to playing – and so made it bearable. (Writing, always a stimulant for him, became in those days a consolation. At one black moment, he remarked about those who were snapping at his heels, 'If I can't out-run, at least I can out-write, them.') Some of the hostility he incurred from film people and journalists at the time came from the feeling they had that Forbes was writing dialogue for himself as he answered their questions: good dialogue it was, always 'quotable,' though some people found it fell too patly from his lips. He 'edited' his replies in the way a good dramatist edits his speeches, or a good actor gives a rhythm to his lines.

It is worth elaborating on this aspect of Forbes because it underpins a great deal of his talent and reinforces the reasons why his remarkable career took the form it did. But it is certainly not to suggest that he is an actor *manqué*. The reverse is the truth. It was because he saw he had fulfilled himself as an actor, at least

[1] Bryan Forbes interviewed by the author, 24 October, 1969. Unless stated otherwise, all subsequent quotations from Forbes come from the same source.

got as far as he could get, that he felt compelled to transform his gifts into something that would take him even further.

Being an actor is an excellent apprenticeship for being a writer. If one has any writing talent at all, the consciousness soon sinks in, during film after film, that one can write better dialogue than one has been given to speak, create better scenes than one is being directed to play. Forbes had had a sound grounding in repertory and stock-company work: he had acted in the 'well-made' and deservedly popular plays of Coward, Rattigan, Emlyn Williams, John Van Druten. There may very well be a connection between the audible reward an actor gets when he hears an audience enjoying itself at these plays, proving at every matinée the old reliable craftsmanship of construction and character, and the concern that Forbes has shown throughout his career to entertain and hold an audience. The greatest reward for him is not necessarily expressing one's own passion or viewpoint, but rather making contact with the emotions of others, moving people to laughter or to caring. 'Being moved' is a phrase that crops up so frequently in the syntax of Forbes's talk that it takes on the character of a shibboleth, 'I like . . . an audience to be moved. I love comedies, but I prefer to be moved to tears . . .'

Forbes has always had an extremely sharp ear for the way people speak as distinct from the things people say: another gift that assists an actor to assume a role and a writer to create one. However, he isn't a naturalistic dialogue writer; he resists the tedium of indiscipline that he believes attaches to unshaped dialogue trying to duplicate the pauses, repetitions and *non sequiturs* of unprocessed speech. He puts construction above naturalism: again it's probably the influence on him of a certain type of play at a certain time in the theatre, before the dam gates were opened to the flood-waters of Jimmy Porter's torrential egotism. Forbes occasionally takes a line from life, an *ad lib* from an actor, and into the script they go: 'but I don't think actors can give you the structure of a script, because they're only really concerned with their own part in it and they're selfish, and under-standably so.' Here, too, experience speaks. Forbes knows the creature called an actor from sharing the same cage with it.

His intuitive sympathy is what has helped to key the actors in his films to give consistently good, often outstanding, performances. One clue to his sympathy is that he hardly ever tests a player for a role. All one tests, he believes, is fear; and one betrays one's own lack of conviction. 'Immediately you give an actor the part, he is 100 per cent better . . . My own experience has helped me spot the reflection of the firing squad in the actor's eyes almost before he's aware of it. I always know when an actor's going to "dry" or has let the scene "go" from him. And I constantly go back to something Carol Reed said to me. "Never cut for an actor," he said, "never humiliate an actor." It's very true. It's so easy to humiliate actors if you are the director. I think you don't achieve much by that. I think you must be kind to actors – always.'

IDEAS IN A DESERT

By the mid-1950s Forbes was finding his knack of writing good, actable dialogue kept him in demand, touching up weak scenes, rewriting other people's lame scripts, adding fresh characters to stale situations in ways that brightened up the whole production. Much of this he did without screen credit (and generally had no regrets on that score). What did depress him was his inability to find film roles worth playing or producers willing to make films of his own scripts. He had sold one of these, *The League of Gentlemen*, to the American producer Carl Foreman; but Foreman was now training his sights on *The Guns of Navarone*, a para-military operation altogether bigger and more attractive to him than Forbes's story of a bank raid led by a band of pseudo-gents. Forbes was also urging Richard Attenborough to turn his box-office popularity into real power by 'going into production' in the way that Clark Gable, Burt Lancaster, Kirk Douglas and other Hollywood stars of the late-1950s were doing. But of course the British film star was in a minor league when it came to raising production capital. Attenborough was suffering the same kind of despair as Forbes over type-casting. As he grew older, more experienced and ambitious, he had found out that his own eternally boyish appearance was a handicap – and in fact the roles he would seek for himself in the next decade were chosen partly in compensation for his unnaturally lengthy screen 'adolescence' by providing him with the chance of sinking his identity untraceably into the false features or impasto make-up of characters many years older than himself. He and Forbes had attempted to set up one production, about the sinking of the Bismarck; but it got nowhere because the German backers failed to come up with the finance and the British backers feared the makers might take a pro-German line because it was a co-production.

In 1958 Attenborough was filming *Sea of Sand* in North Africa, where heat, flies, sandstorms and interruptions in shooting compounded his conviction that he was trapped in an unrewarding career, and that he could make better films than the ones he was paid to act in. Guy Green, his director, and Michael Craig, his co-star, shared this view. And as sandstorms kept them blockaded in their tents, conversation turned to the subjects the British screen never got round to. It was Craig who suggested the story of a factory-hand boycotted by his mates for not joining in an unofficial strike. (Later he attributed the inspiration to his brother, Richard Gregson, who became Forbes's agent before turning independent producer in the late 1960s with *Downhill Racer*.) In due course, the idea was conveyed to Forbes who had, coincidentally, written a film treatment based on just such a theme, called *A Dangerous Game*, which he had laid aside because it hadn't quite worked out. His interest re-kindled, he wrote the screenplay as a speculative venture; and now he had a promise of collaboration from Attenborough, Green and Craig. The 'package deal' – at that time a rare phrase in the industry on either side of the Atlantic – was presented to the chief backer of independent producers, British Lion – and turned down flat. At £140,000, it was considered too costly for a 'risk' subject – the old story. It was pared to £125,000 and re-submitted – and again turned down.

Desperate economies were now made all round. Beyond a fee of about £1,000 for the screenplay, Forbes agreed to take no money for co-producing the film; and Attenborough took no fee either for co-producing or for starring in it. He was to get 9 per cent of the net profit – if any – and Forbes 7 per cent. Every-one else also took miniscule fees and small percentages. By these means the budget was cut to a breath-holding £97,000, of which British Lion put up 70 per cent and the National Film Finance Corporation the remainder. Casting was completed by assigning the role of the non-striker's wife to the Italian actress, Pier Angeli. Considering the essentially English working-class milieu, some regarded this as box-office opportunism. Certainly it didn't harm the film's prospects overseas, but as practical a reason for it was the fact that Guy Green had just directed her and Attenborough in *S.O.S. Pacific* (1959), on the script of which Forbes had helped out, so everyone was familiar with the others' approach to work – a vital factor when there was hardly enough money to replace a button never mind re-shoot a scene. More-over, Forbes reasoned, having an Italian wife helped set the 'odd man out' in the industrial dispute even further apart – and, anyhow, not a few British ex-servicemen had brought foreign wives home with their kit-bags. Such was the self-consciousness of production groups embarking on new subjects.

The *Angry Silence* (10 March 1960) wasn't the first film to be made in Britain about disputes between management and men. There had already been Bernard Miles's *Chance of a Lifetime* (1950), about the factory floor attempting to do management's job, and the Boulting Brothers's satire on labour relations, *I'm All Right, Jack* (1959), which showed the sins of one side of industry to be a mirror reflection of those on the other. But the first film reached benign conclusions (each side needed the other), while the second, for all its cynicism, and Peter Sellers's biting caricature of an ignorant and pathetic shop steward, was essentially good-humoured (each side was no worse than the other). *The Angry Silence*, in contrast, took an unpopular stand and maintained it against a lot of the abuse it incurred then, much of which endures to this day. It supported the individual's right to dissent from the majority when the latter were fundamentally in the wrong. It was itself fundamentally wrathful – its title accidentally emphasised the currently 'in' emotion of 'anger' – and it attacked the misrule, laxness, apathy and intolerance of organized labour as well as

locating, without actually identifying by name, the sinister
political influences behind the scenes with a vested interest in
fomenting industrial strife and economic chaos. The character of
the agitator who passed through the strike-hit factory like a
bacillus through the human body, undetectably but leaving
behind the same seething fever and weakness, had no political
label tied to him: but hardly any was needed. In place of an
amiable oaf like Ian Carmichael in *I'm All Right, Jack* who finds
himself caught between the skulduggery of workers and management, *The Angry Silence* substituted the real tragedy of a man with
convictions who finds himself out on a limb. Into his sufferings
from picket lines with hard shoulders, from workmates who
ostracize him, from shop-floor 'teddy boys' who beat him up so
severely that he loses the sight of an eye, the film built an attack
on union abuses that up to then had never been so scathingly
stated in a British film. It showed its teeth in its picture of the
works meetings which were just a matter of tea and apathy; in
the teenage morons who seized on the right to strike as licence to
run riot; in the way decent men turned into a mindless pack and
harried and savaged the one workmate who went his own way.
Its psychology was accurate, its political reality was recognizable –
the trade unions in Wales and parts of England, who had at first
blacked the film, lifted their ban after representatives had seen
special screenings of it and reported back that abuses of power
were what was under attack, not articles of faith.

Sometimes the film choked on its own anger. An early outburst
of blackleg intimidation – windows being smashed in, cars
going up in flames – was so frenziedly depicted that it needed
only bedsheets and a fiery cross to become a Ku Klux Klan purge.
Other scenes aroused doubts, at least on the cinematic front.
There was an echo of *Room at the Top* in a seduction scene on the
grass, and more than an echo from *Look Back in Anger* in the
domestic set-up of husband, wife and mutual comforter of a
lodger living in rented rooms. The beating-up inflicted on the
hero in the last reel became a terrible retributive cliché of the
cinema's new-found social realism. The ending with Michael
Craig's lodger silencing an angry crowd with a few blurted-out

words ('Tom Curtis has lost an eye . . . I feel dirty') lacked clinching relevance. It was played for sentiment, to shame those responsible back into sense, whereas what was needed was proof of how they had been duped into acting as they did.

In the aftermath, the generally left-wing film unions in Britain have thrown up severe critics of the film and, perhaps mistakenly viewing its intentions through the eyes of their own dogma, have criticized its content and impugned its makers' aims. Without deigning to name it, the Hon. Ivor Montagu breathed Marxist fire on it when he wrote four years after its release, 'Richard Attenborough and Bryan Forbes made a film that heroized (sic) a strike-breaker who was sent to Coventry. The poster publicity proclaimed: "The Most Daring Film Ever Made." What was daring about it? Seeing the income-level of those who control the controlling circuits in this country, such a film, had it been ten times cruder than it was, must inevitably have been certain of distribution and exhibition before even it was begun.'[1] That would certainly have been news to its makers, had it been remotely true. Over ten years after the film had been released, the left-wing film director Ken Loach protested that, although it had an arguable point, it was one that the makers should have hesitated to use to the disadvantage of working men so long as there were no other British films to espouse the workers' grievances with equal zeal. Even more recently a clip from the film showing the agitator at work appeared in a television programme devoted to illustrating the way stereotypes were used to condition viewers into accepting prescribed messages or emotions: it is scarcely necessary to elaborate on the inference one was invited to draw, even though dozens of debates, enquiries and reports on union strife in the intervening years had shown the film's Communist agitator to represent industrial realities rather than any phantom conjured up out of the class war. The film did, however, have considerable power to proselytize: not necessarily by right-wing political example, but certainly by emotional appeal. One critic, Campbell Dixon, recognized this when he wrote, 'One wonders how many other good, well-meaning

[1] Ivor Montagu, *Film World* (Pelican, 1964), p. 271.

trade unionists and employers ready to sacrifice an unpopular man if it means getting on with the job, will see the film, remember acts of selfishness and cruelty, and feel a little dirty, too.'[1] It was temptingly easy to say that what was true of one wildcat strike, where mob law predominated, was true of strikes in general; and in the innumerable references to the film inside Parliament, or on the hustings by week-end speechifiers, the opportunity to turn it into good Tory propaganda wasn't overlooked. Its makers found it all the harder to ward off accusations that they were anti-working class.

At least an artistic rebuttal should have been evident in the performances of a cast who just pre-dated the appearance of genuine young proletarian film stars. Attenborough's show of principle was never allowed to turn into masochistic self-punishment; Pier Angeli's fluttery Latin alarm heightened a dozen moments more naturally than an English actress's hysteria would have done; and Michael Craig's lodger bunched into closed-fist compactness all the contradictions of a chap with three-inch sideburns and a carnal eye, dedicated to looking after Number One, who lets loyalty and affection get the better of his instincts.

The Angry Silence came slowly, very slowly into profit. By 1971 it had earned £58,000 for its makers. Not a large sum; but the film's success in establishing its theme with such force and timeliness in a cinema that had hitherto fought shy of political involvement was much greater than the box-office could gauge. More important to its makers' future, it established Forbes and Attenborough as people to reckon with on the production side, 'artists' who could turn to making films with business-like dispatch and eventual profit; and this was even more forcefully confirmed within a surprisingly short time when the next film on which the pair were associated opened in London exactly one month later.

*   *   *

[1] *The Daily Telegraph*, 12 March, 1960.

ALLIED FILM MAKERS

The strong follow-through of publicity and success which *The League of Gentlemen* (7 April, 1960) made possible was more than an auspicious omen. It consolidated the film-makers' fortunes in a very real way. The screenplay which Forbes had written had passed into Carl Foreman's possession, as has been mentioned. It was intended to star Cary Grant as the leader of a gang of ex-army types, all fallen on hard times, who plan and execute a bank raid with their old military precision. A 'caper' film, it was a type that is always popular with film-makers since it provides blueprint suspense, a variety of featured roles of roughly equal weight and, in dealing with those who set out to acquire large chunks of money, it has the soothing property of nearly always making satisfactory chunks of money at the box-office. Unfortunately, Grant disliked the script and it was put on ice. Eventually Leslie Linder, an agent who would later turn producer, telephoned Forbes to say that his client, Basil Dearden, had acquired it and was preparing to go into production with his partner, Michael Relph. It was proposed to form a new company, a consortium of film-makers which would distribute films that the members made themselves, and also those produced by outside talents. The original idea had come from Sydney Box, who had produced some of Britain's biggest post-war hits like *The Seventh Veil* and was still active as a behind-the-scenes force: but illness caused Box to drop out just as the group established itself, on 30 September, 1959, with the name of Allied Film Makers. It was originally planned to include five partnerships, but with Box's departure could muster only four: Attenborough and Forbes; Relph and Dearden; Jack Hawkins; and Hawkins's brother. Guy Green later joined the Forbes-Attenborough group. Whereas the Bryanston group, formed six months earlier, had close ties with British Lion for the release of its films, A.F.M. liaised with the Rank Organization, which promised them a guarantee of £143,000, while the National Provincial Bank, who were Rank's financiers, guaranteed advances to A.F.M. producers up to five times this sum, to £840,000. (Actually Rank's guarantee was in two parts: £64,000 on setting up the company and a further £79,000 when they found a fifth partner, which they never did.) The four groups had each put up £5,000. The National Film Finance Corporation provided completion guarantees for *The League of Gentlemen:* in the case of the five other films which A.F.M. subsequently made the end money came from the Rank Organization. The distribution fee charged was 27½ per cent for the first year, 25 per cent the second year; and of this A.F.M. took five per cent and Rank the rest. (Overseas distribution fee was 15 per cent: 5 per cent to A.F.M., the rest to Rank.)[1] These arrangements gave the Rank Organization an extremely favourable deal, since its own cinemas could show the films which it helped to finance and on which it already took a distributor's fee; but it also increased the financial muscle of the film-makers as distinct from the front-office distributors – the one had assumed some of the functions of the other. The crucial proviso, however, was that the A.F.M. films should be a big enough success quickly enough to keep the box-office receipts flowing back to the principal financiers who, in turn, would keep the revolving fund topped up. In essence, it was the same make-or-break condition that Bryanston had to meet.

For A.F.M., the year 1960 began excellently. *The League of Gentlemen* was one of the major box-office successes. It cost £192,000 and by mid-1971 its profit was over £250,000. It was a more wry, disenchanted kind of comedy than Ealing would have made, though it was visibly an off-shoot of that same tradition. It maintained Ealing's unflagging belief that the amateurs could outwit the experts, the irregulars could defeat the authorities; and the aggressive band of shady customers, all keeping up a pretence of respectability under Supremo Jack Hawkins, appeared in retrospect to be mirroring Britain's buoyant, acquisitive society in the 1960s. Prime Minister Harold Macmillan had boasted 'Most of our people have never had it so good' as election bait as early as 1957: but in 1959 'You've never had it so good' was suddenly *the* catch-phrase of the year. *The League of Gentlemen,* with its

[1] Information supplied by A.F.M. executive Leslie Baker, interviewed by the author, 6 August, 1971.

target of quick capital gains, was the ideal comedy for a boom-time economy. Forbes's screenplay, directed by Basil Dearden, also drew heavily on the barrack-room iconoclasm of his own Army service: it parodied Queen's Regulations which were now being applied to the masterminding of a bank raid; there was an 'Other Ranks' disrespect about the dialogue that purveyed a tart new flavour in British screen comedy.

One astringent moment deserves quoting. It is when 'Colonel' Jack Hawkins allows a sharp tooth to show under the stiff upper-lip attitudes. 'I took those attitudes and smartly reversed them,' said Forbes, 'so that when a confederate in a scene in the country-house, which the League were using as a "training-college," referred to Hawkins's wife and said, "Is she dead?" the reply that most film-goers expected in those days might have been "I'm afraid she, er, passed away in child-birth," or some such manfully repressed sentiment that would have given a clue to why the widower had left the straight and honest path. Instead of which, I had Jack reply crisply, "I'm sorry to say the bitch is still alive." '

The next A.F.M. film was turned out smartly and premièred seven months later, yet it seemed a throwback to earlier years. *Man in the Moon* (22 December, 1960) was directed by Dearden from a screenplay by Relph and Forbes; and again the launching-pad was Ealing tradition, though this time more fanciful and less well grounded in contemporary attitudes. Kenneth More played a human guinea-pig at a common-cold research centre where gale-force winds meet head-on in the British Summer Simulator Laboratory and a grandstand of spectators sit in rain-stops-play dejection under individual waterfalls in an Exposure to Outdoor Sports (Traditional) Test. Stephen Potter, then at the height of his international 'Gamesmanship' reputation, was the influence here. Expelled because of his too-perfect metabolism, More is recruited for the British Space Programme and has to beat yet another 'league of gentlemen' in the shape of the public-school astronauts, whose higher social class is their justification for pulling every dirty trick in the handbook on the 'outsider.' But there were too many fagged-out elements of earlier comedies in all this: too much a reversion to the good-humoured idolatry of warm-hearted incompetence to catch a public mood which, in the early 1960s, looked for more bitter ironies and more aggressive self-service in their heroes. In spite of starring Kenneth More, then the most popular film actor in Britain, the movie didn't do nearly as well as was necessary to keep A.F.M. happy. Moreover, at £202,000 it had cost a shade too much for what it was, and far too much for what it eventually made: by mid-1971 it was still £37,000 short of breaking even, never mind going into profit. Fortunately, formidable consolation was at hand.

Looking for a subject to follow *The Angry Silence*, Forbes and Attenborough acquired the rights to a novel by Mary Hayley Bell (Mrs John Mills). *Whistle Down the Wind* (6 July, 1961) was a story of childhood innocence which rejected the formalities of religion and achieved a painful but purer understanding of what faith was all about. To Forbes, it had sympathetic echoes of René Clément's *Les Jeux Interdits*. More specifically, it dealt with a band of children who befriend a murderer on the run, mistaking him for Jesus – for they are north-country valley children schooled in fundamentalist religion rather than the television serials of the 'townies' – and finally seeing him (fortunately it's never quite a case of 'Him') caught by the police and taken away in handcuffs. The humanism which that old-fashioned piety sometimes sustained was kept within the understanding of the children by their social responses as well as their religious fantasies – 'Ought I to curtsey?' asks the heroine's even smaller but more formal sister when she hears Christ has come again. The gentle literalism of belief was deftly insinuated into the screenplay, so that when the fugitive is asked for a Bible story, he turns desperately to the first thing to hand and reads his infant 'congregation' a chapter from *Ruth Lawrence, Air Hostess*. Precision in small things – in accents, vocabulary, reactions – kept the larger risks of whimsy at bay most of the time, though the occasional New Testament parallel like the trio of children dancing for joy on the skyline in emulation of the Three Kings was dangerously explicit for all its visual attractiveness. What most attracted Forbes to the story was a quality he had noted – 'the moment in a child's life when he or she is absolutely, completely innocent. The test of being able to capture that without mawkishness was what keyed the film for me.'

It was the first film he directed – and he very nearly didn't, being turned down for the job by the agent representing Hayley Mills, then possibly the highest-paid child-star in films and a carefully nurtured Walt Disney contract artist. Her family felt they had to abide by this rejection and Forbes, too disappointed at losing his chance to direct, or even to adapt the novel for the screen, turned the writing of the script over to Keith Waterhouse and Willis Hall and tried to content himself with co-producing the film with Attenborough. This helps to explain why the story was removed from the south-east of England to the north country, which was the screen-writers' native territory, and thus acquired a tougher, more astringent character than it might have had if left in, the blander county of Sussex. Guy Green had been approved as director when, within weeks of the starting date, he accepted another film offer. Beaver Films, the company established by Forbes and Attenborough inside the A.F.M. set up, faced bankruptcy unless a new director could be found who was approved by Hayley Mills's representatives. The anxious producers drove to the Mills' home and asked point-blank why Forbes wasn't acceptable. After some hours' 'auditioning,' the decision was arrived at – he was.

The film cost £148,000 and very quickly began out-grossing *The League of Gentlemen:* by mid-1971 its profit was over £240,000. But as Allied Film Makers were soon to discover, while having success was exhilarating and invaluable in launching a film director's career, something far more crucial determined the continuing existence of film companies; and this was having the resources to sustain failure.

Chapter Six: The Anglo-Italian Job

What I tend to go for and what interests me is not the hero, it's the coward . . . it's not the success, but the failure. I think there are many more of them.

John Schlesinger, Thames TV interview, 11 January, 1970

Joseph Janni was an unlikely person to speed the new British cinema along on its journey into north-country realism. But then he was an unlikely person to find in the British film industry in the first place. He was part Persian, part English on his grand-parents' side; his father was born in India and stayed in Bombay till he was thirty and his mother in Milan, where her family was 'quite wealthy,' as Janni puts it, in the understated, self-deprecating way he has picked up in the country he has lived in since 1939.

Janni read industrial engineering at Milan University, and one may note in passing how the aptitude for mentally conceiving a structure where none physically exists as yet is one that seems to transfer well to producing films. His urge pointed in that direction from an early age; he joined a university cine-club and was soon working on a co-operative amateur film venture. Few student productions anywhere can have been so prodigiously endowed with the future talents of a country's film industry. The leading actor was young Vittorio De Sica; Valli was a supporting player; Nino Rota composed the music; assistance was given by Luigi Commencini and Renato Castellani; while invaluable financial advice was rendered by a student of accountancy at a nearby institute, Carlo Ponti. An American expatriate, Saul Steinberg, acted as production designer. As Janni recalls *A Gentleman has Arrived* some forty years after its production, it was about a State lottery winner who succumbs to a life of idleness and affluence 'and it contained thinly veiled criticism of Fascist corruption.'[1]

Janni's wealthy background didn't endear him to this radical cine-club, however, and he would very likely have gone into his

[1] Joseph Janni interviewed by the author, 11 May, 1971. Unless stated otherwise, all subsequent quotations from Janni come from the same source.

intended occupation, engineering, but for a *bon vivant* uncle who encouraged him to go into film-making instead, as seemingly the most agreeable way to earn a living while enjoying life. Having a fondness for strip cartoons, this uncle decided that Walt Disney would be the mentor for his nephew and arranged for him to go to the United States and be taught the business at the then expanding Disney studio. Young Joe got no farther than England, where he landed five days before the outbreak of war and stayed put, working for the Ministry of Information until Italy's entry into the war got him transferred to an internment camp. (A fellow internee was Mario Zampi, who was to bring a certain much-needed native ebullience into the post-war British comedies he wrote and produced.) Released after some months' captivity, Janni spent the war writing propaganda material for the BBC's European service, stayed on in England when hostilities ended, and got his postponed film education with a small independent company before collecting the finance to start his own production outfit, Vic Films.

This biography is worth relating in some detail, since it illustrates Janni's wry acceptance of what fate brings him as well as his aptitude for turning whatever that may be to his profit. He belongs to the tribe of those who believe the best way of getting what one wants is to learn to like the way things have of coming about of their own accord when one gives them a gentle push. In time Janni has become one of the film industry's most dogged 'pushers' without ever losing his winning gentleness of manner. And even more important, he has never quite lost the feeling of being an Italian – albeit adapting very comfortably to English habits. More than anything else in his make-up this contributed to his success as a producer. (It also accounted for one of his most bitterly regretted mistakes, which will be related in due course.)

Up to the early 1960s, Janni's career prospered but could hardly be said to have broken any radical ground. For the Rank Organization he produced several conventional British entertainments such as *White Corridors* (1950) and *A Town like Alice* (1956), as well as such multi-national oddities as Renato

Castellani's *Romeo and Juliet* (1953) and Nicholas Ray's *The Savage Innocents* (1960), both of which were co-financed by Rank in its expansionist days when it seemed prudent to have every national box-office that counted represented at least once in the multinational casts. Janni might have settled into the groove of efficient but superficial studio productions if he hadn't hankered so deeply after the international recognition which had been gained by countrymen of his like De Sica, Rossellini, Visconti, Zavattini and others who had pioneered the neo-realist movement in the immediate post-war years. While Janni was making escapist entertainment in studio conditions, he knew his old school-friends were enviably active in creating a national cinema committed to putting on the screen an image of real places, ordinary people and all aspects of daily life in which the individual's predicament was central and the plot was merely a means of facilitating the director's social comment. Of all the aspects of ordinary life which the British cinema shied away from presenting, sex was the one that Janni felt demanded to be discovered. 'Compared to Rome, England was then like a monastery,' he recalled. 'In those days England had forgotten she possessed provinces. She denied that her people even had a sex life: sex was regarded, if it was regarded at all, as an exclusively Continental pursuit. The Italians in the years before the French *nouvelle vague* had made all the best pictures about provincial life, which included the frustrations and pleasures of sex life, and I was bitten by the desire to do the same for England. I began looking around for subjects that would interlock the human and social themes and persuade us we were seeing parts of life that in Britain we knew very little about, though in Italy they had become the foundation of a national cinema.'

Fate seemed to deliver the opportunity into his hands when he encountered Alan Sillitoe at the provincial première of one of his Rank movies and was given the manuscript of *Saturday Night and Sunday Morning* to read. Within a few hours of finishing it, he had bought an option for £1,000. Then he tried to set it up. British Lion, who were the first distribution company he turned to, speedily disenchanted him. You've lived in England all these years, he was told, and you haven't understood the English. It was the wildest imagining on Sillitoe's part that any factory worker in the Midlands should sleep and have sex with his best pal's wife and that the woman should then have to seek an abortion. Such things were simply not done by the workers, said British Lion. Janni retorted, 'They screw all right: maybe they just don't talk about it,' and took the project to the Rank Organization, who deliberated, hesitated, but finally said No, no . . . they couldn't see their studio producing anything like that. As Janni's option was expiring and he couldn't afford to renew it, he reluctantly parted with the property when an offer arrived from Woodfall Films asking if he would sell it to them for £2,000. 'I had just become an independent producer. Possibly for this reason I didn't have enough experience, courage, or the right frame of mind to fight the prejudices of the distributors. Almost everyone told me no one would want to see such a film. I was too easily convinced.' (Another property he briefly acquired and had to relinquish for similar reasons was E. R. Braithwaite's novel *To Sir, with Love*, which dealt with a black teacher's experiences in a London East End school.[1]) Janni contented himself as best he could with the resolve that, come what might, he would produce the *second* English film about provincial life. That chance came when he contracted Keith Waterhouse and Willis Hall to script the film version of a novel by Stan Barstow which he had bought. It was called *A Kind of Loving*.

Waterhouse and Hall were heavily in demand as screenwriters. Their own successful stage play, *Billy Liar*, adapted from Waterhouse's novel, had confirmed their talent for strong, quirky characters anchored in the native idiom of the north country and a freshly observed social scene: it had been directed by Lindsay Anderson in September 1960, with Albert Finney in the title role. Janni would have liked to buy the film rights to *Billy Liar*, too, but lacked the resources until Woodrow Wyatt, the Member of Parliament, publisher and television pundit, who had brought

---

[1] It was sold to Harry Belafonte, but when it was made in Britain in 1967 it starred Sidney Poitier and became one of Columbia Pictures' biggest money-makers of those years.

John Braine's novel *Room at the Top* to national prominence in his
current-affairs programme on BBC TV, offered to put up the cash.
Janni then acted most astutely. Forewarned by his bad experience
with British Lion and Rank, he took *A Kind of Loving* and *Billy
Liar* along to Anglo-Amalgamated, a production–distribution
company owned by Nat Cohen and Stuart Levy. He was offered
100 per cent financing, a rare deal for a British film-maker to get
at that time from an independent distributor. It was more usual
for the latter to put up, say, 70 per cent of the budget, and leave
the producer scratching around feverishly for the rest. But then
Anglo-Amalgamated was – and still is – an unusually sturdy,
independent-minded outfit.

Nat Cohen, its chief executive since his partner's death in the
early 1960s, is in many ways a more urbane version of the one-
man-bands who used to boss the studios in Hollywood's heyday
of the movie moguls. An impresario, a *bon vivant*, a racehorse
owner with many wins in his stable, he applies the lessons of the
turf to the film industry when he affirms that 'there is no such
thing as playing safe' and describes himself as 'a gambler, but an
extremely cautious one. Never reckless. I gamble when the odds
are in my favour, not simply on hunches. I back judgment, not
luck. But, ultimately, gamble I've got to.'[1] Anglo-Amalgamated
had a cautious 'bread-and-butter' build-up in the industry, starting
with half-hour Edgar Wallace thrillers, moving on to hour-long
productions and 'never dropping a profit on one, never a picture
with a red pencil attached to it,' then diversifying into farce with
some early films in the *Carry On* series, and always putting the
profit back into the company. Energy and tenacity permitted risk-
taking and expansion into subjects for which the audience wasn't
ready-made. Here the speed of decision, possible in what was
virtually a one-man operation, began to pay off. 'When the
proposition has merit,' Cohen said, 'I put it into effect without
delay.' I made the decision on a combination of the project and
the individual who brings it to me.

'Janni came into this office almost a complete stranger,' he

[1] Nat Cohen interviewed by the author, 10 May, 1972. Unless stated otherwise, all subsequent quotations from Cohen come from the same source.

recalled. 'We went through his track record, saw he had been one of Rank's most successful producers at different times, then weighed up his projects. I felt they had something which would get across to audiences – though how well and how rewardingly it was hard to tell. But I did feel the change in audiences' tastes taking place at that time – for one thing, television was reflecting back into their own living-rooms a much more realistic picture of the lives they led outside.' All the same, Cohen wanted to do *Billy Liar* first: it was a proven stage success and didn't depart too far from traditional north-country comedy, although its point was the suffocating parochialism which that genre had enshrined and from which one must escape by real means or by the power of fantasy. Janni demurred. No, he said, he wanted to do *A Kind of Loving* first: he had already found the man to direct it. This was not strictly true.

Some time before, watching the *Monitor* current affairs programme on BBC TV, he had caught an item about Italian opera singers in London. 'I laughed uproariously at the view of my countrymen: it was observant, barbed, but not unkind.' The director's name was John Schlesinger and on meeting him Janni told him to wait till he had the right project and then they would both make the Woodfall type of film – 'only we will make it better.' Now, a year later, hearing Janni had bought *A Kind of Loving*, Schlesinger on holiday sent him a postcard saying as passionately as possible within the space permitted for the expression of personal sentiments, 'Let me direct *A Kind of Loving* – please, please, please, please.' Unfortunately, on the point of actually setting up a deal, Janni found himself wavering. 'I was suddenly frightened to death of using a new, untried young director.' Cohen, as it happened, was as uncertain about a new, untried young actor called Tom Courtenay whom he was considering for the title role in *Billy Liar*, since Albert Finney, stubborn about being locked into success as if into solitary confinement, had turned down the chance of repeating his stage success as Billy for the screen. 'I asked John to make a test of Courtenay,' Janni said, smiling shyly at his deception even after ten years, 'though actually it was a test of John, to let me see what he could do directing actors in a feature film. To tell the truth, I hated the test when I screened it. But I shut my eyes and went ahead with John Schlesinger.'

A KIND OF STOICISM

Despite the success that has deservedly come his way since he directed *A Kind of Loving* (12 April, 1962), John Schlesinger still believes in the virtues of being allowed to fail. The several years he spent with BBC TV, prior to 1961, are valued precisely because the speed and relative cheapness of working in documentary features allowed him the luxury of failing, without it being fatal to his career. 'I had the assurance that if something didn't turn out well, it wasn't important, or at least *that* important; there was always the next *Monitor* programme to give you another chance in a month or two.'[1] But this assurance was balanced by an anxiety never to leave anything to chance – an anxiety that actually cost him his job on the BBC's news-magazine programme, *Tonight*, where he was accused of constantly interrupting the production flow by insisting on dubbing his own short reportage films – the BBC TV producers complained in hurt tones that their dubbing facilities were quite adequately manned. So he moved on to *Monitor*, where the slower tempo and greater length of twenty minutes or so allocated to an item made it easier to bear with a director's idiosyncracies – and also stretched his talents, if he had any.

This characteristic of keeping total control over what he did while he was doing it has matured into a creative obduracy of granite-like resistance to anyone, or anything, that is not, as he puts it, 'in synch' with his intentions. 'I am absolutely ruthless in trying to get what I want regardless of where it's going to take us or what it's going to cost to get it. I loathe and detest and resist any form of compromise. I would rather make commercials just to pay the rent – and do frequently, and have absolutely no

[1] John Schlesinger interviewed by the author for Thames TV series directed by David Wickes, 11 January, 1970. Unless stated otherwise all subsequent quotations from Schlesinger come from the same source.

qualms about it – than choose a film subject, even where there's an immense amount of money involved, which I didn't believe in. I am in on a film from the start of the idea to the final première screening: it's like an extremely tempestuous love affair – you have to fuck a film, if I may say so. You really do, when you're making it.'[1]

Schlesinger was pulled towards the world of entertainment and illusion at a formative period of childhood. The memory of being taken to see the music-hall magicians Davenant and Maskelyn perform their conjuring acts has still for him the force of a revelation. He subsequently worked up a magic act of his own – one of some sophistication and skill, too – and he retains something of the conjuror's finesse and daintiness in his movements. Watching him direct a scene, one senses the precision hovering about his fingertips. The 'box of tricks' brought him compensation for the miseries he had to undergo when drafted into the Army; and, more important, this early predisposition towards fantasy, allied with other more fundamental aspects of his personality and temperament, has inclined him to seek or accept certain themes and subjects.

The subjects which Schlesinger prefers are those that deal in lost illusions where heroes and heroines awaken to a reality which is always more painful than their self-induced fantasy that something better is just around the corner, that the distant field is always greener. But the cruelty with which illusion is dispersed by experience is also softened by the director's own understanding of the pain. Schlesinger is an ironist, pessimist and stoic. And of these three qualities, the greatest is his stoicism. He shares Thomas Hardy's view of man as a very small figure in a very large landscape, a human speck in a vast plan he imagines to be of his own devising, but where his best efforts and aspirations are always being knocked sideways by nature, by God, or by his own doing, leaving him only the freedom to pick up the pieces and soldier on.

Schlesinger's own early life, which he now looks back on with

[1] John Schlesinger interviewed by the author, BBC Radio 4, for producer Elizabeth Smith, 4 August, 1970.

a cathartic sense of release, dinned into him the enormous effort he must make to get anywhere – or be anyone. At that time the right to fail wasn't extended to him: on the contrary, the fact of failure was constantly being rubbed in. 'The bleaker part of me, the pessimistic side of my films, probably comes from this source,' he admits. 'For though I had an extraordinarily happy and secure childhood in terms of parents who were like Romeo and Juliet together, which was marvellously endearing, nevertheless the example they set in our largish family was very difficult to live up to. I found that during childhood, and for a long time after it, I was a failure at a great number of things. I was hopeless at school and miserably unhappy. I was no good at games. I couldn't ride a bicycle till I was eleven. I was terrified of fireworks. I was no good in the Army and didn't get a commission. I remember I was frightened to death of going over obstacle courses and on one occasion, when I'd just come back from a six-months' bout of rheumatic fever, I jumped badly, broke my ankle, and I remember swearing at the sergeant who ordered me to carry on. From that day on, I resolved to rebel against any kind of organized group. I could identify very easily with anyone who felt out of it, excluded, or in the minority, or not able to live up to what was expected of him. Even in very personal things, like being in love, I was never very successful. Those years made me realize the necessity for some kind of compromise in life, if not in my art, the question of to what extent you can accept half a loaf of bread – or no bread at all. All these things are so very personal to me that I look for them in the films I want to make – they're so much a part of yourself that you can't escape them.'

The first professional short which Schlesinger made for cinema, as distinct from television, revealed the strength of these sympathies with people who are out of step with life – 'with the lonely people who are suddenly lost, or cut off.' What made this even more noticeable was that the film, *Terminus*, made in 1961 for British Transport Films, was about Waterloo Station and, from all the possible combination of moods and travellers, Schlesinger selected and dwelt on the isolated and the ill-adjusted: the lost child, the convicts being escorted to Dartmoor Prison, the old lady continually dazzled by the swivelling indicator boards . . . all life's pathetic cases. The thirty-minute film, which took two weeks to shoot but six months to edit, was obviously more in the nature of poetry than of publicity for its sponsor: not really surprising since Edgar Anstey, who headed British Transport Films, belonged to the Grierson school of poetic documentary of which he had been a founder member in the 1930s. Much more significant was the way *Terminus* confirmed Schlesinger's skill, already evident in television, in summing up people and places with the vividness of a first impression – which, given the meagre budgets, was likely to be the last one as well. Schlesinger was the first, or, at any rate, the most notable entrant into cinema direct from television, and one can see in *Terminus* the effect of television's professional training on a certain type of sensibility which is already finely attuned to people and moods. Richardson, Reisz, Forbes and others had already their shoulders to the film studio doors: not breaking in, but endeavouring to break out of them and gain freedom. Television, in the days before videotape became the swift means of recording events, though a poor tool for their artistic reworking, already gave encouragement and freedom to its graduates with movie cameras to bring to their subjects the visual precision and emotional sensitivity of top-flight feature writers. The reporter's notebook was opened on the spot as life happened: the film script had *to be opened* before the reproduction of life could begin. Men versed in the former approach were bound to transfer what they had learnt to the latter.

Schlesinger's television work is strongly marked by his curiosity about people: it was the strength of this that first caught Janni's eye quite as much as the national accent of an amusing film about his compatriots abroad. This aspect of himself Schlesinger traces back to the influence of two of the most indomitable women he ever knew, his maternal and paternal grandmothers, both of whom had the authority of old age as well as the distaff side of the Jewish faith to hold and mould young John's interest in, as he later expressed it, 'the difficult thing that living one's life is for most of us.'

His own professional acting experience had deepened this. Unable to break into films after leaving Oxford, he had turned professional actor, working in repertory and occasionally as a bit player in films (one of them a twenty-five-minute episode in *The Adventures of Robin Hood* television series directed by Lindsay Anderson in 1956), and this gave him an intimacy and sympathy with actors that paid off when he had to direct them. Quite a number of directors possess or develop an antipathy to actors, or cover up their apprehension of the species by bending them to their technical bidding. Schlesinger welcomes the interaction of director and cast: just as becoming a director enabled him to extend his involvement with 'make-believe,' so the association with actors enables him to recapture something of himself which he voluntarily gave up. 'On the whole I choose films which leave room for actors and which demand performances. It is through the performance that one says what one wants about the people.' The concept of a 'performance,' of a player assuming a role and not just displaying the most popular aspect of a real or fabricated personality, is so central to Schlesinger's work that he is apt to be touchy if he feels it is not recognized or appreciated. Deeply impressed by the success of *Midnight Cowboy*, one critic telephoned his congratulations, adding his admiration for Dustin Hoffman's 'performance,' but imprudently enquiring how Schlesinger had come to find a 'natural' like Jon Voight. He was brusquely disillusioned. Voight it was, Schlesinger said pointedly, who had really given the considerably more risky and subtle 'performance.' Schlesinger doesn't relish the limitations that 'naturals' might put on the satisfaction he obtains from directing his actors' performances. 'I've never come out of an Antonioni film, for instance, saying what a marvellous actress Monica Vitti is. She may be. She may also be just a personality very cleverly directed. I'm no wiser now than when I first saw her: it's not the kind of film I would want to make.'

As his career has advanced, Schlesinger puts more and more value on the precious bonus of rehearsal time which success (sometimes) permits a director. One feels that rehearsals are used quite as much to satisfy his curiosity about people as to elaborate his craftsmanship: it's then that the 'humanity' is created. 'I don't use this period for plotting where the camera will be, but for pushing the cast further, backwards or forwards, in certain scenes. The more knowledge they have of a character or situation or relationship, the better it will be when we shoot it. They then have a fund of information at their disposal which helps them be more selective when I want to be more precise about any given moment. That's very important.'

To make *A Kind of Loving*, Schlesinger stocked up on his own fund of information, spending much time in the north of England – Lancashire, actually – before taking the unit up there on location towards the end of 1961. Superficially it might seem the same setting as that of *Look Back in Anger* or *Saturday Night and Sunday Morning:* in fact, it had an awareness of social change that Schlesinger carried over from the swiftly annotated news reportage he had done for television. For example, he used a modern factory 'because the whole of the north isn't black and grimy' and a contemporary flat for a young couple instead of a slum terrace. Non-professionals were picked off the streets for smaller parts; the pursuit of naturalism involved engaging the actual caterers and floral decorators who would 'do' a works dance; and a recce patrol of obliging suburban houses as well as a sampling of north-country hospitality yielded such *trouvailles* as the inordinate numbers of Annigoni prints of the Queen on the wall and the way people *speared* their food at meal-times. In all this, naturally, he was encouraged by Joseph Janni, who saw in these virtues of sympathetic research the same kind of persuasive reality which his own country's film-makers arrived at in their streets and tenements so much more spontaneously. To Schlesinger, his producer was 'a father-figure, someone you trust in identifying himself with the project, not with . . . whether the thing is costing too much or whether it's got the right ingredients to bring in the public.'

Then, too, though apparently more ordinary than Karel Reisz's picture, *A Kind of Loving* is actually a more complex description of people at a specific time in English life. With Arthur Seaton in *Saturday Night and Sunday Morning*, we know the answer from the word go: his truculent stream of consciousness tells all that's essential to know about him – 'Don't let the bastards grind you down.' Schlesinger's people have a transitional status in a class whose conventions they don't rebel against so much as try to wriggle out of, until in the end they are forced to live with them. 'It was about the reality of being in love with someone and the compromise one has to make on realizing it isn't all it first appeared to be – about the battle one has against suburban ideas of love or marriage.' Alan Bates's hero, inching his way up from working-class traditions via a white-collar job into the no-man's-land of middle-class gentility gets trapped by the frightening reality of his girl-friend's pregnancy. He does the conventional thing – 'the done thing.' He marries her. Penelope Houston, comparing Schlesinger's picture with Reisz's, said, 'The public response [to *Saturday Night and Sunday Morning*] was fundamentally to a character and an actor, whereas in the case of *A Kind of Loving*, a film very similar in its attitudes, one suspects that it was rather to a situation.'[1] The situation the boy finds himself caught in is strong enough to stop him rebelling against the system like Arthur Seaton, or using the system to his own advantage like Joe Lampton. The films of Reisz and Clayton were dramas, whereas Schlesinger's is almost a documentary predicament, one which, as Eric Rhode perceived, 'involves an analysis of sentiments. We need to be shown how class conditions feelings, how the lovers have to move through the various stages of self-deception before they can possibly arrive at an authentic relationship'[2] – in short, at a kind of loving. The low key in which the film was pitched, along with the director's balance of sympathy for his characters, prevented audiences from reaching any easy, finite judgments about who was 'right' and who was 'wrong,' and compelled them instead to view the separate struggles of Alan Bates and June Ritchie as part of a wider complex of social events beyond their experience and control. In this sense the film fully achieved its producer's intention of transferring to the English screen the Italian neo-realist cinema's grasp of the unstressed

[1] Penelope Houston, *op. cit.*, p. 122.
[2] *Sight and Sound* (Summer 1962), Vol. 31, No. 3, p. 144.

reality of life. It signalled to us that another new director had arrived who could show us something fresh, honest and personal about our society. And in commercial terms, *A Kind of Loving* exceeded everyone's hopes: it cost a well-pruned £165,000, and in Britain alone it grossed £450,000, over four times what the average home-produced feature could expect to do, if it was lucky.[1]

MEANWHILE, BACK AT WOODFALL

When Harry Saltzman quit the board of Woodfall Films at the end of 1960, his place was taken by a white-haired, frail-looking man of scholarly mien who spoke so quietly that one frequently found oneself craning forward to catch what fell from his tight-drawn lips. Oscar Lewenstein was one of the West End theatre's most successful impresarios; and though no film-maker up to then, his connections with the Woodfall management were close and profitable. It was Lewenstein who had suggested George Devine to take on the English Stage Company at the Royal Court, which he was managing at the time; he had 'discovered' Albert Finney's gifts under Macbeth's 'rathery whiskery' make-up in a 'not very good' performance at the Birmingham Repertory Company in 1957; and in 1961 he presented Osborne's *Luther*, with Finney in the title role and Richardson directing. Since Finney was under contract to him, and had just won acclaim in Lewenstein's presentation of *Billy Liar*, it was expected that the film rights to the play would go with Lewenstein to Woodfall. Instead, as we have seen, Janni bought them for a reported £12,000 and Woodfall instead embarked on filming Shelagh Delaney's play *A Taste of Honey* (14 September, 1961) which had been acquired for about half that sum (later increased as the play continued to do well in New York as well as London), but which they had been unable to get Bryanston to finance until the break-through of *Saturday Night and Sunday Morning*.

[1] A sum enhanced, as in the case of every successful British film, by the Eady Levy, or box-office subsidy paid to producers in proportion to their success.

Richardson first went to Broadway to direct the Delaney play there – a popular hit in New York would assist the film's chance of wide distribution – and then on to Hollywood to make *Sanctuary* for 20th Century-Fox, an experience he later called 'the unhappiest time of my life.' 'I went there on the understanding that the atrocious adaptation of Faulkner's novel would be changed; instead I found it had to be shot as it was.' He found that Hollywood gave him all he asked for technically, but had little understanding and showed less sympathy when he wanted to improvise a scene on the spot. The studio's quest for perfection – that old curse – swallowed up all possibility of spontaneity. 'It was like working in a strait-jacket.' When he returned home to start filming in the spring of 1961, he carried his aversion to studios to the extreme and declared that not a single set would be built for *A Taste of Honey* – it would all be filmed on location and in a real house – a derelict mansion in Fulham Road, London, where municipal renovation was temporarily suspended while the top floor served as the rooming-house for the heroine, Jo, and her trollopy mother, and the rest was used as production offices. (The rental was £20 a week, compared with the usual studio fee of £2,000.) Again, one must stop and remember that, although such practice is commonplace today, in 1961 it was deemed exceptionally audacious, or foolhardy, for any reputable film unit to work this way. Richardson's detestation of studio-created 'reality' was abetted by his choice of Walter Lassally as lighting cameraman.

Since the days of the late 1950s, when he had photographed some of the 'Free Cinema' films, Lassally had been trying to break into first-feature work, with little success. Even the Michael Cacoyannis films he had photographed, *A Girl in Black* (1955) and *A Matter of Dignity* (1957), which had made his reputation on the Continent, were ignored by British producers, or else held against him. 'They didn't consider the way they'd been made, entirely on location, was relevant to the British scene. 'Yes, but have you shot a film in a studio?' they kept asking me, not understanding that it's actually more difficult to light on location than on a sound-stage.' He had been vetoed as lighting cameraman on

Look Back in Anger – it was felt that an 'inexperienced' film-director was quite risky enough – and missed the chance of *Saturday Night and Sunday Morning*; but now Richardson moved heaven and earth to get the *Taste of Honey* distributors, Bryanston-British Lion, to accept him and do the whole of the photography on the spot. ' "The English weather," they murmured, with fear in their eyes,' Lassally recalled. Like much else of less changeable disposition in the British character, the weather had played a large, superstitious, but sometimes practical, role in inhibiting any cinema breakthrough.

'If you worked in the documentary tradition,' Lassally said, 'you learned to improvise on location, even though Cacoyannis prepared everything well in advance and seldom deviated from it. Richardson was a more improvisational and sympathetic director, very good at picking elements from everything the team gives him, then putting them together his way. He liked to work quickly, which suited me; the spontaneity must still be there when you have set up the lights. I lit *A Taste of Honey* so as to keep a naturalistic look throughout. I used a grainy stock for the indoor scenes, which gave the film its key feeling, then ordinary stock for the exteriors – all strictly against the advice the laboratories gave us at the time.'

Quite as much as the screenplay, which Richardson and Delaney wrote, it is Lassally's naturalistic lighting which strips away the play's non-naturalistic texture. On the stage it had a dream-projection quality. Jo and her tarty mother, mother's fancy man, the black sailor who gets Jo pregnant, and the lonely homosexual boy who nursemaids her through to motherhood existed in a one-dimensional world that overlapped with music-hall routines and Brechtian confabs with the audience. In the film they were transported into the solid reality of the industrial scene which Lassally's camera runs through like a questing mongrel at home in the back streets, eyeing schoolgirls got up like miniature Bardots, the deserted churches with notice boards proclaiming 'God Washes Whitest of All,' and municipal statues that appear to swivel offended eyes on the mother and daughter doing a flit from one cheap room to the next, with the rent unpaid. Heavy criticism was directed against such an over-sharp focus on what John Russell Taylor called, in writing about the play, 'characters . . . entering momentarily into [Jo's] dream of life and vanishing when they have no further usefulness for it.'[1] Yet Richardson's success in fashioning a film form out of a play tips the balance his way. Recast to fit a very solid industrial topography, the characters are directed, and acted, with total understanding of where they fit into it. Quotation marks aren't used as they were in *The Entertainer* to extract a bit of social reality and comment on it. It is a film about acceptance of life, not rebellion, and the muted note keys the film more confidently than the trumpet blasts that were the metaphor for Jimmy Porter's monologues in *Look Back in Anger*.

Richardson's skill with performers was confirmed by a total newcomer, Rita Tushingham, picked from a Liverpool repertory company, who played Jo in a way that made one feel a female Finney had come to town. She wouldn't turn out to be quite that; but as well as the homeliness of her flat-vowelled Merseyside name, she brought a plainness that was almost eerie, a crow's nest of hair, an acute-angled nose, eyes of doggy loyalty, and a mouth one could fit a saucer into – a cup and saucer when it was wide open. This was a new amalgam of un-starry characteristics that proved touchingly amenable to Richardson's blending of them as Jo learned to accept life's heaped spoonful of bitterness before the first kick of her baby in the womb gave her a taste of its sweetness. Not only did Richardson reject the blandishments of American finance which offered to bankroll the film provided Audrey Hepburn played the part, but he turned down, with half-amused contempt, the 'happy ending' that was to go with Hepburn – a miscarriage, which the backers deemed 'up-beat' as well as solving the miscegenation problem – and he substituted his own oddly moving metaphor of motherhood, with Jo gripping a penny sparkler on bonfire night and the fizzing firework magically embodying the spark of life inside her. Before the glow died down, and the film ended, it had illuminated

[1] John Russell Taylor, *op. cit.*, p. 134.

the new cinema's confidence in making its own stars.
The profits on a film that cost only £120,000 also boosted
confidence.

A BREAKTHROUGH BREAKS DOWN

On 2 November, 1961, Woodfall announced a million-pound
production programme 'in which Bryanston will participate';
and exactly four weeks later the latter consortium announced its
own expansionist ambitions. It had linked up with Seven Arts
Productions, U.K., a production company headed by Kenneth
Hyman, whose father, Eliot, controlled the American parent
organization. Now this meant for Bryanston a considerable
departure from its original modest and cautious intentions. For
one thing, it opened up new finance. Seven Arts was wealthy and
it was fiscally advantageous to make films in Britain; it had just
produced *The Roman Spring of Mrs Stone* (1962) at Elstree and, in
1962, would make *Lolita* there, too. With it as partner, Bryanston
could henceforth offer the full 100 per cent financing to independent producers whose projects got the nod of approval, while
guaranteeing total creative freedom to the film-makers. The
consortium had now, in theory, the resources to underwrite
movies whose size, stars and budgets had – it was hoped – the
power to penetrate the American market. Whereas Bryanston had
thought in terms of films costing between £150,000 and £180,000,
it now was possible, provided pre-sale support was promised, to
consider budgets from £500,000 to £700,000. Balcon's vow of
'no blockbusters' was quietly forgotten; and the first film of this
order that Bryanston-Seven Arts announced was *Sammy Going
South* (1963), to be produced by Balcon. It was a subject whose
star (Edward G. Robinson) and location filming (East and South
Africa, where salaries and wages were approximately two-and-a-
half times the United Kingdom rate) would have meant a budget
of at least £300,000 – too big a fish for Bryanston to fry alone.
In spite of the Hollywood star – or maybe because of him – it was
stated rather defensively that 'this is a purely British film with no
concession to the American market in production terms.' The

words had an ominous echo of past aspirations and disappointing achievements. Filming began early in 1962.

Meanwhile, no concessions of budget or casting were being made in the next film to carry Bryanston's trademark: the Woodfall production of *The Loneliness of the Long Distance Runner* (21 September, 1962). Richardson had tried to set it up the previous summer, but the authorities of the Borstal reform schools refused him access to any of their institutions in order to gather facts and atmosphere. (A large country mansion was to do duty for a Borstal's exterior view, for the film was, of course, to be photographed entirely on location by Walter Lassally.) Richardson postponed production till early spring, 1962, by which time presumably enough evidence of what the inside of a contemporary Borstal looked like had been smuggled out to satisfy his restless impatience with 'make-believe' substitutes for the real thing.

Alan Sillitoe wrote the screenplay from his own forty-page story. Though linked with the themes of 'anger ' and 'revolt,' the film isn't really about either. Its hero is a case-hardened conservative. He is a thief because it is the way things are with him, have always been with him, in his social class where running from the police has kept his leg muscles in trim. Even the premature death of his father from 'some nameless capitalist disease,' as *Time*'s reviewer snidely but accurately put it, has bred no Marxist rage for revolution, but only resentment against a mother who brought her 'fancy man' into the house before his dad was cold in his bed. The token gesture he makes against 'the system' which has sent him to Borstal for 'reform' spring from a romantic reflex rather than a class hatred: he stops dead only a few yards short of winning the race between the Borstal boys and a public-school team. Certainly he is anti-Establishment in a generalized way: but more particularly he retains a vested interest in the *status quo* characteristic of the petty proletarian thief. His opposition to the Borstal governor derives from the same low guile that bamboozles the insidiously chummy prison psychiatrist – 'He's stupid and I'm not, because I can see further into the likes of him than he can see into the likes of me.' Alan Sillitoe, however, had his own interpretation of the story. 'It's really about a writer who regards his integrity as his most sacred possession,' he said. 'But you obviously can't write about that baldly, so you create an objective situation in real life. I put the "Runner" into a Borstal, which is now I see society; society puts its own valuation on you, as the prison governor does, and in many ways it's a totally wrong one.' The script he found easier, but less satisfying to write than *Saturday Night and Sunday Morning*. 'It was difficult to know what to take out of *Saturday Night*, easier to put things into the *Runner* which had to be expanded from a short story . . . but to me it always seemed a bit padded.'

To others, the film had even more serious flaws. It was attacked for attempting to score points on a broader social front than its theme could encompass – and doing so with a crudely propagandist technique and a grab-bag of derivative cinema styles lifted self-consciously from the French *nouvelle vague* directors. *Time*'s critic commented that the film was 'a piece of skilful but specious pleading for the British proletariat . . . the hero is too palpably prolier-than-thou, his case is too obviously rigged.'[1] It's hard to disagree with this. Far from granting the 'Runner' his existential status through his own actions on the limited scale of resistance at his disposal, the film tries to justify those actions by crude references-back to the society he comes from. The technique is nowhere worse deployed than in the attempt to suggest the 'Runner's' stream of consciousness as he nears the winning tape by machine-gun bursts of flashbacks which riddle him with bitter memories of his hovel-like home, his invalid father, his worthless mother, the Fascist police and the Establishmentarian governor. It is like a jockey flaying his mount in the last furlong: it betrays Richardson's anxiety lest his audience miss the 'message.'

Yet the 'message' is inherent all the time in Tom Courtenay's impressive début as the 'Runner.' The label of 'a second Finney' was more inevitable than accurate. Actually he was genuinely nearer working-class bedrock than Finney, coming from a family where his father chipped paint off fisher-trawlers in the Hull dockyards. Liberated from such dead-end prospects by the post-

[1] *Time*, 26 October, 1962.

war Education Act and quickly educated out of his social niche, he reached the theatre only through failing to graduate with a university Arts degree. He stayed nervously conscious of his class origins for a long time: in those early days he had a self-deprecating way of referring to his physical awkwardness and the ironic contrast between his proletarian looks and the pretensions of his aristocratic sounding name (even though in its original French derivation it meant merely 'short nose'). In talking of the theatre, though, he showed an early scepticism about the working-class influence on it. 'Take all this thing now about working-class actors and writers,' he said in 1961. 'It's simply a release of certain talents from that class . . . The real working class has nothing to do with the theatre today. The railway porter, the chap on the fish dock in Hull, they're not interested . . . Why should they be?'[1] Yet his own looks left no doubt on which side of the barricades the characters he played belonged: a nose that would split wood, eyes like gun-sights, a rare smile that opened out like a jack-knife and twisted in the enemy's guts, tons of worry on his brow, weeks of hunger-striking behind his cheeks. In those early years of the 1960s, Courtenay's off-screen temperament rarely lost its pull towards melancholy and scepticism. Like Finney, he was later to beat a retreat, part strategic, part therapeutic, from the suddenness of celebrity, and enlist in the ranks of the provincial repertory actors where it was possible for the refugee from film stardom to regain a proper sense of proportion.

The character of the 'Runner' was self-drawn in Sillitoe's first-person style of the original story: it was greatly to Courtenay's credit as an actor that he retained its truth in a film that insisted on overdrawing it by technical flashiness. 'He needles his way into the character with no mannerisms or calculated effects that are obvious,' said Peter Baker.[2]

He went largely unscathed by critics' blows which rained down on the film's style – or, rather, mish-mash of styles. These ranged violently from one mood to the next: accelerated Chaplinesque farce for the thieves' flight from a baker's shop; satirical punchi-

[1] *Daily Express*, 2 November, 1961. Interview by David Lewin.
[2] *Films and Filming*, November, 1962.

ness parodying television commercials when the 'Rebel's' mother squanders her widow's insurance on a spending spree; the lyrical dreaminess of cigarette ads for the 'Runner's' solitary sprinting through the dawn woods; savagely ironic cross-cutting between a Borstal escapee being brutally recaptured and the rest of the school singing the hymn *Jerusalem*; and those final angry volleys of flashbacks. John Coleman summed up the effect of these un-assimilated styles when he wrote, 'You can almost hear the clashing of new waves, English and French, and it is their head-on confrontation that finally rocks the boat.'[1] The massive arrival of films by Truffaut, Chabrol, Resnais and Godard in the English, or, rather, in the London cinemas in the months prior to *The Loneliness of the Long Distance Runner*, simply reinforced the feeling that the English breakthrough had become derivative and pre-dictable. Peter Harcourt voiced the reaction very perceptively at the end of 1962 when he wrote, 'One of the great limitations of so many of the new British films can be seen in terms of this externality and uninventiveness of technique. Of course there are obviously the limiting physical factors of production in this country, the economic pressures which encourage conventionality of technique, as there are the problems inseparable from the process of adaptation which must undoubtedly contribute to this lack of freshness on the screen. But more important than these, I feel, is the sociological bias which seems such a part of so many of these films. No doubt from their origins in the "Free Cinema" movement, the films set out to explore the less familiar territories of working-class life; and yet, in doing so, they have succeeded in presenting us less with the unique quality of individual life than with the broad general outline of sociological types. They have been less concerned with exploration of the intimacies of day-to-day living than with a pictorial demonstration of what is already known to be there.'[2]

In short, familiarity had bred not contempt, but lack of interest. The surprise had gone, the shock of recognition had been

[1] *New Statesman*, 28 September, 1962.
[2] 'I'd Rather Be Like I Am,' *Sight and Sound* (Winter 1962–3), Vol. 32, No. 1, p. 19.

absorbed by dint of repetition. It was all too predictable – and it had happened with disconcerting speed. 'For years we begged for British films about real people and contemporary themes,' wrote David Robinson. 'Now that we have them (and, as a result, are re-establishing a reputation in the international cinema), it is alarming to detect – among critics, if not, as yet, in the audience – a growing resistance to such a film as *The Loneliness of the Long Distance Runner*. It is a resistance to change belief in the picture palace as fairyland, for the interesting new experience of stories about working-class people in working class and regional situations.'[1] And the then anonymous critic of *The Times*, who had shown a fairly consistent antipathy to these new films, seized the chance to put in the boot on behalf of the Establishment. 'It would be a pleasant change,' he wrote, 'if all this elaborate apparatus of mockery at the expense of the existing order of things were put into action on behalf not of discontented youth, the spoilt darlings of the age, but of the ill, the solitary, the virtuous old who are the real sufferers from it.'[2] Though this was special pleading, it contained much unpalatable truth. One longed for the essential differences of the figures in the industrial landscape to be investigated. One hungered for an indication that under the blanket of industrial smog there were surely unique pockets of resistance to the greyness of life, some residual joy, warmth, humour, release, such as there surely would have been in any similar milieu in Paris or Rome or Lyons or Milan. 'Glumness,' that perfect onomatopoeic word to express the spiritual deflation of the English, was the characteristic that, when the sheer excitement of revolution had subsided, came to dominate the picture. But the film-makers, though they were often sympathetic and always understanding towards the dilemmas of their characters, hardly ever generated the sense that they actually *liked* them. Pity, yes: that was present in abundance. The trouble was, the people to whom it was extended tended to become *objects* of pity unless they had the animating independence of a performance by a Finney. They were representatives more than individuals. The

---

[1] *The Financial Times*, 28 September, 1962.
[2] *The Times*, 26 September, 1962.

E

content of the films was the novel addition to the British screen, but the attitudes towards it on the part of the directors remained tentative or reserved. There was a feeling that they were doing their duty – which of course they were – but as for anything beyond the call of duty, the passionate, intimate commitment of a Truffaut, a sense of shared biography or imaginative empathy, this was locked behind an English reserve bordering on the puritanical. The passions that should have been implicit in the film-maker's involvement had now to be whipped up by means of a style that was applied from the outside and, even worse, had been borrowed from the French, though without the French zest in their own rediscovery of cinema as a means of subjective expression. The industry's very economic set-up ruled that out in Britain: Richardson had impetuously broken the studio strangle-hold, but even he, had he had it in him, couldn't have mustered the personal independence, the total flouting of traditional methods and corporate edicts, which the French *nouvelle vague* talents put to work. 'If the French risk irresponsibility,' Penelope Houston said, 'the British risk the elimination of surprise: a situation triggers off a reaction, and the audience knows in advance what the reaction must be, because it knows – or by now should know – the kind of social thinking at work.'[1]

The one link most enduringly forged between audiences and screen in Britain was that of 'youth' – the excitement aroused by the new young stars these films had made. But excitement implies identification. The audience was changing with great rapidity. And this was bound to reduce the identification which audiences felt with the proletarian heroes of the screen – as would the success that the actors who played these rebels and underdogs gained from acclaim and sought to preserve without risking their popularity through repetition. The 'under-achieved' proletarian heroes would begin to look their age when the imagination of the youthful audience had been seized by the over-rewarded pop heroes of their own generation. At the beginning of 1960 there

---

[1] Penelope Houston, *op. cit.*, p. 123.

were just over 5,000,000 teenagers in Britain.[1] They were drawing
11 per cent of the personal incomes; 60 per cent of them went
to the cinema at least once a week as against only
13 per cent of the adult population. (Nearly 50 per cent of the
adults never went at all.) Even more important, the great majority
of teenagers no longer wanted to feel, be or be treated as adults:
they wanted to stay young and they were increasingly assisted to
believe it was within their power, as their ever-rising income soon
put it within their means, to remain so by the enormous increase
in all the commercial pressures that by the start of the 1960s had
identified youth as the richest potential market. In 1955 advertising expenditure in Britain totalled £277 million a year: by 1960
it had risen to nearly £500 million a year, a large part of it aimed
directly at youth, endowing youth with a corporate identity and
going a long way to wiping out the more obvious social distinctions. Aspirations were on the way up; pride and even consciousness in belonging to a particular social class was growing blurred
as the economic boom brought more and more consumer goods
within everyone's range in spite of pay pauses and wage freezes
which had to be imposed in the summer of 1961. 'Prepare to
Meet Thy Boom' had been *Queen* magazine's irreverent slogan in
its issue of 15 September, 1959. The editorial struck the note of
the coming decade with remarkable accuracy, allowing for the
consciously eupeptic note of knowingness which gave *Queen*'s
pages much of their *élan*. 'Have you woken up? Do you know
you are living in a new world?' it asked. 'You are half-aware of
it perhaps. You don't use words like ersatz or economy label.
You don't even say credit squeeze. But here we are, 20 years after
the war started, in an age better than any even our grandfathers
can remember, for all their grumblings. Better, in fact, than any
in the history of the world. Material, yes, but pleasant. You are
richer than ever before. You are spending more than you have
ever done. Our hope is that you realise it and enjoy it. We don't
want you to miss it. Don't wait till years after to realise you have
lived in a remarkable age – the age of BOOM.' And in the same

[1] Defined by Mark Abrams of the London Press Exchange, as young
people over fifteen and under twenty-five and unmarried.

magazine Robert Bolt anticipated one of the changing aspects of this new age of affluence. 'In the first 18 months of the sixties,' he said, 'the thing that is different is the widening gap between our beliefs and our actions.'[1]

On the cinema, all these changes would have an impact; and it, in turn, would have an impact on them. Given this new mood, it was hardly surprising to encounter so strong a reaction against *The Loneliness of the Long Distance Runner*. 'Already, in this film, the original spirit of rebellion is seen to be turning towards sterile fretfulness,' said Penelope Houston, and she added, 'The post-*Room at the Top* era has come near to running its course; and the directors who have emerged from it have to find their own way towards a more cinematic cinema, unaided by influences from across the Channel.'[2] As a prediction, this was precisely half-right. The 'post-*Room at the Top* era' was indeed almost over. But as for the influences, particularly the economic influences, that were going to affect the fortunes and, to an increasing degree, set the style of the next era of British films – well, they were going to come from across a wider stretch of water than the Channel.

[1] *Queen*, July 1961.
[2] Penelope Houston, *op. cit.*, pp. 121, 124.

Chapter Seven: The One that got away

This is our holiday film.   Tony Richardson

Early in 1962, before spring had reached England, Bryanston's managing director was spending the better part of a sunny fortnight in Acapulco in the company of Tony Richardson and John Osborne. The film festival there had invited Bryanston to show the Woodfall production, *Saturday Night and Sunday Morning*, and Max Setton felt it a good opportunity for thorough discussion of Woodfall's next project, the one immediately after *The Loneliness of the Long Distance Runner*. It was a considerable break with the company's commitment to contemporary, often radical, subjects. For one thing, it was to be a roistering eighteenth-century social comedy; for another, it was to cost 'about £300,000' – an appreciable sum.

Tom Jones (27 June, 1963) was a fairly free adaptation of Fielding's novel. Osborne had scripted it, Richardson would direct, Albert Finney was set to star. All this looked attractive to Setton; but the price made Bryanston pause. Linked though it was to the American company of Seven Arts, which now made higher budgets feasible, the consortium had embarked on another expensive project, *Sammy Going South*, which has already been referred to, and two 'blockbusters' totalling at least £600,000 constituted a high risk that would have to be spread. There were Bryanston members who would have preferred *Tom Jones*, which they felt more likely to appeal to the modern mood, to the rather old-fashioned, sentimental emphasis of *Sammy Going South*, the story of a small British boy's odyssey through former colonial territories from Port Said to South Africa. (Children and the Empire had been part and parcel of Ealing's faith, and the film was to be directed by an old Ealing hand, Alexander Mackendrick.) However, Bryanston was already committed to *Sammy Going South*; so Setton looked around for other investors in *Tom Jones*.

It is at this crucial point that accounts of what then ensued begin to differ, until some aspects of the pre-production history

of *Tom Jones* are difficult to reconcile. Actually, this is not uncommon in so tense and even traumatic a business as film production; and there is no reason to doubt that all those involved
in the *Tom Jones* deal believed – and still believe – they acted
sincerely and honestly. Each, of course, acted with a different
purpose uppermost in his mind; and as anyone knows who has
tried to co-ordinate the efforts of a group of people, not
necessarily film people, the opportunities for misunder-
standing present formidable and not always foreseeable obstacles.
It is best, therefore, in view of the pivotal effect that the *Tom
Jones* film had on the future pattern of film-making in Britain, to
present the separate accounts as they were communicated to me
in the 1971–2 period, a lapse of time that is certainly long enough
to have blurred some impressions and softened others, but also
to have freed some people from the embarrassment they may have
experienced at the time.

As Max Setton recalled the events, it was agreed that Bryanston
should put up 70 per cent of the estimated budget of £300,000,
and he set about raising the rest. First he approached Mike
Frankovich, then based in London where he was in charge of
European production for Columbia Pictures. (Setton and Frankovich already knew each other well, having produced some
earlier British films together.) He asked Frankovich to put up
30 per cent – in short the remainder of the budget. Frankovich
demurred at providing all, but promised part of the 30 per cent.
Fifteen per cent was then guaranteed by Elliott Hyman, head of
Seven Arts, and the National Film Finance Corporation chipped
in 'with a little, too.' It all looked set, and at the Cannes Film
Festival in May 1962 the parties met in the hotel suite of Abe
Schneider, president of Columbia Pictures, to celebrate the deal.
At this moment, according to Setton, 'Tony Richardson took a
call from Woodfall's London offices, came back and whispered
in my ear that, on a recheck, the budget might not be enough.
We would have to raise more. 'We'll raise it,' I promised. 'How
much?' When he told me, the champagne went flat in my glass.
It was a pretty hefty sum.' Accounts differ on how hefty was
'hefty,' but between £50,000 and £60,000 seems a likely sum.

Balcon affirmed in his autobiography that 'we should have agreed to increase our various contributions to the cost.'[1] This would have let Bryanston in for finding 55 per cent of the extra money. Setton tried to do this, but found Columbia wanted to hold Richardson to his original figure. He telephoned Elliott Hyman, who was at his Westport home recovering from influenza and coincidentally reading the *Tom Jones* script, which was causing him some surprise. 'Do you know,' he said, 'that there's a character in this who talks to the camera?' Setton advised him to put down the screenplay and pick up his cheque-book.

Tony Richardson's recollection of these events, perhaps not surprisingly, differs somewhat from the previous account, though the difference is probably one of emphasis more than fact. Bryanston certainly wanted to make *Tom Jones*, a project he had discussed with them 'for a long time,' but they wanted to do so for a sum he considered 'totally unrealistic.' The additional amount he needed was 'relatively small' and the total budget of some £350,000 was 'the absolute nitty-gritty in which no one took anything you could call "money." I didn't take any money. Albert Finney would get paid about £9,000 and the only person who would be paid anything that could be called substantial was one of the leading actresses who would get £20,000.' Finney was already under contract to do the film, through options on his services when he signed for *Saturday Night and Sunday Morning*, but when he notified Richardson of a desire he had to be associated more closely with the production than simply playing the title role, the former replied, 'Well, if that's what you want we'll tear up the contract and become partners, you, me and John (Osborne).' According to Richardson, the decision to film the picture in colour was not the make-or-break element in the budget it has since been rumoured to be. 'We had spent every penny we had on developing the film and preparing the production,' Richardson recalled, 'and if it wasn't made, we would probably go bankrupt at Woodfall – even the money starting to come in from *Saturday Night and Sunday Morning* was committed. Bryanston reckoned that, by making me cut corners on the film,

[1] Michael Balcon, *op. cit.*, p. 197.

it could be made for £50–60,000 less. I kept saying, "Show me how. Send over your experts. Tell me what to do." It got to absurd lengths. I would call and say, "I can get such and such an actress, who's got quite a growing reputation, for £1,200 to £1,500: would you agree to that?" And they'd reply, "Oh, we'd love to have her, provided you can find her fee out of the budget." Of course it couldn't be done. We had got within weeks of our shooting-date, the cast were signed up, the crew contracted, and we knew that we simply could not make *Tom Jones* on the budget we had.'

At some point, either around this time, or prior to it – no one's recollection of this is perfectly clear – Richardson's agent, Cecil Tennant, remarked that there was a new man in charge of production in United Artists' London office. He might be interested in backing the film. After all, what had they to lose?

The 'new man' at United Artists was George H. Ornstein, an American then in his early forties, a tall, well-built man who looked as if he could take good care of himself. Ornstein had flown V.I.P.'s to Britain through the thick of the North Atlantic air war, and it had been not at all a bad preparation for his initiation assignment as a post-war trainee salesman with United Artists, selling product that included Rank's British films to the tough Irish neighbourhood-cinemas in Brooklyn where, he was told, 'the Micks throw bottles at the screen the second they see a British trademark.' With a flash of perhaps not entirely ethical inspiration, the young salesman asked if there was any reason why such irksome national characteristics couldn't be snipped off before the film was run. He returned to his office – and general amazement – with two contracts. A later transfer to U.A.'s foreign division had taken him to Latin America, then to Europe and a lengthy, eight-and-a-half year spell in Spain –Ornstein spoke fluent Spanish: then, and perhaps now, a rare asset for resident Americans – before he was transferred to London in the early 1960s to involve himself in production. By marriage, Ornstein was connected to the Mary Pickford family – his wife's aunt had been a founder of United Artists in 1919. But this had been no asset in his early years with the company, when it had passed into the control of new, more efficient management. By experience, he knew the world sales markets at a level and with a detail certainly not shared by any British film executives, and by hardly any other American production chief in London at that date. By temperament, he was able to talk the artists' language as well as the financiers', and he was ready to go out and bat for a project. But he had no final say-so. This power didn't reside in London – and never would – but with the legal and financial triumvirate who headed United Artists in New York: Arthur Krim, Robert Benjamin and Arnold Picker.

'The London agents in 1962 were just realizing I was alive,' Ornstein recalled. 'Cecil Tennant told me to come over and see him: he certainly wasn't stepping over to my office. He gave me the *Tom Jones* property and I read the first twenty-odd pages in bed, and fell asleep unimpressed by what seemed its old-fashioned style. I woke up about 3 a.m. with the realization that this just wasn't so. I reread it twice before breakfast and later that morning told Tennant I was recommending it highly.'[1] New York, though, remained adamantly unconvinced that costume epics weren't box-office poison and Ornstein's only ally in New York was Arnold Picker's nephew David, then being brought into production. By wearisome insistence, which brought him near to being fired, Ornstein manoeuvred a meeting between David Picker, Osborne and Richardson which resulted in Picker saying to him, 'Move your head over on the block and I'll lie down with you.' Ornstein and he composed a lengthy cable to New York – a practice which that frugal management sternly discouraged – and adjourned to the White Elephant, a Curzon Street dining-club where many film deals of the 1960s were set up, to await the transatlantic reply. They later learned that the initial response to their cable had been distinct displeasure. However, when the call came, it brought not dismissal, but approval of *Tom Jones* and a £350,000 budget. 'David and I told Tony Richardson,' Ornstein said, 'and his immediate reaction was, "Marvellous, but why is it merely a

[1] George H. Ornstein interviewed by the author, 9–14 September, 1972. Unless stated otherwise, all subsequent quotations from Ornstein come from the same source

50–50 deal? If the picture is a success, don't we deserve more than that?" ' When United Artists' profit equalled the cost of the negative, he was assured with a certain sardonic inflection, he could have 75 per cent to their 25 per cent. At the time it looked a safe bet: it proved one of the most generous deals in movies.

Maxwell Setton, at Bryanston, took the news philosophically when a 'slightly embarrassed' Richardson broke it to him. United Artists had guaranteed 100 per cent financing, the director's and producer's fees in cash, and a percentage of the picture. 'I really couldn't blame him for accepting: it was a much better deal than we could ever have offered . . . Tom Jones made a fortune, between thirty and forty million dollars. If Bryanston had had it, we would have been set for life.' Sir Michael Balcon, too, accepted the inevitable and later wrote, 'For my own part, I can only say that if I had had the courage to pawn everything I possessed and risk it on Tom Jones it would have been a wise decision. It could be said I lacked the courage of my convictions, but to have taken that gamble quite soon after having contemplated retirement might also have been called foolhardy! No doubt Tom Jones is engraved on my heart.'[1]

PARTIE DE CAMPAGNE

I have dealt with the pre-production history of Tom Jones in some detail because it is such a watershed film in the period under review. Subsequent chapters will illustrate the immense influence its success had on the production pattern of the film industry in Britain: but every facet of its making, as well as its financing, is significant. When Tony Richardson in the early summer of 1962 dubbed it 'our holiday film,' he was considerably understating its impact. This film, the sixth Woodfall had made since 1959, was the one that put the company's fortunes on a solid footing for almost the rest of the decade and allowed Richardson what was virtually a blank cheque in the choice of future films, secure in the knowledge that Tom Jones's world-wide profits would enable him to turn aspiration into achievement without the heartbreaking

[1] Michael Balcon, op. cit., p. 198.

haggling that most directors had to undergo with their money suppliers.

It gave a fillip to the creative spirits of even the people not directly profiting from it, though Richardson was generous when it came to making separate packages of Woodfall's percentage in the film and distributing them among his close associates. Just when the 'new realism' was drooping for want of refreshment, its energies were revived by *Tom Jones* and redirected away from a scene that had staled from over-familiarity and repetitiveness. The sense of having a 'good time' spilled out of every frame of *Tom Jones* and, in the phrase then in vogue, audiences found themselves 'switched on' by it. That it *was* an intoxicating film is paradoxically due to the fact that Henry Fielding's eighteenth-century novel permitted Osborne and Richardson to carry their commitment to social realism with a light conscience. The 'two Englands' of the rich and poor, the 'haves' and the 'have-nots,' had been the basis of that conscience: now that they intermingled so rowdily and colourfully in a picaresque comedy, Woodfall were freed from the patronizing sympathy which the screen had begun extending to the poor, trapped, inarticulate people in the depressed areas of the mid-twentieth century. The landscape of contemporary naturalism had been excavated for what it yielded about the substance of life: the philistinism of Fielding's time, over which he moralized, may have reached the screen with much of its didactic force diminished, but what a relief it was from the present-day puritanism of provincial England!

Tom Jones's appearance also coincided with an accelerating candour in English public life, a revision of opinion about conventions and taste and a tolerance of attitudes once thought wayward, not to say aberrant, which the successful defence of Penguin Books, the publishers of the unexpurgated edition of *Lady Chatterley's Lover*, in October 1960, had helped get under way. 'A healthy freedom of expression has been established,' Bernard Levin wrote of a trial that was not so much a legal wrangle as a conflict of generation and social class.[1] And *Tom Jones* helped extend, as far as the screen was concerned, the limits

[1] Bernard Levin, *The Pendulum Years* (Cape, 1970), p. 294.

of the permissible which the printed word had managed to push forward. Its candid acknowledgement that human conduct was less than perfect, its dislike of bigotry and hypocrisy, its tolerance of the whole range of behaviour unconfined by class restraints, its frank enjoyment of the sensual, and at the same time its endorsement through its hero's character – 'a lover without being a lecher,' David Robinson called him – of a general fund of good sense and honesty: these elements were even more acceptable to the mood of the public by being assimilated into a robust historical romp.

The liberation was visible in everything Richardson and company did. Walter Lassally, his lighting photographer, was called in after Richardson had parted company with a photographer who, in Lassally's opinion, had been trying to 'pull him back to orthodoxy.' And a lot of the film's freshness comes from Richardson's willingness to 'stick his neck out' artistically, and Lassally's ability to follow suit technically. 'We didn't want to make *Tom Jones* look like a Hollywood epic,' Lassally recalled, 'so we agreed to incorporate the style of *A Taste of Honey*; so long as the staging, costumes and locations were impeccably in period,[1] we were determined to use very modern camera techniques, documentary ones in many of the sequences – the hunt, for instance.' The gathering pack of hounds and huntsmen was shot with a hand-held camera, with rapid cutting and sometimes deliberate visual distortions to induce the stirrup-cup feeling of mounting intoxication that would be followed by a brutal hunt in which shots taken by a camera on a low-loader vehicle were intercut with views from a helicopter. Naturalism in *Tom Jones* was forever overlapping with a subjective view of things: the audience was either having its nose rubbed in eighteenth-century life, or sharing the hero's personal predicament, or both. Either way, there was no 'distancing' effect: the film reached out directly by every means, by narration as much as by the visuals, to keep audiences at the same kind of elastic stretch as a Keystone comedy. Lassally believes that possibly no film of this size had been shot totally on location *and in colour* before *Tom Jones*.

[1] Not quite. The 'period' allowed itself some expansive liberties.

'Colour-film stock was then half the speed it was in the late 1960s,' he said. But he had recently lit interiors in St Paul's Cathedral in colour for an American television film using a newly developed Eastman stock which required one-and-a-half times less light than the customary colour-stock then in use; and this made it feasible to shoot the whole of *Tom Jones* on location by manipulating or supplementing natural light. 'This is not so much improving on nature,' he later told an interviewer, 'as rendering it closer to what the human eye sees. The eye adjusts to a dark area, the lens does not, or at any rate it is unable to compensate for extremes of light and darkness *in the same frame.*'[1] *Tom Jones*'s colour had a softness that not only complemented the eye's view of the landscape, but also suited the way Richardson, in slightly up-dating the novel, muted Hogarthian caricature into something nearer the verisimilitude of Rowlandson. Tempering the colour tones was achieved in the camera, not the laboratory – 'The trouble with labs is that they're run by chemists, not artists,' Richardson lamented after viewing one attempt at desaturating the raw stock. Instead, Lassally found the softening effect he sought by using an extremely fine piece of veiling of the sort that used to decorate ladies' hats. Once the property of Georges Perinal, the veteran French cinematographer, these two scraps of net imparted to the landscape and its figures the visual fluency of the watercolour sketch which Richardson, as I have noted, preferred to the worked-over oil painting.

Lassally's camera was a blimped Arriflex. It only held a short, 400-foot length of film, but was lighter than the Mitchell or B.N.C. cameras then in common use on British and Hollywood movies, and 'it was the only camera available then which allowed me to see what I was getting in the lens. On the other cameras, you had to use a view-finder. With a view-finder, you have to give the actors "marks" to hit, which means they have to rehearse for the camera-man with some precision. The picture you get in the view-finder may differ considerably from the one on the cinema screen, for if the actor doesn't hit his mark, it may not be

[1] Ivan Butler, *The Making of Feature Films – A Guide* (Penguin Books, 1971), p. 122.

apparent till the rushes are viewed. A reflex camera like the Arriflex, on the other hand, saves time and technical rehearsal, but needs quite different lighting. With a non-reflex camera, only specific areas were lit, whereas I could light locations so that the actors could move all over them if the director wanted. It made for a much more mobile relationship between Richardson and the cast.'

If one dwells on these technical details, it is because they seldom get referred to when the question is asked why some films turn out the way they do. Style may be attitude, as Lindsay Anderson would have it: but technique is frequently temperament, too. The more mobile relationship Lassally mentions fitted in perfectly with Richardson's characteristic impatience and habit of improvising with whatever was at hand. Even the concept of the film confirms this. 'In *Tom Jones*,' Albert Finney recalled, 'we wanted to create a Latin feeling, not to ponder too much but to leap in. We would rehearse a scene very little, but plunge haphazardly into it. Tony was in his element, picking, blending, substituting, rearranging – if a scene took two days to shoot, the odds were he would change it all on the second day.'

Not that this entirely suited Finney's temperament. Though it shows nowhere in the edited film, Richardson's way of shooting wasn't one Finney took to easily. 'I tend to be cautious in building a character,' he explained. 'I walk around the poolside, so to speak, testing the temperature before I lower myself in. With Tony, it's instant immersion. As it turned out, it worked well, but I found it hard to sustain my enthusiasm for the role over the shooting period. Certainly I couldn't have made *Saturday Night and Sunday Morning* like that: in *that* film my conception of the role came slowly, by jettisoning what didn't work, by doing what Lee Strasberg counsels: "In the long run, reduce a performance".' That Finney's concern showed itself in interviews with him nearly ten years after *Tom Jones*'s enormous and still-continuing success only emphasizes how deep-seated the worry was at the time. On reflection, he attributed it to the wish that 'you want to show them you're an actor, not a puppet.' The same desire was at the back of his request to Richardson to be co-producer on the film. For him, film acting was a question of controlling what you were involved in. He was asserting that very stubborn, self-protective side of his nature which has already been noted. 'If you have strong feelings about aspects of your work, you've got to be in a position to express them. I wanted it to be stated clearly, on the screen, in the credits, that I was now in a position to make my voice heard in the production, as well as contribute my acting talent to it.' The reason he finally didn't co-produce *Tom Jones* was that he had not reckoned with all the multifarious wheeling and dealing needed to set up a film, which can exhaust an actor's creative energy even before the camera starts turning.

He nevertheless added much to the role – and the film – through sheer dissatisfaction with it. Philip Oakes accurately diagnosed this when he wrote, '(Tom Jones) is a hero whom things are done to. He is loyal, loving and kind, but his nature is a composite of amiable shallows. He has no depth and for Finney to play the part is like asking Harold Pinter to write a nursery rhyme.'[1]

Finney kept restlessly trying to take a hand in Tom's fate by adding 'business' that would illustrate an independent will behind the hero's good-natured compliance with his destiny. One of the most successful, which he claims the director inventively enlarged on during shooting, was the famous 'eating scene' with the courtesan Mrs Walters, a mutual seduction in which not a word is spoken, but Finney and Joyce Redman munch their way through a meal in which lobster claws, chicken wishbones, roast ribs, oysters and outsize pears connote an appetite that is not for food alone. 'At first the scene had been mainly chat,' Finney recalled. 'I had the idea of letting the characters displace their carnal longings on to the supper they shared. We shot the scene silent.' Arthur Knight called it 'the funniest and lewdest eating scene ever set to celluloid.'[2] The oral eroticism with which every mouthful is charged was a joyous shock to audiences the world over in those pre-permissive days and neatly frustrated the objections which censors would have been bound to mete out to any fleshly encounter. Richardson's term 'our holiday film' is even more apt

[1] *The Sunday Telegraph*, 30 June, 1963.
[2] *Saturday Review*, 5 October, 1963.

if one interprets 'holiday' in the sense of 'taking French leave.' The bold stylistic borrowings from the French *nouvelle vague*, which looked like an after-thought in *The Loneliness of the Long Distance Runner*, now worked a treat. The silent-film titling, the under-cranked camera accelerating the riotous consequences of being found in the wrong bed, the frozen close-ups, the old-fashioned 'wipes' from one scene to the next, the times the characters address the camera directly, or Tom whips his tricorne hat over the lens at an indelicate juncture: all these permitted Osborne and Richardson to telescope the novel into a period précis of the social scene where a nod and a wink were as good as a chapter of moralizing comment. It had an exhilarating effect on audiences.

According to Ornstein, the biggest problem was finding a proper opening for the film. 'It seemed to take ages before we got into the action. One idea tried and rejected had Tom resting his head on his elbow, telling the story. There were over a dozen screenings of the rough cut to try and find an opening – during which some of the "out-takes," like the slow fall of the horse under the drunken squire, were put back to great effect. Finally Tony Richardson came up with the speeded-up action and the pounding pianola. It worked so beautifully the first time it was screened that we knew we had it there and then.'

Isabel Quigly estimated the gains and losses between the book and the film when she wrote, 'The book is (perhaps inevitably) much diminished. The film has got much of its fun and most of its bawdiness, a good sense of the 18th century social condition, a (justifiably) tighter plot and more dramatic ending (with Tom Jones brought to the gallows and indeed a little beyond) but little of its style (in the director's style, that is: what there is of it is in the script and the acting), none of its moral preoccupations (which Fielding hammers pretty hard) and scarcely any of its richness of heart.'[1] The cast was almost a National Theatre in itself and flaw-lessly deployed: eye-cocking Finney, Diane Cilento's lewd gamekeeper's wench, Joyce Redman's over-ripe courtesan, Susannah York's English rose waiting to be plucked, Hugh

---

[1] *The Spectator*, 5 July, 1963.

Griffith's barnyard Squire Western aflame with oaths and punch,
George Devine's good-natured Squire Allworthy forever believing the best of tearaway Tom, Edith Evans's haughty-vowelled
Lady, the throaty temptations put in Tom's way by Joan
Greenwood, the plunder almost made of sweetheart Sophia's
virtue by David Tomlinson, Peter Bull's apoplectic Thwackum
and his venomous pupil Blifil – played by an actor who would
shortly pole-vault to stardom, David Warner. All these embodi-
ments of period colour and swagger showed how pallid the
customary 'costume' genre had become. Something else was
present, too. For the first time the screen was decked out with a
prophetic sense of the tone that would play a dynamic part,
whether actually justified by fact or not, in shaping the foreigners'
impressions of Britain in the mid-1960s. That's to say, its
'swinging' mood. Though it was eighteenth century which
'swung' on the screen, there was a dimension of audacity, style
and high spirits relevant to the scene that was taking shape in
contemporary London. The past seemed to carry over vividly to
the present: the look, feel, smell, finery, coarseness and cruelty
of Fielding's England was still visible, though only just in some
cases, as Londonderry House, in Park Lane, the location used for
the film's high-society milieu, was being pulled down around
Richardson's crew while they made use of its refurbished splend-
ours. And all this was combined with, as *Time* put it, 'the primitive, illimitable will to live the whole of life.' Here was an
irresistible international package. As it started to bring back one
of the biggest box-office fortunes at that date, *Tom Jones* had even
sweeter significance. 'While such mundane matters as money
should be the last of a critic's concerns,' Arthur Knight wrote,
'I find it impossible not to add as a footnote that this sumptuous,
satisfying production cost only 1,300,000 dollars. In this age of
super-budgets, such a modest statistic might prove sobering.
The race is not to the rich, it seems to imply, but to the talented.'[1]

It is only fair to add, though, for its own sobering emphasis,
that during that dangerously unsettled period between a film's

[1] *Saturday Review*, 5 October, 1963. (Knight's estimate of the budget is
on the high side, but this hardly affects his argument.)

being completed and its being released, hardly anyone at United
Artists was sure who had won the race, or, indeed, if it had been
worth running at all. After a viewing had been held in London
of the assembled footage, Ornstein was told from a high level
inside the company that he had cost it a million dollars! Of the
dozen or so United Artists people who saw the first cut, only
Ilya Lopert thought it would get its money back. A British
executive confided to Ornstein that he didn't think it would make
£25,000 in Britain – 'and I'm going to tell you the truth,' he
added, 'I feel I have just crawled through a sewer.' Another was
more optimistic: he thought it would make £75,000 in Britain,
'but of course you won't get a cinema circuit release.' Censorship
raised a couple of unexpected problems. One was the stag hunt,
which the censor at first thought too cruel, but subsequently
allowed himself to be converted when the aid of an anti-blood-
sports league was enlisted. Then he decided it must be given an
X. because of a bedroom scene. Ornstein, by now fairly despond-
ent, accepted the X. and wasn't much cheered when an exhibitor
told him, 'I've got to have an X. if I'm to sell such a film at all.'
'The box-office results came in and the film was a resounding
success,' Ornstein said, 'and I don't remember anyone telling me
they'd been wrong.'

FINNEY, FAME AND FRUSTRATION

On Albert Finney this immense success had rather more ambivalent effects, which deserve examination now, even though it
entails a 'flash forward' in time to practically a year later when
Finney's next film, *Night Must Fall* (21 May, 1964) was premièred
in Britain.

Immediately after finishing his role in *Tom Jones* Finney had
been all set to make *Ned Kelly*, the story of the nineteenth-century
Australian bandit of the outback, which Karel Reisz was to direct
from a screenplay by David Storey, author of *This Sporting Life*.
Finney and Reisz flew to Australia in October 1962, and spent
ten weeks picking locations and delving into local lore about
Kelly. They intended to start shooting in March 1963, with the

British production office of Columbia Pictures putting up 100 per cent financing. But British labour union regulations and the necessity of flying out a large crew from Britain and maintaining them on location for several months began to inflate the budget until it came to well over a million dollars, at which point Columbia insisted on a drastic cut-back. After Finney and Reisz had made vain tours of Ireland and Spain, that all-purpose country for film-makers who needed to travel far afield for the sake of their plot but didn't have the cash for the journey, the project was abandoned. (Columbia at that time hadn't seen *Tom Jones* and, like everyone else, had no inkling that it and Finney would amass a fortune.) The experience taught Finney one of the most frustrating lessons of film-making: the belief that all is settled and that creative energies can be released when 'a telephone rings and suddenly – it's all off.' It was at this juncture, when he and Reisz were in the depths of despondency, that M.G.M. proposed a remake of their successful thriller of the 1930s, *Night Must Fall*. 'Six weeks later,' Reisz recalled, 'we were on the floor.'

Night Must Fall, adapted from Emlyn Williams's melodrama, had first been filmed in 1937 with Robert Montgomery as Danny, the working-class psychopath who totes the head of his last victim around with him in a hat-box. It seemed an impoverished theme for a socially conscious director like Reisz and an acclaimed actor like Finney to be remaking in the 1960s. Finney's memory of the early film was merely that 'it didn't strike any spark in me.' As projects went, however, it was typical of M.G.M., a film company which clung more tenaciously than most to the remake rights of its successful pictures.

Suddenly Reisz conceived the idea of bringing *Night Must Fall* up-to-date by using Danny's murders to reveal the attitudes of the society in which they took place. At once he and Finney were galvanized by the possibilities: it would now be much more a character study than a melodrama, they hoped, and as such might regain a social validity and prove attractive to Finney, who had just played what he regarded as the very unchallenging role of Tom Jones. Thus with the purest of motives and soberest of intentions, the two approached a project that would draw upon their luckless heads a great volley of criticism and even abuse. Clive Exton, then making his name as a dramatist of fine sensibilities and sound construction, did a quick and fairly full rewrite of the play, trying to supplement the penny-dreadful suspense of 'will he, won't he, chop off her head?' with a more thoughtful analysis of a psychopath shut up inside the unfriendly class structures of British society. Danny's urge to kill now derived from the man's envy, resentment and hopelessness. He fought back with his only weapons: a cunning charm that took care of his immediate needs, and the hatchet that satisfied his unspoken need for dominance and revenge. Although some reviewers subsequently found in the film a deliberate breakaway from social realism, Exton did try to relate Danny realistically to the class structure inside the country house where Danny found employment as an odd-job-man. Yet even he conceded that all was not well with the concept when, as Reisz recalled, he remarked only a week prior to shooting, 'We could make a very good film if only he didn't have to be a killer.'

In retrospect, Reisz admitted that 'we only half-converted it from a melodrama into a social study.' And Finney agreed. 'We meant to stick to sociology, but that damn head in the hatbox proved too powerful.' The finished film shows signs of everyone's dissatisfaction; yet many elements in it work strongly to its advantage. In particular, the powerful opening juxtaposes the two worlds of light and shade, sanity and madness, calm and violence, as the camera starts moving deeper into the woods, away from the girl day-dreaming on the still garden swing one hot summer morning. A bird cries. An axe hacks at something hidden by ferns. A body slithers under the surface of a lake, and minutes later Danny is rolling and diving like a dolphin amidst the dark waters in a delirium of lunacy. Finney's performance is based on the choppy gestures that recall the initial hatchet-work. With his polished, waxy complexion and his hair brushed up into a cockatoo cut in front, he alters his outward appearance and, even more skilfully, manifests an inward frenzy in ways that suggest how barely suppressed it is. He discussed in advance with Reisz the character's relationships with the three women in the story: as he meets each one, his performance shifts into a different key. Towards the housemaid, he is a violent buffoon; towards the household's spoilt young daughter, an envious and brutal lover; towards the wealthy widow, he adopts the child-like attractiveness she would seek in a son. Danny adapts his image to people's expectations of him; but where Finney himself felt he went wrong was in never satisfactorily finding a way of getting to grips with Danny when alone. This was certainly not this critic's opinion: nor was it shared by the psychiatrist prudently consulted by the British film censor, who confirmed that it was these moments, particularly his horrid little caper round the hatbox before the mirror and his whispered 'Hello' to the contents as he peeps under the lid, which are the most accurate intuitions of a dissociated personality. However, these were minority reports. The film was assailed by a barrage of criticism that chilled Reisz to the bone. 'I knew it was an incompletely realized work, though the last twenty minutes' – the old lady's murder and Danny's withdrawal into insanity – 'contain some of the best things I have done. But what staggered me was the violence with which I was told from all quarters that I was "selling out" and "going commercial".'

Such reaction was partly prompted by a 'committed' director's involvement with a murder melodrama that had been a popular hit with the pre-war generation: as Finney said, the power of a severed head was just too strong. But *Night Must Fall*, which was not premièred in Britain until May 1964, almost a year after *Tom Jones* had opened in London and eight months after its New York screening, caught the full force of two continents' objections to Albert Finney in such an 'unsympathetic' role as a mad axeman. Finney's popular image of virile charm and natural candour as regards the normal man's appetites had been well and truly (and profitably) fixed by *Saturday Night and Sunday Morning* and, even more, by *Tom Jones*. And the image was so absolutely denied by his character in *Night Must Fall* that many of those with reservations about the film's success now hated it with an almost militant antipathy. 'All the wives at M.G.M. who had seen the star as Tom Jones, adoring him, rounded on me like avenging Furies screaming, "What have you done to this beautiful boy?"'

Reisz ruefully recalled. He might protest that he was only doing
what he had done in *Saturday Night and Sunday Morning*, showing
people as both the aggressors and victims in society. It was in
vain. People persisted in thinking the film was somehow un-
worthy of the talents in it; and, paradoxically, Finney's serious
character-study was pushed into the background by the public's
preference for what *he* regarded as his lightweight 'personality
performance' in *Tom Jones*: 'a facile exercise,' he later termed it.

Finney had left for New York immediately he finished *Night
Must Fall* and there he enjoyed an enormous double triumph in
the autumn of 1963, playing Luther in the Broadway production
of Osborne's play and Tom Jones in the American première of
Richardson's film. It is hard to think of another English actor
before him – or, for that matter, since him – who was so fêted and
courted. He was only twenty-seven: *Tom Jones*'s receipts, though
just beginning to flow back substantially, were calculable and,
along with his percentage, guaranteed his financial independence
for the foreseeable future. At this moment *Newsweek* produced a
perceptive report on him which predicted that 'he will not
squander his talent, or sell out in the belief that he is buying in.'[1]
But one can fall into another kind of trap just the reverse of this
– that of husbanding one's talent, of being over-cautious and too
scrupulous about the use one commits it to. It was round about
this time that Finney began seriously questioning whether being
a great actor was what he wanted, *really and truly* wanted. Was it
worth it if a performance as facile as his in *Tom Jones* was greeted
with such adulation? Later he was to say wryly, 'I may have
questioned myself out of acting.'[2] 'I wanted to go into the world
unencumbered, in control of my own destiny,' he also remarked,
referring to all the attractive offers he had refused while he was
still at drama school; but now that he had had a double dose of
success, the 'encumbrances' were being thrust on him. Had he
been in London, things might have been different: there the
problems of success were not so immediately felt or presented to

[1] *Newsweek*, 28 October, 1963.
[2] Albert Finney in a BBC radio conversation with theatre director
Michael Elliott, for producer Charles Lefeaux, 4 April, 1972.

one as they were in New York. When one is uncertain about the direction to take, the safest course is to walk away from success – and that was what Finney now did. (Characteristically, he had only signed a four-month contract for *Luther*.) There and then he resolved to take a sabbatical, 'to do nothing, because I wasn't sure what I wanted to do.' What helped clinch his determination was a deeply felt response to the news of President Kennedy's assassination in November 1963. It summed up for him the frailty of human accomplishment in a way that impinged on his own uncertainties of the moment and the irrelevance of the future.

For a more personal analysis of his state of mind one had to wait for the film, *Charlie Bubbles*, which he would make as actor and director six years later. For the time being, however, at the very height of his fame and in the prime of his career, when he felt he owned the space he walked on, Albert Finney put films aside and without plans or maps set out to wander slowly round the world. After *Night Must Fall* he was not to be seen on the screen again for three years.

THE END OF BRYANSTON

The consortium members of Bryanston Films bore the loss of the *Tom Jones* film to an American distribution company with as stiff a lip and as good a grace as they could muster. But they had a hard job hiding their chagrin as the film's receipts began to roll in; and while not immediately fatal, the loss of such almost inexhaustible revenue was ultimately to prove mortal.

Shortly afterwards Max Setton was offered the position of production chief for all Columbia Pictures' European projects by Mike Frankovich, who was returning to Hollywood where he hoped to put some new vigour into the West Coast studios. Setton left Bryanston on amicable terms, but since his headquarters were to be in Paris he felt he could not perform any further useful functions for it. Bryanston continued to back the films of independent British producers, but the latter dwindled in numbers and importance as the major talents turned increasingly to American companies for the finance that was now extended readily to them in the wake of *Tom Jones*'s success. Bryanston also ran into trouble getting some of its later films distributed quickly and profitably on the two main cinema circuits, Rank and A.B.C., and since the company depended on a continuous cash flow to keep its production fund revolving, the lack of liquidity proved as severe a blow to its prospects as did the lack of attractive projects. Sir Michael Balcon recorded the last chapter: 'Independent pictures were taking longer and longer to be released . . . Our bank payments had to be made within eighteen months of the delivery of a film to the distributors and in the pile-up which developed at this time (1963–4) it was often taking that length of time for a film to be released. Those films which were eventually released, although produced as first-feature films, were often forced to share the bill with another film. Two films for the price of one – and thus anticipated revenues in these cases were cut by 50 per cent. So there arose not only the danger of default in terms of bank repayments but also the grim fact that our costs were being artificially increased by our having to pay interest on borrowed money for longer than had been anticipated.'[1]

In January 1965 this increasingly dismaying situation was resolved in a sadly ironic way. The independent television company, Associated Rediffusion, made a bid for the issued capital of Bryanston Films, whose most attractive asset was some thirty features including the early ones from Woodfall. They paid 'a fair price,' Balcon noted. But he added ruefully, 'sometimes when I have seen the films of ours that they acquired coming up on the television screen for repeat showings, I think they got a wonderful bargain.'[2]

Maybe: but nothing like the bargains that were to be picked up from 1963 onwards by the American film companies in Britain.

[1] Michael Balcon, *op. cit.*, p. 201.
[2] Ibid., p. 201.

Part Two
PLAYTIME

Young people today are
eager to face the exciting
problem of prosperity.
Prime Minister Harold Macmillan, October 1960

Chapter Eight: Escape from Reality

I don't believe in being fashionable. Try to be, and you are usually out of date before you start.   Jack Clayton

Excess has as much to do with change in the film industry as originality. When the public no longer make the profitable response to a stimulus that has become commonplace through repetition, then conditions are right for renewal. By 1962, as we have seen, social realism on the screen in Britain had become commercialized and conventionalized: what had been genuinely innovative was now predictable; what had been an individual vision was now an industry formula.

It wasn't a development peculiar to Britain: the same thing had happened in France, where the multitude of *nouvelle vague* films which had got made quickly, cheaply, and sometimes immaturely after the 1959 breakthrough soon confined themselves to an endlessly repeated view of society which critics and public found wearisome. 'All French films are beginning to look alike,' Jacques Siclier was complaining barely two years after Chabrol, Truffaut, Godard and Resnais had given the *nouvelle vague* its first great international success.[1] Quite early on in Britain, films appeared that tried to have it both ways – to give the sensation of up-to-dateness without any of the substance of contemporary reality. Sometimes the device employed was akin to the *exposé* – the emphatic 'frankness' familiar in the columns of confessional journalism, which was now applied to 'respectable' Establishment figures in order to reveal that they, too, had a few homely frailties of an appropriately classless kind. Into this *exposé* was packed a knowing cynicism combined with a sentimentalized understanding of, or else a reformative concern with, some social or legal injustice. *No Love for Johnnie* (9 February, 1961) and *Victim* (31 August, 1961) fitted these categories perfectly, one dealing with adultery by a Member of Parliament, the other with the homosexuality of a Queen's Counsel barrister. Tracing a

[1] 'New Wave and French Cinema,' by Jacques Siclier, *Sight and Sound* (Summer 1961), Vol. 30, No. 3, p. 118.

commonplace screen 'sin' like adultery to Westminster, in fact to a Labour M.P., imparted a modernity to the story in line with the sexual frankness of *Room at the Top*. The novel on which it was based had the additional savour of being the posthumously published work of a noticeably disenchanted Labour M.P. Otherwise, the film might well have been called *Room on the Front Bench*, since ambition was its real theme, and strength: it charted the rise of a Joe Lampton-type from the back streets of the sooty north who has mended his manners, lost his accent, served his time and done all he can for preference in his political party. It even matched the three women in *Room at the Top* with its own schematic trio of females, respectively a conscience-keeper, a comfort-giver and a pace-setter; and its ironic ending, with promotion being offered the hero as a *quid pro quo* for abandoning his Communist wife, provided the same kind of ambivalent success as attended Joe Lampton's 'good marriage' after the loss of his life's true love. In every way *No Love for Johnnie* shows the running down of impetus, the softening up of authenticity, the working-over of freshly broken ground till all the vitality has been extracted from it, leaving the soil stale and unprofitable.

Victim was the fourth film from the Allied Film Makers consortium, produced and directed by Michael Relph and Basil Dearden, and was itself a spin-off from the tradition of the social thriller profitably established by *Sapphire* two years before by the same screen-writers, John McCormick and Janet Green. That's to say, it presented a social problem in thriller terms, including every viewpoint that could have a bearing on it or yield a suspect. In *Sapphire*, it had been colour prejudice; in *Victim*, it was homosexuality, at the time still a criminal offence in Britain, punishable by a long jail sentence with or without hard labour, but increasingly the concern of law reformers backed by the tolerant recommendations of the Wolfenden Report of 1957. *Victim* is thus a difficult film to judge with fairness, though one contemporary critic in *Sight and Sound* asked, 'Could *Victim* have been more frank than it is?' and answered, 'It is only fair to say that it could not (in the Britain of 1961).[1] A sense of concern lay somewhat

[1] Terence Kelly, *Sight and Sound* (Autumn 1961), Vol. 30, No. 4.

solemnly over the shooting of the movie, which was preceded by a lecture to the cast and technicians by the director who advised that, to save embarrassment, the subjects of their film should be referred to as 'inverts.'

Perhaps inevitably, considering public ignorance on the subject, all the characters in the film came equipped with an over-explicit attitude to express. (That this was prudent, if not artistic, was proved by the reactions of middle-class provincial audiences who were baffled by the damning graffiti scrawled on the hero's garage door accusing him of being 'queer.' In the vernacular of audiences outside the metropolis, 'queer' still meant simply 'ill' or 'poorly.') More serious is the objection that the barrister, played by Dirk Bogarde, although by inclination a deviant, is never allowed to get as far as the act. Thus the film sidesteps the less comfortable qualifications of its resolutely middle-class sympathies. For Bogarde, the film was a calculated gamble: he hazarded the box-office popularity he had earned in a string of light comedies about medical interns, produced for the Rank Organization, on the type of character with whom his 'normal' fans could hardly be expected to sympathize. Nor did they. They deserted *en masse*, though Bogarde bore this with easy fortitude, since his performance not only stretched him as an actor but proved the turning-point in his career by revealing the sensitivity on which Losey and Schlesinger were soon to play brilliant variations. It was at least a comfort to Allied Film Makers that the film didn't end up in the red, but made a slow profit that in mid-1971 stood at £51,762: it had cost £153,756. Whether such a 'slow' profit was a great *practical* comfort at the time is, of course, another matter which will be considered in its place.

It is significant that it took a younger director, Sidney J. Furie, using unfamiliar actors, in a working-class environment and with a discreet use of improvisation, to make a fresher, less fraught statement on homosexuality in *The Leather Boys*: but it came two years after *Victim*, when public opinion had clearly shifted on to the side of such 'victims.' Homosexuality was one of the early subjects that appeared on the cinema screen almost solely as a result of its prominence on the television screen. Home viewers had been made much more sharply – and painfully – aware of social issues than had film-goers: they were accustomed to hearing a vocabulary that seems pathetically formal today but at that time pioneered terms like 'homosexuality,' 'abortion,' 'VD' and so on, and the presence of this more tolerant or, at least, curious audience provided an incentive for film people to make money, not just debate, by dramatizing the same issues.

Because of the airing which homosexuality had on television, the British film censor found himself able to assent not simply to one, but to two films on the subject of Oscar Wilde in 1960, though he had declared eighteen months earlier that the theme would be banned 'until it becomes one that can be mentioned without offence.'[1] On 24 March, 1960, Warwick Films began production on *The Trials of Oscar Wilde* in colour and on a £270,000 budget, starring Peter Finch; and four days later Vantage Films began shooting *Oscar Wilde*, a black-and-white version of the same subject on an undisclosed but obviously much smaller budget, starring Robert Morley. Ken Hughes directed the former, Gregory Ratoff the latter, and both films were premièred in mid-May within a week of each other – an example of production endeavour that could have been profitably emulated by other sections of the industry which didn't have to rush to the box-office ahead of a rival. The Ratoff film emerged markedly the inferior, stuffed with epigrams which made it sound like *The Wit and Folly of Oscar Wilde* and only coming to life in a courtroom scene whose material was piquantly unusual on an English-speaking screen. (Its free use of facts may be charitably attributed to the same over-concern for clarity which led the makers to clean up the mis-spelling 'sondomite' on the accusing visiting card left at Wilde's club by the irate Marquess of Queensberry.) The Finch film was at pains to deepen, develop and round out the tragedy by revealing the corrosive effect of Wilde's downfall on himself and his family, though in retrospect its implication that medicine, not the law, was the suitable means of treatment for offenders like

[1] John Trevelyan quoted by David Robinson in 'Trevelyan's Social History,' *Sight and Sound* (Spring 1971), Vol. 40, No. 2, p. 71.

Wilde stands out for what it was, a piece of 1960-ish special pleading just before the reform of the law, as recommended by the Wolfenden Report of 1957, was put into effect. The contemporary pressures put on public opinion in 1960 to 'accept' homosexuality as less a crime than a condition probably account for the film's omitting the grotesque side of Wilde's character so that, despite Finch's excellent and unsentimentalized performance, he seemed at times to be simply a decent family man who preferred stimulating small talk in the cafés to dull nights at home. Neither Wilde film was a noticeable financial success, though this was partly due to the politics of film distribution as well as to the banning of the subject from American cinema screens. (One of the acts the British censor performed somewhat later in the 1960s was to intercede with a new and more reasonable directorate at the National Catholic Office of Motion Pictures, formerly the old and bigoted Legion of Decency, and ask them to take the Finch film off the 'condemned' list.)

Two films that reflected the contemporary social scene in Britain, in varying degrees, also continued the steady *embourgeoisement* of working-class realism. One was Bryan Forbes's *The L-Shaped Room* (15 November, 1962). Though set in a Notting Hill bed-sitter and described as an attempt to do for London what other films had already done for the English north country and midlands, its central compromise was immediately apparent by the casting of Leslie Caron as the girl who decides to have a baby instead of an abortion. It hopefully turned the clichés of a banal situation inside out, trusting to the momentary insights it achieved into the female psyche, but all the time being vitiated by the cinema tradition to which its star belonged. Realist by intention, or at least emulation, it prudently warmed the water to body heat before inviting anyone to try it; appealing to popularity, it lost a vital hold on authenticity; and in the days when the revealing details of location shooting were co-opted more and more by film-makers, its plethora of 'character touches' appeared too pat by half. Open any door in the studio-bound lodging-house and one might have thought that all the stock characters, made homeless by more ruthlessly realistic film-makers, had found fixed abodes again. In Forbes's favour, for he wrote as well as directed it, it must be said the film found the popularity it sought. The subject had originally been prepared for Jack Clayton, who had unaccountably gone cold on it, and then characteristically been offered almost as an afterthought to Forbes by its producer James Woolf. If it put social realism a step or two back, it at least confirmed Forbes's gift for blending intuition with experience when directing actresses and making the result show on the screen. Inside the well-drafted *L-Shaped Room* was a knottier theme trying to break out: occasionally, in Caron's performance, it did.

In *Term of Trial* (16 August, 1962) the feeling of bits broken off from earlier, better British realist films was even stronger. Where it had been an exciting novelty to see Olivier assemble a clever characterization of a broken-down human being in *The Entertainer*, it was now the pale ghost of Archie Rice he let be seen in this film, directed by Peter Glenville, as he played a north-country schoolteacher grasping at the cane as he drowns in domestic misery and professional frustration. Without Archie's naturally theatrical extensions into self-caricature, Olivier's attempt to diminish himself and fit together the tics and traits of a man smaller than his own dramatic stature painfully revealed the limitations of a great actor who can be anything but common-place. Casting Simone Signoret as his wife merely evoked memories of *Room at the Top* to the disadvantage of a film that, in any case, sensationalized every aspect of its plot – a master escorting a school party to Paris was certain to encounter a prostitute – and underlined every effect to the point where it killed it. It wasn't simply enough to trust to Olivier in a scene like his night of sleepless vigil while waiting for the next day's appearance in court on a charge of indecent assault. The clinking bottles of the milkman make him realize the merciless hour is nigh – and then the scene is finally killed stone-dead by the superfluous comment, 'It's the milkman.'

The film, however, had some compensations to offer. It introduced two players of the new, classless generation. Though Sarah Miles belonged to this category by sympathy rather than by

'Permissiveness' in an earlier era had Isadora Duncan as one of its symbols: 'liberation' in the 1960s found Vanessa Redgrave ready to shed conventions in the same role. (*Universal*)

Released from the confines of studio artifice, the cameras of 'realist' film directors in the early 1960s made the industrial landscape their habitat. The new generation of actors were now placed solidly in the context of factory work-bench, backstreets and soot-streaked brick. Whether shirt-sleeved, like Albert Finney in *Saturday Night and Sunday Morning* (above), or white-collared like Alan Bates in *A Kind of Loving* (below), they seemed to have grown out of their environment. At the end of their films, they had rarely escaped from it. (*Bryanston/British Lion* and *Anglo Film Distributors*)

As 'social realism' caught on, it swiftly lost its freshness. One knew what one was going to find before the film began and, all too frequently, one found it: the pub brawl, the funfair or playground high jinks, the beating-up in the alleyway . . . A romantic weekend between Laurence Harvey and Simone Signoret on a wet sea-shore appeared as a kind of breakthrough in *Room At the Top* (left); by the time the sodden, raincoated lovers, played by Tom Courtenay and Topsy Jane, idled beside the sea in *The Loneliness of the Long Distance Runner* (right), we expected the beach to be as full of stars' footprints as the concrete pavements outside Grauman's Chinese Theatre, Los Angeles. (*Romulus* and *Bryanston/Woodfall*)

The 1960s cinema showed the transformation of the provincial girl as she moved from her bleak North Country origins to the fantasy life of the South and the Big City. (left) Julie Christie, first of the liberated 'swingers', almost lured Billy Liar on to the train to London with her . . . (*Anglo Film Distributors*). As Rita Tushingham in *The Knack* (right), her naiveté helped her survive all the perils of a London that belonged to youth . . . (*United Artists*)

Sometimes the girl from the provinces was a corrupting, rather than a liberating force. In *The Servant*, Sarah Miles (left) became the pawn in a game of seduction played by master and manservant . . . (*Anglo Film Distributors*). Judy Geeson in *Three into Two Won't Go* (right) portrayed the footloose girl, almost without origins now, who used the ruthless candour and sex appeal of youth to break up the hypocrisies of a middle-class marriage. (*Universal*)

Icon of the Era: the Image Maker. Classless, sexy, hard-working, the Pop historian of the novelty generation and chief creator of the 'swinging' scene: such was the magazine photographer of the Sixties. David Bailey personified him in life, David Hemmings played him in *Blow-Up*. By turning his camera on the cameraman, Antonioni revealed him as the captive of his own illusion. (M.G.M.)

Icon of the Era: the Secret Agent. A male chauvinist patriot, Bond internationalised each country's licence to kill and personalised everyone's fantasies of sex and violence. Sean Connery as 007 was a hyperstar: as himself, only a superstar. Like other icons, the role classified the performer and the public frequently confused him with it. (*United Artists*)

Icon of the Era: the Model Girl. The ascension of the photographer's model to the status of international idol, outwardly glamorous and successful but inwardly restless, unsatisfied and an object of male manipulation: Julie Christie's *Darling* incarnated the type so vividly that she spawned a string of imitators — and could never quite escape from her own incarnation. (*Anglo Film Distributors*)

Pioneer: Tony Richardson, who freed the camera from the captive artifice of the film studio, on location with *The Loneliness of the Long Distance Runner.* (*Bryanston/Woodfall*)

Non-Conformist: Karel Reisz instructs David Warner in the anthropoid posture of *Morgan's* hero, a man more in sympathy with apes than humans. (*British Lion*)

Stoic: John Schlesinger with Tom Courtenay behind the big drum, arranges a fantasy sequence in *Billy Liar,* the story of a failure saved by his daydreams. (*Anglo Film Distributors*)

birth, Terence Stamp was genuinely the first of those South London actors from across the Thames, that natural frontier for his working-class parentage. Playing respectively the sexually promiscuous schoolgirl who threatens her teacher's emotional self-control and the tearaway young devil who breaks his class-room discipline, they succeeded in making these 'blackboard jungle' clichés into characters who were all of a piece. Just over a month later, in September 1962, Stamp let us know he had definitely arrived when he played the eponymous hero of Peter Ustinov's *Billy Bud*, doing that extraordinarily difficult feat of making goodness attractive and sweetness credible – a perform-ance of immense delicacy fingered entirely on the white notes of guilelessness.

The Wild and the Willing (16 October, 1962) also cosied up to the 'new realism,' and only succeeded in bringing it into absurdity by the compromises it made in order to make everything pain-lessly palatable for the middle-class mass audience. It was the Rank Organization's attempt to be in fashion, which was a surer sign than almost anything else that the fashion was long past. Its hero, a scholarship boy at a provincial university, was a rebel, but he looked washed; the cast of youthful 'unknowns' in the Stamp and Courtenay style radiated the charm school, not Salford smog; and its social problem – the 'red-brick' blues – came a poor second to a melodrama about a professor's wife who apparently had the run of the men's hall of residence and spent her time angling for the hero in the student union's jazz club or knocking back a bottle of Scotch with him in her convertible.

Francis Wyndham was referring to another film, *The L-Shaped Room*, when he asked, 'In its dogged attempts to combine the old theatrical conventions with the new social subtlety . . . is the commercial British cinema having its cake and eating it, or merely falling between two stools?'[1] But his scepticism could be directed just as accurately at any or all of these productions. Among the original pioneers of the new cinema were signs that this was being recognized, that the directors were moving away from social realism into territory that wasn't either so well explored or so

---

[1] *Sight and Sound* (Winter 1962–3), Vol. 32, No. 1, p. 41.

F

well defined. It involved the creation of a more subjective cinema in which exterior reality was yielding place to private worlds of fantasy and memory.

MYSTERY AND IMAGINATION

The film that marked the beginning of the flight from social realism was Jack Clayton's *The Innocents* (23 November, 1961). Coming from a director popularly credited with starting the British 'new wave,' his decision to film Henry James's ghost story, *The Turn of the Screw*, looked idiosyncratic to say the least. Some critics put it more strongly. 'Abdicating his social responsibilities,' was a phrase frequently heard as Clayton created an 'outdoor' location inside Shepperton Studios' silent stage where the papier-mâché willows with gummed-on leaves seemed emblematic of the film's painstaking artificial and theatrical conventions. But it served to remind us that Clayton wasn't really a social revolutionary so much as a traditional craftsman with a well-developed – some would say over-developed – literary 'feeling' for a scene, a character, a story, a subject. If one remembers that the film which first found him a producer was another ghost story, Gogol's whimsical *Bespoke Overcoat*, then it is *Room at the Top* which marks a temporary diversion in his career, not *The Innocents*.

Clayton has no manifesto, resists belonging to any group, and quietly refuses to let himself be typed by subject rather than by inclination. After *Room at the Top*, he was offered *Sons and Lovers*, *The L-Shaped Room* and *Saturday Night and Sunday Morning* – and turned them all down. To turn from the contemporary issues everyone else was burrowing into or borrowing from in 1961 and depict the white-upon-white perceptions of a nineteenth-century story of a haunting showed an eclecticism that, however misconceived the result might be judged, certainly set Clayton apart. A choosy talent. And an intuitive one. He believed that 'to make films is to create an illusion: you have to feel it, not think it . . . If I make the illusion work *for me*, that feeling is the victory.' Remembering, too, that he entered films aged fifteen and waited twenty years for a chance to direct, then one can only see him as a patient observer, not a thrusting visionary. But certain elements to which Clayton consistently responds help to explain why his choice fell on *The Innocents*. An attachment to places – a very English characteristic – is a strong element in his temperament. More than once he has referred to his own country home near London with a strong affective quality like that possessed by Bly House in *The Innocents*, or the old mill that figures in the last scenes of *The Pumpkin Eater*, or, of course, the whole run-down Victorian ambience of *Our Mother's House*. Then, roles that create a language for the inner emotions of women are ones he's drawn towards: like Forbes, he is an impeccable director of actresses, particularly those in middle-age with the capacity for deeply-felt responses that they only have to 'think,' not act: Signoret, Kerr, Bancroft. Finally, children: the two 'innocents' of the Henry James *novella*, the household of 'numberless' youngsters in *The Pumpkin Eater*, the motherless brood of *Our Mother's House*. 'I adore working with children, seeing them embody my concept,' Clayton said later. 'It is totally "pure" directing. It brings out the best in me.'

All these elements are present in *The Innocents*. There is an additional pleasure in the satisfaction Clayton takes in setting himself a problem to solve: in this case the problem of deciding to what degree the phantom manifestations of the dead valet and governess are projections of the emotionally disturbed heroine's mind and to what degree they lead their own independent existence. This time the problem could be solved in the comparative quiet of an 'untrendy' subject.

20th Century-Fox had bought William Archibald's stage adaptation of the James story, and Archibald and John Mortimer worked on the screenplay, with Truman Capote making later additions. The budget was high, about £430,000, and it is doubtful if the finished film justified such an investment quickly in pure commercial terms. As an artistic venture, it was a qualified success, elegant and tasteful and occasionally condensing the psychic disturbance beneath the surface into images of real disquiet and fear. But it was fatally indecisive where it should have been surest, in the matter of its psychological undertones, and it was over-emphatic where it should have been most oblique, in the matter of its supernatural ones. Having dispensed with James's framework of a story told by someone uninvolved in the haunting of Bly House, the film created more a sense of its own indecisiveness than any intentional ambiguity when it refused to face up to the problem of 'real' or 'imaginary' manifestations, parapsychology or psychopathology. Clayton sometimes finds most successful atmospheric images for Deborah Kerr's inner fears: the beetle 'dribbling' out of the stone Cupid's mouth, for instance, or the sudden falling of dying flower petals in a still room. The most effectively suggested touch of corruption comes with the affectionate goodnight peck on little Miles's cheek by his governess which she suddenly feels returned by a pair of infant lips that convey the hard passion of a man who, in his lifetime, was a notorious womanizer. Unfortunately, some of Clayton's other supernatural effects are the stock ones of the Old Dark House and no match for the Magritte-like 'reality' of the dead governess, still and black as Whistler's mother, seemingly floating on the airless summer lake water. And, whatever its faults, *The Innocents* makes Clayton's nature unmistakable – a stylist, not a revolutionary. In the film's warmest and most perceptive American review, Pauline Kael wrote, 'James was a man of taste, and the film-makers, even when they fail as artists, remain gentlemen.'[1]

If Clayton's choice of subject had appeared like a romantic time-slip back into the past, John Schlesinger's second film stayed in the present but used it to take off into fantasy. *Billy Liar* was premièred on 15 August, 1963, just six weeks after *Tom Jones*, and shows Schlesinger arriving at a similar sense of liberation to Richardson by a different route. Billy Liar, the middle-class provincial boy with the over-active imagination, is a Tom Jones in his fantasy life. And just as Richardson's film had its intentionally Italianate flavour, that of Schlesinger and Joseph Janni had sometimes the undertones of a suburban English *Vitelloni* with its emphasis on provincial stagnation and the day-

[1] Pauline Kael, *I Lost It at the Movies* (Cape, 1966), p. 166.

dreams of a boy who believes that Life, intense and capitalized, begins in the metropolis, though he himself only gets as far as the railway lines leading away to it . . . Escape is the theme of *Billy Liar*, but it is escape only into fantasy, not physical escape, that Billy achieves. He is trapped just as much by his dream-life as he is by industrial drabness, social conformity, unimaginative parents, and girl-friends who are either brazen flirts or chicken-brained dollies. He lacks the essential courage to get up and get out of his dull rut when his girl-friend sings him her 'Song of the South' and tries to entice him to hop aboard the early-morning milk train to London and put his dreams to the test with her. 'The train for London with Liz aboard is waiting. Billy is putting sixpences into the machine for milk they neither of them want in a desperate, unacknowledged effort not to come to London . . . The two containers of milk clunk down on the scales of fate. The train chuffs out. Liz, in a last gesture of understanding, has put his suitcase out on the platform, where it waits, a tombstone to success.'[1]

Billy Liar is an offshoot from *A Kind of Loving*, and encapsulates Schlesinger's persistent themes of belief in the greenness of distant fields, sympathy with the emotionally crippled, the pardonable necessity of accepting compromise and even the myth of 'making it' in the Big City which he was to take up again, in a drastically altered context and very different latitude, in *Midnight Cowboy* seven years later. The Keith Waterhouse–Willis Hall screenplay had the deadly accuracy of talented provincials who had made their own escape and could now cast a satirist's backward glance at what they had left so unchangingly – and unchangeably – behind. But whereas the stage play had confined itself to verbal fantasy, the film script veered into visual conceits, with Billy picturing himself as soldier, convict, dictator, blind man, best-selling novelist, the usual ups and downs of the hero-martyr complex. It ended disturbingly with him imprisoned, perhaps for good, inside the trappings of power as he marches at the head of his phantom army down the suburban avenue: it is

---

[1] Anne Sharpley, *Evening Standard*, 15 August, 1963.

the lighter side of Danny's far more hideous incarceration in his own lunacy in *Night Must Fall*.

Billy in the film is a far more vulnerable and palpably serious person than the figure of farcical frustration he had cut on the stage when Albert Finney played him. Part of the reason for this is the casting of Tom Courtenay. Finney had been harassed but dogged and had retained a residual Jimmy Porterish faith in the sheer power of verbal virtuosity to get him out of scrapes – hence his nickname 'Billy Liar.' But Courtenay's naturally worried face contained the desperation of a man in flight, and the visual fantasy – somewhat top-heavy in the set-pieces like his review of the army, but stunningly apt in the simpler shocks like his sudden machine-gunning of his Pa and Ma – made him out to be the victim of an illusion far more inimical to sanity than any domestic-comedy situation. Finding an actress to play the liberated Liz led to one of the timeliest discoveries of the new British cinema. 'We had still a sizeable inferiority complex as regards Woodfall Films,' Joseph Janni later recalled, 'and we first of all tested Topsy Jane, the girl they had co-starred with Courtenay in *The Loneliness of the Long Distance Runner*. After quite a few of her scenes had been shot, she fell ill and it was vital to find a replacement quickly. A year or so earlier, while setting up *A Kind of Loving*, I had seen an enchanting girl at the Central School of Speech and Drama. Her name was Julie Christie. I thought she should be in films. 'If you really mean it,' she said then, 'put me into *A Kind of Loving*,' but I told her it wasn't the right part for her. Now I asked John to test her for *Billy Liar*. He disliked the idea of her in the role. But when Topsy Jane dropped out, we rushed down to a London cinema on a Sunday to see a farce called *Crooks Anonymous* with Julie Christie in the cast. As we came out, John said, 'Right, we go ahead with her.' It can't have been the best circumstances for any actress to take over a role, in the middle of shooting, when we were harassed by budget troubles aggravated by the need to re-shoot scenes.' Schlesinger at first feared Christie might be 'too gorgeous' for Liz the provincial swinger. 'But when I look back on it,' he said later, 'her first entrance gives the precise feeling of liberation I was after.' In fact her carefree jauntiness, the unselfconscious swing of her body as she comes down the street, side-stepping obstructions, nipping between cars, mugging at herself in the shop-window reflections, all of it heightened by the camera's tracking and zooming, remind us less of an English girl than an Italian one. Here for what seems the first time is a provincial kid who takes her pleasures gladly in the Latin manner, not glumly in the Anglo-Saxon tradition. The strangeness is exhilarating.

In *Billy Liar* one feels at a cross-roads in cinema. The sad-faced boy who stays behind and conforms, a rebel only in his dreams, has been passed by the new type of girl swinging confidently and joyously out into a future that is part and parcel of an affluent generation's life-style centred on youth, dreams and metropolitan delights. With Julie Christie, the British cinema caught the train south.

A sense of the flux and change going on in Britain, as well as in its cinema, is present in *Billy Liar*. *The Times*'s critic remarked, 'Mr Schlesinger gives us perhaps the sharpest and most persuasive picture yet of that northern town in the throes of reconstruction.'[1] Philip Oakes, complimenting Schlesinger on once again, as in *A Kind of Loving*, avoiding 'the easy poetry of the North,' also perceived that 'he has hit upon something much more valid. The world he shows is a world of change . . . where new flats sprout from the rubble of back-to-backs, and a supermarket opens for business to the skirl of a band of girl pipers. The face-lift is impressive, but nothing can touch the heart of the provinces. This is the deepest irony of *Billy Liar* and it is the reason why the escape routes are sedulously kept open.'[2] That social and artistic changes take place around the same focal points is a hypothesis to treat with caution and, possibly, to despair of ever being able to prove conclusively; but what films like *Billy Liar* remind us of is the extraordinary power the cinema possesses, against all the odds, of anticipating as well as reflecting social change, so that the films seem to be at one and the same time prophecies of and metaphors for what is happening or going to happen. The state

[1] *The Times*, 14 August, 1963.
[2] *The Sunday Telegraph*, 18 August, 1963.

of Britain as a society feverishly spiralling into a consumers' paradise, a period of rising excitement and dream-like gratification, is kept satirically in the background of *Billy Liar*. But it is there, all the same, and it had found much more savage expression in a film that, because it lacked the pedigree of known 'names' and the hard sell of a major distributor, got scant attention at the time. This was *Live Now – Pay Later*, premièred on 25 October 1962, well before its time, but a most accurate and acerbic criticism of the conspicuous consumption that allied itself to the 'swinging' escapism of the mid-1960s.

Written by Jack Trevor Story and directed by Jay Lewis, whose previous record as a maker of war and comedy films (sometimes together) was scarcely distinguished, this vision of lower- and middle-class society in Britain was Jonsonian in its savagery and almost Bosch-like in its variety of creatures who wriggled out from under every post-war stone: speculative developers, civvy-street 'majors,' suburban housewives filling the shopping basket with a bit of amateur prostitution, cynical vicars rattling collecting boxes with the slogan 'Pay Now – Live Later,' estate agents out to turn a quick profit by collusion and corruption on the town council, credit-store bosses gloating over the new altars of free enterprise in the shape of credit-capped skyscrapers ... The film's cynicism was total, its targets were ruthlessly demolished, and everything had the vigour of a cartoonist's world where the action is carried an instant beyond its naturalistic conclusion. Its hero was a door-to-door salesman played by Ian Hendry, a slicker son of Archie Rice in a length of gigolo suiting, with a plastic smile, a heart that beat like a cash register and a built-in waste-disposal unit for chewing up and flushing away any decent thought or conviction. Like Billy Liar, he was a mythomaniac, a pathological fantasist, hooked on the never-never narcotic as hopelessly as the mugs to whom he sells goods they don't want and can't afford, relying on his smooth patter and imagination to keep a jump ahead of the law or the women on whom he has fathered his illegitimate children. The well-stocked van in which he tours council estates is a mobile Aladdin's cave of easy credit; and the same fantasy element that punctuated the social realism of *Billy Liar* is duplicated in a near-surrealistic scene in a supermarket at night where the hero has brought his current mistress – played by June Ritchie, the trapped young wife of *A Kind of Loving*. He plies her endlessly, frantically, with consumer goods, almost burying her in an inebriated orgy of vicarious getting-and-spending before collapsing with his arms round a plastic window dummy.

'All we need is love, Love is all we need' the Beatles would soon be singing: but 'love' in the new morality that boasted to the British they had 'never had it so good' ('nor so often,' the cynics added) was allied to 'an ever-mounting spiral of demand,' as Christopher Booker diagnosed it, 'ever more violent, more dream-like and fragmentary and ever more destructive of the framework of order.'[1] 'Love' in this film was the 'love' of the Big Sell: 'love . . . and a telly . . . and a fridge . . . and a washer . . . and a mixer . . . and a freezer,' went the chorus. That would do to be going on with. Other films would make increasingly sophisticated use of, or attacks on, the affluent society in Britain: but *Live Now – Pay Later* deserves the credit of being the earliest to distinguish the fantasy element working away in it like yeast.

THE LAST PURITAN

It was inevitable that, as the tide of social realism turned and ebbed during these early years of the 1960s, some films which were conceived when it was high and triumphant would find themselves badly beached. One that did was nevertheless so original that its isolation seemed particularly appropriate. It was the high-water mark reached by this particular 'new wave.' It drew richly but not parasitically on its predecessors; its maker's identity was impressed on every foot of it – uncompromisingly. Its subject was working-class: but what it illuminated was the emotional space inside its characters, not the industrial landscape around them. It was puritan in the self-denying English tradition, yet romantic in the self-destructive Byronic one. The film was

[1] Christopher Booker, *op. cit.*, p. 71.

This Sporting Life (7 February, 1963); its director, Lindsay Anderson.

After 'Free Cinema' had run its course, Anderson returned to the theatre, refusing to participate in the commercial cinema except on his own terms. Between 1957 and 1962 he made no films at all, an abstinence which makes *This Sporting Life*'s appearance all the more startling. Anderson's lengthy immersion in theatre work may have been the furnace that hardened him for film-making: what one feels in *This Sporting Life* is the toughness of someone who has undergone a professional annealing elsewhere. Anderson himself said, 'Working in the theatre I'm always conscious of rhythm and a kind of precise timing, and this is my most uncomfortable obsession when cutting a film. I am slightly at odds with certain contemporary developments which place more emphasis on disintegration than on integration. My tendency is towards a very controlled and rhythmic form. I am not sure if that makes my theatre work "cinematic" or my films "theatrical".'[1] Of the eight plays he directed (seven of them at the Royal Court Theatre), before his first feature film, two starred Albert Finney (*The Lily White Boys, Billy Liar*); one was written by Alun Owen (*Progress to the Park*), who would script the first Beatles film; one by Willis Hall (*The Long and the Short and the Tall*); and one by Hall and Keith Waterhouse (*Billy Liar*): so Anderson was at least in close touch and sympathy with talents that were – or soon would be – transforming the screen, even if his own involvement with it was delayed by his customary wariness, not to mention lack of opportunity. Ealing Films had snapped up *The Long and the Short and the Tall*. The lost patrol, cut off in the jungle, had an obvious box-office tradition, except that what made the play so timely and original was the fact that not one of its Army characters came from the officer class. 'I had a flirtation with Ealing,' Anderson recalled dryly, 'but of course as a stage director how could I be regarded as fit to make a film? – so Leslie Norman directed it. And Peter O'Toole who was then virtually unknown as a film quantity, how could he be considered fit to star in his

[1] Lindsay Anderson interviewed by Paul Gray, *Tulane Drama Review*, Fall, 1966.

stage role? – so Laurence Harvey got the part. The position altered with *Saturday Night and Sunday Morning*. The fact that an "unknown" actor (Finney) and an "unknown" director (Reisz) had achieved a commercial hit made itself felt immediately. The defences fell, which showed there had been no reality to them at all. But the very same people who had manned them showed they still didn't know what their business was about when they went around saying, "We must now get an unknown director to make a film for us".'

Tony Richardson had always wanted Anderson to do a film for Woodfall and had had his eye on David Storey's novel *This Sporting Life:* but it was published in 1960, just before Woodfall's commercial bonanza with *Saturday Night and Sunday Morning*, and they were outbid by Julian Wintle and Leslie Parkyn of Independent Artists, who made films for release through the Rank Organization. Their company had produced the Joseph Losey film *Blind Date*, but although Losey was also attracted to the Storey novel, with Stanley Baker in mind, Wintle's approach was to Karel Reisz, the currently 'hot' director. Reisz demurred. He didn't want to direct another north-country subject, but he did want to learn about the production side: in fact he performed for Lindsay Anderson the very function that Tony Richardson had performed for him. 'Karel came to me while I was at the theatre directing *Billy Liar*,' Anderson said, 'and asked, would I direct *This Sporting Life* if he produced. Two days later he said, "They've agreed." I am quite sure "they" agreed because they had the belief that *This Sporting Life* would turn out to be another *Saturday Night and Sunday Morning*. But it certainly didn't. And it never could have been.' To Anderson, it was all a practical illustration of what he regarded as most vital to him and his work-connections, that's to say, the network of professional loyalties and emotional sympathies that tie an individual in with the group, yet give him the freedom to function freely. 'From the start,' he said in an interview at the time, 'the film was essentially a collaborative affair.'[1]

[1] Lindsay Anderson, 'Sport, Life and Art,' *Films and Filming* (February 1963), Vol. 9, No. 5, p. 16.

Looking back on that collaboration in a programme-note he wrote for Storey's first play, in 1967, Anderson added, 'At that time I still believed or wanted to believe that (English society) could become "better." David, whose father had not been some sort of General,[1] and who had managed to fill out his Slade School scholarship by battering and being battered every Saturday during the Season as a forward in the Leeds Rugby League "A" team, was not under this misapprehension. Also he was not interested in surface, but in essence; not to find what was representative but what was exceptional. This made him, and makes him, a very exceptional kind of English writer . . . He seeks to penetrate the soul; yet he never forgets the relevance of the social world in which souls meet, conflict, and struggle. He labours, often desperately, to balance the ambiguities of our nature, our situation: male and female, tenderness and violence, isolation and love.'[2] As Elizabeth Sussex has remarked, this is as good a description of Anderson's working processes as of Storey's.

At first, though, the collaboration was disappointing. Reisz and Anderson both agreed that Storey should write the screenplay if he wanted to: but Storey started out feeling he had both fulfilled and exhausted himself in the book and the draft script, in Anderson's opinion, was 'a bad one.' This view was shared by Richard Harris, to whom Anderson had sent a copy of the novel in the hope that he would play the lead in the film. Harris was then filming the remake of *Mutiny on the Bounty* in Tahiti and feeling depressed by the experience and in sore need of someone to come up with a reassuring project for his future. 'I flew out to Tahiti,' said Anderson. 'The tears and tantrums everyone was going through were a godsend to us.' Harris turned to *This Sporting Life* with relief and gratitude and his intuition that the book was so well constructed that any departure from it would be to the film's detriment proved absolutely right. 'Storey wrote another script beginning with the patterned "flash-backs" as in the book, when Arthur Machin, the hero, has his memories revived while under

---

[1] Unlike Anderson's, who had been an officer in the Royal Engineers.

[2] The play for which this note was written was *The Restoration of Arnold Middleton*, directed by Robert Kidd at the Royal Court, 1967.

a dentist's anaesthetic. But it still wasn't right and the third script, which was the one we used, stuck even more closely to the book. So you see, the film's structure which some critics believed we derived from the style of Alain Resnais is explicit in the script almost from the first, because *its* interweaving of past and present was based on the first quarter of the book.' Nevertheless, it is the boldness of the subjective editing, evoking emotional states or implying events elliptically by direct cuts in time and place, which is Anderson's indebtedness to Resnais. The audience is made to work for the links and, if it grasps them at all, does so by instinct: it must be confessed that some audiences in 1963 found the labour involved too heavy.

But it is this technique that enables Anderson to operate inside the character's consciousness, at least for half the film, rather than batter him with the hurricane of shock cuts that Richardson launched at his long-distance runner. Where *This Sporting Life* differs significantly from the social realism of its predecessors is in the introduction the audience gets to the interior landscape of the protagonist.

Anderson was only a few weeks into shooting, however, when it looked as if he might have to surrender the direction to someone else. Things went badly for him. He can look stoically back to this period: at the time, though, it must have been agonizing – presented with the long-awaited opportunity, a 'test' he was to refer to in terms of medieval chivalry, and aware that he was falling well short of what was needed. 'After four weeks they wanted to take me off the film,' he said. Harris was being 'obstinate': Anderson was being just as 'difficult': neither man was ever willing to 'let anything go' if he felt the rightness of his viewpoint. Constant argument was draining Anderson of nervous energy, and not being able to 'get a run' at the film because of these incessant interruptions meant slow, expensive progress. He found the hundred-and-one things to be attended to, the multitude of often unnecessary crew members, a sore trial after the relatively unfettered control of the 'Free Cinema' days and, to put it bluntly, he did not know the first thing about getting some of the technical effects. (Nor, he remembered, did the technical experts do much to assist.) What probably saved him was his consummate assurance with players, in particular with Harris and Rachel Roberts, who played the self-denying, life-rejecting land-lady. Anderson fell back on traditional theatre methods of rehearsing them prior to shooting: for ten days he took them through their scenes in continuity, then continued during the evenings of filming and over the week-ends, too, whatever production troubles were threatening his tenure on the set. This contributed immensely to the feeling both players project of performances that come from within: both have 'found' the characters in the way Anderson 'found' his film, by understanding and intuition of what *should be* which, in turn, becomes what *is*. The intensity of the felt performance seals it into the character, just as the whole film seals itself off from the familiar working-class genre by its own felt intensity – though none of this necessarily helped ease an audience into sympathy with it, or, in some cases, even understanding.

It didn't help its commercial chances to be represented in some quarters as the story of a footballer, since exhibitors told Anderson that sporting stories were box-office disasters before they got screened. But its chill reception, Anderson believes, was due to something deeper and more complex about the film. 'The central character, Frank Machin' – he had been 'Arthur' in the novel, but this was altered lest it recall Arthur Seaton in *Saturday Night and Sunday Morning* – 'was immensely striking, with an ambiguity of nature, half overbearing, half acutely sensitive, that fascinated me without my being fully aware that I understood him. The same was true of his tortured, impossible relationship with the woman in the story, a bleak northern affair of powerful, inarticulate emotions frustrated or deformed by puritanism or inhibition. Their background was rough and hard, no room here for charm or sentimental proletarianism. It was an intimidating subject for a film.'[1] The story was one of self-punishment, of masochistically 'missed connections' in which the male partner can't embody his love in tenderness, and the female one won't accept the pleasure of her own repressed sexuality. As Karel Reisz observed sadly,

[1] *Films and Filming, op. cit.*, p. oo.

'There was a hard, intransigent, ruthless quality about it . . . rightly charmless in the acting . . . But people came away having been pained rather than cheered.'

Its artistic success, however, was another matter. It was on a par with Anderson's ambitions; and both were pitched high – incredibly high for a *first* feature film. The sophistication of the time-shift structure brilliantly subjectified the complexity of a 'simple' man, while Harris suggested in a hundred subtle ways the dammed-up aggression that would have found its release in sensual enjoyment had his Lawrence-like primitivism been matched by a partner of fire, not ice. The only place it *did* find release was on the rugby field where Anderson's technique of slow motion, combined with deleted 'frames,' turned the mud-encrusted players into nearly dehumanized forces whose inter-locking limbs jerked with the spasms of martyrdom. What he himself called 'the motif of force' dominated the film, rather than that of love, sympathy or understanding – and it is the more forceful for coming almost consistently from within the hero. The power to *feel*, not to *rail against* in the Jimmy Porter manner, but to *give vent to* the inner, inexpressible emotions: this was the new note sounded by *This Sporting Life*. 'Here pain *is* called pain, and the feeling is one of liberation,' wrote Robert Vas, an ex-Free Cinema member, in one of the most perceptive of the partisan reviews.[1] And the editorial writer in the same issue of *Sight and Sound* said boldly, 'This looks like the moment for the real break-through.' But if anything, it was just the opposite.

'The most completely achieved of the "new wave" films, because the most passionately felt and ambitious,' Karel Reisz later called *This Sporting Life*. But it was the last of stature in its line, not the first progeny of the new breed.

The temper of the times, the tastes of the public, were against it. 'The Rank Organization were genuinely stirred and impressed when they saw it,' Anderson recalls. 'But they didn't honestly know what to do with it, how to sell it or to whom, short of pushing it out on their own cinema circuit with a decent send-off

[1] Robert Vas, 'Arrival and Departure,' *Sight and Sound* (Spring 1963), Vol. 32, No. 2, p. 59.

and then hoping for the best. It did well enough in the United States, where Walter Reade secured the rights for about £70–80,000 – the whole film cost around £230,000 – but its non-success in Britain was taken by Rank as confirmation of a basic reluctance to invest in social realism any further. When it was seen not to be doing well, it was immediately disliked . . . But none of these things really means anything. The movies are made that will be made – that's all. I'm sure that nobody has slept less well, eaten less well, lived less well because *This Sporting Life* was made at that particular time. I look back on the making of it as a fantastic ordeal – the kind of *épreuve* they had in chivalry. I emerged from it purified and much stronger.'

Finally, *This Sporting Life* is illuminating about the film industry of the time in quite another way. From the list of 'cautions' prepared by the censor, John Trevelyan, after reading the screenplay, it is clear that the 'permissive' tide had not yet begun to rip through society or film-making. Although the sex scenes were deemed to present fewer difficulties than those in *Saturday Night and Sunday Morning*, nevertheless the censor correctly appreciated that 'there is a "feel" of violence about this story which is bound to come out in the film . . . What adds to the difficulty is that Karel Reisz has a documentary approach to film-making which results in his characters becoming real people . . .' This consideration and the fact that the film was full of 'what is called "language",' made the censor feel that an X. Certificate, instead of the milder A., was the more likely rating. But even so, he cautioned, 'for an X. film there are limits to what we would accept and we think that this script goes beyond them.' He then went into some detail. He drew the line at locker-room expressions (' "Put your foot in it, you noisy bastard" is a bit crude and dialogue between two nude men in the showers examining each other ribaldly is even more crude and would be unacceptable'), and vulgar locutions ('We are trying to keep the phrases "get stuffed" out of films since its meaning is only too obvious') and even scenes that audiences would be likely to find embarrassing ('crude dialogue between Frank and the trainer . . . a lot of women would find offensive').

The sex scene in which Frank forces his landlady to let him make love to her was the subject of a particularly solemn caveat. 'We would not want to see Frank moving his hands over Mrs Hammond, bearing down on her and lying on top of her, and we would certainly not want what I imagine would be the visual described by the phrase, "Their bodies are suddenly in spasm".' Physical sickness was also judged undesirable. It would be nauseating, said the censor's caution. Finally there was a caution on nudity. 'There are scenes of men in showers and changing rooms. We do not want any censorable nudity and even full-length back-view shots should be few and discreet.'

A caution of one's own has to be sounded about such counsel as this: this kind of prior 'advice' tends to err on the side of discretion. When the finished film comes up for certification, the censor may find less cause to be censorious than the printed word offered him. Remember, too, this is an opinion delivered in mid-1961 and Trevelyan's reservations would almost certainly have been milder by the time the film actually appeared on the screen eighteen months later. For the cinema was by then embarked on a joy-ride which progressively threw all such cautions to the winds.

Chapter Nine: Man of the Decade

All was incarnated in a hero specially designed to attract the sympathies of the public, with the danger of one who is above the Law because he has a licence to kill and he is everything normally forbidden. But we had the ingenuousness to hope that the film would not have met with such a wide success.

Osservatore Romano, 17 May, 1965

When United Artists opened its production office in London, in 1961, with George H. Ornstein in charge, it was the best organized and possibly the most profitable film-making outfit in the world. It had *esprit de corps*; it was enterprising; most of all, it was economical. 'My office,' Ornstein said, 'was never sufficiently staffed to do more than four or five films a year. In those days the company was highly selective – rightly so – and very cautious of overheads. The operation wasn't penny-pinching: but it was definitely frugal. If an airmail stamp could deliver the message, then you didn't use the telephone or cable service. If you were called by phone from New York, you had to be ready with the answer in the minimum number of words, then hang up: no shit about the weather – *verboten!* Very few people had total freedom on expense-account spending; even the company president filed his expenses weekly. Where properties were concerned, we were very selective. Many film companies then had overstaffed story departments and even invited submissions: I'd have been dismissed if I'd overwhelmed United Artists with projects, invited or unsought. We weren't greedy, either: you could never sell United Artists anything by saying, "Okay, if you don't buy it, I'll take it over to Fox." We never operated a policy of "We don't want it, but we'd better have it." Producers knew that – knew that if we said "Yes" we meant business. Decisions were swift. A "turndown" or a "let's talk" usually came within days of my submitting anything that involved major policy or expenditure to New York, which was the channel I went through. Decisions were usually final, but not always so: if there was a decent doubt and you put your head on the block, they could be reversed. It was flexible, though it could be fatal!'

United Artists had one special advantage over all the other Hollywood majors. It was not a Hollywood-based company: which is another way of saying that it owned no permanent film studio. Mary Pickford's proffered use of her share of the Goldwyn lot had been politely turned down when the company was reorganized in the early 1950s, with the observation that it wasn't desirable to influence producers about where they made their pictures. This proved a godsend; it relieved United Artists of the escalating financial costs of having to keep a studio open for business, even when the business was not coming in or was proving wildly unprofitable, which in the middle-1960s began to eat the guts out of the old-established Hollywood outfits. Independent producers appreciated it, too; it meant they could make a film for United Artists distribution without being tied to some probably padded-out production facility whose labour force, rather than the picture, was the reason for their being there.

When Ornstein moved into his Wardour Street office, a dowdy, old-fashioned suite of rooms reached after a dizzy scramble over cast-iron cat-walks from the main-street block, there were four chief men at United Artists' New York headquarters. Arthur B. Krim and Robert Benjamin were tough company lawyers, but shrewd enough to listen to people, patient enough to tie up the smallest detail in a secure knot: their speciality was the financial side. Arnold Picker controlled the day-to-day running of the corporation, re-established its identity in the early days after its ailing years as the once famous and profitable company set up in 1919 by Pickford, Chaplin, Fairbanks Sr and D. W. Griffith. It was Picker who met censors in America and abroad, wooed producer associations, and kept mental tabs on cinemas in every land where United Artists released their films. The fourth top executive was Max Youngstein, whose artistic bent was possibly the strongest of the four: he resigned in 1962 to join Cinerama, then returned to United Artists' fold as an independent producer late in 1965. Arnold Picker's nephew, David, had been brought

in to assist Youngstein and, as already mentioned, had gradually
moved over to the production side. Krim, Benjamin and Arnold
Picker were so close that they thought alike and hardly needed to
speak their minds – which they did, frequently, none the less.

   Their decision whether or not to back a picture was based on
an appreciation of its market potential and also on how many
pictures United Artists could physically distribute each year.
Obviously, ties with independent producers who had brought
them projects that had turned out well tended to build up more
or less stable relationships, more favoured and even *most* favoured
partners. United Artists tended to 'go along with' directors, or
director-producers, rather than with stars; and they 'went along'
until unprofitability couldn't be ignored: sometimes that was
quite a long trip, for the gamble that some directors represented
could be borne with financial fortitude, provided a few sure
money-makers came from the groups that enjoyed special ties
with United Artists – the Mirisch Company, for instance. (All
Hollywood majors had guaranteed suppliers like this.) United
Artists offered 100 per cent financing to producers they backed:
if not, they offered a reason for the turn-down. The reason could
be as simple as a similarity between a project on offer and one they
were already backing; it could be as complex as a director's known
rate of progress balanced against the fact that the film had to be
made in one of the 'zones' in the United States where union labour
was most costly. Some types of film United Artists did rarely and
sometimes there was no logical reason for the top echelon's turn-
down: horror films, for example, which Arnold Picker believed
the company had had no luck with. (Every film company has such
taboos.) They had also had a bad experience with a Micky
Spillane series that hadn't worked out. So it would have been
logical to think that adventure stories with tough-guy heroes who
left a wake of blondes and bodies as they forged their way towards
some criminal 'Mr Big' would have been poor starters in 1961.
Logical thinkers, however, are not the people who build film
companies: lucky accidents do that more frequently. And a few
months after Ornstein got to his London post, an extraordinary
piece of luck – backed by good judgment, but luck in the first

place – brought him and the American company he represented the most profitable phenomenon of the decade under review.

JUST WILD ABOUT . . . JAMES

Early in the 1960s Albert R. Broccoli, known familiarly as 'Cubby,' and Irving Allen, co-founders of Warwick Films, the British company which had produced *The Trials of Oscar Wilde*, as well as much else less distinguished but more profitable, began to grow restless in their partnership. Each felt his usefulness to the other had petered out. 'Any time one of us particularly badly wanted to do something, the other didn't,' Broccoli commented later. 'I was ready to go solo.'[1]

Gnawing at Broccoli, an impressively built Italian-American whose grandfather marched with Garibaldi and who owes his patronym to his descent from a prosperous line of broccoli farmers in Italy and his nickname to the popularity at school of a comic-strip character named Abe Kabibble, was the feeling that his contribution to Warwick had been overshadowed. His partner had a better grasp of public relations, and Broccoli wanted to establish himself as very definitely *the* producer of any film to carry his credit in future. The Oscar Wilde film was their last together and Broccoli, along with the author and screenwriter Wolf Mankowitz, was working on a concept for an Arabian Nights film for distribution by Columbia Pictures. Columbia had had a fifty–fifty deal with Warwick, a deal that sweetened to forty–sixty as the box-office returns came in. But Mike Frankovich, who controlled Columbia's production in Europe at this time, was lukewarm about the Arabian Nights fantasy; and when Allen and Broccoli amicably parted company, it was with Allen that Frankovich decided to go along, after offering Broccoli 'dollar for dollar' financing for his project. 'That wasn't my scene,' the latter said. 'I had been a proven success at Warwick and felt I had earned a distributor's cash backing by putting up my own

[1] Albert R. Broccoli interviewed by the author, 25 February, 1972. Unless stated otherwise, all subsequent quotations from Broccoli come from the same source.

talent as collateral in the deal.' But he privately admitted that Frankovich's hesitation was understandable. 'The Arabian Nights project just wasn't working out and Wolf and I were intelligent enough to know it. "What exactly do you want to do?" Wolf asked me one day. "What I'd really like to film are the Ian Fleming books," I told him, "the James Bond thrillers." "Then do them," said Wolf. "Call his agent and find out where the film rights lie".'

Thus out of one abortive fantasy emerged another that was to make more than a sultan's fortune for everyone concerned with it.

Looking back on the Bond phenomenon, it is almost unbelievable to realize how slow and hesitant a start it had. Even after writing four Bond books, one a year between 1953 and 1955, Ian Fleming still hadn't achieved a really profitable breakthrough: he had failed both to make the best-seller lists in England and America and to clinch a Hollywood deal. Sir Alexander Korda had asked to see the MS. of *Live and Let Die* (1954), and returned it with polite thanks but no contract; Columbia Broadcasting System had done a one-hour version of *Casino Royale* (1953) (retitled in the United States as *Too Hot to Handle*) and gratefully forgotten about it; the paperback market found sales sluggish. 'Certainly, judged by the hopes of fame and fortune Fleming had had of his hero,' wrote the fiction-writer's biographer. 'James Bond was a great disappointment.'[1] Fleming had almost made up his mind to kill off 'that cardboard booby' in one more book, then find an easier way of getting rich, and in this mood he sold the rights of *Casino Royale* outright for 6,000 dollars in the spring of 1955 to Gregory Ratoff, the same man who gave Warwick Films such cause for financial heartburn when his Oscar Wilde film rushed theirs to the box-office five years later. The mass public didn't really get to hear of Ian Fleming till he had inveigled an endorsement for *Live and Let Die* out of Raymond Chandler; he was still better served by vicarious celebrity when the then Prime Minister, Sir Anthony Eden, rented Fleming's Jamaica villa in February 1957 to recuperate from his breakdown in health over the Suez débâcle. Eden's visit made Fleming 'news' and, as John Pearson has recounted, he saw that, if he could stomach 'the great

[1] John Pearson, *The Life of Ian Fleming* (Cape, 1966), p. 257.

splurge' of personal publicity, it would promote the Bond books. But how indifferent the film industry was to him in 1957 is revealed by the reception Broccoli got when he tried to interest a vice-president of Columbia Pictures in filming the Bond books. There and then the executive called for details of 'the Fleming properties' from the story department and received the reply, 'Apparently all he writes is travel books.' They had, of course, confused Ian Fleming with his (then) better-known brother Peter. In the intervening years Broccoli had 'somehow got the notion that Columbia Broadcasting System had taken options on the books.' This mistaken impression arose from a fruitless series of thirty-two scripts which Fleming undertook to write for C.B.S., some of which later found their way into Bond short stories. (*Dr No*, published in novel form in 1958, had begun life as an outline for a National Broadcasting Company television script: Fleming, a lamentably poor plotter, never liked wasting anything.)

But when Broccoli made enquiries from Fleming's agents, he learned that an option on the Bond books had already been taken by another film producer. So far nothing had been clinched – and the option had only twenty-eight more days to run. 'I was uncertain whether to wait for it to expire,' says Broccoli, recalling this decisive moment, 'or start talking there and then. Anyhow I wrote the producer's name down on a memo pad and showed it to Wolf Mankowitz. "I know him," said Wolf. "If I call and ask if he'll do a deal, can I write the screenplay?" ' The name was that of Harry Saltzman.

Harry Saltzman had caught Fleming at, as he put it, 'a propitious moment,' which must have been some time after March 1961, for Fleming was recovering from the first of two heart attacks, the second of which, in August 1964 would kill him. His financial advisers were urging him to capitalize himself and invest the money in a family trust; so now he sold Saltzman an option on all the available Bond novels, although he remarked that he himself hadn't seen a film since *Gone with the Wind* – a condescending exaggeration characteristic of a man whose attitude to films was that they were a plebeian amusement. 'Well,' said Saltzman, 'I'd like you to see one of *my* films' and sat him down in front of

Saturday Night and Sunday Morning. It is unrecorded what the fastidious Fleming thought of the grubby sex scenes and parlour abor-
tions that, he was told, constituted a 'breakthrough' for British
films, but he was apparently impressed enough to give the go-
ahead for his own books to be filmed, provided a backer could be
located. Even in 1961 this wasn't certain despite the biggest break
that James Bond's creator coincidentally received when *Life*
magazine, on 17 March, named *From Russia, with Love* amongst a
list of President Kennedy's ten favourite books. It was ninth:
Stendhal's *Le Rouge et le Noir* was tenth, but as far as Saltzman
was concerned, he might have been trying to set up the Stendhal
property instead. 'I've tried to set the Bond books up with every
studio in the business,' he informed Broccoli when they met, 'and
it's just not a proposition.' However, he *was* interested in going
into partnership with Broccoli. Both men had just severed highly
successful relationships with their respective companies, Broccoli
with Warwick Films and Saltzman with Woodfall Films. Broccoli
at that moment was not sure if he wanted a new partner: but he
certainly did want James Bond, and therefore he wrote out an
agreement guaranteeing an advance of at least £1,000, and the
two producers started hunting for financial backing.

One thing they had agreed on made this additionally difficult.
They wanted an 'unknown' to play Bond, whereas distributors
would have preferred an established star. 'We felt the books were
the "star," ' Broccoli said. 'If the films were successful, they
would make whoever played Bond famous. A star couldn't have
been tied up for a series of pictures; and we felt this to be vital.
United Artists had failed with Micky Spillane because they used
a different star each time and the public got no chance to form an
affectionate identification with him.' One reason for approaching
United Artists, in spite of the Spillane failure, was Broccoli's close
relationship with Arthur Krim, dating back to the years when the
latter had been the company lawyer on 'a smaller kind of Bond
nonsense called *Treasury Agent*, which I'd made on a six-day
schedule and an $80,000 budget, mostly borrowed from my
cousin Pat De Sica.' ('My cousin,' Broccoli added, with familiar
stoicism, 'took producer credit, Irving Allen got co-producer

credit, leaving me coming in at the tail-end as production manager. Krim had helped us rent the house and a boxer dog we used.') At least they felt that Krim, now a powerful corporation executive, would give them a polite hearing and not the brush-off. After gaining Ornstein's blessing and recommendation, the two producers flew to New York in mid-June 1961. 'It was a mixture of optimism and apprehension that I carried into the meeting with Krim, Benjamin and David Picker,' Broccoli said. 'David said, "I'm familiar with James Bond." Krim said, "If David likes the idea, we'll talk." Frankly, they were reluctant to make the series using an unknown actor; but eventually, after some talk, we did get an understanding that the picture would be done, if it could be done cheaply. In short, a million dollar budget – tops.' (Broccoli recalls that the figures discussed included a 50 per cent participation in the profits after the deduction of distribution and other fees, which is normal practice; Saltzman believes the figure mentioned was nearer 30 per cent, 'which was the lowest you could receive as producers,' he said. But the confusion here may simply be due to each man recalling a different participation figure for a different world territory. In any case, it was on a 50 per cent of the net basis when the film was released.)

Broccoli and Saltzman left the meeting with a verbal understanding, though not yet a written agreement. They accordingly went across town to Columbia Pictures 'to test the reaction there' – a by no means unusual precaution in film financing – and after being kept waiting in an outside office, they met with two executives who asked which Bond book they wished to film first. Broccoli recalled the conversation. ' "*Dr No* or *Thunderball*" – "How much?" – "A million dollars" – "Out of the question." They saw it as just a low-budget film and wanted us to consider making it for $300–400,000. I said the cheapest film we'd made for Columbia at Warwick was *The Red Beret* and that had cost $700,000 and made eight million worldwide. When we got back to our hotel we found awaiting us a letter from Arthur Krim. "Harry, we now have a contract," I said. "We are in the Bond business".'

*   *   *

'ALL THIS HUCKSTERING'

It had been intended that *Thunderball* would be the first Bond book to be filmed; and if it had been, some people considered it would have been the end and not the beginning of the series. Ornstein's view was that, since much of the film happened underwater, it couldn't have been done well – or at all – on the budget allocated, even in black-and-white. But *Thunderball* ran into litigation early in 1961 – the rights in it were disputed by the film producer Kevin McClory, who, along with Jack Whittingham, had worked on the film treatment on which Fleming had based the book – and the dispute wasn't settled till late in 1963,[1] by which time *Dr No* had become the first Bond film: it was in colour, which added $50,400 on to the budget, at which some United Artists executives jibbed. If not the most exotic Bond book at that time, it was the most topical. Cape Canaveral was having an embarrassingly bad international Press as its missiles either misfired or went dangerously astray. *Dr No* provided an appealing rationalization for this in the activities of the Jamaican-based villain who was beaming confusing 'instructions' at the missiles. The plot was one that a million-dollar budget would be stretched to encompass; an attractive heroine; and exotic locations in Jamaica, which was a useful 'mid-Atlantic' setting for a film that had to appeal to Anglo-American film-goers and, at the same time, comply with the British cinema's quota nationality requirements if it hoped to enjoy a share of the box-office subsidy, the Eady Levy, paid to British productions. To have made a film entirely based in the United States would have meant using American technicians or doubling up with a British crew: both impossible on the budget. Jamaica, being British territory, fitted all quota and union requirements.

Finding a Bond was crucial. One thing that definitely swung the scales in favour of a 'cheap' unknown was a cut-back in the budget, just after production had begun, to between $800–900,000, much of which was ear-marked for 'production values,'

---

[1] McClory got the film rights to *Thunderball* and produced it for Eon Films, the Saltzman-Broccoli company, in 1965.

that vague term encompassing the conspicuous 'above the line' expenditure on things that will actually show up to striking effect on the screen. At one time Fleming had considered David Niven, James Stewart, James Mason or Richard Burton for Bond. That was now a nice daydream. In any case, Broccoli and Saltzman had their idea. 'I'd always regarded Bond as a real shit,' Broccoli said, 'tougher than Fleming's model.' After vetting about a dozen candidates and drawing up a short-list of three, he and Saltzman finally looked long and closely at Sean Connery.[1] They saw him first in – of all things! – Walt Disney's whimsical comedy *Darby O'Gill and the Little People*, then took in the character parts he had played in a string of unmemorable films. 'He was dreadful in most of them, we thought,' Saltzman said later. 'He had suffered a small but fatal miscasting all the way down the line.' But they arranged to meet him and, despite his turning up in loafers, baggy trousers and a heavy five o'clock shadow, immediately liked his face, accent and especially his walk. 'As he left the office,' Ornstein recalled, 'we all went to the window and watched him cross the street.' 'What impressed me,' said Saltzman, 'was that a man of his size and frame could move in such a supple way.' Broccoli put it more plainly. 'He looked like he had balls.' Fleming's only recorded comment was somewhat more generous in its estimate. 'Saltzman thinks he has found an absolute corker,' he wrote to a business associate, 'a thirty-year-old Shakespearian actor, ex-Navy boxing champion, etc., etc., and even, he says, intelligent.' And he added, with characteristic disdain for the vulgarity of the film world, 'I am staying away from all this side of the business and dodging all those lunches and dinners at the Mirabelle and the Ambassadeurs which seem to be the offices for all this huckstering.'[2]

Connery made a screen test, dressed in beach togs and surrounded by pretty girls: it was meant to put his virility on show, but evoked a lukewarm response when viewed by United Artists

---

[1] Number two or three on the list saw Roger Moore, who, in 1973, became the 'third' Bond.

[2] John Pearson, *op. cit.*, pp. 333–4.

executives in New York.[1] Their spirits picked up, though, when they saw the man himself. Terence Young had directed *The Red Beret* for Warwick and, even though his recent films for United Artists had been somewhat short of expectations, Broccoli unhesitatingly picked him for *Dr No*, knowing his capacity for contributing ideas to a film above and beyond those in the script. Young's boyish enthusiasm for a 'good yarn' proved just what was needed, though at the start, Broccoli claims, his enthusiasm for Connery didn't rate as high – he would have preferred Richard Johnson. The screenplay wasn't proving straightforward. Wolf Mankowitz and Richard Maibaum had produced several drafts, 'but I couldn't get it into anyone's head,' Broccoli said, 'that Bond was an important character, to be taken seriously. I believe one version had it that Dr No turned out to be – a monkey! "This won't do," I said, "do it again".' Honeychile Rider, the first of the Bondmaidens who materializes Venus-like out of the Caribbean on to the beach where 007 has made landfall, was cast by the happy accident of Ursula Andress's portrait being the only one in a slew of photos on Broccoli's desk which showed a girl with her hair wet. 'She looked very attractive – wet – like a sea-lion.' There and then he ordered her dispatch to Jamaica; and, like Esther Williams before her, one could soon agree that, wet, she *was* a star. Connery, according to Saltzman, was the happiest person on location when shooting began. 'He knew as well as we did that Bond was a real leading-man role, one that went through the film from first scene to last.' He was also paid about $30,000. Fleming got $100,000 and the deal at this stage was, roughly, that Saltzman and Broccoli, incorporated as Eon Films, had options on all the available Bond books: each year they had to pick one up for the same price as above; they also had rights in the character of Bond, so that if ever they ran out of the published books and wished to make a Bond 'original,' Fleming, or, as it turned out, Booker Brothers, who acquired 51 per cent of Fleming's company in 1964, and his estate would still be paid an

---

[1] They were staunch Kennedy supporters and one report had it that they would have preferred Peter Lawford, John Kennedy's film-star brother-in-law in the role.

agreed sum. When the enormous returns became evident, the producers assigned part of their percentage to the Fleming estate. At first the films were to be cross-collateralized, which meant roughly that any profits one happened to make could be used to offset the losses another might incur; later this was renegotiated, but by then it was of academic importance, since every Bond film was making a fortune.

At the time, though, not a single person had the slightest inkling of the phenomenon they were launching. Indeed, there was no belief that anything but a routine commercial 'actioner' would emerge, and the budgetary cut dictated by United Artists indicated that even here there was room for caution. Even when *Dr No* was finished and ready for screening, the distributors showed no great enthusiasm. On *that*, both Saltzman and Broccoli are in complete accord. 'When we first ran the film,' Saltzman said, 'some genius said, "Well, all we can lose is 950,000 dollars, Harry",' – which is what *Dr No* finally cost, somewhat above budget – 'and Ilya Lopert gave it as his opinion that, "It simply won't work in America, Connery will never go over".' Of this dismaying reception, Broccoli said, 'It opened in the United States in what we thought a very disappointing way. We were telephoned from New York and told the film was opening in drive-in cinemas in Texas and Oklahoma, so as to get the investment back quickly. From which, I gathered their confidence in it was low.'

It was, in fact, the public who, in the face of such dismaying predictions, made James Bond's success secure. Not that it was by any means a tearaway success from the word go; nor were many of the notices it received, at least when it opened in London on 4 October, 1962, any more clear-sighted than the distributors' prophecies. 'Perhaps Mr Sean Connery will, with practice, get the "feel" of the part a little more surely than he does here,' wrote *The Times* critic,[1] cavilling (as usual) at the 'faint Irish-American look and sound' of the Scottish-born Connery which he inferred was part of the film's bias towards the American market. In fact this accent was probably a vital part in public acceptance of Connery; for being 'non-English,' it avoided pigeon-holing Bond

[1] *The Times*, 5 October, 1962.

anywhere in the Anglo-Saxon class system, yet it was authentically 'British' enough to avoid any accusation that he had been located in some mid-Atlantic limbo. Connery's burry drawl travelled well the world over and the very novelty of hearing a dialect tone that wasn't noticeably lower-class issuing from a leading man's lips usefully distinguished Connery from the now multiplying numbers of young newcomers on the British screen.

Connery was – and has remained, despite his replacements in the role – the chief reason for people's impatient anticipation of the next Bond film and the next and the next . . . Unlike most English actors, the trades he had plied before taking up acting actually appeared to have formed his persona in a visible, all-male way: something much commoner with American screen stars, especially those of Connery's generation, than among the English acting-school intake who generally go there on scholarships and not after hard labour as boxer, bricklayer, truck driver, merchant seaman, etc., etc. Connery's features in *Dr No* were really quite rough-cast: it was with the second Bond film, *From Russia, with Love*, that Connery–Bond began to acquire exterior polish. But from the first, his movements were distinctive. He had the model's ability to carry his height with an easy, unbound grace – he had been a male model, too – and he had none of the fashion model's narcissism. (The Bond character maybe had that, but 007 saw his own flattering virility in terms of the women he attracted or the action he handled: the ironic quips with which he dispatched his victims, or secured his sexual advantage before a tactful fade-out, was the most obvious form of self-satisfaction he was permitted.) Connery's boxing reflexes lent his most ordinary movements a degree of dangerous anticipation: as *Time*'s critic put it, 'he moves with a tensile grace that excitingly suggests the violence that is bottled in Bond.'[1] Though he was certainly no Cary Grant at this stage, it is nevertheless the confident physicality of the American star, who had also started off along athletic lines as a circus artist, that Connery recalls. And under both men's exterior charm lies the same hint of cruelty. Connery once defined it in an interview comment which, whether or not it was consciously prepared to

[1] *Time*, 21 April, 1963.

fit the accreting image of Bond, is very appropriate: 'The proper sadist is always aware of what he's doing. He is never completely passionate. His mind is always working. That's where the dividing line is.'[1] (It was perfectly in keeping with this image that Alfred Hitchcock, who had employed Cary Grant so adroitly in earlier films, should have picked Connery for *Marnie* and there used him as a 'proper sadist.') To this quality the Bond films added the enormous dimension of fantasy. Scarcely ever afflicted with doubts in the Ian Fleming novels, and *never* in the films, Bond is a man who makes his own rules: he is never really in love with the girl, never plagued with doubts, but absolutely sure of what *he* wants. To the vast majority of men, and many women at that relatively unliberated time – so soon to change! – sexual decisiveness of this stamp was infinitely gratifying. Bond was a dream figure in a traditional mode, not a social rebel like the screen figures at war with the reality of society around them. Unlike them, he was not aggressively youthful: at the age of thirty, Connery could scarcely be that. He was not anti-authority: obedience to the father-figure of M and a worshipful distance from the surrogate sister-figure of Miss Moneypenny were carefully preserved in each film. Bond served his country at a time when that country's confidence in its old imperial potency had been shaken by Suez and the retreat of the old certainties; so in that sense he was both a salve for the wound and a sentimental, nostalgic bandage. The timing of his appearance was perfect.

He was also one of the earliest symptoms of permissiveness in the 1960s. He was licensed to kill and enjoyed it. He took death as he took sex: both provided gratification *now* without remorse or complications *later*. The antithesis of 'now' and 'later' is what separates fantasy from fact, playtime from reality. Connery–Bond always lived in the daydreamer's present tense. Theodore Roszak was writing some years after the phenomenon had been exhaustively analyzed, and was specifically concerned with the strategies used by technocratic society to defuse men's aggressive sexuality, but he has given a vivid précis of the type of playboy

[1] Connery interviewed by Susan Barnes, *Sunday Express*, 31 December, 1961.

fantasy which Bond represented. 'He practises a career en-
veloped by noncommital trivialities: there is no home, no family,
no romance that divides the heart painfully. Life off the job itself
is a constant run of imbecile affluences and impersonal orgasms.
Finally, as a neat little divider, the ideal of the swinging life . . .
gives us a conception of femininity which is indistinguishable
from social idiocy. The woman becomes a mere playmate, a
submissive bunny, a mindless decoration.'[1] Kingsley Amis read
Bond's lineage back to the Byronic hero. 'Mr Fleming has brought
off the unlikely feat of enclosing this wildly romantic, almost
narcissistic and (one would have thought) hopelessly out-of-date
person inside the shellac of a secret agent, and so making it
plausible, mentally actable and, to all appearance, contemporary.'[2]
Amis saw the secret agent as the most universal focus for day-
dreaming; since he must not seem to be different from other men,
he gives to the widest possible number of ordinary men a corresponding range of vicarious experiences to savour. By the time
the fourth Bond film was made – *Thunderball* (1965) – the fantasy
was rendered even 'purer,' since the 'secret agent' aspect of 007
was played down in response to improved relations between East
and West which in turn led to the popularity of Bond's only
dangerous competitor, the Russian 'secret agent' played by David
McCallum in *The Man from U.N.C.L.E.* film and television series,
whose loyalties, whatever his nationality, were at the service of
'the world community'.

If one finds Christopher Booker persuasive when he analyzes
Britain's developing society in the 1960s and sees it as a spiralling
fantasy – and I must affirm my own belief in the essential rightness
of this view – then Bond has played a generative role of immense
power in the national 'dream fantasy' which Booker describes in
The Neophiliacs. 'Just as every individual neurotic feels the need
firstly for a dream to escape into, secondly for a dream projection
to identify with, and thirdly for the illusion of self-assertion, so
every collective neurosis displays these characteristics writ large
– the common dream which binds its members rigidly together,

---

[1] Theodore Roszak, *The Making of a Counter Culture* (Faber, 1970), p. 15.
[2] Kingsley Amis, *The James Bond Dossier* (Cape, 1965), p. 36.

the dream heroes who attain their hypnotic glamour by embodying and acting as projections of the group neurosis and the
common fund of aggression, whether expressed towards the rest
of society in general or just one or other group in particular.'[1]

It was enough in the first Bond film to offer an assembly kit for
fantasists. When novelty was required later on, it was supplied by
the gadgets with which Bond armed himself or, alternately, was
trapped by: for a spell, the films redirected their appeal away from
the romanticism of Bond and towards that of the inanimate
object. The hardwear became more fascinating than the hero.
Perhaps that was the penalty of being superhuman: the life and
death forces flew straight into the machines. For *Dr No*, though,
Connery simply lent Bond an engagingly unfamiliar personality
which was moulded into an 'image' as the film unreeled. What one
recognizes behind *Dr No* is the technique used in advertising to
establish brand images, though probably it was not engineered as
deliberately as that – not yet, anyhow. Since Bond had already in
the books a history as an ad-man's all-purpose hero, there was a
natural carry-over; but the film's structure, its rapid editing,
elliptical progression for at least the first and more gripping half,
even the stylised opening titles, all recall a highly accomplished
television commercial. At a time when the cinema's 'lost audience'
was far more accustomed to the condensed consumer fantasies
which commercial television showed it, the Bond films were that
much more easy and attractive to identify with whenever the
television audience made the rare return visit to the movies. The
films had the pace and nervous stimulation of the hard and fast
'sell' as well as the highly efficient nonchalance of the 'class'
commercials which would set up an elaborate scene in order to
dispose of it with a throw-away gag. *Dr No* had some of the
earliest 'black' (some said 'sick') jokes that later on got to be as
regular (some said 'monotonous') as a cabaret 'black-out.' 'I think
they must have been going to a funeral,' quips 007, as the enemy's
Cadillac hearse crashes in flames. 'It's a Smith and Wesson and
you've had your six,' he tells an adversary who has clicked the
trigger of a pistol he has already emptied into the bed he thinks

[1] Christopher Booker, *op. cit.*, p. 62.

G

holds Bond – and, the rules of the game thus politely observed, Bond shoots the fellow dead. He was, as Derek Hill noted, 'exactly the right mixture of strong-arm Fascist and telly commercial salesman.'[1] Like *Tom Jones*, the film swiftly recruited the audience into sympathy with it by its own degree of self-parody: it had gusto and sociability built into it. Arthur Knight, terming it 'the best bad film of the year,' added, 'Connery meets such wild improbability with such grim inflexibility . . . that one is soon shouting warnings to him as at the Saturday afternoon serials.'[2] As in *Tom Jones*, there were moments when the hero addressed the camera-audience directly, intimately, cheekily – Tom Jones with eye-to-eye candour, Bond through his lethal asides. *Dr No* had a submerged complicity with the audience that formed a large part of its attractiveness and made its dull plot pardonable or forgetable. It was this factor that took the makers by surprise. Most fantasy thrillers worked with the screen: Bond was the first film series at that time to work *with an audience*. In a way, it *was* a return to those Saturday afternoon serials. People who went to see the Bond films henceforth knew the game and anticipated playing it and even working at it as the film-makers fed them the clues. Once Broccoli and Saltzman had tumbled to this factor, which they soon did, then the formula was theirs and Connery–Bond gave them a world patent. Ornstein ascribes another reason. 'Anyone's ideas were welcomed and, if good, they were used.' That's to say, Saltzman and Broccoli worked closely on the script, but 'it was soon like a 24th of December Christmas tree, the whole family came in to decorate it, in Bondian style.' With such flexibility, the series preserved for a long time its freshness and good humour.

THE ADAM STYLE

To keep the mind boggling amiably at the Bond fantasy, the sets created by the production designer Ken Adam were of powerful assistance and even, for a period, of dominating importance.

[1] *Scene*, 5 October, 1962.
[2] *Saturday Review*, 1 June, 1963.

Born Klaus Adam in Germany in the 1920s, he arrived in England as a refugee from Hitler and studied architecture before the Royal Air Force recruited him as a war-time fighter pilot – one of the few instances of an ex-German in that particular role. Even before Bond, he had always leaned towards the theatrical style in film designs: the Bauhaus had less influence on him, even as a student architect, than had a boyhood visit to *The Cabinet of Dr Caligari*. William Cameron Menzies, the American designer of extravagant settings like those in *The Thief of Baghdad* and *Things to Come* had also a lasting effect, and when Menzies was associate producer on *Around the World in Eighty Days* he had Ken Adam as his designer. Adam also admits to a liking for Andreyev, who designed some of Korda's films, and for Wakhevich's grotesque stage sets; but, with him, the baroque imagination was at odds with the architectural functionalism of his training and if he had not broken free from the latter, then the Bond films might have evolved in a very different way. 'The irregularity of your lines on the sketchboard is what makes a set come alive,' he was advised by John Bryan at an early stage and, following the senior designer's counsel, Adam immediately dispensed with the fine, sharp pencil of his architectural classes and found liberation in a felt-tipped pen which gave him the ability to loosen up as well as the impulse to depart from reality. 'I found I could create more sense of cinema "reality" by abandoning naturalism, finding a concept to match a film's content and then extending it into the imagination of the audience – however irrational it might be in real life.'[1] *Goldfinger*, made two years after *Dr No*, at a time when the romanticism of the machine had begun to take the spotlight away from Bond, illustrates how far Ken Adam's 'reality' determined the sense of space and size that had become associated with the Bond series – 'space' he traced back to the U.F.A. films of pre-Hitlerite Germany, 'size' to *Things to Come*. For example, in his designs for the interior of Fort Knox in *Goldfinger*, he sought the feeling of a gigantic goldsmith's showcase, and designed a set

[1] Ken Adam interviewed by the author, 25 June, 1971. Unless stated otherwise, all subsequent quotations from Adam come from the same source.

dominated by a huge vaulted arch, a shining grille with elevators gliding up and down it like the camera platforms in Leni Riefenstahl's film of the Berlin Olympic Games in 1936, and, behind it all, pyramids of gold bars. The 'reality' of nearly any of the world's major gold repositories was very different. Gold, being so heavy, is hardly ever stacked more than two feet high; and the one national gold vault which Adam was permitted to inspect, at the Bank of England, turned out to be a depressing warren of branching corridors, with the dusty gold bricks stacked away in little alcoves like refuse that had been swept out of sight. Yet Adam's Fort Knox 'came off conceptually if not functionally.'

This was the intention he brought to *Dr No*, although its plot, never mind a tiny budget of £14,000 for his set designs, hardly supplied the opportunities of the later Bonds. Nevertheless, with a budget of almost the same cramped proportions he had shown what dazzling effects he could obtain when he designed Warwick's production of *The Trials of Oscar Wilde*. Like the others, he concedes, his enthusiasm for *Dr No* was hardly unbounded at the start of the production; but he had been bogged down for months in Morocco and Italy, working on Robert Aldrich's costly débâcle *Sodom and Gomorrah*, and 'I felt I needed to work in England pretty soon, lest I be forgotten. I said "Yes" to *Dr No* and thought I was prostituting myself.' After supervizing the location-filming in Jamaica, he returned to Pinewood Studies several weeks before the unit. The sets were to fill four or five stages. 'I began to realize that here was an opportunity to be slightly ahead of contemporary feeling by giving the thriller-genre – which, remember, had been out of fashion for several years – a larger-than-life atmosphere with a tongue-in-cheek touch to it here and there. I decided to break away from routine materials and experimented with the effects of copper, stainless steel and plastic, though there was some resistance to this on the grounds of cost, and the design budget eventually finished up nearer £20,000. We used lots of real fabrics and finishes, but fortunately I evolved a nitrate process which could give wonderful chrome, brass and copper effects. It was all new to the Pinewood construction people and they responded with enthusiasm, which in turn encouraged me to go beyond what was considered "safe" in a commercial movie at that date. So everything in *Dr No* was being pushed further and further away from naturalism; and when Harry, Cubby and Terence Young returned from Jamaica, they said, "Good," and stimulated me to go further still.' Part of the décor provided one excellent topical joke, typical of the way the film-makers soon learned to make the audience share in the fun by sowing 'clues' around the scenes. This was the Goya painting of the Duke of Wellington which had been stolen from London's National Gallery a few months earlier and, in the film, turned up in Dr No's luxurious living-quarters. 'The Goya was Harry Saltzman's notion,' said Adam. 'I only had to paint it.'

By the time *From Russia, With Love* was screened in the autumn of 1963, the Bond formula had been well and truly processed: the outsize action, the superman panache, the self-parody, the eroticism that carried just a hint of what the then currently fashionable term dubbed 'kinky' and the brutality which was so nonchalantly dealt out that the moral shock was absorbed almost before the blows landed or the bullets struck home, and it became what I termed, in writing of *Dr No*, 'sadism for the family.' From mid-1963 on, when audiences everywhere had discovered their novelty-dimension, the Bond films became established as a world cult. Their fantasies were continually fed by fact, as the real international espionage plots which the 1960s revealed kept underlining the films' repeated theme of a vast conspiracy. Even the hardware items of their trade used by real secret agents and professional assassins – like the false cigarette packs that dispensed bullets when squeezed – might have come out of Fleming's fiction. Nightmare was combined with plausibility, as Kingsley Amis noted, so that in going to see the Bond thrillers one embraced the reality of the nightmare while escaping into the re-assurance of the fantasy. Almost by accident Saltzman, Broccoli, Connery, Adam and all the other contributors had discovered one of the era's great recipes for alternately stimulating and soothing a captive audience.

But as well as their appeal to a restless, thrilling sense of global disorder, which is miraculously cleared up in time to catch the last train home, the Bond films profited in a much more practical, down-to-earth way from the distribution strategy evolved for them in meetings between Ornstein and the producers. Very early on it was apparent that there would be immense commercial advantage to the series if each picture could be made at a certain time of year, got on the screen at a specific season and, most important of all, got out on distribution in a tremendous number of prints supported by peak publicity. It would be possible to recoup the negative-cost within a few weeks, instead of reckoning on up a year, perhaps, as in the case of other successful films distributed with less saturated strategy. This gave the makers an incalculable advantage on the foreign accounting of their box-office profits – or, rather, the advantage was reassuringly *calculable*, since there was literally no time for exhibitors, and others, to lump on all the charges that can cut a hefty profit down to slim proportions when it is returned to the film-maker at the end of the line, perhaps a year after his film has been released. Foreign accounting tended to be months behind the actual payment, the accumulated backlog constituting a very attractive free loan to whoever happened to hold it in their hands *pro tem*. United Artists and Eon Productions eventually got things so streamlined that for *Goldfinger*, for example, 1,100 prints were in use globally: in Germany alone there were between 80 and 100 prints, whereas normally that particular market was served by a mere twenty prints. In the United States the average well-received film ended up with 350–80 prints: *Goldfinger* began its release with at least that number. The plethora of prints has meant that the Bond films can be kept in almost continuous re-release in virtually every territory in the world. The mechanics of money worked hand in glove with the metaphysics of sensation to provide the British cinema of the early 1960s with an image it could impose world-wide for the remainder of the decade and into the 1970s. Except, of course, that being 'British' really had nothing to do with it . . .

Chapter Ten: The Servant Problem

> What disturbed me most in watching the film was the reaction of the audience – smirking and chortling at the portrayal of the English gentleman brought low by his servant. There was a total lack of indignation at the covert Communist propaganda.
>
> Reader's letter, *The Sunday Telegraph*, 2 February, 1964

Most of the influences evident in Joseph Losey's British films had already been shaped by his life and character before he decided to settle in England. But it was this enforced residence, as a fugitive from the black-list of Hollywood film-makers deemed to be Communists or Communist sympathizers and thus denied the right to work in the United States or even to have films bearing their name shown there, which relaunched Losey on a new career and permitted him to contribute so forcefully to changing the cinema in Britain in the 1960s.

Again and again in his work and his conversation he emphasizes that the tragedies his films explore aren't simply those of the characters' own making: they spring, instead, from the interaction between people, time and place . . . 'the layers of life that people leave on their environment, the layers that the environment leaves on people.'[1] So is it with Losey himself. His Mid-Western upbringing, in Wisconsin, left many such under-layers. One was the river, a tributary of the Mississippi which flowed through the community and a source of entertainment and disaster, dances on steamboats, picnics, swimming, ice-skating in winter, floods, constant drownings, drawing lives together and taking lives, above all leaving him sensitized for life to the treacherous duality of the mirror image that the surface water created, the fear of seeing oneself repeated or reversed which threatens one's sense of unique identity. The houses familiar to him in his youth have haunted him, too. The house-design in a Losey film is true interior design, illuminating the characters'

[1] Joseph Losey interviewed by the author, 24 March, 1970. Unless stated otherwise, all subsequent quotations from Losey come from the same source.

inner lives as well as furnishing their exterior needs, the unconscious construction of the resident personality that assumes
the shape of their passions or their crimes. It's no accident that
the one name accompanying Losey through his English film-
making, from *The Sleeping Tiger* (1954) right up to *Secret Ceremony*
(1968), with the sole exception of *Accident*, is that of his design-
consultant (later production designer) Richard MacDonald, an
artist whose relationship to him, Losey has said, is that of 'a
sounding board . . . somebody I could talk to, not to get ideas
from necessarily, but just to hear my own ideas, test them or
reject them in the telling. Richard and I had a language worked
out over many years which is partly drawn and partly verbal.'[1]
MacDonald's designs represent a process of imaginative accretion
– the 'layers' again – which is then stripped down to the illuminating essentials – a highly selective form of naturalism.

One notices this hypersensitiveness to surroundings in Losey's
own London home, or homes, for his residence in Chelsea is
actually two houses knocked into one. The patterned exoticism
is extraordinarily precise: severe glass dining-tables and walls of
black-glass mirrors mingling with the sharp leafy spikes and
emaciated trunks of semi-tropical shrubs and elongated ottomans
fabricated on the spot from the dissected pieces of Oriental
carpets. Even a pinky-beige chrysanthemum petal that falls on
the floor is seized on as exemplifying a corrective tone to the
figured beige carpet. It is upstairs, in Losey's study, that his
Wisconsin ancestry has been tucked: dozens of small, framed
album photographs of plain, confident, townsfolk, flanked on one
side by a manuscript letter from Bertholt Brecht, and on the other
by a French artist's *fantaisie* of Losey as a winged Fallen Angel in
the manner of Michelangelo. (What passions and events would
this environment reflect if he decided to shoot a film in it?) Until
one gets to know him – and even afterwards, if the vibrations are
bad or lack of sympathy for his current film is communicated to
him – Losey responds to questioning from a defensively physical
posture in which scatter-cushions are unconsciously enlisted as

[1] Tom Milne, ed., *Losey on Losey* (Secker & Warburg / British Film
Institute, 1967), pp. 107–8.

an extra barricade, the asthma he sometimes suffers from adding its tension to pressures that start off as cloistral and frequently end by becoming claustrophobic for both subject and interviewer. Such a man couldn't help being acutely sensitive to his living-conditions, interpreted figuratively as well as solidly. He is not obviously a rebel – his life-style hardly suggests discomfort, much less spiritual liaison with the have-nots of the world – in the way that Lindsay Anderson instantly reveals himself to be. Anderson is a sceptic whereas Losey is a pessimist: though neither scepticism nor pessimism precludes the romantic impulse, And this beats incessantly through Losey's work, giving it a lot of its ambiguity, his half-love for a world he politically rejects and sees to be the social sham which his films expose.

This layer of romanticism was probably formed in the sixteen years of his life spent in his hometown of La Crosse. Home was 'a pleasant, strange kind of Victorian affair'; Thursday nights were spent reading aloud in French to an aunt; at other times he read avidly by himself 'all of Dickens, all of George Elliot, all of Dumas, most of Scott.' Religion had its allotted place; the domestic servants had theirs as well. 'These were things that were influences in the sense of rebelling against them later,' he recalls. They are things to bear in mind while examining the part of Losey's career that belongs to this book. For very often the early influences in life are the ones intensified by an event that traumatically separates one from them in the most complete way possible – in Losey's case the blacklisting that brutally annihilated one career in the United States and forced him abroad as an expatriate who eventually settled in London at the end of 1954 'on the very night of Eisenhower's first election.'

'It wasn't a question of fleeing,' he recalled, 'but one of existing.' He was in a greater state of shock than one can nowadays appreciate, viewing the complex 'European' artist he has evolved into. At that time, in his mid-forties, his youthful idealism had been abruptly called into question. He had discovered how quickly intellectual freedom could vanish into the ground, like a river drying up, and that his belief in the possibility of ultimate solutions for all human ills had failed to take account of the less benign kind of reality that had struck him down. Statements about the human condition, fostered by friendship with Brecht, a pre-war visit to Russia, a stint with the Rockefeller Foundation, lost their altruistic certainty in the sheer necessity of personal survival. Losey had to work on a closed set and use the name 'Victor Hanbury' on his first film in England, *The Sleeping Tiger*, with another prudent pseudonym, 'Derek Frye,' covering the identities of his blacklisted writers Harold Buchman and Carl Foreman: it all conspired to make him feel trapped. He was also trapped in a subtler way: he was a foreigner in that most deceptive of all situations in which understanding the language persuades the stranger he understands the society. Losey wasn't that naïve, of course; but his early films do show the strain of an expatriate trying to shake off an old morality that had been proved vulnerable to attack and to feel his way into a more complex set of values, where short answers like 'yes' or 'no' and simple verities like 'good' or 'bad' weren't sufficient. He absorbed the subtleties of the English scene very slowly at first, and tended to fall back on Hollywood's inadequate view of life when trying to give social reality to the bread-and-butter melodramas he directed. The fellow-blacklisted exiles he worked with didn't help him to find his social footing swiftly: they were too busy finding theirs. All of which explains 'the five years of nothing,' as he put it cruelly but with more than a mite of truth, till *Blind Date* (1959: U.S. title *Chance Meeting*), perhaps the film he would prefer to date as the start of his 'European' work, although *Time without Pity* (1957), an anti-capital-punishment tract, has its appositeness to his own professional 'death' and 'reprieve.'

But in *Blind Date* he confidently challenged the values specific to his adopted society: and with only a couple of exceptions this remained the theme of all his British films. In it he took a characteristically American theme, the use and abuse of power in the community, and absorbed it into a critique of the English class system. For the first time a British film seriously challenged the acceptance of the police as an institution above class interests. The corrupt cop had earlier appeared in Losey's Hollywood thriller, *The Prowler* (1951), although, as he later pointed out, its theme was the peculiarly 1950-ish one of 'making it,' being a 'big man' in the community in terms of material possessions. *Blind Date* anglicized this: it was about 'preserving it' – about the 'haves' covering up the evidence of their crimes from the scrutiny of the 'have nots.'

The English class system had intrigued and appalled Losey from the day of his arrival – and nearly twenty years later he could still say, 'There's no place I know of where the class system is so horrifying and so unchanging as it is here in England.' The system struck him initially through the efforts of so many of those he met to maintain a false front, and there were obvious ironies between their hypocrisy and his necessity as he worked under a false name in a closed set. 'Having to maintain some sort of truth in your existence and your work while not being allowed by society to work out the things that are intellectually vital,' is how he described it: it was another way of stating that it is not people who are destructive of each other, but people in relation to particular situations in place and time. Though *Blind Date* was basically a banal and unbelievable melodrama, one short scene in it struck through one's social wadding like a scalpel through cotton wool: it is when Scotland Yard's assistant commissioner and another executive out of the same top drawer hob-nob with a telepathic collusion in their voices that excludes the lower-class detective inspector played by Stanley Baker.

Losey's view of the class system was still fairly simplistic: you must be a rebel or a hypocrite, go for the 'essence' at whatever the cost, or else support 'appearances.' One can see the fearful attraction that Brecht's play *Galileo* had for him when he had staged it in 1947, and why he has always wanted to film a work that deals with his own personal tragedy of a man who is driven to taking sides, compelled either to make a hypocritical declaration of a dishonest belief or else to be 'willing to make the desperate fight and take the desperate consequences of standing up as individuals.'[1]

If Losey had stayed in Hollywood and been able to work, he would probably have been a pioneer in the Peckinpah country and dealt with the violence in American society. As he was forced to continue his career abroad, what shaped his films were the non-violent contradictions of English society.

Not at first, though. The Hollywood brand of action-melodramas persisted through *The Criminal* (1960) and *The Damned* (1962). (These two films were retitled in the United States *The Concrete Jungle* and *These are the Damned*, respectively.) Like other directors who personally abhor violence, Losey is fascinated by its manifestation in society: both films dealt with this. *The Criminal* allowed him to use Stanley Baker again, an actor with a too explicit tough-guy exterior under which Losey discerned a whole new field of aggression turned inwards on itself, and so served notice that he was a director who could extract from a star something only partially guessed at from his prior performances. It's been said by one of the actresses he worked with that Losey is at his strongest when things go wrong, and one suspects that he sometimes puts himself in situations with stars or pictures where the 'suffering' can be most intense and at the same time meaningful. *Machismo* is an overworked term: but it is relevant to the background in American movies that Losey springs from. As I've remarked earlier, where it doesn't destroy, it anneals. A gangster-on-the-loose film like *The Criminal* explodes with the director's own sense of liberation from confinement. *The Damned*, on the other hand, is the work of a man now picking up native vibrations at full strength – in this case the violent vibrations of Britain's 'teddy-boy' phenomenon, the earliest manifestation of the country's aggressive youth culture. Teenagers who took violence on to the streets in the outmoded clothes of their Edwardian grandfathers were themselves already out of date when *The Damned* was made: they had yielded place after 1958 to the slick, Italianate 'mods' and the butch, leathery 'rockers' as vitality symptoms of working-class youth. But Losey presciently linked the phenomenon they represented with the presence of an underground branch of the Establishment engaged in the propagation of itself by 'grooming' its secret classroom of captive school-children to form 'the ruling class' on the day that megadeaths have extinguished the rest of the country not immunized against radiation. The official violence sanctioned by the State, from which there is no appeal, corresponds to the primitive violence of the 'teddy boys' marching down the street whistling 'Colonel Bogey' in a parody of the River Kwai's tattered legions. Both are mutations of the social order.

By the time Losey made *Eve* (1962), he had completely internalised the violence of destructive relationships as far as the characters were concerned, though, as he admitted to James Leahy, it was still an 'over-subjective and over-personal' film and he should have stood outside it more than he did.[1] No such misjudgment was evident in the next film; and it is with this one, *The Servant* (14 November, 1963), that Losey's hour struck massively. Everything was right for it: a director fascinated by the milieu in which he now lived and moved freely, a writer who could take him into the innermost recesses of such representative figures as master and manservant, and above all a society that had undergone an extraordinary mutation of its own social fibres in the months before the film appeared, so that, when it was shown, it held the mirror up to England and let it recognize the process of change in its image of corruption.

PRIVATE STANDARDS, PUBLIC MORALS

By the time *The Servant* was premièred in mid-November, public reputations in Britain had come apart in the way family heirlooms are traditionally supposed to do in the hands of careless domestic servants. This year, 1963, was the year of rumours, doubts, suspicions and scandals about public figures and people in high places in England whose confluence was such that, by the time the Losey film was ready, it threatened virtually to destroy all credibility in our rulers and 'our betters.'

The scandals had actually begun in September 1962 with the so-called Vassall affair, involving Admiralty espionage for the Russians mingled with totally baseless but extremely hurtful and ultimately harmful sexual innuendoes, which ended with the imprisonment of a junior Civil Servant and the resignation of a

[1] James Leahy, *The Cinema of Joseph Losey* (Zwemmer/Barnes, 1967), p. 110.

wholly innocent Junior Minister. Then in the early spring of 1963 another Junior Minister in the Macmillan administration, who had been imprudent enough to lend his official car to a former reform-school boy, gave in his resignation. 'The public,' as Bernard Levin wrote, 'was ready to be scandalized; the Press was eager to provide the material.'[1] Much of the material was available in the reports of a divorce action involving a celebrated Duchess, non-political, perhaps, but contributing to the sense that the national stock of official virtue was declining while that of private licence was positively overflowing. Richard Ingrams, editor of the fortnightly satire sheet *Private Eye*, then with a circulation of 80,000, declared that 'a scandal can only flourish in the right soil. There must be a prevalent atmosphere for an incident, which might in other circumstances be totally ignored, to emerge as a symptom of all that is wrong with the times. In 1963 conditions were perfect. At the back of it all was the growing feeling that the Macmillan Government was steeped in favouritism and corruption . . . The Government ranks were thick with Earls and Marquesses, the Cabinet gave the impression of being a grown-up Etonian "Pop" (society) and it was obvious that Macmillan revelled in this anachronistic state of affairs, even boasting at one point that his powers of patronage made all those years of reading Trollope seem worthwhile . . .'[2] In March 1963 came the first whispers of indiscretions by the Minister for War, John Profumo, with a professional model, Christine Keeler, coupled with allegations of a security risk. The wretched Minister at first denied all, then in June 1963 admitted to the House of Commons that he had lied, and therefore resigned. The sequel was a commission of enquiry headed by Lord Denning into the security (and inevitably the moral) aspects of the 'Profumo Affair' with a report which appeared in September 1963 and proved a document that would nowadays be inevitably termed 'a scenario,' for not only was it written with unaccustomed regard for narrative shape and dramatic climaxes, but also it recalled the most sensational

[1] Bernard Levin, *op. cit.*, p. 62.
[2] Richard Ingrams, *The Life and Times of Private Eye* (Allen Lane, The Penguin Press, 1971), p. 12.

type of B. picture. Life, one felt, didn't ape art so much as bad art.

Levin has written that the Profumo scandal, while not exhausting all the aspects of society's changing attitudes, did help to bring people face to face with truths they had been very good at concealing from themselves. Robert Bolt, in a *Queen* magazine quotation already alluded to, had been prescient enough in mid-1961 to distinguish the trend of the 1960s towards a 'widening gap between our beliefs and our actions.' The Profumo Affair enlarged this to Grand Canyon dimensions. The Press was filled with endless self-questioning homilies, sermons preaching to those already half-converted by facts that were more exotic than fiction. The *Guardian*, for instance, saw the year out with the reflection, 'The orgies of sex and security have exposed us to some vigorous self-criticism and we enter 1964 purged of a lot of humbug both about the nature of our own society and about our part in the world.'[1] 'Humbug' that had tried, for a long time successfully, to ignore such truths as those 'that men have lusts, that they sometimes go to extraordinary lengths to satisfy those lusts, that this applies to men in positions of responsibility and power as well as to men in positions of obscurity and unimportance, that whatever a man's desires there is always somebody willing to supply his indulgence of them at the appropriate price, that greed and selfishness, pride and vanity, revenge and self-seeking, true righteousness and false righteousness run through all sections of society, that all human actions are determined by a complex play of motives and forces because all human beings are subject to many springs of action.'[2] Bernard Levin, in these words, might have been describing the flux of forces at work in *The Servant*.

Not that I am suggesting any *post hoc, propter hoc* relationship: *The Servant* was scripted, shot and ready for release long before many of these scandalous events were even publicly hinted at in the gossip columns, never mind set forth with varying degrees of sensationalism and sobriety in the news columns. But a film is an

[1] The *Guardian*, 31 December, 1963.
[2] Bernard Levin, *op. cit.*, pp. 86–7.

effective work of art; and the strength of the resonances it sets up, if society is in a receptive state to echo what is on the screen, can prove to be such that the film will be referred to constantly, in the terms of a popular metaphor, to describe events which have occurred in real life before or after its release. This is what happened in the case of Losey's film.

I can still vividly recall the impression in London, shortly after the first reviews appeared and its critical and commercial success were assured, that within its own terms *The Servant* had managed to conceptualize a state of change in British society which, as Levin and other commentators have since said, was forcing self-knowledge on to people who had been hidden from it by their own sedulously fostered division of life into public and private sectors with appropriate, though hypocritically unreconcilable, standards of conduct for each. *The Servant* was one of the events that breached this moral *cordon sanitaire*; it isolated something British society already felt stirring, and because it was a work of art that was all of a piece (or very nearly) it permeated one's cultural consciousness more profoundly than any British film had done since *Saturday Night and Sunday Morning*.

Andrew Sarris correctly speculated that what must have attracted Losey was 'the opportunity provided by Robin Maugham's conventional novel of decadence to dissect British class society within a controlled frame.'[1] Losey had first read Maugham's *novella* – published in 1948 and a mere sixty-nine pages in length – in 1956 when he was still something of an 'outsider' in England. Dirk Bogarde told him that Michael Anderson, director of *Around the World in Eighty Days* and *Yangtse Incident*, and essentially an 'action' director, had bought the rights and commissioned Harold Pinter to write a screen treatment. Bogarde would have liked to play the role, for he felt a growing need to extend his powers and shatter his matinée-idol image, but he confessed he was 'afraid of it' and not till *Victim* in 1961 had given him his freedom and cost him his pop following did he overcome his hesitation. Anderson had failed to set up the

---

[1] Andrew Sarris, *Confessions of a Cultist: On the Cinema*, 1955/1969 (Simon and Schuster, 1971), p. 130.

film for two reasons. He could not find any sizeable star to play the title role: Peter Finch was attracted, but he listened to advice which dissuaded him. Secondly, it was budgeted at £250,000; and at that price, plus the incomprehension that Pinter's elliptical script elicited from likely backers who read it, the money was just not forthcoming. So Losey secured an option on the film rights to Pinter's script and set about reworking it along with its author to serve his own concept. Leslie Grade, a producer and artists' agent, had Sarah Miles as his client: she had finished her first film, *Term of Trial*, in 1962, and needed a quick follow-up in order to consolidate her début opposite Olivier. Grade promised to find finance for *The Servant* provided the budget could be cut to £150,000. Grade was part of Elstree Distributors whose other partner was the Associated British Picture Corporation: this gave him quite a lot of muscle and he used it in an interesting way. Losey got the budget down to £141,000, neither he nor Bogarde taking much of a fee, and it actually wound up costing £135,000. But although the A.B.P.C. studios, through Grade, had money in the film, Grade insisted on the film's being put out to tender by other film studios and it wound up being shot at Shepperton, the studios owned by the British Lion group who distributed the movies made by independent producers. In the film boom that was just getting under way in Britain in 1963, competitive bidding of this kind was the exception, where it should have been the rule. Had it been the rule, it might have helped to reduce the service fees that studios charged film-makers, which as the decade advanced tended to put a lot of unnecessary 'fat' on the budgets. The National Film Finance Corporation supplied most of the 30 per cent of *The Servant*'s budget not included in the distributor's guarantee.

THE SCENARIO OF SERVILITY

Robin Maugham told his story through a narrator, thus gaining a valuable Jamesian distance from events which, to be frank, dealt with a rather conventional kind of corruption by one

individual of another.[1] In the book it was the servant's 'nannyish'
relationship to young master Tony which received the accent of
interest: 'He became comfort incarnate.' And to the same source,
Tony's old nanny, is traced the congenital weakness of the upper
classes: nanny was the only woman who had really loved the boy.
Now Losey's film follows the story very closely indeed – even the
kitchen seduction pulsing to the rhythm of the dripping tap is
in both film and book – but the 'nanny' theme is only one of many
elements that have been added to Maugham's narrative or else
expanded from it by Pinter and Losey. Since retarded infantilism
would clearly be too simplistic a diagnosis of the ruling class's
sickness in the Britain of the 1960s, the film is extended into a
critique of a way of life. The film thus lends itself more fully than
the book to socio-political interpretation: the hypocrisy of the
ruling class manifests itself in the tic-like reflexes and mannered
speech of Tony's world and this gives it a wider contemporary
resonance than the 'nanny complex' of the book.

Most of this 'class' background occurs in the film's first third,
the section that Pinter and Losey elaborated when Pinter was
doing a rewrite of his original script. 'The main thing in [our]
discussions was on what is taking place in each scene,' Pinter said,
two months after the British première. 'He [Losey] questioned a
lot most acutely and I was able to answer him on such points.'[2]
It is easy to appreciate the transfusion of the script, reworked in
his way, by Losey's Marxist view of society, and indeed he made
no secret of his view that 'all the characters are products and
victims of the same thing – class. The same trap. It's a story about
the trap – the house and the society in which they live . . . the
servility of attitudes of all kinds of people in different classes and
situations who are afraid of not being loved or not loving . . .
of not having money . . . of their wives, mistresses . . . the
atomic bomb or whatever. It's about servility as an attitude of

[1] Though 'unconventional' enough at the time for Robin Maugham's
parents to try to dissuade him from publishing it. In his autobiography,
Escape from the Shadows (1972), Maugham traces the story's genesis back to
an attempted homosexual seduction of himself by a manservant and the
latter's attractive young 'nephew,' who becomes a girl in the book.
[2] *Isis*, No. 1456, 1 February, 1964.

mind.'[1] Losey's account of the origin of one small, penetrating sequence indicates how the social background gathered density. 'The little vignettes in the restaurant were all written during shooting. I suddenly realised that stylistically I needed a bridge between the first country-house scene and the end sequence' – the orgy – 'as I planned to do it. I called Harold and asked him to write me some little bits to go into the restaurant scene and he asked what and I said, "Two lesbians, a bishop and a curate, a society girl and her escort." So he wrote them overnight and I had them in the mail the next day . . . They were *part of the background of the characters and the social background of the whole film.*'[2] The restaurant vignettes are sharp summaries of people's crooked relationships, self-indulgent and domineering in the areas of sex, religion and society. The country-house scene, besides casting an amusing sidelight on the dilettante nature of Tony's grandiose plans to better the lot of peasants in Asia Minor by building cities for them in Brazil, shows the characters' old colonial reflexes towards their natural inferiors the moment the butler enters the room, and the tableau noticeably stiffens into the attitudes of upper-class superiority. Pinter's screenplay had only indicated 'the bare lines of the activity' and he said later he had had no idea that Losey was going to use those physical postures to indicate the formality of the scene.

In all these subtle ways the film enlarges the social relevance – the hypocrisy of people who, in Losey's words, 'live in a society where they pay lip service to all sorts of ideas which are not, in any sense, acted on; ideas which educated people hold intellectually, but which they use emotionally as the basis for their privileged existence . . . If you don't know the basis of the kind of life you're leading, eventually this must corrupt your mind. And if it happens to be a very comfortable life and there's someone around who is interested in making use of it, it may become actively corrupting in other ways.'[3] In short, like master, like

[1] Ibid.
[2] Ibid. (italics mine).
[3] Joseph Losey interviewed by the author, Thames Television, 25 March, 1970.

servant: both are fraudulent and spurious, but one is more vicious and intelligent in the use he makes of his position.

Like most films that are successful in extending their events into a critique of society – Bunuel's *Tristana*, Renoir's *La Règle du Jeu*, for example – the casting of *The Servant* was extraordinarily precise: once one saw Bogarde and James Fox in the roles, one could see no other actors doing as well. Just by existing, they brought the division of society into the domestic circle, yet never failed to draw portraits of precise individuals. 'I usually wear every character I play,' Bogarde said later. 'But I wore Barrett with a zip-fastener down the back.'[1] Fox was Bogarde's suggestion for the role and became Losey's choice 'at first sight' when he met him at the Connaught Hotel – again a totally precise background – 'dolled up to the nines,' as Fox later put it, unconsciously employing Tony's rather dated 'in' slang. ('Being American,' Bogarde said later, '(Joe) was rather uncertain and said, "Maybe the boy's a queer or something." I said, "He's not, he's rather effeminately British, we often are like that in this country, you know. You get used to it".'.) A screen test of Fox, which Losey himself paid for, later confirmed him as the ideal choice. Fox himself, though, was far from uncritical, viewing Tony as 'a little too stupid' and too much in the 'Oh, I say' public-school tradition he had already had to suffer when he played the well-bred young athlete who beat Tom Courtenay to the tape in *The Loneliness of the Long Distance Runner*. Reginald Mills the film's editor, was later quoted as saying that Fox's performance owed much, perhaps most, to Losey's creation. This is unfair. In the interaction of Fox and Bogarde one can see how the character's conventional aspects assume a pathetic unawareness of his own imminent decay and destruction. He suggests the flaccid, inert, charming stupidity of a class too long sustained by the efforts of his inferiors who have now grown actively resentful – not wholly malevolent, though, but ultimately a destroyer impelled by some kind of historical dialectic.

This is important; for Losey stated at the film's première that 'it is the story of Faust' and has never ceased to regret this over-

[1] *Isis, op. cit.*

simplification. For *The Servant* is not a simple allegory of good versus evil. Both men are the servants of their desires and if Tony is corrupted by the pandering to his comforts and lusts, then Barrett also is coarsened by the dissoluteness for which his master's weaknesses give him the opportunity. As Andrew Sarris summed it up, 'a fine house where everyone once knew his place has been converted into a seedy brothel where everyone now knows his vice – in short, Losey's vision of contemporary England.'[1] Philip Oakes related the film even more specifically to the aftermath of the political scandals that had occurred a few months before it reached the screen. 'What it suggests . . . is that indulgence is the chosen weapon by which all our masters (*vide* the Denning Report) can be relied on to commit *hara-kari*.'[2]

THE SPACE BETWEEN THE WORDS

It is commonplace to the point of banality for a house to symbolize the dissolution of society: but seldom has the deteriorating state of the English class system in 1963 been so well suggested as it is in Richard MacDonald's designs and Douglas Slocombe's photography. 'The furnished space,' Penelope Gilliatt wrote, 'is a take-over of power every bit as much as the master's evacuating personality.'[3] Losey decided that the house should have three overlapping moods reflected in the lighting and furnishing: at first it is an empty shell that becomes bright and smart, then it is gradually rotting away, and finally it is as garish and ambiguous as the odd 'happenings' staged in it. Losey used quite a bit of deep-focus photography, enabling shifts in the relationships to be recorded with great finesse and without the interruption of close-ups or out-of-focus shots. More than in any previous film, he also used long takes – some four minutes at a time – and while this technique gave Slocombe innumerable lighting problems, it enabled the 'logic' of the relationships to be maintained unbroken. Slocombe later credited Losey with leaving to him the patterns that the camera should make within the predetermined movements of the actors.

Of the way the lighting assisted the dialectic of the piece, he said, 'I shot the opening scenes in an overall grey tone that showed the bare bones of the building and its intrinsic coldness. Then we wanted to make things look exciting with new furniture, new belongings, so I shot it with a certain glossy contrast. Then, as the servant takes over, we wanted things to show meaningfully for their own sake, wanted to find sinister meanings in things that seemed merely pretty and inoffensive. I used the lighting to rub out a number of things that had to be forgotten, and bring forward new elements that had to be given sinister implications.'[1]

Pinter's response to Losey's fluid camera movement inside an enclosed situation throws interesting light on their working relationship in this and later films. 'His camera never becomes complacent, never says "I'm doing fine, I'm very happy where I am." Even when it is still, you feel it really wants to move, but it can't, it's trapped. A kind of anxiety which I find is always stimulating.'[2]

When he was asked what had drawn him to the film, Pinter replied in an odd phrase that it was 'the closeness' of the characters 'like a couple of crabs getting nearer and nearer to each other.' It is precisely in the later movements of this 'dance' to destruction, which begins with the re-engagement of Barrett by a lonely Tony, after he has sacked him, that Pinter impresses himself most characteristically on the film. It is the sublimated power struggle between the two men as they play games in which each tries to dominate the other while both draw physically closer. First, the bitchy stalemate of the crossword-puzzle-solving leading to the servant's explosive 'I'm a gentleman's gentleman and you're no gentleman.' Then the aggressive ball-game, in which Barrett gives Tony his first order ('Well, go and pour me a glass of brandy'), and clinches his dominance. Finally, the ambiguous hide-and-seek episode which culminates in Tony's fainting. The

[1] Roger Hudson, 'The Secret Profession,' interview with two lighting cameramen, *Sight and Sound* (Summer 1965), Vol. 34, No. 3, p.117.

[2] Harold Pinter interviewed by the author, Thames TV, 8 January, 1970.

role-playing is switched from sequence to sequence, so that sometimes Barrett and Tony are like nagging wife and shiftless husband, sometimes like barrack-room buddies, sometimes like a schoolyard bully and his trembling victim: there is a sense of regression that passes into decadence at the orgy. As Losey has indicated, these sequences belong to an earlier Pinter scenario and in their more deliberate 'confrontations' they have echoes of the controlled horror in his 'comedies of menace' which preceded *The Caretaker*; while the earlier sections of the screenplay, written in close association with Losey, tend to resemble *The Caretaker* in that the balance of power is triangular, two individuals constantly combining against one.

Losey had never before had to work so tightly within the disciplining limits of another man's 'frame.' Yet instead of confinement, *The Servant* signals his breakthrough to a freedom of expression that, just because it is controlled by underlying rhythms, as a sea is by its tides, never lets the unity of vision slip out of focus.

Pinter curbed Losey's tendencies to baroque romanticism: Losey amplified Pinter's economy by visual suggestiveness. It was the first film in which one sensed a two-way process of reduction and expansion. In none of his previous collaborators had Losey tapped such hidden harmonies of relationships. And the communication existing between a master and his servant is perfect for Pinter's purpose, since words are often used to conceal feelings and thus imply a world of unspoken deference and authority. Much has been written about Pinter's dialogue technique: but Losey's own estimate of its effectiveness deserves quoting in full. Issued with the synopsis at the Press show, it has curiously enough passed out of circulation: it has the generosity as well as precision of the man most indebted to Pinter:

'I strongly believe in the essentially visual language of the cinema,' Losey wrote in 1963, 'almost to the point of making the dictum that a good film should be intelligible even if no word of the original language is understood. This doesn't mean we should still be making silent pictures, nor does it minimise the importance of the writer, his words, or of sound and music. In fact, I find

increasingly that I as a director must usually make as much of a
fight for the kind of sound effects and the balance of sound, music
and words that I want, as for the image itself. In the case of *The
Servant*, the writer of the screenplay is Harold Pinter. It is his first
screenplay (its first draft preceded the screenplay of *The Caretaker*[1])
and . . . in spite of the fact that it is a first work in cinema, and
not his original work, the mark of Pinter is very strongly im-
printed on the whole film, not just its dialogue – and the dialogue
therefore becomes in this film far more important than dialogue
often is, even in films where there is much more of it. As you
might expect, Pinter's words are few, economical, exact – they
have their own rhythm, and he quickly appreciated that the
spoken word in films may have many different values and functions; sometimes it is the word itself: sometimes it is the scene
played out in full with a beginning, middle and end, almost as if
lifted from a theatre piece, but with images *between* speeches
playing as long and even longer than the words themselves.

'Pinter also appreciated the usefulness of the overheard inci-
dental lines of dialogue used as sound effects, of words which are
music and poetry and which help to determine the rhythm and
style of the picture. He understands, too, how often the human
creature uses words to block communication. Pinter himself says,
"The desire for verification is understandable, but cannot always
be satisfied. There are no hard distinctions between what is real
and what is unreal . . . Given characters who possess a momentum
of their own, my job is not to impose on them . . . by which I
mean forcing a character to speak where he could not speak . . .
making him speak of what he could never speak." With such
values at stake, the problem of translating and sub-titling becomes
enormously treacherous.[1] Sub-titles may obscure the images, or
distract from the rhythm. The pace of one language is never the

---

[1] The film version of Pinter's play was premiered in London on 12 March,
1964, after a long wait for a screening. See Chapter 12.

[2] When *The Go-Between* was presented at the Cannes Film Festival in 1971,
where it won the Palme d'Or, Pinter confessed to me he could hardly look
at the images, so great was his concern over the sub-titling.

same as another – nor is its length – and yet the exact word and exact rhythm is of primary importance.'[1]

I have thought it valuable to quote this statement at length because one is unlikely, at this date anyhow, to find a better first-hand account of how Pinter and Losey work together. Very shortly afterwards both grew increasingly reticent about discussing their 'collaboration'. A screenplay of theirs is a telepathic meeting of minds as well as crafts, and neither has worked separately in the cinema with such fulfilment as is represented by their three screenplays to date, *The Servant*, *Accident* and *The Go-Between*: three films that deal strongly in portents, evasions and silences and all illustrate perfectly John Russell Taylor's percep-tive definition of Pinter's 'musical orchestration' as 'a tightly knit and intricate texture of which the "naturalistic" words being spoken at any given moment are only the top line, supported by elusive and intricate harmonies . . .'[2]

Only where the film became over-explicit in relation to what had gone before did the critics, generally, find it unacceptable: this was the final scene of the orgy. Losey possibly meant to alienate the audience from any sentimental pity for the characters and to make the scene so unendurable that there would be no cosiness to offer a refuge to those who were predisposed to 'identify' with some part of the characters' fate. But two things rarely work on the cinema screen, however successful they are in theory: one is the technique of alienation which the hypnotic nature of the film experience resists, and the other is the difficulty of communicating depravity in physical terms, even though Losey deliberately arranged a very English type of orgy in which really nothing takes place. The upshot was that instead of being a coda, the last sequence in the film feels like overload. Various

[2] But it is worth noting, lest too oracular an impression be created, the down-to-earth comment of Reginald Mills, who edited *The Servant*, and, unimpressed by Losey's 'theoretical remarks', was quoted by *Isis* in almost heretical tones: '(Pinter) repeats everything about six times – he should write the libretto for an opera – think what he could do with "I love you" . . . I cut out a lot of his lines and I'm sure he never knew; it just meant one repetition less.' *Isis, op. cit.*

[1] John Russell Taylor, *op. cit.*, p. 358.

critics, of course, saw various meanings in *The Servant*. 'The parable of a man and his *alter ego*' (Richard Roud, *The Guardian*); 'Is it, by implication, a study of homosexuality?' (Eric Rhode, the *Listener*); 'a film about possession, not merely who owns what, but who owns who' (Philip Oakes, *The Sunday Telegraph*); 'an all-out attack on Britain's caste system' (*Time*).[1] But so far from creating a case for an explicit final sequence, such diversity of opinions is proof of the metaphor's success in containing many meanings, to a much richer degree than any previous Losey film. 'The truth which *The Servant* conveys,' James Leahy writes, 'is the truth which results from the dialectic between the movie and the individual members of the audience; the only clarity of vision that it expresses is the clarity of vision of the individual spectator which may result from his viewing the movie.'[2]

After *The Servant* had been finished and was awaiting screening, there were very few people in the film industry who saw it as an 'audience picture.' Losey had the sweet satisfaction of saying, some months after its opening, 'they've been wrong, this majority of people in the distributor set-up and the producer set-up, at every point they've been wrong about how the picture would be received by audiences, about the kind of business it would do . . . I'm sure the next step is they will want other people to make them remakes of *The Servant*.'[3]

In an odd way it was Losey himself who came nearest to a re-make of *The Servant* with his next film, *King and Country* (3 December, 1964); for although the milieu was far removed in place and time – from a Chelsea house with an eighteenth-century façade to the rain and ankle-deep mud of the front in World War One – in it Losey was again essentially examining the disparity between what society believes itself to be and what it actually is. Like *The Servant*, it is again about a peasant's revolt, though this time the gentleman wins. Based on a television play called *Hamp*, it was made for a company, British Home Entertainment, that saw the possibility of making films for theatrical and also tele-

[1] To which one could add, 'This is a film about two men' (Harold Pinter).
[2] James Leahy, *op. cit.*, p. 133.
[3] *Isis, op. cit.*

vision release and, as Losey said, it had to be made for a particular budget or not at all. It had Bogarde as the officer at a court-martial who puts up the best show he can in defence of a private soldier, played by Tom Courtenay, who has been stricken by a fatal moment of sanity amidst all the madness of war, so that he quite simply and totally trustingly starts to walk home, only to be pulled up sharp by a trial and execution. No one must break the rules: those who do must die. The gentleman, too, has his rules, his code, which permit him to sympathize theoretically and legally, yet in the end force him to stick a gun in the dying Hamp's mouth and finish him off 'painlessly,' in the way he might finish off a horse that's fallen in a hunt and broken its leg. The ethics of those who ride to hounds are the same as those who ride to war: the master's code overcomes temporary embarrassments occasioned by his servant's incompetence. At the moment the bullet is fired, Losey has said, the gentleman dies, too: but it was not a coda that became generally accepted, or even perceived in these terms. 'What I was really thinking of when I did *King and Country*,' Losey said to an interviewer, 'was the terrible situation every human being is locked in, and progressively so in this century.'[1] Of course, some 'traps' are more easily borne than others: those of birth, affluence and insulating hypocrisy. Hamp's body goes to the lime-pit; the soul of the gent goes marching on.

Whatever its limitation – the film was a mere eighty-six minutes and necessarily confined to a composite set – *King and Country* revealed how well Losey without Pinter had learnt to fill in the society attitudes he had formerly improvised out of his not altogether congruent Hollywood experience. Pinter had given him a social sounding-board, in the way that Richard MacDonald continued to put his drawing-board at his disposal, to test out his feelings about society, the contradictions one has to resolve and be a rebel or embrace and be a hypocrite. It couldn't be said that Losey, with *The Servant*, had ceased to be an 'outsider,' but he was now a foreigner with an understanding of his adopted society

[1] Tom Milne, *op. cit.*, p. 125.

fully developed and able to fix a state of change in one vivid entity. Having taken the measure of the social climate, he had now, with Pinter's assistance, learned to gauge that even more indigenous characteristic of the English people indoors – the room-temperature.

Chapter Eleven: Running, Jumping, Never Standing Still

I'd spent my early life working in television in the United States, and I felt that there was a great possibility that I would be a has-been at twenty-two; so I thought that before this happened I'd escape and see whether the rest of the world existed. There was a general feeling, I think, at that time in America that the earth was flat, and once you went east you'd fall off the edge of the world.

Dick Lester to author, Thames Television, 24 September, 1969

'One doesn't expect novelty in a film called *It's Trad, Dad!*' I wrote in 1962. 'One hardly even expects a story when twenty-five numbers are packed into seventy-three minutes. But Helen Shapiro's first film is more than a piece of high-density syncopation. All kinds of unexpected hip, flip and far-out tricks are played by the director, Dick Lester, with the story of a pompous mayor who bans pop music in a new town – then has to reckon with an invasion of disc jockeys and artistes battling for the right to 'swing' their way . . . A door marked 'Music Department' in a TV studio conceals musicians stacked up on shelves. The mayor's chauffeur breaks a flag over the limousine every time His Worship steps aboard. A man pruning tropical foliage in an espresso bar casually uses his trimmers and greenfly spray on the lettuce sandwiches. Characters talk back to the narrator, action stops, accelerates, runs backwards . . .'[1]

What we were witnessing in this quickie about rock music was the advent of one of the most successful new talents of the decade. In it were influences I did not have the space to spell out then – the op and pop art-work, for instance, borrowed from the ad-men's graphics, even from the screenprint 'dots' of Lichtenstein's strip cartoons which Lester duplicated by the simple means of putting wire mesh in front of the camera and photographing Acker Bilk's band through it. And there were so many sight-gags piled prodigally two on top of each other that one hardly had time

---

[1] *Evening Standard*, 29 March, 1962. The film's title in the United States was *Ring-a-Ding Rhythm*.

to catalogue more than the most strikingly surrealist ones. A second viewing of *It's Trad, Dad!* nearly a decade later confirms its innovatory thrust – now with the bonus that familiarity with its director and the whole visual explosion of the years between enables one to locate the influences with the jubilant eye of a pinball player totting up the winking score. *It's Trad, Dad!* was the first feature film that successfully made the presentation techniques of television commercials and the pop shows on the small screen designed for the teenage and sub-teenage audiences into an integral part of its jokey structure. The words 'trad' and 'Dad' in the title had the flip, mocking emphasis of a generation growing more aggressively conscious almost daily of their own identity and creating heroes who were certainly not those of their fathers. Lester said later, 'I prefer the social attitudes of the young people to the disapproval of their parents . . . If you deal with a subject, you have to take sides somewhere, so I've chosen the side I have most sympathy for and therefore I suppose it could be called anarchy, because it is a youth revolution. But it isn't a conscious attitude – it's not irony in the political sense.'[1]

As George Melly, jazz singer and critic, pointed out in *Revolt into Style*, producers and directors working in television, being younger than those who worked in the cinema industry, had brought to the presentation of pop shows a new ingredient – speed. And speed was built into the television commercials on the ITV network as well as into the once-weekly big spot on BBC TV, the early evening mix of jazz, skiffle, rock and trad called *6.5 Special*. The producer, Jack Good, who later created shows like *Wham!* and *Oh Boy!* for the commercial channel, did more than anyone else to invent the pop style on the box in which pop personalities were marketed with the same ingenuity as the goods in the commercials. *It's Trad, Dad!* moved at the speed of the hard-sell merchandizing. From Good's pioneering ventures, Lester undoubtedly borrowed a lot of the expectations of his audience, as well as some of the television man's techniques; but he also reached back beyond the electronic innovations to the

[1] Dick Lester, quoted by Philip French in *Movie* (Autumn 1965), No. 14, p. 9.

inconsequential humour of English literary tradition, the surrealist movement in modern art, and the whole contemporary manifestation of zaniness incorporated in the free-form cameraderie of the Goons, whose stars, Peter Sellers, Spike Milligan, Harry Secombe *et al.*, had made the transition from radio to television without losing their subversive zeal. Into all these phenomena, ancient and modern, Dick Lester was supremely well equipped to plug himself. No film-maker in this decade appeared more punctually when his hour struck; and for a long time he succeeded marvellously in synchronising himself to its every trend and eruption.

Born in the early 1930s in Philadelphia, he apparently possessed a precocious mental agility – he learned to read at the age of three and later quipped, 'My mother fed me a bit of royal jelly' – taught himself to play and compose music when he was no more than twelve. Music, more than his studies in clinical psychology, he credits with influencing his film-making. A director sufficiently well versed in musical technique to supervise this side of his films is a rarity. But testimony to Lester's capacities has come from such an authority as John Barry, the composer of some of the age's most identifiable call-signs, who noted how Lester 'knew the whole line of the score, starting it off in a very hard, austere way and winding up the movie in a complete Hollywood attitude to romanticism – the development from this to that was essentially his concept. And it is incredibly helpful in viewing a picture of such complex design that he knows how to be specific: it's a very strong leader for a composer.'[1] The rhythms of all Lester's films reveal how sharply cocked he keeps his musical ear: and this talent certainly gave him quicker and more empathetic access to the pop scene than another, less musically inclined film-maker might have had when he met the Beatles; while the latter, for their part, were at the point in their career when they had ceased being 'grateful' and had become touchily intolerant to 'insensitive' vibrations around them. ('At least,' said Lester, not entirely facetiously, 'if we found a time when we couldn't bear to talk to

---

[1] John Barry interviewed by the author, 9 October, 1969. He was referring to Lester's film *Petulia* (1968), for which he composed the score.

each other, I could always sit down and play the piano and they could make jokes about it.'[1])

Another thing that the competitive business of early television work drilled into Lester was a severe sense of timing. Television's most exacting influence on its programme-makers is to make them aware of time passing not in days or weeks, as in the lengthy schedules of film-making in a studio or on location, but in seconds and minutes. Lester was a stage-hand in the television studios in the early 1950s, when it took a sharp talent to nip through the crowded avenues of promotion to floor manager, assistant director and finally fully-fledged director; and one of the keeping-in-trim techniques he and his fellow-workers practised was 'to give ourselves a particular time, say fifty-five seconds, and, at a given instruction, we would all engage in normal conversation until someone decided fifty-five seconds was up – and check it against the stop-clock. We'd practise it till it became second nature and we were able, subliminally as it were, to guess at any particular time-span very accurately.' Again, Lester's working metabolism both conditioned and matched the reaction speeds of young audiences increasingly accustomed to the fifty-second commercials bombarding them with quick cuts and rapidly delivered messages.

One other feature of American television at this time favoured Lester's own quirky vision of a life in which people and things transposed themselves into other states and conditions by some event that dislocated one's normal expectations. Videotape was not then in common use by television directors; many programmes went out live 'and anything that went wrong was on the air, on the screen, and nobody could do anything to cover up the mistake. I did about fifteen shows a week and lots of strange surrealistic effects were always happening – like the dog that went mad in the studio and ripped down the set, revealing another one behind it, so that our actors who were in eighteenth-century costumes suddenly found themselves part of a 1944 prisoner-of-

[1] Dick Lester interviewed by the author for Thames Television, 24 September, 1969. Unless stated otherwise, all subsequent quotations from Lester come from the same source.

war camp. Live television was the best medium ever devised for creating surrealistic effects – and I think the accidental, documentary quality of such "happenings" is what I try to reproduce in films.' Live television also made it essential to employ as many cameras as a programme could afford to have; and this practice, too, Lester continued, using two and even three cameras – and not simply for the musical numbers. The plethora of choice he thus gained was bound to add to the staccato rhythm he preferred to work in. (It was also a gratefully acknowledged means of masking mistakes!)

When Lester arrived in England in the mid-1950s, by way of supporting himself through Europe with jazz piano-playing and freelance journalism, he found a market – a goldmine – in the making for his talent: the newly-fledged commercial television network needed all the food that the advertising agencies could ferry to it, like a mother bird and its young, and Lester was employed on making commercials, which gave him the chance to learn about film, something his experience in live television had ironically deprived him of experiencing. In time he worked his way into the programmes, creating the style of comedy shows like *Idiot's Weekly*, *A Show Called Fred*, and *The Dick Lester Show*, which ran for one performance only, but caught Peter Sellers's eye and led directly to doing the Goon Shows.

Lester and the Goons took an instantaneous liking to each other and this persisted so closely that it is virtually impossible to say who influenced whom the more. They had a common meeting-ground in their relish for the logic of the absurd, the apparently accidental association of words and images which overlapped in the audience's consciousness, dislocating its expectations and forcing it to respond, to 'fight back' in Lester's words, with gratified and reassuring laughter. Absolutely no pause for breath was allowed. The chain explosions of Lester's style echoed the manic rhythm of the Goons and could only have worked with a team who knew each other so intimately that communication was almost telepathic, and even improvisation was welcomed as a spur to ever wilder combinations and associations.

Lester found a special sympathy with some of the Goons –

H

Spike Milligan in particular – in the affectionate mockery of militarism and past imperial greatness. In part this was nostalgia for the war-time closeness of a common cause which had temporarily seemed to sink class differences; but it was also sharp sniping at the class attitudes which had surfaced again once Civvy Street and mufti reasserted themselves. The Goons aped and mimicked the officer class to perfection; and from this 'other ranks' attitude of satirical subversion Lester took the tone of his own anti-war protests in some of his later films. The cross-fertilization of talent that ensued would baffle anyone in search of specific origins: it would be like trying to trace a bee's flight back to a particular pollen head from the 'evidence' it had accumulated *en route*. But the potent forces at work were apparent when *The Running, Jumping and Standing Still Film* was made in 1959. It was completed in a day and a half for £70. The half-day's work on it was ascribed to Peter Sellers, who had shot 'a bit of footage' with his own 16mm. zoom Bolex, which he showed after dinner at Lester's one evening and which resulted in the available Goons, along with props 'borrowed' from Granada Television, whose prop-master was Bruce Lacey, another joker on the Goons' wavelength, using the daylight hours and the first field their van stopped at to finish off the reel. Topping and tailing the takes, 'like French beans,' took two hours, and the film, with a music track composed by Lester, ran for all of eleven minutes – 'every shot we did is in the finished film.' The shared enjoyment and professional *rapport* are tangible elements in the film. But it is an excellent catalogue of every tool that Lester had by then assembled in his comedy kit: the telegraphic funniness of the silent-movie techniques, the surrealist gags like the scrubbing brush used on the grass, the inverted logic of racing round a stationary phonograph disc with a needle, the ramshackle nationalism of the box-kite decorated with Union Jacks as Britain's entry in the space race, and the famous subversive booby-trap of the hand that beckons a distant figure nearer and nearer till he is within reach of the boxing-glove on the hand outside the frame.

'Having made this and done quite well,' Lester later recalled, 'I said I would like to concentrate on film work. And everyone that saw it thought it was very funny and producers thought: "Whenever we want a large version of *The Running, Jumping and Standing Still Film*, we'll certainly let you know".[1]

Lester filled in the time – two years – with advertising films and a television pilot for a jazz programme until on the strength of these he was offered *It's Trad, Dad!* produced by Milton Subotsky for Columbia's British set-up. The chance to make a feature film, plus the confidence he had in handling pop musicians, decided Lester's acceptance: economy dictated his approach. He once referred to a television thriller series, *Mark Sabre*, some of whose episodes he had shared with Joseph Losey in 1957 (when the latter, still blacklisted, had to use a pseudonym) and he related how the economy-minded producers of that show almost required the sets to be designed so that an Adam fireplace could be stood upside down and become an Arab doorway. *It's Trad, Dad!* was constructed on similar lines. Shot in three weeks for £50,000 – it took £300,000 in Britain alone – its script was a twenty-two-page story outline and, within the space of its seventy-three minutes, opportunities to do things highly characteristic of themselves had to be created for fifteen soloists and groups: in all there were twenty-six numbers. It was more an invoice than an artistic entity.

Two weeks were taken up by the numbers alone. 'Every day three groups of singers would come into the studios and I would attack them with three cameras and they would go out gasping and the next ones were brought in – we devised a set that would turn upside down and inside out.' Speed, improvisation, a magpie attitude to any eye-catching effect he could pull out of the contemporary consciousness of op or pop: the intention made so exuberantly apparent by *It's Trad, Dad!* was, in George Melly's words, 'to make the maximum impact *now*, to hold the moment, freeze it, show it and let it melt.'[2] It was a perfect way of gratifying the needs of the 'novelty generation' who saw their fantasies projected with the sharp impermanence of a thousand lantern

---

[1] Dick Lester interviewed by Ian Cameron and Mark Shivas, *Movie*, No. 16, p. 18.

[2] George Melly, *Revolt into Style* (Allen Lane, The Penguin Press, 1970), p. 167.

slides – *click! click! click!* Never a second's hesitation, lest bore-
dom set in, but always passing on to the next excitement.

Soon, though, Lester was to be caught up in a process that was
considerably more ambitious, altogether more significant – one
designed not to let it melt, but to make it last. And in this a fellow
American played an essential part.

'THE BEATLES – WHO ARE THEY?'

Walter Shenson was an excellent partner for Lester. Like him, he
had come out of the advertising and publicity side of films. He
had a disenchanted sense of humour, a cynical relish of the
absurdities of the business, a quirky approachableness, a swiftness
in seeing the possibilities latent in a project, an obvious enjoyment
of the continuous crisis of film production, a fatalistic belief that,
though the worst was always certain, it would maybe happen
tomorrow, not today. In the 1950s, before he came to Britain, he
had worked in the publicity department of Columbia Pictures,
one of his responsibilities being to vet the movies and trailers that
Columbia made abroad, especially the ones financed by the
company's British office, and purge them of any 'Anglicisms' that
might be baffling to an American audience. A buzz from Shenson
in the screening-room signified that he had heard a line of
dialogue or glimpsed something that fell strangely on American
sensibilities, and the projectionist would insert a piece of paper
in the unwinding reel so that the discrepancy could be traced
back, threshed out and (hopefully) put right later. Shenson also
advised on how the British-made trailers could be adapted for
American theatres: it wasn't deemed to be a drawback if some
film-goers took away the impression that the forthcoming films
were Hollywood product that for some reason or other had been
made on location abroad. With a few exceptions, this was fairly
standard Hollywood practice at the time.

In recent years agents and publicists, who see at first hand the
way films are put together and have developed an expertise from
the inside, as it were, have tended to turn more and more into
producers or 'packagers' of films: it is a trend that will be

examined more fully in due course, for one of the most striking things about American production in Britain in the 1960s is the number of agents who ended up as production chiefs. So it is not surprising that Shenson had a script in his desk drawer and approached Harry Cohn, Columbia's dreaded president and production chief, with the proposition that he put some of the company's money into producing it. Shenson dramatizes events that happen to him with wit and fluency when recalling them – as in this case. Cohn: Have you worked on the script yourself? – Shenson (cannily): Only at nights and week-ends. – Cohn: Have you put any money of your own into it? – Shenson: Yes. – Cohn: You lost your money. Get back to your job. – Shenson: I want to make this film, Mr Cohn. – Cohn: Would you be ready to resign to do so? – Shenson: Yes. – Cohn: Good luck. You just lost your job.[1]

The result was that Walter Shenson moved himself and his family to England, got finance and made the script into the film *The Mouse that Roared* (1959), an Ealing-type satire of power politics in which the inhabitants of a mythical Grand Duchy successfully invaded the United States under the command of Peter Sellers, who took several other roles in the film, including that of the Grand Duchess. A 'typical little English film,' modestly rated in its home country, *The Mouse that Roared* made a fortune in America, was for long the biggest moneymaker in proportion to its cost of any Peter Sellers film (and may still be), and convinced Shenson that, contrary to all his last job should have taught him, a British movie need not speak with an American accent for it to be a hit across the Atlantic. Later on he would insist that it might even be allowed to speak with the accent of provincial Liverpool without damaging its American chances. This is more important than might at first appear: for when Shenson came to produce *A Hard Day's Night* in 1963 the Beatles cult had not then reached America and a less resolute producer, whose confidence in local accents hadn't been boosted by a

[1] Walter Shenson interviewed by the author, 14 January, 1971. Unless stated otherwise, all subsequent quotations from Shenson come from the same source.

fortune at the international box-office, might have yielded to pressure to give the film an American slant.

When Shenson planned a sequel to *The Mouse that Roared*, to be called *The Mouse on the Moon* (1963), he turned to Peter Sellers again; but Sellers, then at the start of his immense critical and public popularity, had no taste for repeating a past success and was kicking and stretching his way into the skins of new characters. But he broke the news gently by suggesting a director who could get the kind of results that he (Sellers) was rightly famed for. 'He has a big talent,' he told Shenson. 'I could see that even with people who couldn't act, he had their faces turned away from the camera.' He meant, of course, Dick Lester.

All that need concern us about *The Mouse on the Moon*, apart from its box-office success and its commendable economy in using the sets built at Pinewood for Cornel Wilde's historical pageant *Lancelot and Guinevere*, is that it gave Shenson and Lester the experience of a compatible partnership, not necessarily a common outcome of film-making, and one that was to be vital in their next project.

As Shenson tells it, he was in Los Angeles at the end of the summer in 1963 when George H. Ornstein, European production chief for United Artists, who was in the same city, called him and said he had to see him urgently. They met a few hours later and Ornstein immediately asked, 'Would you produce a film that United Artists want done?' – 'What's the subject?' – 'The Beatles.' – 'The Beatles, who are they?' – 'Four boys with a guitar.' – 'I don't think I'm interested.' Ornstein then said, 'Would you do it as a favour to me? Our records division want to get the album to distribute in the States and what we lose on the film we'll get back on the discs. Just say "Yes" so that I can get on to New York and tell them.' Reluctantly, Shenson said yes, and was told, 'Take some money, about £800, and develop a script as quickly as possible.'

Thus George H. Ornstein was about to deliver the third of the three most remarkable films produced under his aegis in Britain; but being a resolutely frank man, he certainly would not have claimed to know it at the time. He was riding high in London, though not so high as he would be when *A Hard Day's Night* was premièred on 6 July, 1964. The box-office receipts for *Dr No* were coming in nicely, but the huge potential of the Bond series would not really show itself, like a mountain in avalanche revealing the gold seams, until the film's almost continuous re-release and *From Russia, with Love*, premièred on 10 October, 1963, revealed the phenomenal public taste for it. *Tom Jones* would be an instantaneous hit, but it had only opened at the time when Ornstein put the Beatles proposition to Shenson in that summer of 1963.

The Beatles film had actually begun in United Artists' music department in London, which Ornstein had discovered was rarely brought into film discussions in advance of production – 'which was wasteful, since music was an important source of revenue.' Its departmental head was invited accordingly to sit in on the *Dr No* conferences and came up with ideas that won approval, tending to replace original thoughts about Jamaican music with something more in the 1960s idiom; so that when he suggested that United Artists should do a British musical, Ornstein listened. Tommy Steele and Cliff Richard were then the indigenous idols, both with successful films behind them; but what was laid on Ornstein's desk early in 1963 was the sleeve of the first LP, entitled *Please Please Me*, cut by a new group called the Beatles from Liverpool in the north of England. Issued in mid-January, it had climbed to the number-one position by mid-February, notching up sales in excess of 150,000 – the highest previous sale of an Elvis Presley LP was 250,000 for his *Blue Hawaii* album in 1960. Ornstein decided to 'make something inexpensive' with the Beatles; but his intention lagged behind his decision until he heard that the *Daily Mirror* newspaper had had to print a million extra copies of one of its issues containing a centre spread devoted to the Beatles after they produced their fourth single, *She Loves You*, in August. Ornstein met the Beatles' manager, Brian Epstein, one evening at 9 p.m., and by midnight, contrary to the strict United Artists rule that no one but Picker, Krim and Benjamin should 'commit' the company to any expenditure, he had made a deal for a film with options on three others with escalating scales of pay and percentages. Epstein asked for 7½ per cent of the net on the first picture, plus £20,000. Ornstein shook hands – and knew he was in trouble as far as United Artists were concerned. He now had to inform his bosses. At that time United Artists was deep in *Mr Moses* and *Khartoum*, two spectaculars carrying high hopes and a lot of money, and Ornstein figured that New York's imagination wasn't likely to be set on fire by the announcement of a pop musical involving four boys barely known inside Britain except to fans and the disc industry, and not at all known outside the country. Hence his request to Shenson to do the film 'as a favour' and his suggestion of a mere £800 to develop a screen treatment. 'If I'd asked the company for any *real* money,' he said later, 'I'd have been thrown out of the window and been out of a job by the time I hit the ground.'

He assembled as much publicity as he could on the Beatles – it wasn't much, for the only serious notice taken of the Beatles for the first six months of 1963, outside the music industry Press, had been an article by Maureen Cleave in the London *Evening Standard*. 'The simple explanation,' wrote Hunter Davies, explaining this lack of publicity in his authorised biography of the group, 'is that as (Beatlemania) had never happened before in Britain, the British Press had no way of recognising it. They had to wait until it jumped out and hit them over the head.'[1] However, Ornstein sent what he could collect to David Picker in New York, remembering that David had graduated from the company's music department, but still thinking it prudent not to mention that he had 'committed' for four films. David Picker liked the idea: so did United Artists' music department chief, who felt that his own status was enhanced by the company producing a musical, then a fairly rare genre, owing to the escalating costs; and when Arnold Picker's first query – 'How much is the outlay so far?' – had been reassuringly answered by a mere £800, the project was agreed.

The pace now picked up – how fast may be judged from Ornstein's first act after the green light had been given. He re-

[1] Hunter Davies, *The Beatles* (Heinemann, 1968), p. 184.

negotiated the deal with Epstein, raising it to 20 per cent of the net and £25,000 cash. He also limited it to three pictures. It was well that he satisfied early on the naturally suspicious mind of Brian Epstein about the probity of the film company to which he was now about to entrust his precious Beatles; for, in Ornstein's words, from this moment on 'the scene exploded.'

FOUR BALLS OF MERCURY

Beatlemania didn't break out till October 1963. On two tours, in February and June 1963, the Beatles had actually played second fiddle to Helen Shapiro and Roy Orbison, though the fans' reactions, the hailstorm of emblematic jelly-baby sweets tossed on to the stage and the soaring success of their discs all presaged the phenomenon unleashed when they topped the bill at the London Palladium on 13 October, 1963, were televised to fifteen million viewers and pulled thousands of fans on to the streets outside the theatre, setting up a continuous screaming sound like the moment of mass extermination in a pig factory – the tribal sound of the early 1960s. On 11 November, 1963, an estimated twenty-six million viewers saw the television recording of their appearance at the Royal Variety Show a week earlier; and from then on there were daily convulsions of Beatlemania, reported with a regularity that swiftly became monotonous. Hectic moves were made to merchandise the phenomenon into its hard-cash equivalent in Beatle wigs, suits and sweaters. Opinion quickly polarized into those who reviled the mass hysteria as a dangerous symptom of unbridled youth and others who delved solemnly into its meaning, finding the guitar to be a potency symbol and the group a conditioning factor in the orgasmic emotions that many teenage girls reported experiencing. As for the Beatles, they were still amenable to discipline, though Epstein noted signs of incipient rebellion. 'I have an uneasy feeling that every time they get a big hand, they return the compliment with two fingers.'[1]

When Shenson arrived back in Britain, everything the Beatles

---

[1] Brian Epstein quoted by David Bailey and Peter Evans in *Goodbye Baby and Amen* (Condé-Nast/Collins, 1969), p. 73.

did was a headline and Ornstein was in a state of mixed excitement and anxiety to have the deal he had set up blessed by the Beatles. 'Don't let them get away,' he urged Shenson, sending him in alone to do the negotiating because he figured, correctly, the boys would respond to someone dealing with them on an intimate basis, rather than to the distant moneymen. Shenson knew Lester was as eager as he was: he had called him on his return and the two had met at the Hilton coffee-shop just outside Shenson's Hertford Street offices. 'I might be able to do a film with the Beatles,' Shenson said tentatively. By then there was no doubt in anyone's mind about what *that* meant or who *they* were. 'Dick jumped up and said, "I'd love to direct them".' But at the first meeting Shenson sought, only Epstein turned up: his Famous Four he said, with a tinge of helplessness, were off watching Gerry and the Pacemakers recording. Jumping in a cab with Epstein, the harassed Shenson, feeling a fortune ebbing through his fingers, just managed to pick up the Beatles at their rented apartment and all six – a couple more than the maximum number of passengers a London cab was licensed to carry – pushed on to the recording studios. It was actually from the physical discomfort of the overcrowded cab, intensified by worry lest he lose the deal, that Shenson suddenly conceived the shape that the film later to be called *A Hard Day's Night* would take. Though it would gain an imaginative complexity from the inventiveness which Alun Owen and Dick Lester brought to it – never mind the Beatles' contribution – the film never lost this early, brutally simple concept of being about four boys who were in captivity, physically imprisoned by their fans, and resorting to all kinds of strategies to evade the consequences of their celebrity.

Along with their current confinement, what struck Shenson was their restlessness, in itself a response to their frustrating celebrity. 'Every time the cab stopped in traffic, one or more of them would dash out and buy a newspaper, open it to see if they were featured in it, and once inside the recording studio they were like mercury – it took an hour to run them together into one room. I told them "I don't want to make a Hollywood style pop musical about four unknown Liverpool boys who smuggle the tapes of their home-made compositions into the disc jockey's studio. I want to make a broad comedy based on a day in your life." To my immense relief, they all said, "Gear! you're the producer, who's the director?" – "I'm thinking of Dick Lester." – "What's he done?" – "He did *The Running, Jumping and Standing Still Film.*" – "Gear!" So Dick was in. Of course, I didn't say Dick had directed *It's Trad, Dad!* – for the Beatles, that would have been all wrong.'

Thus from the start Shenson showed the care and tact he would continue to bestow on the four-headed *monstre sacré* whose ring-master he had been appointed.

At first United Artists talked in terms of a £150,000 budget. This was realistic for a pop group whose fame was localized inside Britain, who could be relied on to have hoisted themselves up the record charts by the time of the film's release, and to keep (or be kept) there while the film went the rounds in a quick play-off. England, Germany, Scandinavia and the Commonwealth: these were the territories Ornstein had in mind to recoup the cost plus a profit: he frankly confessed that what the film would lose in America could be made up on the sale of discs there. But once Beatlemania broke out, he knew he had a much more lucrative deal; and when the Beatles gave their Carnegie Hall concert at the start of 1964, followed by two television appearances on the Ed Sullivan Show, he was aware that United Artists possessed one of the most potentially profitable deals it had made in recent years. It is greatly to his credit – to that of everyone with a say-so in the film – that he resisted the temptation (and the pressures) to inflate the budget in keeping with the new importance of the project. In one way the growing concern lest the Beatles become 'over-exposed' assisted this. For the film had to be made quickly – a première date was set in July 1964, well before shooting began in March. There was also a limit to what an 'unlimited' budget could usefully do for the *ciné-verité* style that Lester and Shenson had decided on. More money simply meant more material – which meant more time would be consumed in editing it.

Lester's television background made him welcome the kind of improvisation of location that might have unnerved a studio-bred-and-bound director. He saw the chance, from very early on, to show the Beatles against the contemporary social revolution in art, architecture, clothes, language, and class which they had in part helped create. 'I was aware when we were filming it that they were producing an effect on the entire population of Britain, for better or worse, which badly needed to be documented. I think they were the first to give a confidence to the youth of the country which led to the disappearance of the Angry Young Men with a defensive mien. The Beatles sent the class thing sky high: they laughed it out of existence and, I think, introduced a tone of equality more successfully than any other single factor that I know.' Something else helped Lester's desire to make more than just a pop musical: the apprehension that Beatlemania might subside as rapidly as it had blown up. After all, why should *they* be immune to the built-in obsolescence of the pop industry? From the first, therefore, it was deliberately intended to use the film to extend the Beatles' popularity – and hence their longevity – with a maturer audience than the one which had responded to the aphrodisiac sing-song of *Yeh, Yeh!* This concern increased while filming went ahead and the Beatles' pop rating was knocked by the discs of other groups which replaced them in the record charts, however briefly, and by the backlash of Press cynicism and even hatred for the phenomenon which publicity had helped to promote and which was now monopolizing so much of the news and features pages. (The attention-span of readers, it is sometimes forgotten, is matched by the patience-span of newspaper editors: both tend to react against what has grown over-familiar; then, if it survives, to bear it resignedly before it transforms itself into other novel and interest-worthy mutations.) The sexual jealousy that the group's much photographed girl-friends aroused in their fans became worrysome; previously the Beatles' girl-friends, where they had been visible at all, received only vaguely directed feelings of curiosity from the fans. Then the Beatles' cohesive image was loosened for the first time when, with filming over, they separated for their free-wheeling holidays. Finally, the film-makers knew that fans grow older and the twelve-year-olds of last winter might not find the Beatles pubescently exciting next summer.

'For survival's sake,' I wrote at the time, 'the Beatles film had better make some appeal to adult audiences.'[1] George Melly shared this feeling. 'I was certain that once their sexual charisma had burnt itself out, they would join, as the other talented products of pop had joined before them, the ranks of traditional show business . . . I'd heard of course that the Beatles were making a film, but this was in itself no revolutionary departure. (Tommy) Steele too had made films and they had, if anything, accelerated his propulsion into the mum-and-kids belt. What I hadn't catered for was Alun Owen's script.'[2]

Getting Alun Owen to script the film was the first important move to have the Beatles taken seriously. Owen had acted with Dick Lester in television: he was the other half of the two-man ad-lib *Dick Lester Show* which had had its single night of glory in the 1950s. He was also a *persona grata* with the Beatles, who wanted a writer with no barriers between him and them, and readily approved the half-Irish, half-Welsh playwright who aroused the same affability around him as they did and had the blessing of a Merseyside upbringing in a family 'just down the road' from Paul McCartney's. He was the perfect choice to turn pop into art. He viewed the Beatles as an insider; he was paternal towards them without seeming so – a Big Brother, if not a Big Daddy. From his own observation, he had reached the same view of them as Shenson had – physical prisoners of success. 'One thing I'm putting into the script, if I die for it,' he said at the time. 'Ever noticed how much celebrities are pushed around in public? Really pushed around? Managers guiding them, fans pulling at them, compères patting them. You get to feel so much moveable property. What it *feels* like to be a Beatle: that's the first priority.'[3] The second was not to have any story as such. 'The usual one's the rags-to-riches plot: but who'd stand for the boys playing character roles, like hard-up Beatles? They'll play their famous selves, established right at the start with dozens, scores, hundreds

[1] *Evening Standard*, 19 June, 1964.
[2] George Melly, *op. cit.*, pp. 72–3.
[3] Alun Owen interviewed by the author, 11 March 1964. Unless stated otherwise, all subsequent quotations from Owen come from the same source.

of fans chasing the boys. A street riot almost. If anyone, anywhere, hasn't heard of the Beatles, they'll be hard put to it not to get a hint that the four boys must be fairly well known. The form of the film is "a day in the life of . . ." We pick them up on a train, off to keep an engagement, show the larks they get up to *en route*, in a hotel, a gambling club, all over town, in a television studio – finally they blast off by helicopter to another date. What Shenson and I want to avoid is a "slick" movie: a rough-cast look is the aim, a documentary feel. This may seem apostasy, but I want a film that can stand on its own io *without* the Beatles.' Ornstein confessed he 'fell in love' with the first draft (which was fortunate, for the screenplay had to be ready in five weeks) and only challenged one sequence which he felt inappropriate. It showed Ringo in a second-hand clothing store, chatting to a 'typical Jewish' proprietor, going behind the counter and selling a top hat and cutaway coat to East Indian sailors, making them, in Ornstein's opinion, 'look stupid niggers.' As a replacement for a scene that wouldn't obviously have had the same racial explosiveness in Merseyside as it might in Harlem, Owen wrote one of the best sequences in the film – the encounter between Ringo, playing truant from the group, and the school-kids also playing truant from the classroom. Owen shrewdly constructed most of the dialogue so that the inexperienced 'actor' Beatles had only one line, one sentence, to speak at a time; if there were difficulties even then, Dick Lester got the expression and inflection he wanted by making the speaker repeat the line after him.

To some extent this pulled the Beatles apart; for in close-up the individual differences that the group status had effaced were for the first time accentuated. Though the risk was that the camera might play its favourites against the wishes of a pop impresario like Brian Epstein, it was decided to capitalize on the separateness of each Beatle by devising a strong sequence showing each on his own for a stretch of the film: so Paul had a quiet, melodious solo turn; John had a 'kookie' interview with a high-brow girl who knew the face but couldn't put a name to it; George was quizzed by a designer of teenage fashions, and Ringo had the lonely encounter already mentioned. By thus emphasizing their differences, the film paradoxically lengthened the life-time of the Beatles as a group, for opening up their individual identities to inspection averted the then considerable risk of the public's being sated and wearied with the Beatles as a four-headed monster.

The film in the making was being shaped almost daily by accident as well as design. I think this helps to account for its spontaneity. The Beatles' talent for ad-libbing had made Shenson and Owen fear that the carefully pointed humour of the dialogue – a 'knocking' humour typical of their personalities and Mersey-side background – would be blunted. But Lester turned this natural talent of theirs to acidly funny effect by staging a British Press conference – suggested by the ordeal they had surmounted so well in the United States a few weeks earlier – in which the Beatles improvised jokey, 'unphoney' answers to Owen's scripted questions which were sprung on them without forewarning. As with so much else in the film, the skill lay in pitchforking the Beatles into situations they had met many times – then standing back and viewing them that little bit obliquely or oddly.

The dubious life-expectancy assigned to them at the time may be judged from the debate, that continued till almost the first day of shooting, over whether the film needed 'stars' besides the Beatles. Lester and Shenson resisted this: and finally the only other 'name' signed for the film was Wilfrid Brambell, then nationally famous as the grouchy senior partner of the *Steptoe and Son* series on BBC TV. Cast as Paul McCartney's troublesome Irish grandfather – parents, of course, had no part in the scenario – who scuttles through the film like an ancient fighting crab, he turned out to be the professional mainstay of the early sequences where the Beatles were still a trifle unsure of themselves, and he provided an astringent figure with whom the older generation of film-goers, to whom the film was now being hopefully directed, could feel on familiar terms. Lester later admitted that the character's Irish accent somehow allowed an uncalculated aggressiveness to emerge that was different from the passive cunning of Steptoe Senior. But he added, 'I didn't dislike that.'

The title of the film was one of the late thoughts that came

accidentally during a lunch-break at Twickenham Studios, when
Paul McCartney was telling Ornstein about Ringo's early days
with the group and how he had had a habit of putting things
backwards, a kind of Merseyside 'spoonerism,' such as the time
the group turned-in in the small hours and Ringo remarked that
it had been 'a hard day's night.' Ornstein recalls that he said,
'We just got the title.' The next day the title-song was ready. The
photographer Lester used was Gilbert Taylor, who had worked
on *It's Trad, Dad!* To both of them the television-influenced style
of *ciné-verité* was highly attractive; and so was the experience in
the 'presentation' of pop acts they had gained in the earlier film
where Taylor, a tough pragmatic professional, had proved how
inventively the whole extent of the black-and-white scale could
be used, not just what was known as 'middle of the strip' shooting.
'By using absolutely white backings and a key light we could
make the people who played against this "white-out" environment take on the definition of steel engravings.'[1] In *A Hard Day's
Night*, there were effects that even he didn't bargain for, but
inventively recruited into the film's style. 'We were shooting the
exteriors behind the theatre where the Beatles were performing.
A helicopter was there at the time, while the Beatles were larking
about in the field, alone without the press of the crowds for the
first time. Unfortunately when we came to do a shot from the
helicopter, the battery I was handed for the hand-held camera
wasn't fully charged – we started the shot and the speed went
down. I was able to correct it and by managing to 'stop down'
we finished shooting at four frames. I didn't tell Dick till we
finished and then I said, "We shot this in accelerated motion."
His face fell, but when he had the rushes screened it was so
successful that we shot a complementary sequence in slow motion.'
This famous sequence is the 'time-out' pause from serfdom that
refreshes the Beatles – and to some extent the whole film – as the
joyful acrobatics assume a dimension of frantic relief from the
pressures of fan worship just by being shot in the way to which
mischance contributed and the inventive imagination of director

[1] Gilbert Taylor interviewed by the author, 17 April, 1972. Unless stated
otherwise, all subsequent quotations from Taylor come from the same source.

and photographer abetted. For the sequences of the Beatles concert they used no fewer than six cameras simultaneously with 10 × 1 zoom lenses – 'and since there was not much work then,' said Taylor, 'we were able to engage crack operators on every one of them and give them orders to shoot and shoot and shoot . . .'

The budget finally wound up somewhere between £175,000 and £189,000.[1] But such were the guaranteed advance sales of the discs bearing the music and lyrics that the film was close to 200 per cent profit before it had opened at a cinema anywhere. The world-wide gross came to about eleven million dollars by mid-1971, six million of it in the United States and Canada alone, and has been increasing yearly since the film, like the Bond pictures, received a mass saturation release in 1964 and has been showing virtually continuously round the world ever since. For just four screenings, an American television network paid the sum of $2,500,000.

Critics generally received the film with surprise, relief, even rapture, though *The Times* reviewer found it 'so rough and gritty, so choppy and 'new wave' in its editing, so insistently hand-held in its camerawork that by the end, more than a little dazzled and deafened, one may find oneself thinking back nostalgically to the good old straightforward days of *Orchestra Wives*.'[2] And though Penelope Gilliatt compared it, to its disadvantage, with the *cinéma-verité* report on the Beatles, entitled *Yeah! Yeah! Yeah!*, which the Maysles had made in America, she observed acutely that '*A Hard Day's Night* is better described . . . as a piece of feature journalism; this is the first film in England that has anything like the urgency and dash of an English popular daily at its best. Like a news feature, it was produced under pressure and the head of steam behind it has produced something expressive and alive.'[3] The Beatles' unanticipated charms for the middle-aged or middle-

[1] The lower figure is Ornstein's estimate, the higher Shenson's: it may include bonuses the latter paid from a contingency fund that, he said cryptically, 'I had held in reserve lest Brian Epstein wanted an associate producer's credit.'
[2] *The Times*, 7 July, 1964.
[3] The *Observer*, 12 July, 1964.

class parents put them firmly into place in the pantheon of family favourites and not just pop idols. The film was fantasy, yes – but it was fantasy enriched with fact: people felt this *is* what the boys would do, not just what their director thinks would make a funny gag. This is the main reason why the film, which is otherwise firmly anchored in the world of the television commercial, finally evades the synthetic sell of packaged personalities. The personalities at that period of their development behaved as if they resented being sold, and there was still enough credibility in their stance to adhere to Lester's style and give it honesty as well as appropriateness. 'They accept one another with the stoicism of clowns,' wrote Penelope Gilliatt, 'none of them tries to tell you that their personalities are a sign of the traumas of modern man . . .'[1]

Maybe not. All the same, the film very successfully told one that on every level it was a manifestation of the compulsive up-to-dateness one felt strongly everywhere in daily life in Britain. For various reasons, chiefly to do with the restrictions placed on shooting the Beatles against the open, unprotected face of architectural London, within reach and grab of the hordes of fans, Lester did not manage to make the film a documentary on actual physical change. But he caught and intensified the appetite for 'Now' excitement that the Beatles amplified: the 'classlessness,' 'youth,' 'revolt,' and 'professionalism' that his 'Inside Report' projected were precisely the ingredients of the collective image which, Christopher Booker observed, dozens of epiphenomena were starting to feed into the media – the Press, television networks, and cinema – which in turn would feed them back in magnified form into society, creating the illusion which in fact became the reality that Britain was the place where, in a phrase that came into vogue in 1964, 'it's all happening.'

[1] Ibid.

Chapter Twelve: What Price Independents?

> You'll never change the pattern, not while all those Philistines
> are in Parliament.
> John Osborne, quoted in *The Sunday Times*, 22 December, 1963

By the middle of 1963, just as the British-based company of one
of the American film-making 'majors,' United Artists, saw the
opportunities that were opening up, the specifically British
independent film-makers sensed that the squeeze was on them.
Portents visible in previous years suddenly became painful
realities. One such portent was the steady drop in the number of
films needed to support the remaining cinemas, which gave the
cinemas in the Rank and A.B.C. circuits an even freer hand in
picking the movies they believed would be profitable from among
all the available ones, small-budget and blockbuster, independent
(and often shakily financed), and American-backed and (therefore
solidly) guaranteed. The independently owned cinemas, or the
less favourably sited Rank and A.B.C. ones, had withered away:
the so-called 'National Circuit,' comprising these 'inferior' houses
had anyway been abandoned as part of the tripartite release
pattern in 1961. A rather visionary plan devised by the film
industry's trade bodies to pump confidence into the old, decaying
cinemas by 'recommending' films for them to select predictably
came to nothing. A crisis was in the making, but as usual it was
experienced when it was too late to do anything but issue charges,
counter-charges and recriminations. The outcome shaped the
pattern of Anglo-American film-making for the rest of the
decade.

The problem was that the Rank and A.B.C. circuits between
them required only 104 new movies a year: even that didn't allow
for films held over for several weeks at a theatre. Yet for a
producer to have any chance of a profit he simply had to get his
movie generally released on one or other circuit. Not that this by
itself guaranteed anything. The Rank Organization in 1961 had
established that an average return to distributors from a film

released in its cinemas would be about £90,000 – against £80,000 on the A.B.C. circuit and a mere £35–40,000 on the 'National Circuit,' that was to be absorbed into the other two as a direct consequence of this economic weakness. When distributors' fees, print costs, publicity and advertising came off these sums, the butter left on the bread was hardly enough to be tasted and needed some subsidy spread on it from the Eady (box-office) Levy to keep many a producer from starvation. It all drove home the continuing fact of film-making in Britain that operated most harshly against a strong native industry: only in the most exceptional cases could a British-made film hope to make a profit inside Britain.

In mid-1963 there were about 2,430 cinemas in Britain and while the Rank and A.B.C. circuits owned only 651 of these (or 21 per cent) they were usually the plum sites, accounting for 42 per cent of all seats sold in a year. 'Circuit Power' was dominant – yet it was not competitive. Although legislation forbade films to be booked into cinemas 'sight unseen' by the circuits' booking managers, a shadow area existed in which films financed by reputable guarantors (mainly Hollywood majors) were 'pencilled in' – and the Hollywood majors had traditional links with one or other (very, very rarely with both) of the circuits. An independent British film-maker had no such traditional ties and, with a film that was shakily financed and perhaps represented an unknown entertainment appeal, he was doubly at a disadvantage. It didn't help much to appeal to patriotism and cry 'A fair deal for the British.' Figures could be produced – and were – to prove they were already getting it. In the first fifty weeks of 1963, for instance, the Rank circuit showed twenty-three British first features and twenty-seven foreign (mostly American-made) ones: in the same period the A.B.C. circuit showed twenty-six British and twenty-four foreign films. The Quota Laws at that time made it obligatory for cinemas to devote 30 per cent of their playing time per year to British films; so, as things stood, the circuits were devoting half the year to the home product, though of course a proportion of this 'home' product was financed by Hollywood through British subsidiaries, and the proportion was about to increase dramatically. By the end of 1963 enough films were stock-piled in the distributors' vaults, or had finished shooting, to meet the quota requirements without a single new British film needing to be shot throughout the whole of the next year, and gloomy groups of film-makers were desperately seeking ways of (a) getting their new films shown and (b) raising cash to make their next one. Among these groups was British Lion, the chief distributor of independently financed films; and as the year wore on they asserted that 'some twenty films' were unable to get a screening widely enough, or early enough, on either circuit to give any reasonable hope of ultimate profit.

Now if there was more than six months' delay in showing a film in Britain, the producers would have to start to pay interest charges on it out of their own resources. (Interest rates at that time were averaging 6 per cent: before the decade was out they climbed to 14 per cent and even higher.) It was claimed that £2,250,000 was tied up in eighteen of these unreleased first features, some of them ones on which British Lion would also draw a distribution commission – hence their particular anxiety. The average budget was in the £100,000 to £200,000 range.

Of course, the issues were not all that clear cut. The exhibitors defended their preference for films from the majors by claiming that the independents were falling down badly on quality. John Davis, head of the Rank Organization, said that a realistic budget for a British first feature should be between £250,000 and £400,000 and the independents were geared to much smaller – i.e. inadequate – sums. And much the same point was made by John Terry, managing director of the National Film Finance Corporation, when he urged the independents, in October 1963, to pool their resources and rationalize production – or perish.

But cost was only one of the reasons why the independents were being hurt. It was easier to assign their difficulties to that neutral cause than to admit that some of their films were not being 'sold' to the public because the bookers couldn't fit them into any clear-cut category. Exhibitors believed, probably with some cynical justification, that the public liked what they knew: any-how, it was less risky and expensive than gambling on the public knowing what they might like. As Joseph Losey said after the success, totally unexpected by the exhibitors, of *The Servant*, 'The film industry constantly rejects one year what it is crying to have repeated the next year.' The unfairnesses of the situation could hardly be better illustrated than in the continuing fortunes of the group of Allied Film Makers which had been begun so auspiciously – and even profitably – with *The Angry Silence* three years earlier.

BEAVER IN TROUBLE

Bryan Forbes and Richard Attenborough, whose Beaver Films Company was an A.F.M. founder-member, put *Séance on a Wet Afternoon* into production late in 1963. Its story might have looked a clearly categorized one: a child-kidnapping thriller with a strong emotional conflict between the kidnappers, a female medium and her submissive husband, to stretch the tension further still. But though the kidnapping and ransom sequences wound one's apprehensions up tight, with the serpentine to-and-fro-ing of the camera in the streets and subways of Central London (and this was when such location shooting was still relatively rare), the film's accent of interest was placed on the oblique relationship between the kidnappers. The film had really grown around *it* and not the crime. Forbes had written the screenplay for an actor and actress; but failing to cast it, he then rewrote it to turn the two protagonists into males, an ageing homosexual and his boy-friend, with the hope that Alec Guinness and Tom Courtenay might be interested in the complexities of the roles. Guinness declined at once. Another rewrite: then, feeling he had shot his bolt, Forbes asked the playwright Giles Cooper for advice and, though this pre-dates Edward Albee's play *Who's Afraid of Virginia Woolf?* Cooper came up with the idea of locating the woman kidnapper's urge in the idea of a stillborn child who, for its mother, had obstinately refused to 'die.' Shelley Winters declined the part, Anne Bancroft was unavailable, and it was with time running out and pre-production costs adding up like a cab meter that Forbes impulsively offered Kim Stanley the role. She accepted. Attenborough played her paunchy, beak-nosed husband, relishing the visibly ageing persona he could exhibit after his years in bondage to eternal boyhood.

But Forbes's problems and at least certain aspects of the film were now shaped by Kim Stanley's approach to the part. Though an actress of mesmerizing power, her unshakeable dedication to the 'Method' style of acting and her infrequent film appearances made for a performance that was difficult to standardize from take to take. Her timing was an acutely personal decision, too, and since many of her scenes were between the medium and her husband, Attenborough had the task of accommodating himself to the actress's varying emphases and responses. His performance consequently tended towards the generously self-effacing, like those of a man waiting to be spoken to before venturing to speak. Fortunately his character was just such a docile servant of his wife's desires. But to save time – and money – as well as comply with Kim Stanley's penchant for altering a response if she 'perceived' a more truthful inflection, Forbes and his photographer, Gerry Turpin, had to employ several cameras that would preserve the continuity of the star's performance in at least one take; and this in turn required a form of lighting that, considering the Victorian *chiaroscuro* of the hermit couple's suburban mansion, was extremely difficult to evolve.

The film cost about £139,000, a small sum, owing to Attenborough and Forbes accepting small fees and percentages; and it was critically well received when premièred on 4 June, 1964, but never achieved anything like a widespread release in Britain. The bookers were unable or unwilling to determine where its appeal lay, or at which section of film-goers the bizarre complicity of its plot was aimed. Its income was slow to materialize. After all deductions had been made, its world gross by mid-1971 was only £195,688. Since the bulk of this revenue came from overseas, in particular from America where Artie Shaw, the former band leader who had turned film distributor, made it into a profitable 'sleeper,' the money it received from the Eady Levy in Britain was mortifyingly low, just about £9,330 – evidence in itself of the restricted exhibition it got. (The Eady Levy is payable for only five years after a film's first screening: then the tap is turned off. So if there are long gaps between play-dates, the time available for levy money to accrue is lessened.)

Other financial blows now fell on Allied Film Makers. The Basil Dearden-Michael Relph team went ahead with a social drama, *Life for Ruth*, on the ethics of whether a couple of fundamental religionists should refuse a blood transfusion to their child. It cost £126,800 and by mid-1971 it had grossed world-wide only £53,788. The Eady Levy was only £18,626, which did not even help it cover its cost, much less get into profit. The slow receipts from the restricted release that the first film got and the failure of the second brought about the demise of Allied Film Makers as an active force when it was £300,000 to £400,000 in debt to the Rank Organization. Rank's distribution side, Forbes insisted, 'treated us fairly throughout' and never interfered in production, although its cinema circuit was less altruistic when it came to exhibiting the films. That A.F.M. continued its corporate existence at all was due to Leslie Baker, its company secretary. This astute executive nursed its dormant affairs so well from two small offices with a weekly outgoing of £60 that by the early 1970s nearly all the six-figure debt owed to the Rank Organization had been repaid. 'The experience proved to me,' Forbes reflected, 'that films can be profitable but must be well handled; and that the distribution company can come successfully out of the deal well in advance of the actual film producers having anything to show for their efforts.' The total negative cost of the seven A.F.M. films made for Rank was £1,042,157, the distributor's gross was £1,820,940 giving them a gross profit of £778,783. But the producers of the films had to carry a loss of £142,934. Moreover, after the cinemas had taken their cut, some 65 per cent overall, there was still a return of over 75 per cent on initial capital investment. Thus the distributors did well, the exhibitors did very well, and the producers did modestly and were eventually forced to shut shop.

*   *   *

A VICIOUS CIRCLE

The satellite film-makers orbiting round British Lion had had their production paralysed just as effectively by the latter's failure to get their films shown early or widely enough; and this position worsened as 1963 went on. Part of the trouble was that British Lion felt a moral obligation to hold itself independent from each circuit of cinemas and at the same time to trade with both. British Lion's managing director, David Kingsley, later claimed, 'Both were out to get us. We were the exception that set a bad example to the tied suppliers, in particular the American companies. It cost the circuits more to book a British film than one from a tied supplier: consequently there was a good reason for perpetuating the tied supplier system and viewing the long-term position of British Lion as undesirable. Had we been a public company – which in 1963 we weren't – it would have been reasonable to have done a deal with one or other circuit; but we tended to see any departure from independence as a breach of faith. The circuits did propose to use the "alternative film" plan – giving one film in turn to each circuit. But even this struck us as unacceptable. Today there is a much more flexible "floating release" system for films: at that time one either went on a circuit or didn't go on release at all. Today's flexibility came seven years too late for us.'[1]

But one cannot ignore the quality of the films that the cinema circuits were hesitant to book. The adroit campaign that British Lion ran among a sympathetic Press in 1963 very carefully refrained from ever naming more than one or two of the twenty-odd 'martyred' films; and a few sceptics wondered if the ones that *were* named over and over again might not be the sturdier, better-groomed 'martyrs' who could be relied on to attract sympathy and succour. When the full list did get known, little by little, months after the 'indignation' had passed, it was such as to make one look more charitably on the exhibitors expected to screen them. Some were genuine hard cases. *The Leather Boys*

[1] David Kingsley interviewed by the author, 25 June, 1972. Unless stated otherwise all subsequent quotations from Kingsley come from the same source.

which has been mentioned earlier as the most worth-while of the films dealing with the then fresh issue of male homosexuality, certainly did get harmed artistically and commercially by being finished in March 1963, then held up for release till nearly a year later: it had cost only £100,000 to make, but any delay added appreciable interest charges to this 'absolute minimum' budget. Another victim was the screen version of Harold Pinter's play *The Caretaker*, a privately capitalized production directed by Clive Donner, which cost only £30,000 and was made without any assurance that it would be commercially shown. (The money came from private sources, because the National Film Finance Corporation was expressly forbidden by its rules to advance money to a film that had not a reasonable chance of commercial screening, meaning that it would have to get a sizeable advance from an interested distributor. No distributor evinced much interest in Harold Pinter's screenplay; and it was not till mid-March 1964, nearly a year after shooting, that it got a London screening, having actually opened earlier in New York. But these were films of exceptional quality – too exceptional for their own good, as they did not fit into the exhibition pattern. Other films in the list were more dubious quantities, though one or two in fact did exceptional business when they *were* shown. They were routine farces like *Ladies Who Do* (charwomen picking up Stock Market tips with the wastepaper); *Lunch Hour* (a two-hander based on a duo of one-acters by John Mortimer), *Hide and Seek* (a poor man's *Charade*); *Two Left Feet* (a comedy of working-class manners); and *A Place to Go* (an anthology of every British 'new wave' backstreet cliché, including pub sing-songs, flick-knife fights, loneliness in the new tenement, eviction from the old street, Dad forever on the dole and Mum just as eternally laying the table for high-tea).[1]

What is glaringly obvious about this list is that much of it consisted of films that had got left behind as trends changed, or

[1] A full list of these 'martyred' movies, together with the long waits they had to suffer before being released (and some never were) can be found in *A Competitite Cinema*, by Terence Kelly, with Graham Norton and George Perry (Institute of Economic Affairs, 1966), p. 35.

had tried to play it safe by repeating formula subjects and imitating earlier successes. They were what is called 'programmers,' films made to fill a bill and now, in 1963, seeming little different from the plays that were weekly attractions on both the BBC TV and ITV networks, except that there the themes and treatment were often more adventurous and radical. They had in fact come out at a time when the public taste had changed, and only their producers could have believed, as an editorial in *Sight and Sound* put it, 'that what held the screen a decade ago ought still to hold it today, that the circuits owe them a living.'[1] The unfairness was that, as well as producers who had played safe being the ones who were penalized, those like the makers of *The Leather Boys* and *The Caretaker* who had creative originality but no guaranteed public appeal were also fatally handicapped. The problems were enough to contribute to the hesitancy of other independents to get involved, whether their films were 'old hat' or 'new wave,' so long as the cinema circuits were in a buyer's market. 'The difficulties facing those wishing to make good, intelligent, and commercially valid films in this country stem from economic instabilities (and for independents, particularly, the uncertainty of exhibition outlets) on the one hand, and, on occasion, a lack of passion and real creative involvement on the part of those on the top and bottom of the production spiral.'[2] Thus wrote John Gillett, reporting back from a field trip on films being made on location and in the studios at the end of 1963. At the very time of his writing these words, the independents' troubles were dramatically increased by an event that reverberated through the rest of the 1960s and on into the 1970s. This was the decision taken by the Conservative Government in December 1963 to put that awkward odd-man-out, British Lion Films, on the public auction block.

LION HUNT

Some of the principals involved in the fate of British Lion have still to write their versions of this event. Any account of it is

[1] *Sight and Sound*, (Winter 1963–4), Vol. 33, No. 1, p. 50.
[2] 'State of the Studios,' *Sight and Sound*, (Spring 1964), Vol. 33, No. 2, p. 61.

necessarily partial – some would say partisan – and almost the only thing beyond question is the regret of the wretched British Government at ever having got involved in film-making – an indulgence akin to that of eighteen-century English gentlemen who built romantic follies on their private estates. It is a pleasant pursuit, provided one can afford it.

The Government had 'got into' films after the war, when they were big dollar-earners and when, for a time, the imported Hollywood movies had to pay a swingeing 75 per cent surtax which had tempted their makers to boycott the British market. The Labour Government in 1948 set up the National Film Finance Corporation with £5 million to its account to finance production through the channel of the distributors – i.e. it was not to dole the money out directly to the producers. In November 1948 the British Lion Film Corporation, which was controlled by Sir Alexander Korda, obtained a loan of £2 million, later increased to £3 million; by April 1949 it was anticipating a loss of £700,000. By the end of 1949, Korda's own production company, London Films, owed British Lion over £1,300,000; and in spite of the ever-ebullient Korda continuing to turn out films, which in the long run have proved good investments, the expectations that the N.F.F.C. loan could be repaid at the end of 1951 were, well, poor. In 1952 the N.F.F.C. stoically accepted that perhaps £1 million of it would never be back in their hands and, as George Tabori remarked in his biography of Korda, even this was somewhat optimistic. It was announced in November 1953, that the total loss was £2,200,000; and in June 1954, the Government, now wringing its hands and wishing it could wash them of the film industry, too, called in the loan, put in a receiver in voluntary liquidation and bade a cold farewell to Korda.

The new British Lion was formed in January 1955, and acquired by issue 600,000 shares – the old company's net assets were valued at £600,000 – and these the N.F.F.C. accepted in satisfaction, if that is the word, of its £3 million loss. It also advanced another £567,000 of tax-payers' money to prime the pump of inspiration and creativity. In December 1957 the British Lion board was reorganized and into the managing director's chair came one of the film industry's shrewdest accountants, a boyish-faced, deceptively mild-mannered Old Etonian, whose zeal in the private pursuit of rare old maps and topographical charts was carried on as zealously as his public encouragement of new films, but perhaps more tranquilly. David Kingsley was already managing director of the N.F.F.C. and it was now his job to strengthen British Lion with *working* directors – direct from the industry. 'I went down the list of independent producers and selected the ones with good track records who weren't tied to any of the American majors. I found five names and, believe me, they were almost "the only ones." I said, "Would you be prepared to give up your total independence and come into British Lion and help pull it together?" John and Roy Boulting said yes immediately; so did Frank Launder and Sidney Gilliat. John Woolf at first seemed likely to join, too, but ultimately declined.' All five board directors acquired holdings in British Lion, though the N.F.F.C., whose managing director became John Terry, preserved certain options that it could exercise if it chose after a five-year period, that is after 1962. And in 1963 this Government watchdog, at the bidding of its master, decided to exercise its option and to put British Lion up for auction, which would allow the Government, with a sigh of relief, to get itself out of the business of film-making.

So on 19 December, 1963, the N.F.F.C. acquired the equity shares held by the five executive directors of British Lion for £750,000. Each director is believed to have got around £150,000 – and this was before the introduction of the capital gains tax a couple of years later. There was immediate criticism of their 'good fortune.' But Kingsley later offered a convincing defence – if one were needed – when he said that, when they came on to the board, they were successful film-makers and British Lion was a bankrupt company. Their undertaking to write, produce and direct films for it meant, in effect, that they would be making only about 10 per cent of what they were capable of making, and indeed had already been earning, as independents. They could have worked very lucratively for Hollywood companies, but instead they received only small direct fees for such huge successes as the Boulting Brothers' comedy *I'm All Right, Jack* and the films Launder and Gilliat made about the St Trinian's schoolgirls. Had they failed, they would have been condemned for losing tax-payers' money again. Instead, they succeeded and hence were condemned when they realized the assets that, of course, had increased along with the value of the company. 'We got a very good return on our original investment, but what really annoyed people was that it was free of tax.' Were the assets of the old company undervalued? they were asked. 'I would say they were "conservatively" valued. There is no doubt that with television's insatiable demand for old movies, those in our vaults increased considerably in value: this affected the situation in degree, but not in principle. Had we not gone into British Lion, there is no doubt the old films would have had to be sold there and then, for a very low price perhaps. When we did sell, we had good films of our own to sweeten the deal, as well as the Korda backlog, and all this increased the company's value.'

It was the very success that the new blood had made of British Lion which ironically contributed to the Government's decision to sell it. In July 1963 British Lion had made a profit for the fourth year running, with films like *Only Two can Play, The Wrong Arm of the Law* and *The L-Shaped Room*, and had repaid the Government debt of £600,000. The prosperity of British Lion, plus the virtual exhaustion of the N.F.F.C.'s uncommitted resources caused by purchasing the British Lion directors' shares for £750,000, were given as the two main reasons for the sale. The thought of putting even more State money into films caused shudders in Whitehall. And taking the Government out of businesses best run by private enterprise was then an article of faith of the Minister at the Department of Industry, who was politically responsible for the sale. He was the same Edward Heath who in 1970 became Prime Minister.

But the Treasury now also felt confident enough to let British Lion go without fearing that the film industry might expire with it; for by this date, the start of 1964, it was appreciated that more and more American money was coming into film production in Britain and there would be no need to go on financing the chief independent British company. If this calculation *was* made – and the N.F.F.C. had those on its board who believed it was – then it was a thoroughly cynical but not inaccurate piece of stock-taking. There was a third, more shadowy, reason advanced for the sale. When David Kingsley went to see Sir Nutcombe Hume, chairman of the N.F.F.C., on 27 November 1963, he was told, in his words, 'Of course, you know, you chaps are *persona non grata* with the two cinema circuits. You're a bit like pantie manu-facturers arguing with Marks and Spencer.' That's to say, you're a bit like those who make the goods to specification having the *chutzpah* to argue with the wholesaler-retailer who orders and markets them. Kingsley replied that the analogy was hardly apposite: Marks and Spencer, Britain's most flourishing chain-store group in the 1960s, did not have the monopoly of the pantie market that Rank and A.B.C. virtually had of the film market. But he certainly didn't rebut the charge of being un-popular with the circuits. British Lion had been spear-heading the independent film-makers' attacks on the circuits, and with the enforced sale of British Lion it now looked as if the troops were having the castle sold up before they could let off any more cannons.

Actually, it is generously incorrect to describe British Lion as being put up for auction. As more facts emerged, it became clear that a mystery man had already been selected, to whom the com-pany would be sold for £1,600,000 – the price fixed by the Government valuer. His identity was soon a mystery no longer: it was Sydney Box, producer of many British films in the post-war years, a man backed by City money (Standard Investment Trust) and advice, but independently wealthy and partnered by Ted (later Lord) Willis, playwright, screenwriter and founder member of the British Writers' Guild. It seemed he could count, too, on the gentlemanly English tradition of honouring the first comer. But some people argued that Box had been closely associated with the Rank Organization, and it looked to them that selling British Lion to him was as good as amalgamating it with a major circuit: it would give the death-blow to any hope of setting up a strong, competitive third cinema circuit for independently-financed films.

British Lion, as we have seen, had strong links with Bryanston-Seven Arts and it was from this quarter that an alternative bidder suddenly emerged in the shape of Sir Michael Balcon, Bryanston's chairman. His own group was swiftly mobilized behind him: it included such film-makers as Tony Richardson, Oscar Lewenstein, John Schlesinger, Joseph Janni, Karel Reisz and Walter Reade Jr. The Government was forced to suspend the tentative agreement to sell British Lion to Sydney Box and battle now flared, with new bidders appearing on the horizon almost daily: among them were reported to be Sam Spiegel, John Woolf, Leslie Grade, Tony Tenser and Michael Klinger (who were producing Roman Polanski's first British film), John Bloom (the washing-machine tycoon who was to suffer one of the 1960s' most spectacular bankruptcies) and even (some said appropriately) the two north-country comedians Morecambe and Wise. The ardour of many of those who aspired to save the British film industry was cooled when the terms of sale were announced early in January 1964. Edward Heath stated that the N.F.F.C. would retain a single special share in British Lion with certain rights vested in it: these were the right to veto its voluntary liquidation, the right to veto the sale of the undertaking, the right to veto the repayment of any capital to the shareholders, and the right to veto the disposal of the sixty-acre Shepperton Studios except in well-defined circumstances which would be judged to exist by the special shareholder. To have been free to sell Shepperton, already zoned as a permitted property development area, which was a much more lucrative vision than running a film studio with a high and continuous overhead, would clearly have been worth paying £1,600,000. After this douche of cold water, the ranks of bidders thinned. And when the dead-line drew near in mid-March 1964, it was a fairly straight contest between the Balcon group, the Box group and a bizarre contender called the Freedom Group run by Edward Martell, one of those sturdy, not to say stubborn-minded independents close to the political grass-roots in every country. Balcon won. And the Union Jacks suddenly appeared at the windows of British Lion's London offices, off Wardour Street, leading passers-by to believe that a public holiday of some unconstitutional but undoubtedly jubilant kind had just been declared.

And for a time it *was* like a holiday inside British Lion. Balcon became chairman and David Kingsley vice-chairman; and because Balcon believed 'that the best people to run British Lion were the people who had been running it before,'[1] he brought on to the board John and Roy Boulting and the Launder–Gilliat team, and strengthened it, as he believed, with other groups: Tiberius Films (Joseph Janni, John Schlesinger, David Kingsley), Long Distance Films (Woodfall Films, Border Television, of which Balcon was, or had been, a director, and Brian Epstein, the Beatles' manager); and Walter Reade. The new British Lion and the two cinema circuits made noises of love, or at least reconciliation, in each other's direction, and the *Kinematograph Weekly* announced, 'It is expected that the new management will handle about twelve pictures a year. Each of the five groups will probably supply one picture a year. This leaves room for about half-a-dozen pictures from outside sources.'[2] Shepperton Studios, which had been idle since the last shots were taken on Jack Clayton's film *The Pumpkin Eater* in mid-December 1963, prepared to hum with activity again.

Yet at the end of 1964 the newly constituted British Lion had only one film shooting at Shepperton, a farce called *Joey Boy*; it had four films still in the planning stage, some of which got no further; and it had signally failed to attract back to it the independent producers who, it had hoped, would make it roar powerfully again. The truth was, frustration set in depressingly early, almost as soon as the new board met. It did not radiate the confidence to bring back first-rate independents and consequently, as Kingsley said later, 'the second-raters were the ones who tended to come to us with a project which, almost inevitably, would already have been rejected by the American majors. At the N.F.F.C. there was a similar problem. There was also a psychological resentment of us as a consortium of film-makers daring to pass judgment on other film-makers' projects. The attitude of potential film-makers towards the N.F.F.C. had been, "Why

[1] Michael Balcon, *op. cit.*, p. 205.
[2] *Kinematograph Weekly*, 26 March, 1964.

I

should salesmen read our scripts?" The attitude towards British Lion was, "Why should producers read our scripts?" Undoubtedly there were people who simply did not want anybody to read their scripts but only wanted to be handed the money.' The same difficulty, however, existed within the British Lion board: each of its five groups was relatively autonomous, each with veto rights that were unusual for a public company. Consequently it was enormously difficult to get decisions to make films. Equally ominous was the fact that some board members were, by contract or inclination, preparing films for companies other than British Lion. At the very time Woodfall Films took their place on the board they had embarked on a programme of film-making for United Artists; and other co-directors, namely Schlesinger and Janni, would make *their* next films for Anglo-Amalgamated and ultimately for American majors, too.

But in the last analysis it was the lonely exposure of 'independence' which militated against a swift return of confidence and production. Looking back, Kingsley (and no doubt some of his co-directors as well) felt it might have been better had British Lion agreed to split its projected output fifty-fifty with the Rank and A.B.C. circuits, or even go completely over to one of them, for this would have given it leverage for its 'risk' ventures and confidence for its 'safe' ones. But to do so at the time would have meant a hasty abandonment of the status its new owners had striven to maintain, without developing the resources to make it realistic. The hope that was still held out after March 1964 was that the Government would 'do something' – something economically fruitful but at the very least something psychologically sustaining – to help the group. As the authors of *A Competitive Cinema* correctly predicted, 'If the structure of the industry remains unchanged, one must take a very pessimistic view of British Lion's future as a truly independent company.'[1] In other words, what British Lion prayed for was to have the rules of the game altered, so that its players could get it under way with a fairer chance of winning. And in September 1964, after a long campaign of public and private lobbying, it looked as if their

[1] Terence Kelly *et al.*, *op. cit.*, p. 33.

prayers had been heard, if not exactly answered, when one R. D. Serpell, a secretary at the Board of Trade, in pursuance of Section 2 (1) of the Monopolies and Restrictive Practices Act 1948 as amended by the Restrictive Trade Provisions Act 1956, referred to the Monopolies Commission 'the matter of the supply in Great Britain of films to exhibitors for exhibition in cinemas' and asked the Commission to 'investigate and report' on, amongst other things, 'whether the conditions in question . . . operate or may be expected to operate against the public interest.'[1]

'Against the public interest . . .' They were joyful words to British Lion's ears. It looked at long last as if 'something would be done' now that the investigative heat was being turned on the all-powerful circuits. And to all intents and purposes independent film production in Britain was prepared to await the outcome in the expectation that the news would be good, practical and enriching. While it was waiting – and it had to wait for all of two years – there was no doubt where the action was to be found. It was with the Americans.

[1] Board of Trade Reference, 23 September, 1964.

Chapter Thirteen: Symptoms and Symbols

> If you ask me, they're a new breed of person altogether.
> Dyspeptic middle-aged onlooker in *The Knack*

Broadwick House, where British Lion had its headquarters in 1964, was scarcely a hundred yards from Film House, where United Artists operated at the time; but the two groups might have been thousands of miles apart in their operation, philosophy and results.

In the former a suspicious coalition tried to grapple with the common management of a salvage operation. 'But the main trouble,' said Oscar Lewenstein later, 'was that we had no common outlook, which isn't helpful when the arrangements are supposed to facilitate co-productions with other members of the consortium. We mistrusted each other. We wanted to make our kind of pictures at Woodfall, "they" wanted to make theirs; we didn't respect their films as important or good, "they" didn't show much faith in ours, either. We could never find films that we *all*, or even several of us, wanted to do. It is extremely difficult for producers and directors to have projects judged by other producers and directors with whom they have nothing in common. United Artists people were never producers or directors; they were lawyers, not film-makers; they had access to money, they left the taste to you. It is always better to go to a patron than a rival.' Especially, Lewenstein might have added, a hard-up rival. There was no shortage of cash flowing through United Artists, much of it now coming from their British productions. By February 1964, for instance, after playing in eighteen theatres in only twelve American cities, *Tom Jones* had grossed a spectacular $1,424,108. The ideal situation for Woodfall would have been to have United Artists subsidize whatever they wished to do: but, even with receipts on the *Tom Jones* scale, this went against the financial tradition of the American company; and though a multi-picture deal was swiftly negotiated, it was apparently never actually signed. From George Ornstein's point of view, as the responsible man on the spot, it was better to go from picture to picture and keep the negotiations on the boil. This was good enough for Woodfall. As Lewenstein said, 'The simplicity of the deal was what counted, of being able to get 100 per cent financing and no interference till delivery. We started off very sensibly. After *Tom Jones* we did three films on very low budgets: we hadn't then grown giddy with success. We did *The Girl with Green Eyes* for £140,000; *One-Way Pendulum* for £50,000; and *The Knack* for £125,000.'

Lewenstein acted as executive producer on all three films, for Richardson, much in demand internationally, had yielded to the desire to return in triumph to Hollywood, scene of his anguished 'serfdom' directing *Sanctuary* three years earlier, and make *The Loved One* for Metro-Goldwyn-Mayer, this time resolving to keep total control of the film. That M.G.M. had at last got Evelyn Waugh's satire of Californian burial customs into production says much about the way the success of 'British' film-making was impinging on the Hollywood studios; for besides such trendy influences as the Beatle-style hero, played with a game shot at a north-country accent by Robert Morse, the film was conceived by Richardson, and accepted by M.G.M. without a corporative murmur, as a blend of satire and realism which he aimed to shoot on location in and around Los Angeles. It must be appreciated that at the time this was as radical a departure from form for an M.G.M. crew as it had been for British technicians when Richardson put it into practice in *The Entertainer* and *A Taste of Honey*. It showed the Hollywood envy of 'the British look' that was going down so well at the American box-office.

The three British films Woodfall made bear their company identity very strongly. First, in the selection of new talent. Desmond Davis, who had been camera operator on *Tom Jones*, was given his chance to direct *The Girl with Green Eyes* (1964), and showed himself an apt but not slavish disciple of Richardson in location shooting, and probably an impressionable fan of François Truffaut in the *Jules et Jim* feeling he displayed intuitively for the many moods of Irish landscape and its poetic interaction with the characters. The screenplay was Edna O'Brien's first and had her characteristic shocked delight at the pleasures that freedom from a Catholic education offer to a young girl in love with a married man. And Lynn Redgrave also got her starring opportunity as the big, bouncy, saucy and sharp convent school-girl tittering at her own shamelessness, with the devil's wink for every available male and a fund of girls' magazine wisdom on how to hook him – 'Fascinate him with your bust or somethin'.' Her comedy partner was Rita Tushingham. The tart, true-tempered co-existence of the two actresses in this film is worth stressing, for when they were next joined together, under the same director, it was in *Smashing Time* (1967), a film whose crude exploitation of them once more as innocents-at-large in the big city was to show how coarse and knowing the freshness of the cinema had turned once Britain was 'swinging' and the movies had to swing with it.

N. F. Simpson's *One-Way Pendulum* and Ann Jellicoe's *The Knack* had been produced at the Royal Court Theatre in 1959 and 1962 respectively; and Woodfall's decision to film them in 1964 can only be interpreted as loyalty to the old school. As it happened, in at least one case virtue was more amply rewarded than anyone expected.

Not, however, by *One-Way Pendulum* (1965), a surrealist comedy and a financial flop – 'but at £50,000,' Lewenstein said, 'it was the sort of flop we could afford to have' – though it re-introduced Peter Yates who had two years earlier directed the American-styled musical, *Summer Holiday*, with Cliff Richard. (Extraordinary to think this was the same director who would find his forte with the American action-thriller like *Bullitt*.) *One-Way Pendulum* revealed the *idées fixes* of an 'ordinary' suburban family, whether it was conducting a murder trial in the model of an Old Bailey court-room which the father had run up in the living-room, or the son's patient training of a group of 'speak-your-weight' machines to sing the *Hallelujah!* chorus. The multifold delusions of one person like Billy Liar had now spread out to produce the single obsessive delusions of a multitude of people in a suburban terrace house. Appropriately enough, it was photographed by *Billy Liar*'s camera-man, Denys Coop.

The Knack (3 June, 1965) was luckier in its timing. Instead of an idiosyncratic and dated film version of a play from the end of the 1950s, the film Dick Lester made of it reached the screen at precisely the moment when society was ready for its celebration of youthful hedonism. A new generation had come to earning and spending power and though 'permissiveness' wasn't then in general use in Britain (or over-use, some would say) the extension of economic independence into the sexual sampling of experience was in the air and it was what the film caught and defined and welcomed. The joyful assertiveness of a mass of teenagers was something the mass medium of the cinema embraced much more affirmatively than did the play, which dealt in a series of nearly abstract permutation of relationships. What had been a demonstration on the stage became on the screen a manifesto. A French critic for once sniffed the breeze blowing towards his side of the Channel and wrote, 'Voici que des jeunes gens, pas forcément en colère, se libèrent des contraintes... *The Knack* participe joyeusement à ce moment d'emancipation...'[1] The key phrase here is 'pas forcement en colére' – for the old sour 'anger' had now given way to the new freedom of opportunity. Which meant sexual opportunity. In place of revolution, fun and games.

To promote promiscuity among young people certainly was not the film's anarchic intention. The sexual contest between Tolen, the boy with the knack with girls, and Tom, the absolute beginner, left one in no doubt that a settled relationship with a girl from the provinces was worth more than innumerable hits with the dolly-birds of the Town. But the film deflected attention from its preachy centre by the centrifugal energy it threw off everywhere around it. As George Melly wrote, 'It was optimistic. It believed in pleasure at its most intense. It proposed love and fucking because it felt that this was more pleasurable than fucking without love... *The Knack* was the new Pop gospel, over-rosy in retrospect, but at the time a revelation, an exhilarating "yes".' I saw it one morning and remember coming out afterwards into Piccadilly in a state of euphoria.'[2]

[1] *Films*, 18 July, 1965.
[2] George Melly, *op. cit.*, p. 169.

The Knack had come about in this way. A week after seeing
A Hard Day's Night, Oscar Lewenstein approached Dick Lester,
who set to work at once with Charles Wood, a playwright then
staking out his particular territory in the grandeur, servitude and
folly of military life which he viewed with a minute naturalism
and a Pinteresque sense of humour. Lewenstein suggested Wood,
though, because of his skill with words. His dialogue rhythms
matched Ann Jellicoe's mannered, yet speedy exchanges, one-
liner and often one-word recitatives. He shared Lester's affectionate mockery of Britain's imperial past: a thing that was to shape
their subsequent films together. Between them, they treated
Jellicoe's text like a fragmentation bomb, detonating it, then
rearranging the shrapnel in a surrealistic mosaic. The play had
been a 'psycho-drama' on the stage: the characters had practised
the technique of *s'imposer* on each other as the 'knack' was
illustrated, acquired, adapted and assimilated. All this in the film
was supplemented by a witty series of social attitudes perceived
on the run in the streets of London. *The Knack* is really the first
of the 'London' movies. It contains the alfresco experience of the
capital in the summer of 1964, at which time all who lived there
had become vividly aware of a great sense of unleashing – that
young people had taken it over, or were about to stage a *coup de
jeunesse*. The Beatles had of course enormously assisted this
feeling: by the very over-reporting of them, the mass media had
given shape to the crowd's expectancy, and though their natures
were pre-eminently provincial, localised in Merseyside, it was to
the capital that they had transferred their work-base and all the
hysteria that was attached to it. Carnaby Street was in full blast,
and had about another eighteen months to dominate the fashion
forum of youthful trendiness before the diaspora of boutiques run
by even hippier entrepreneurs took over its energy (and much of
its custom) and changed the image of the clothes to tie them in
with ever more extreme styles of life. The wealthy young who
fancied themselves as dandies but wouldn't patronize their
fathers' tailors had had their own fashion shop, Blade's, since
1962. Now their fathers' stuffier establishments, the custom
tailoring businesses in Savile Row and the smart haberdashers

in Jermyn Street, spruced up *their* image in 1964–5 with bright suits, frilly shirts, vivid ties. Middle-class kids found that Simpson's, the conservatively safe department-store in Piccadilly, had caught a whiff of the youth revolution (and the money in the wind as well) and opened a special section, Trend, in 1965. Youth had its violent side, too. This was brought home in 1964 by the gang-fights between Mods and Rockers – 'West Side Story on English Coast' – which were over-reported by the Press because their first manifestation happened at Easter, a notoriously slack time for news on the home or foreign desk. But as Stanley Cohen argued persuasively in his book on the phenomenon of violence, and its reception by the media, 'Any item of news thrust into an individual's consciousness has the effect of increasing the awareness of items of a similar nature which he might otherwise have ignored.'[1] The continuous reporting of 'youth,' especially its rejection of the work ethic and its wholehearted adoption of the play ethic, sensitized people to the phenomenon of youth so that it was what one expected to see wherever one looked – and frequently all one *did* see.

Lester's television technique was never so appropriately used as in the Greek chorus of middle-aged 'squares' photographed with disapproving expressions on their faces and one-liners on their lips, after the style of a telly commercial for a digestive mint, and all commenting on the kids in the lapidary wisdom of *vox pop*, 'It will all end in tears,' 'I blame it on the National Health,' etc., etc. The over-thirties in the film are represented as 'processed people' programmed by conformity into giving set replies to the most absurd encounters – like Rita Tushingham vibrantly crying 'Rape!' on a housewife's doorstep and eliciting only the blank-faced reply, 'Not today, thank-you.' All liveliness and spontaneity reside in the kids: the lines of the generation gap are sharply and flatteringly drawn. The film's metabolism corresponds to that of young bodies doing acrobatically all the contortions denied to the hardened attitudes of their elders.

The sight-gags at their best convey the sharp observation of

[1] Stanley Cohen, *Folk Devils and Moral Panics* (MacGibbon & Kee, 1972) p. 77.

their victims through the gratifying invisibility of a 'candid camera' technique – like Tushingham stuffing a shopping bag beneath her coat and stopping the road traffic by feigning pregnancy. 'Beware of the dreaded Indian hemp,' says someone, then calls out to a dusky Asiatic, 'Hi, Hemp!' Even Tushingham's repertoire of shouts of 'Rape!' attach themselves to objects and seem to animate them, so that the brakes of a bus appear to shriek the word out in alarm. The film borrows deliberately but happily from other men's styles, like the didactic demonstration *à la Godard* of how to nail up a hall door, the screen having such slogans as 'The Use of the Saw,' 'The Hammer,' etc. super-imposed on it in the kind of stencilled freight-crate capitals that exhibitions of the work of Jasper Johns and Larry Rivers were at that date making familiar to London gallery-goers. The 'knack' itself is treated as if it were endowed with the aphrodisiac quality of a posh deodorant or bath lotion in a telly-commercial. The film opens with just such an image of a bleached-out line of waiting girls filling passageway and staircase as the boy with the knack polishes each one off on the conveyor-belt of his ardent sexuality. And fashion photography is adapted to accentuating individual quirks, like the all-white living-room which one of the boys has painted over 'in case the bomb falls': against its blankness the human shapes are photographed with all their dynamics picked out and emphasized.

The Knack illustrated a force, not a thesis, even though the lustful womanizer turns his coat at the end and becomes a moral prude among the tongue-clucking chorus. But one leaves the cinema remembering the revolt, not the renegade. This is where the film makes common cause with *A Hard Day's Night*, even though Lester observed that *The Knack* was about 'four people who spoke endlessly without any communication – a direct opposite to the Beatles who had enormous communication with-out speech.' Both groups were, as Hollis Alpert wrote, 'an island in amongst an older generation' and what emerges in both films is 'a story . . . of young people finding ways of asserting in-dividuality in a bleak and crowded city-world full of people all too willing to behave as people have always behaved.'[1]

[1] *Saturday Review*, 17 July, 1965.

The film won the principal award, the *Palme d'or*, at the Cannes Film Festival in May 1965, and opened in early June in London, where it was an enormous success – particularly in proportion to its frugal budget. Barely six weeks later Lester had his second Beatles film on the screen: it was the high point in his fortunes and appeared to mark the complete take-over of the entertainment media by mass youthfulness. But inevitably the strains were starting to tell.

EUPHORIA AND DISENCHANTMENT

George H. Ornstein had given the second Beatles film top priority, and United Artists' euphoria showed itself in the budget. Whereas *A Hard Day's Night* had been bought in by Walter Shenson for £189,000, *Help!* (29 July, 1965) cost over £400,000. But even at that sum, it was safe. In the year between the films, Beatlemania had become a world-wide phenomenon. The earlier film had lived up to Epstein's hope – and partial reason for making it – that it would be a celluloid trail-blazer for his flesh-and-blood quartet, and the group had now toured Europe and the Far East as well as doing two North American tours. Their one-night stand at Shea Stadium, New York, on 23 August, 1965, grossed a record $304,000. With that evidence, United Artists could open its purse with a smile.

Help! was the last film, however, that the Beatles made as a group, without contractual compulsion, and even then the celebrity wear-and-tear was showing itself. They were trapped, physically and metaphorically, in their fame. As their biographer wrote, they were rich and powerful and famous enough to open any door they wished, yet always they had to remain behind closed doors for their own bodily protection. The narrative concept of their first film had now become the permanent condition of life for them. And finding a new concept was a headache. Their private lives still could not be shown: it would have meant involving the Beatles in non-public activities like drinking, smoking, and sex. They were still official 'good examples' – 'responsible' public idols. Before very long they would shatter their own images like fun-fair revellers invited to break as much china as they could: Epstein's death and their own intra-group tensions would speed up the process; but film-makers were still obliged to preserve the success pattern, not break it – so 'leisure life' was *out*. Nor could *Help!* be a heightened documentary: all this had been done in the last film. 'So we found we had to do a biographical film about four people without talking about their leisure hours or their working life,' Lester said. 'We had to make them totally passive. As John Lennon said, accurately and ruefully, "We felt that we were extras in our own film" . . . they did, in essence, wander about being attacked by various plots.'

Yet the 'various plots' sprouting out of a Wilkie Collins type of plot about a stolen gem illustrate Lester's deftness at weaving together an extraordinary variety of themes, styles, allusions, and techniques and giving them all a perfectly logical validity.

From strip cartoons came the basic story that immediately branched out into the colour, dialogue and even 'baloon' captions consistent with strip styles. The characters are intentionally two-dimensional: Ringo is 'lovable,' George 'mean,' Paul 'sexy,' John 'sardonic.' Sinister Indians in contemporary London, who assume the protective coloration of military uniforms, clerical vestments and safari gear were emanations of the Goonish love-affair with our imperial past. The gags were a card index to contemporary film hits: a turban that turned into a rather limp 'offensive weapon' recalled Oddjob's razor-sharp bowler hat in *Goldfinger*; the seemingly endless rubber tubing in the Buckingham Palace sequence was a nodding tribute to a similar Jacques Tati gag in *Mon Oncle*. Asprey's, the Bond Street jewellers, the Lambeth Palace Eucumenical Conference, Army exercises on Salisbury Plain, the royal palace itself: the collision with such traditional things as these in the new, youth-possessed London was noticeably more brutal than in the earlier film, which put the emphasis on the escape from tradition. All over, it was a more surrealistic film too, and we are tipped the wink that, behind the façade of normality – 'Success hasn't changed them a bit,' says one of those *vox pop* choristers – lie the personal extravagances that in the years ahead would sunder the Beatles's 'togetherness.' The camera cuts behind the front of four seemingly 'separate' terrace houses to show an open-plan interior like a Dyak 'long house' where the communal living has taken on the fantasy side of incarceration. Drinking, smoking and endless card games, the solace of captive celebrities everywhere, were here turned into the 'gracious-living' accoutrements promoted by the colour supplements recently issued by several national newspapers, or else into the pop trendiness of home-vending machines, or the downright surrealism of a lawn-mower which is used on a grass carpet. (The machine is actually one of the ex-Goon Bruce Lacey's inventions, consisting mainly of a pair of false teeth, and it echoes the hedge-shears used on the lettuce sandwiches several years before in *It's Trad, Dad!*)

Help! hangs together remarkably well – the sheer density of the gags is amazing – but behind it lay a history of dissension and dissolution. The Beatles were disenchanted when they saw it finished, partly for the reason already mentioned, and even while working on it they had become sharper, harder, sourer talents. They didn't want to go through another film in a hurry; a project for a Western hung fire; and when the third film due under the original deal was eventually made, long after Epstein's death, *Let It Be* (1970) might have been taken as a gesture of resignation. It was a *ciné-verité* record of an already fragmenting group in rehearsal or recording; no doubt United Artists agreed to the format with the consoling thought that the music would be worth it, anyhow. But the media were already critical of the Beatles, one ground for complaint being the allegedly harmful effect they had on pubescent fans, which incidentally was the reason that Gil Taylor, photographer of the first Beatles film, gave for not doing the second one. 'I really disapproved of the effect they were having when I witnessed the hysteria our multiple cameras recorded,' he said.

Ornstein, too, had been unhappy about *Help!* At one time he considered abandoning the shooting and starting on a new concept, for his personal view was that *Help!* was 'fourth-rate Marx Brothers stuff' and very hit-and-miss – not really suited to the group's talents. 'But I guess the train was on the track and demand for a new Beatles picture so great that I didn't get anywhere, not even with Epstein.' The film did 'about as well' as *A Hard Day's Night*, but one might have expected the second Beatles picture to do significantly better. The cost, owing to colour and location shooting, didn't help.

Nagging at Ornstein was a feeling experienced by every major production chief if he makes a success of his film company's projects. It is the feeling that others are making more, vastly more money than he is: in particular the producers, directors, writers, stars, etc., of the films he has often laboured long and hard to bring about, supervise (and sometimes more than supervise), launch, and sometimes salvage. It was strictly against United Artists policy for an executive to play producer; and while the company was in many ways an ideal one to work for, its idealism was not expressed first and foremost in the salaries it paid. (Mike Frankovich, who had headed home to Hollywood to be responsible for Columbia's production, would later turn independent producer for much the same set of reasons.) In 1964 two Hollywood majors, noting the fantastic receipts accruing to United Artists from its British productions, offered Ornstein similar posts with them. Instead, he elected to leave United Artists and join Brian Epstein in a production company; but even at that time, early in 1965, Epstein's increasingly erratic habits – his constitution was being sapped by the dosage of barbiturates which killed him in August 1967 – drove Ornstein to despair of anything ever coming of their projects, which included a Richard Condon scenario for the Beatles and a bull-fighting film with Cordobes and Orson Welles. By March 1965 he joined Harry Saltzman and Cubby Broccoli in their Eon production company. But after renegotiating the contract for the Bond films with United Artists, this time from the other side of the table, Ornstein found too little for a man of his energies to do – he also found how difficult it was to do it for two masters – and when an offer was made to him from Paramount Pictures, who were eager to expand their European film-making, he accepted it, hoping to work the production miracle a second time. But *that* story belongs to a later chapter.

Dick Lester remained with United Artists after *Help!* and went to Rome to direct *A Funny Thing Happened on the Way to the Forum*; but his partner, producer Walter Shenson, took leave of the company, and the comments he made some years after *Help!* illustrate an aspect of the distributor–producer relationship which is not peculiar to United Artists. He did not have any cause to regret his relationship: quite the reverse, considering the attractive percentages he owned in the Beatles films. 'When one talks about a company, one talks about the people in it. The United Artists people are tough, laconic, intelligent. Like any company, they are shrewd when it comes to distributing profits, but they give fair shares and if there are disagreements they are negotiated. None of the top people ever indicated he could direct or produce a film better: *that* kind of trouble comes from companies whose management have been producers, directors, agents, or even actors. But I never made a film for United Artists after *Help!* In common with other distributor–producer groups, they will 'go' on a director almost every time if the experience with him has been good, whereas a producer's plight is one of proving himself afresh each time with a new 'package.' You would have thought they'd have been at my door saying, "What have you got?" Instead, the situation was simply that of saying, "Our door is always open." I think that these days when distributors do not develop their own properties they should get down on their knees and thank God for the producers, without whom they would not be in business. The money they pay one is not enough. A producer's pride, his mettle, his vision has got to be recognized just as much as a director's. If he weren't there, the picture wouldn't be there either.'

ANYONE FOR SATIRE?

By the time the first Beatles film appeared, the satire industry in Britain was running at full blast. Satire is, of course, a symptom of social change, very rarely a cause of it; yet the success of the satirical movement helped to define the system of beliefs, and hence to influence the expectations, possessed by the audience it created as it expanded steadily and swiftly in theatrical revues, the satirical Press, the television series, and ultimately into two films which contributed to the now highly marketable image of Britain in the mid-1960s. The first was premièred at the beginning of 1964, perhaps a fatal few months before the home market was ready for it; the second was begun about half-way through 1964 and ultimately shown at exactly the right moment in time for its portrait of British society to be instantly recognized and readily accepted at home and abroad. Both *Nothing but the Best* and *Darling* were scripted by the same writer, Frederic Raphael, and both derived, at least in their basic assumptions, from the identifiable cynicism of a society where the governed no longer accepted as gospel the virtues once attributed to their governors and the established institutions.

The 'credibility gap,' opened up to gulf-like dimensions by the scandals of 1963 which ended fourteen years of Tory rule when the Labour Party won the General Election in October 1964, had begun as the merest hair-line crack in the edifice of power and complacency when the satire show called *Beyond the Fringe* arrived on the London stage in the spring of 1961. Its begetters, who were also its performers – Jonathan Miller, Peter Cook, Dudley Moore and Alan Bennett – had tried it out the year before at the Edinburgh Festival: but it was in the capital that their shafts were most savoured, sometimes, it must be confessed, by the very targets sitting in the front rows of the stalls. A reputation has grown up around them that they were pre-eminently *political* satirists: but it's hard to sustain this view when one inspects their material. As regards the political content of it, they were patent failures, if satirical success is judged by the standards Henry Fairlie referred to at the end of 1961, when he wrote that it was impossible to recall any wounding name or label they had fixed on anyone, 'a single telling phrase or jest, an unforgettable mocking image which has entered the vocabulary of day-to-day political conversation or which has gone to the heart of its intended victim.' The reason, as he saw it, was obvious. 'They know almost nothing of men and affairs, of the way in which power is sought, how it is won and how it is exercised.'[1] One cannot disagree with this: even the Fringe satirists were disturbed by their ready acceptance, their easy popularity. The audience, as Michael Frayn pointed out, became accustomed to being shocked. But probably this was also the extent of their victory: they won too easily, *but they did win*. They pushed forward the barriers of acceptable taste just when they were ready to be pushed. Things like race, royalty, religion and politics, all things that had hitherto been regarded as above comment or simply not thought of as material for 'entertainment,' found a place in the format of their intimate revue. Their bias was refreshingly evident: Penelope Gilliatt called them 'flagrantly biased' and compared them to Mort Sahl in their presumption to be tasteless *and* funny.

Their example was followed, though still inside the metropolitan limits which could be very 'in' indeed, by the appearance of the satirical magazine *Private Eye* in October 1961, marketing gossipy scandal and junior-common-room humour with an increasing sense of moral chastisement to be administered to the ambitious, the complacent, or simply those who were too publicity-worthy to escape whipping now and then. *Private Eye* prospered instantly. By February 1962 it was a fortnightly with a circulation of over 15,000, and in May 1962, it bought the Establishment ('London's First Satirical Night Club') which had been opened in Soho towards the end of 1961 to purvey a sicker brand of social comment than either *Private Eye* or *Beyond the Fringe*, and had swiftly put 11,000 members on its books. Satire was fashionable, profitable, yet still largely restricted to the residents of the parish, the members of the club. As Christopher Booker wrote, '. . . to a large extent the underlying message of the satirists was simply that of the "What's-Wrong-With-Britain?" journalists – only carried to a newly irresponsible, unreal, and more destructive level; particularly in their violent attacks on "Establishment" figures, on Royalty and judges and Conservative Ministers and upper-class accents and the class system, on Britain's pretensions still to be a great nuclear power

[1] *Queen*, 6 December, 1961.

and, above all, on the "decrepitude" of the father-figure, Macmillan himself.'[1]

What changed satire from a thing of incestuous delight to
something of national entertainment was the television show
launched by the BBC in November 1962, with the title *That Was
the Week That Was*. David Frost compèred it and it was inspired
by (and employed) many of those who were already dug into the
satire industry of print or stage. It is important to note that this
belonged to the 'Current Affairs' section of the BBC, not to its
'Light Entertainment' corral, so that its brief was to feed on the
news and not simply to amuse. This was quite a breach in the
tradition of impartiality in the treatment of news laid down for
the BBC by Lord Reith, its first director-general, and it probably
owed its inspiration to three people's recollections of their own
'salad days' which had been stirred by the current fashion in
satire. One of these three, Ned Sherrin, the show's producer,
was just down from Oxford with the glow of undergraduate
satire-shows bright on him; Kenneth Adam, then BBC Director
of Television, was nostalgic for the intimate revues of London's
immediate post-war years; and Hugh (later Sir Hugh) Greene,
the BBC's director-general, thought back to the cellar cabaret of
his pre-war days as a foreign correspondent in Germany. So the
show was blessed by personal predilections; and with encouragement from Donald Baverstock, the show's caustic overseer,
'TW3,' as it got to be called, turned satire and satire's news-
worthy weekly targets into a not-to-be-missed event for an
audience that in the show's eight months' run rose to twelve
million viewers. The majority of these viewers now desired to
be actively shocked or scandalized, while the vocal minority's
protests at actually being so shocked and scandalized ensured the
programme a saturation consciousness throughout the country.
The cinema could no longer ignore satire and, indeed, was all
too eager to promote it.

From the satire show on the small screen some talents passed
rapidly to satirical roles in films on the large one. David Frost,
lifted out of the anchor man's chair, played a barnacle-sized role

[1] Christopher Booker, *op. cit.*, p. 166.

in *The V.I.P.s*; Eleanor Bron from the same show flitted in and out of *Help!*; Millicent Martin, whose harsh rat-tat-tat voice gunning for the current 'Week's' follies supplied the show's signature song, actually played the female lead in *Nothing but the Best*; while one of the show's resident wits, writers and impersonators, William Rushton, also editor of *Private Eye*, made a guest appearance in the film as a sale-room patron murmuring, 'Is Rembrandt "square" or "hip" this week?'

Nothing but the Best (27 February, 1964), produced by Anglo-Amalgamated, was based on the (correct) assumption that class was still a way of life for some and a part of nostalgic memory for most in Britain in the mid-1960s and that the path to advancement was open to him who could convincingly impersonate the life-style, speech-patterns and value-systems of the class above him. The social and political Establishment, even in its shaken condition, still helped to conceal the difference between appearance and reality. Into this vulnerable chink Frederic Raphael inserted his script. Its resemblance to *Room at the Top* was strong, except that class replaced sex as the foot-hold whereby the upstart from the lower levels climbed to the perch of power. It didn't entirely replace it, though, since the men on the make in both films married the boss's daughter. In both, the social consequences shaping the hero's ruthlessness are sketched in bitterly: Laurence Harvey's brief return journey to his childhood slum, Alan Bates's crippled pensioner father who is the victim of an industrial accident. This vulnerability of the working classes is intended to anaesthetize any sympathy we may have for the bourgeois class that the hero is out to exploit. But there the similarities end. The affluent metropolitan society of *Nothing but the Best* is far more rigidly selected and stylized than the north-country milieu of *Room at the Top*: in fact, its graduations are charted as precisely as an advertising agency's market breakdown. This is a world where the company chairman arriving in a Rolls-Royce to a smart salute from the commissionaire is followed by his prospective and titled son-in-law who drives a two-seater Jaguar. Rank bows to commerce where the impetus of such a society is acquisitive. At the same time, a society which is accessible to those who tacitly consent to conform to its values is open to exploitation by others who have acquired the form without the substance. If one has the form, one can forge the title. Indeed, one is accepted so unquestioningly that one hardly needs to forge anything – it would be bad form even to question one's face value.

Alan Bates's impostor is a timeless figure of social satire; but the fraud at the heart of *Nothing but the Best* was particularly characteristic of Britain at that time. It was experiencing the nervous stimulation of young people with talent – and indeed without it – who were crashing through the class barriers. The solid comforts that could be provided by the still relatively tax-free capital gains passed easily into the possession of those who found it simple to create affluence (or the appearance of it). Nothing was for sure, except maybe a cynicism about everything.

There is one passage that not only shows the film at its wittiest, but also adds up to an inventory of mid-1960s attitudes. It is when the intelligent upstart is being coached in the fluent manipulation of class symbols and vocabulary by the upper-class renegade, played to the life by Denholm Elliott. The catechism of question-and-answer is staged as a pre-breakfast work-out in a squash court where the hard rubber ball, slammed back and forth, underlines the callousness of the game of proper prejudices and correct responses which will gain the Top People's acceptance:

'What's wrong with the Socialists? – They're out-of-date. No need for them. – And the Conservatives? – Going pink at the edges. – The Liberals? – Who? – What's wrong with the British workman? – Too bloody middle-class by half. – British Royalty? – Too bloody middle-class by half. – Bloody management? – It ought to pull its finger out. – Negroes are . . .? – Very fine cricketers. – Americans . . .? – Let us down over Suez. – French . . .? – Let us down in 1940. – Germans . . .? – Best infantry in the world. – Indeed they are.'

But Raphael's concern for characterization was frequently coarsened by the influence of the 'telly satire' on the film. Where illumination was required, he too often settled for a lampoon. In compensation, Clive Donner's direction located the film with precision in the perfect conceptual setting: the offices of a fashionable estate agent and auctioneering firm, a business that set the tone for everything bogus, fluctuating, pretentious and would-be respectable in society. He knew his way around the rites of such a society: the film's hunt-ball looked like a devilishly true representation of all the similar events still heavily reported at the time in the society journals. But Donner went beyond mere surface reality. Again and again the smoothly calculated photography of Nicolas Roeg – who was anticipating his own début as a director fascinated by the 'seemingness' of things in a film like *Performance* – revealed the treacherous world of appearances out of which such a society was composed. His effects reminded us of its deceitfulness, in the way the story did, but even more subtly, since they could rely on a precise shift of focus rather than a hit-or-miss bit of dialogue. The close-up opening shot of a stately home is revealed by the camera pulling back to be simply a picture on a cheap biscuit-tin; and the 'mood' sequence of the hero and his girl apparently dancing the night away in some plush club, like those that were opening almost monthly in London, adjusts its focus to let us discover that they are actually moving to the music of a car radio on a dilapidated old Thames barge. Donner was one of the most successful directors of television commercials between his film assignments, and the over-elaborated effects of the advertising medium were deftly appropriate to a picture that emphasized the acceptability of the spurious. The inferior class could be packaged and sold as if it were the real thing. Who would have the effrontery – and very soon one was asking who would have the taste and discrimination – to tell the difference?

THE GIRL MOST LIKELY ...

Yet in spite of its air of smartness and knowingness, *Nothing but the Best* fell dismally flat. It almost seemed as if satire was of consuming interest everywhere except at the cinema box-office. Or perhaps it was simply that the cast had lacked a star whose very *presence* was a guaranteed draw and constituted such a strong contemporary image in his own right that he hardly needed the supplementary benefit of a satirical performance or social attitude. The point of reference of *Darling* (16 September, 1965) was lodged securely inside its star, Julie Christie, in the same way as the eponymous heroine's every whim and desire was narcissistically referred back to her own advantage. Julie Christie incarnated the good-time girl of the era so vividly that the parts she played subsequently appeared to many people to be Darling's distant cousins or historical ancestors.

Though the film appeared when the litany of 'Swinging Britain' was being proclaimed, its origins actually lay three years earlier; and what appealed to its director, John Schlesinger, was not primarily a satirical view of society but the more personally haunting theme of loneliness and disenchantment. '*Darling* was really about choice,' he later reflected, 'about a girl who had the possibility of always thinking there was something better round the next corner, but was never capable of settling for anything, whether emotional stability or professional career . . . I think it was very much a disease of the age.' The germ of the idea for *Darling* came from a man who was professionally in very close touch with popular sentiment and 'in' society – the writer and journalist Godfrey Winn, who was good-humouredly caricaturing himself in *Billy Liar* when he suggested it to Schlesinger and Joseph Janni. He based it on the true case of a call-girl who was maintained by a syndicate of men and who had subsequently committed suicide. Janni paid him £500 for a ten-page treatment. But Schlesinger did not warm to the idea. 'Set in Italy, it would have been a very funny story of the men's warm relationship with their mistress. Set in Britain, it was just ugly and rather nastily sexual,' he said. In any case the 1963 affair of the unhappy John Profumo clearly dictated caution on the film-makers' part, and the basic plot was gradually abandoned while its theme, the turning of a person into a commodity, became more and more timely as society itself, society's entrepreneurs, and society's trumped-up celebrities discovered the profit to be made out of just such a commercial process. In any case, by 1964-5 it was getting harder and harder to scandalize a public which was then receiving its 'fix' of satire thrice weekly in the BBC TV series *Not so much a Programme, more a Way of Life* that had taken over from *TW3* with roughly the same band of satirists and an escalating vulgarity of tone and content that soon provoked the emergence of right-wing moralists and 'order' figures calling for a return to 'decent' values. One thing *Darling* was never intended to be in the beginning was – satire. As Janni and Schlesinger together dictated ideas for the film, based on what they had personally observed of the 'wrap-up and throw-away relationships that people tend to have today more than at any previous time,' the accent was placed even more firmly on individual loneliness.

The character of 'Darling' was based on a girl who had had much the same outwardly successful kind of career and who talked freely about her life, attitudes and acquaintances to Janni, Schlesinger and Frederic Raphael. Janni and Schlesinger had a three-picture deal with Nat Cohen of Anglo-Amalgamated, and it was to him that they turned when they had discovered that 'nobody wanted to back *Darling*. It was turned down right, left and centre. People thought the girl was unsympathetic. "Immoral" was Walter Reade's word, as far as I can remember. Columbia turned it down as unsavoury.'[1] Ultimately Cohen and Janni put up the money. Neither was Julie Christie everyone's first choice. Indeed, Schlesinger decided on her only when he had spent three days in Philadelphia, watching her play in *The Comedy of Errors*. 'Afterwards, I knew that she would be right,' he said, though he added, significantly in view of how the film turned out, 'and that she would be very good for the serious, bitchy moments, but not so good with the comedy. We had to tone that down a little.'[2] This helps to explain why, as he also admitted, 'a lot of the things I thought were funny have turned out to be ironic.' Not

[1] John Schlesinger interviewed by David Spiers, *Screen*, Summer, 1970 Vol. 11 No. 3. Columbia's reluctance may be attributed to the 'morality crisis' then raging in the United States which certain films had provoked. For a fuller discussion of this, see the chapter on American censorship in my book *The Celluloid Sacrifice* (Michael Joseph/Hawthorn, 1966) (also as *Sex in the Movies*, Pelican, 1968).
[2] *Daily Mail*, 14 September, 1965.

surprising, then, considering the way the theme evolved, that the viewpoint finally turned out to be oddly unfocused. Films that depict people with no values ought to be very sure in advance where their own lie. *Darling* was not.

What it lacked was any strong moral positive to offset the heroine's restless negative as she adapted her ambitions to any opportunity the moment brought. The intended ironic counter-point between the life-story as she is heard relating it to a glossy-magazine journalist and the life-story as we saw it happening was used so fitfully and vaguely that many people might have missed it completely, and accepted the excuses the woman was making for herself, especially when they are impaired by the ambivalent view of the Julie Christie character who had to be shown to be a bitch and yet kept 'sympathetic.' Either it should have been a more astringently moral film or she should have been a more defiantly amoral person. The film caught the compromising, opportunistic infection of the very times it was trying to diagnose. But what it also captured, this time very successfully, was a picture of the compulsive promiscuity, professional as well as sexual, of a figure of the times, the freelance female whose ambition barely outlasts her attention span and who moves from bed to bed on the presumption that fidelity means having only one man in it at a time. She either ignores the emotional mess she leaves behind, or believes it is up to others to clean it up. Seemingly the exploiter, she is continually the exploited party. Yet even this, good enough as it goes dramatically, does not go nearly far enough. The comeuppance reserved for 'Darling' is her marriage to an Italian prince who sets her up in style in his *palazzo*, where none of the servants is under fifty, while he shoots off to Rome and a likely mistress. To quote the synopsis of the film, she is 'the prisoner of a world she has conquered.' Maybe. But even with Schlesinger's adroit direction, all this appeared as implausible as it was modish. And it was very modish. A girl of 'Darling's' temperament would hardly have comprehended the notion that loneliness is to be her particular hell, any more than she would have tolerated her 'imprisonment.' Within five minutes of the film's ending, one feels, she would have had the spare

Ferrari on the road to Rome to have herself a little *dolce vita*.

The influence of Antonioni had been just as inappropriate in Jack Clayton's *The Pumpkin Eater* (7 May, 1964), which told the story of an English middle-class marriage in breakdown, by means of the Italian director's favourite peripatetic style of fastidious sensibility. The neurotic destructive relationships between people living out their spiritual desolation amidst high-income comfort demanded a quality of introspection that Clayton and Antonioni both possessed, but it was peculiarly out of place in an essentially English story of a household bursting at the joints with the children who were the one means that the philoprogenitive heroine could use to give meaning to life. It was difficult to imagine an Antonioni heroine's spiritual journey towards self-discovery being interrupted by anything so determinate as a bawling baby. Clayton always thought his film would have done better had it come out eighteen months later; maybe he had *Darling* in mind, for although Antonioni's note of disenchantment looked all too 'barrowed' for the occasion in Schlesinger's film and really fitted no better, it did meet with a welcome from the public that had stayed away from *The Pumpkin Eater*. Clayton's film (scripted by Pinter) probably started a noticeable reaction against him: Schlesinger's film confirmed that he could make an entertainment that was serious and popular and a significant film in spite of its faults.

Raphael's apparently irrepressible tendency towards caricature of the Top People whom 'Darling' moved among at least provided many a spitefully satirical moment. The clutch of unscripted television interviews of the *vox-pop* style; a parody newsreel paying sycophantic tribute to 'the British girl who is Italy's newest *principessa*, no stranger to the palace kitchen, she' (shot of Christie tipping a glassful of wine into a cooking-pot while her chef looks on); a suburban supper-party's painfully accurate colour-supplement small-talk; a charity ball in a gambling club where the camera takes in the phonies, queers, pseuds and parasites and then rises to a full-length portrait of the Queen at the Trooping the Colour ceremony, apparently saluting this section of her subjects under the chandeliers. The critic of *Time* described *Darling* as a 'caustic picture-essay on London' and this was true enough; but the naturalism after which the story was always striving fitted awkwardly into the context of these scenes, and since Schlesinger said the film 'was never intended to be a satire,' we can see where the betrayal lies.

But besides sticking a pin through the heroine and stapling her to the background of her times, the film's social significance derives from the three men in her life. For the characters played by Dirk Bogarde, Laurence Harvey and Roland Curram are all, by profession and inclination, image-makers. Bogarde's character was originally written for an American star who was to play a journalist writing a food column and getting sent in error to Lord's to cover a cricket match. But Paul Newman and Cliff Robertson both turned the part down and a quick rewrite was needed when Bogarde took the role. He became a television interviewer, a man of muddled conscience trying to be true to himself in a medium that encouraged him to be false to his view of society. Schlesinger knew the job from the inside; and it may be more than affection that caused him to cast his own former tutor, Hugo Dyson, as an eminent writer now in retreat from the rottenness of society and representing for Bogarde a small symbol of integrity. But if Bogarde also represents the man striving to tell reality from illusion, Laurence Harvey is a totally cynical advertising executive skilled at manipulating the values of a consumer society by presenting an infinitely more attractive illusion of reality. And Roland Curram, as a smart magazine photographer, battens parasitically on the images of the society that his lens abstracts from reality.

All three men also contain much of the sexual confusion characteristic of the mid-1960s, when the legal tolerance of homosexuality in private was being fortified by the social acceptance of the homosexual – and the coming commercial exploitation of him. Bogarde's 'average sensual man' seeks the fulfilment that wife and family cannot give him by deserting them for 'Darling.' Harvey's character is the bitchy, aimless voyeur: after a surfeit of consumer selling, even a Paris orgy has for him only the faint appeal of a spectator sport. Curram's photographer is overtly a cuddly homosexual who competes with 'Darling' for the favours of a young waiter on Capri. Locking 'Darling's' fate into her manipulation by these three image-makers was a more accurate picture of what was happening in British society than the makers may have realized. Like many a film where the unconscious intention proves stronger than any overt one, *Darling* hit a responsive public nerve in Britain – and not only Britain. Joe Levine bought it from Anglo-Amalgamated for a million dollars and distributed it with success in the United States, where it probably made him his largest profit from a 'quality' film before *The Graduate*. Its box-office appeal there stimulated the rush that was now well under way among the Hollywood majors to finance films with the 'exciting' British label on them.

Yet it was a bad model to follow. Because it relayed the sensations of the 'Novelty Generation' without any corresponding success at judging and condemning them, *Darling* was subject to the same charge that its responses were those of the immediate moment with nothing deeper or more lasting to it. Schlesinger was very pleased with his film at the time. Making it, he said, had given him the keenest enjoyment of any of his films to date. But he found its novelty wore off dismayingly quickly; and two films later he acknowledged it to be his 'least good' movie and added, 'It hasn't stood the test of time.' Recalling its origins in the story of a girl kept by a syndicate of men, he said wryly to me as we were selecting a clip from it for a television programme, 'I only wish we had made *that* story instead.'

Part Three
SHEER FANTASY

I suppose if we can't make our living
in any other way, it will have to do.
But let's not kid ourselves about a renaissance.
This is national senescence, the Road to Ruritania.

Paul Johnson,
quoted in *Newsweek*, 10 May, 1965

Chapter Fourteen: Living the Illusion

> I think the cinema is the greatest thing today. I want to be a director. I want to make epics. I've started already. I've been consultant on a few commercials. But suddenly it's all happening. Everybody's after me. About 20 different people have been trying to sign me up as a director. That's what I want to do – direct.
>
> David Bailey interviewed by Felicity Green, *Daily Mirror*

The vogue phrase in the 1964–5 period in Britain was 'It's all happening.' It was, indeed, in the film industry, at least as far as the American companies were concerned. The National Film Finance Corporation's report for the year ending 31 March, 1966, was a mixture of bitterness and pride: bitterness that so many of the truly British 'independents' were finding no alternative but to seek finance from the American majors: the N.F.F.C. doubted if they could really be called 'independent.' Nevertheless, with British Lion in a state of virtual suspended animation, awaiting the Monopolies Commission report, and the N.F.F.C. itself about to have its lending powers brought to a halt by the 1966 credit squeeze, it recognized reality when it was brought face to face with it and restrained its pessimism by the reflection, 'British film technicians are among the best in the world. British film directors are much sought after, British actors and actresses figure prominently among those who command astronomical fees; and London is fast becoming, if it is not already, the greatest film-making centre in the world.' The N.F.F.C. reckoned that while it was able to assist only 17 per cent of the films made in Britain in 1965, 64 per cent of them were financed in whole or part by American money, and these were on the whole the more important productions made in Britain that year.

The year 1965 was the one in which several of the major American companies, as well as some of the important American 'independents,' committed themselves to setting up, or expanding, production programmes in Britain. By the end of the year

Columbia had so decided, and appointed Maxwell Setton to head its growing British production office. Into the same office came a former actor-turned-agent, John Van Eyssen, who had headed the literary arm of the Grade Organisation which had set up *The Servant*. He was to become Columbia's head of European production in mid-1967. Also at the end of 1965 it was announced that Universal Pictures were setting up a production office in London and putting an ambitious programme of films into preparation right away. It was to be directed by another agent, Jay Kanter, a vice-president of Universal's parent company, the vast Music Corporation of America. Thus the day of the agent-turned-production-chief came to Britain. By the end of the year such American 'independent' producers as Joe Levine, of Embassy, and Martin Ransohoff, of Filmways, were opening offices in London. They, too, had read what was written in the balance sheets. But the message wasn't simply that a growing number of British-made films were racking up huge grosses in America: United Artists, for example, announced record profits in March 1965, a large part of them contributed by their British successes, and as a sign that the goldmine had only been scratched, the appropriately titled *Goldfinger* was producing receipts by early 1965 that were running ahead of *the first two* Bond films. This kind of success proved the boom to be no overnight one; but it scarcely allowed for the feeling, that grew steadily from this year on, that to make a film in Britain was somehow to acquire a touchstone for success everywhere it was shown, especially in the American home market. In the mid-1960s it was estimated that for Britain's 2,000-odd cinemas there were 20,000-odd in the United States; and at a major number of these there were people, particularly young people then constituting the largest and most faithful section of cinema-goers, running at some 65 per cent, who would pay to see, or, more accurately, to experience vicariously the exciting phenomena taking place in Britain. Yet the word 'Britain' is probably casting the social net too wide: a more accurate assessment of the area where 'it's all happening' would be 'London,' and some even thought the events could be confined within a few parishes of the capital, notably the ones in which the media people worked, fraternised and played.

Time magazine in its famous issue of 15 April, 1966, was not by any means the first publication to note the extraordinary flux of professional, commercial and cultural talents composing young London society; but it was the first to term it 'London: the *Swinging* City' and so create a label that was a form of currency wherever its promissory sensations could be turned into hard cash, and in particular at the cinema box-office. Now London is a very small place for many who inhabit its centre and scarcely venture to its sprawling periphery. It is a cliché of American commentators on a first visit, or indeed returning State-side after a prolonged stay, that it is a 'city of villages.' And the film people who flocked there, in ever-increasing numbers from 1964-5 onwards, were more than usually content to settle in one or other of the 'villages.' For without moving far from their home door-step or place of business – in some cases needing only to open the windows and lean out – they could participate in the 'swinging' life of the 'village': a 'village' where every talented inhabitant seemed to know everyone else, where filmworthy properties were to be picked off the trees, where dollar salaries gave the life-style of the 'village' an added boost and where every talented person one wished to meet could materialize in one's presence at a moment's notice (or at least as long as it took to telephone his agent) without the drag out to New York or Los Angeles. It was the Americans who did something for the 'village' that it probably never could have done so successfully for itself: they brought it to market. Imagine bringing a whole village to market! But when the market is the world and the movies are the mode of transport, it does not seem such a Herculean achievement. It was, in fact, for a few short years, an unbelievably rich and hedonistic one.

The British cinema had been moving geographically ever closer to London since the 'social realism' of the early 1960s had obligatorily located nearly every major film hundreds of miles north of the metropolis. It appeared that when Julie Christie had boarded that train south at the end of *Billy Liar* she had brought

K

the British cinema along with her in the baggage van. A capital city is always a magnet; but it is extraordinary how many of the 'social realist' movie characters do an about-turn and reappear, often played by the same actors and actresses, in films that are now more or less built on the dream (sometimes the nightmare) life of the metropolis. Thus Julie Christie, the liberated shop-girl of *Billy Liar*, turns up as 'Darling' the good-time girl; Rita Tushingham moves out of grimy tenement reality in *A Taste of Honey* and into the bleached-out limbo-land of *The Knack*; even the Beatles have to come south to make their film debut; Sarah Miles's classroom flirt in *Term of Trial* becomes bait for Chelsea's upper-class masters in *The Servant*; her co-star Terence Stamp will shortly play the sidekick to Modesty Blaise, heroine of a strip-cartoon originating in London's *Evening Standard*; Alan Bates breaks out of the provincial suburbs in *A Kind of Loving* to take on the capital and win in *Nothing but the Best*; and even Joe Lampton, the boy who might be said to have begun it all in *Room at the Top*, appears again as Joe Lampton (and Laurence Harvey) in the sequel *Life at the Top* seeking his fortune in London – where else would 'Life' begin?

THE VILLAGE GOSSIPS

Iconoclastic, hedonistic and increasingly incestuous, the daily fraternization of age-groups, occupations and financial interests which *Time* was to term 'Swinging London' eventually created the myth of a 'magic village' of such extravagant proportions that later commentators queried whether it had actually existed outside the overheated imagination of journalists and copy-writers. The answer – and it must be a highly personal one – is that, Yes, in a limited but real and increasingly influential way, 'Swinging London' did exist for many of us in the early 1960s, at least for a period of months before the Americans took it up as part of the 'Love Anything British' phenomenon. I have already referred to Stanley Cohen's study *Folk Devils and Moral Panics* and, though one must bear in mind that his concern was with delinquent groups, from which society fled in apprehension, his analysis of the ways in which various forms of sub-culture emerge in society, their growth hastened by the media, seems to me to furnish a structure that can be cautiously applied to the appearance of 'swinging-ness' as a 1960s phenomenon. It was not a threatening fantasy, like the panic that the 'mods and rockers' gave rise to in the media magnification of their occasional gang clashes: on the contrary, it provided a sense of continuous vitality as the fresh events on the London scene were seized on and reported. It not only sensitized readers or viewers who stood outside the 'swinging' scene looking enviously in, but also prompted the 'swingers' on how people expected them to behave.

'Newness' was the quality that, if present, excused the absence of all others. One could have quoted Wordsworth with just a single substitute word and said, 'Bliss was it in that dawn to be alive, / But to be new was very heaven!' The new vocabulary ('gear,' 'kinky,' 'fab,' 'birds,' 'way-out,' 'with-it') created a gratifying sense of belonging; the new boutiques; the new Italian restaurants; the new discotheques; the new gambling clubs; the new pop artistes; the new pop art dealers; the new music groups; the new paperback imprints; the new playwrights; the new morality; the new classlessness. Reporting all of this breathlessly and usually uncritically, the newspapers and magazines, and to a lesser extent the television shows, inevitably exaggerated and heightened it. But this, as Dr Cohen observes, is characteristic of the 'inventory phase' of a phenomenon and he reports how the sharpening up process that occurs produces emotionally toned symbols that eventually acquire their own momentum. People who are thus sensitized to expectations that are not fulfilled when they experience 'reality' rather resemble those who have found the image more stimulating than the object of which it is a reflection. Dr Cohen quotes Daniel J. Boorstin's similar observation on the effects which television and colour photography had on the imagination. 'Verisimilitude took on a new meaning . . . The Grand Canyon itself became a disappointing reproduction of the Kodachrome original.'[1] The 'inventory,'

---

[1] Daniel J. Boorstin *The Image* (Penguin Books, 1963), p. 25.

Dr Cohen reminds us, is not reflective stock-taking, but manufactured news involving elements of fantasy and selective
misperception.

But even this is 'creative' when it comes to be believed; and as
these random events that are making up the sense of daily novelty
and vitality are repeated often enough, they come to 'reverberate
through the social system, creating the conditions on which
subsequent stages are built.'[1]

Now one of the occupations which was both part of the
'show' and also a creative element in the myth-making which
surrounded it was – commercial photography. A better description of it, or the most potent part of it, might be 'cult' photography. The photographic revolution of the 1960s was a violation
of tradition just as much as the satire movement on stage or
television. In both cases the attack was on class-bound attitudes
that predetermined the way one perceived things as well as the
things one perceived. But the impact of the new young photographers on journalism, on pop culture and on mid-1960s cinema
proved to be far more potent, enduring (and ultimately more
corrupting) than that of the satire movement. By 1965, satire had
already got itself a bad name. Its targets were tediously predictable.
Its practitioners had programmed people how to respond, and
now what many people wanted was simply to clear their system
of satire and be grateful for the decades of congested thinking
that had been broken up. But photography had the power
constantly to create new fantasies, not simply to shatter ancient
prejudices; and this made it altogether more seductive, resilient
and commercially viable as it created the 'swinging scene' of the
village-capital. This scene it then sold to the world; so that, by
reproduction and repetition in tens of thousands of international
magazines and newspapers, the reputation of London as the
place where 'it's all happening' was given a fantasy perspective
both sharper and more alluring than reality. 'One perceives and
selects according to certain orientations already in existence,'
Dr Cohen writes, 'and then what is perceived is shaped and

---

[1] Stanley Cohen, *op. cit.*, p. 50.

absorbed into more enduring clusters of attitudes,'[1] The visual power of the image to act on people's beliefs was what fed this spiralling fascination with London.

David Bailey, Terence Donovan and Brian Duffy are the trinity of photographers who contributed to this process. The real world somehow did not look 'real' until they had isolated it on the glossy surface of the fashion magazines – just as it eventually did not look 'real', either, until it pulsated in the coloured flux of the cinema screens. All three came from working-class backgrounds; but they did not emulate the 'classlessness' of people who tuned the (generally upper) class pitch out of their voices for reasons of idealism or commercial expediency and assumed the flat, classless accent that predominated on the London scene, and soon on the London stage and screen. On the contrary, they used their origins with the same aggressive flair as they used their cameras. 'Before us,' Duffy said, 'most fashion photographers were tall, middle-class and a bit camp. We are short, working-class and heterosexual.' They imposed an egalitarianism on whichever group they chose to enter: everyone was equal before the camera shutter. And that, too, was part of the newness. Even royalty had married into the profession in 1960: and the Queen's brother-in-law, the Earl of Snowdon, or plain 'Snowdon' when it was a matter not of letters of nobility but of professional accreditation, would go to work for the new offshoot of the print media, the Sunday newspaper colour supplements, and help make up the mosaic of the 'swinging' life-style.

Several of these photographers, while still in their late twenties and early thirties, had a yearly income in excess of £100,000. Their East End approach shattered many a cultured shibboleth of the West End world across the Thames without their even being aware of it – at first, anyhow. Bailey had photographed in 1962 a model called Jean Shrimpton standing, walking and sitting down quite normally without the 'distance' deliberately interposed between the potential client and the commercial mannequin by reason of the latter's frozen posture. A small event, perhaps. But it meant there was an immediate identification with the girl, not

[1] Ibid., p. 49.

just with the clothes on her back. The model whose life is reported in every detail had been a feature of the American scene for some time: from the early 1960s on she was increasingly a person of interest in Britain, too. Soon she was absorbed into the photographer's life-style, a symbolic relationship not uncommon between the star and her director at some periods in the film industry. And as the image was repeated in the public prints until it detached itself from their pages and became a part of the look of young people everywhere, the photographer became a pop tastemaker in far more than the fashion world he originally inhabited.

In December 1965 there was published a book – no, not a book but a box, a container with a stack of thirty-six photographs in it. Pasted on card, with lengthy captions by Francis Wyndham on the back, they represented not the best work that a photographer might wish to preserve from his folio, but David Bailey's own nominees – 'the people who, in England today, seem glamorous to him.' David Bailey's *Box of Pin-Ups* was not an aesthetic statement; it was a social one. And what defined his choice was life-style, not breeding. Wyndham described it as 'London Life in 1965,' and he added, 'Many of the people here have gone all out for the immediate rewards of success, quick money, quick fame, quick sex – a brave thing to do.'[1] Among the 'brave ones' were Lord Snowdon, Cecil Beaton, P. J. Proby, the Beatles, Mick Jagger, Gerald McCann (a fashionable milliner), Jean Shrimpton, Nureyev, James Woolf, and the Kray twins (notable gangsters of the Town). Around nearly all of them hung an essentially narcissistic satisfaction. Later on, when some among them had died or been sentenced to long terms of imprisonment, people avowed that the photographs also conveyed an impression of impending doom. But it is very easy to pronounce such a verdict once the coroner has assembled his court. At this time it was very much the photographer who had *his* court grouped around him. 'The camera,' said Malcolm Muggeridge, 'the most characteristic and sinister invention of our time, has ushered in

---

[1] *David Bailey's Box of Pin-Ups* (Weidenfeld & Nicholson, 1965).

– perhaps, better, crystallized – a religion of narcissism, of which photographers such as Mr Bailey are high priests.'[1]

The predominance of the image facilitated that psychic longing to break out, to 'take off,' as the 'in' phrase of the later 1960s had it, which the Bond films had been the earliest to tap publicly. Pop culture lent it impetus. It gave the fantasies sharper focus, magnified their brilliance, promoted their ubiquity. Mid-way through 1965 the venerable yet ageless super-heroes of the American comic strips, Batman, Superman and all the other caped crusaders, were enjoying a great camp revival in the United States and the craze swiftly spread to Britain where, at the beginning of 1966, the fifteen-part serial film of Batman and Robin made in 1940 and lasting 248 minutes (if you sat it out from one cliff-edge to the next), was packing in the pop crowd at one of London's West End cinemas and generating a camp affection for what everyone knew was really bad but, if one were to approach it from a smart and knowing vantage-point, could really be considered good. Fantasy heroes, only several degrees removed in coloration and capacities, it seemed, from the all-stars in the Bailey box of public heroes, took over the pantheon of images that had been once inhabited by the old social rebels. The image could scarcely solve social problems, but there was no better way of releasing personal fantasies. For the American film-makers resident in London there was also the gratifying reassurance that Britain's fantasies were America's, too, and that for once the box-office of one country couldn't resist what the film-makers of the other turned their cameras on.

This rapidly emerging fantasy community, a Camelot-on-Thames, had been strongly foreshadowed a year earlier by the appearance, within a week or so of each other, of two new newspaper colour supplements, *The Observer*'s and *The Daily Telegraph*'s, both dedicated to creating the feeling of Living, intense and capitalized and, wherever possible, in enriching colour.[2]

[1] *The Observer*, 12 December 1965.
[2] *The Observer* colour supplement was launched on 6 September, 1964, the *Weekend Telegraph* on 25 September, 1964. *The Sunday Times* had published its first colour supplement on 4 February, 1962.

Earlier that same year, 1964, the *Sunday Times*'s colour supplement, which had been first in the field, declared that 'Taste '64' was above all else 'a way of looking.' And Christopher Booker wrote, 'Now (in 1964) the coalescence of one form of fantasy with another to make up a sort of overall "pop culture" was taking place so fast that, within a year or two, no one would be surprised to see the pages of the "quality" Press regularly taken up with rapturous reviews of the latest pop records, or prominent pop singers being starred in plays and films by directors of impeccable "intellectual" credentials.'[2] The *image* was the factor that unified the pop and the *avant-garde* cultures, as far as the young were concerned. There can never have been a period of post-war Britain when the eye had to organize so much perceptual experience. The Gulbenkian Foundation's art exhibition entitled 'Painting and Sculpture of a Decade: 1954–64' proved immensely popular when it opened at London's Tate Gallery in April 1964. It conveyed to a wide, youthful and generally non-gallery-going public the powerful feeling of the image-ridden environment from which artists like Rauschenberg, Dine, Lichtenstein, Johns and others (but as yet no Warhol) could borrow directly, dressing up, mimicking, punning upon and claiming the familiar object for their own purposes, and giving 'the common images of the day' a magic that they didn't possess in the real world. The movie camera was about to do the same; and we have already seen how Dick Lester happily incorporated such influences in *Help!* and *The Knack* which came out the following year. The impact of such an exhibition, increased many times over by its coverage in the newspapers and magazines, assisted the restless dominance of the image so that it could scarcely be overlooked by the resident Americans, who were invariably swifter at spotting and absorbing, and more enterprizing at merchandizing, whatever was saleable among the elements of pop phenomena.

With the exception of Alan Aldridge, Peter Blake and Allen Jones – I am not forgetting David Hockney and R. B. Kitaj, but they were eventually 'gallery' stars, not 'market-place' performers – British pop artistes played a smaller part in influencing this

[1] Christopher Booker, *op. cit.*, p. 231.

'way of looking' than British photographers. The record companies, then the paperback publishers and only later – paradoxically – the film-poster people put this trio of graphic artists to
work (or simply picked up ideas from them and put others to
work on them), so that the environment outside the art galleries
and museums became full of tantalizing polychrome images and
playthings. One gallery artist who burst on the scene with
historical promptness in 1964 was Bridget Riley, whose 'op art'
paintings were exhibited at the Robert Fraser Gallery, Fraser had
been one of Bailey's 'Pin-Ups' and was later to share the flash-
light glare with another of them, Mick Jagger, in Richard
Hamilton's painting of their arrest on drugs charges in 1967:
among themselves, pop 'priests' were great cannibals. Riley's
violation of visual orthodoxy in favour of constantly moving
neural patterns gave the eye a continual jag of excitement. It was
a sensation akin to the restless movement, the daily stimulation,
the after-images of a bright 'swinging' existence which the media,
and in particular the movies, were projecting with increasing
frenzy from the mid-1960s on.

The image would surrender more and more of its content as
the record of recognisable social reality transformed itself into
catering to increasingly fragmented fantasies and sensations, and
at last reached the point where no more could be absorbed and
fatigue set in – the fatigue of the nervous breakdown. Towards
that fatal overloading, the British cinema, powered by the booster
motors of American finance and opportunism, was now directing
itself.

CULT GOES PUBLIC

One of the earliest uses of 'op art' effects in a commercial feature
film was the coloured-light show assaulting the captive hero of
The Ipcress File (18 March, 1965) in a brainwashing sequence;
while the opening credits of *Goldfinger*, premièred at the end of
1964, showed the floating, shimmering influence of 'op' as they
were projected in soft, intangible form on to the burnished
bodywork of one of the villain's gilded victims. No accident that

both were films made by the Saltzman or Saltzman-Broccoli team which had always shown itself so alert to the manifestation in their films of whatever stimulus was passing through the collective consciousness of the public.

But if one sought the key film that cross-pollinated the cults of op and pop with the world of commerce, it would have to be *Modesty Blaise* (5 May, 1966). That it should have been directed by no less a personage than Joseph Losey was evidence enough of the mingling of *avant-garde* and popular entertainment. Based on a Peter O'Donnell strip cartoon featuring what might have been called a female James Bond and her cockney sidekick, one Willie Garvin, the film had originally been announced in February 1965 as part of a programme on which British Lion, as if it were whistling in the dark to keep its courage up, declared its willingness to spend £2,000,000 'over the next year or two' on a dozen features.[1] *Modesty Blaise* was to be the first, at a budget of £600,000, and it was to be directed by Sidney Gilliat and produced by Joseph Janni. The film at that stage was uncast; but the same programme included mention of 'a Monica Vitti subject' to be produced by Joseph Janni. What ensued in the interval is still far from clear, but the *Modesty Blaise* project soon afterwards passed – along with Jenni, but not with Gilliat – on to 20th Century–Fox's British production roster. Monica Vitti was named for the title role, and Joseph Losey was set to direct.

With his screenwriter Evan Jones, who had scripted *The Damned* and *King and Country* for him, Losey set about remoulding the story; and gradually the element of plot was demoted more and more in favour of drawing into the scenario the maximum amount of currently fashionable images and experiences. This succeeded so well, declared one critic, that 'if a social historian were faced with the task of citing the film most representative of

[1] Other films announced were *Lord Byron*, with John Schlesinger directing from a Frederic Raphael screenplay (never made); *The Great St Trinian's Train Robbery* (directed by Launder and Gilliat, 1966); *All in Good Time* (directed by Roy Boulting, 1966, under the title *The Family Way*); a film version of Doris Lessing's *A Woman Alone* (never made); *Pimpernel of the Vatican* (never made) and a Malcolm Muggeridge original *Who's for Sex?* (never made);

the age, *Modesty Blaise* would be a strong candidate.'[1] To this deliberate 'fashionableness' may be attributed some of the subsequent irritation the picture produced, though Losey's supporters among the critics chose to regard it as the director's 'caprice'; his permissible 'fun' picture; a 'folly' which distinguished artists could indulge themselves in constructing; and even, in Penelope Houston's memorable phrase, as Losey's disposable 'paper handkerchief.' (This notion of instant disposability was timely, too, as the auto-destruct mobiles and sculptures were all the rage in art shows when the film made its appearance.)

But chiefly *Modesty Blaise* (even the first syllable echoed the 'mod' trend) was regarded as a toy for intellectuals, akin to those calming desk-top playthings for overworked executives which began to pop up in the gift boutiques towards the end of the 1960s. Coming from a radical like Losey, some thought it a most surprising piece of chic. What had drawn him to the project? Possibly the intriguing question of what kind of film might be turned out if a director of real distinction got to work on the 'Bond' formula. Possibly, too, the chance to work with Monica Vitti, hitherto the *avant-garde's* playmate, the passive and passionless embodiment of Antonioni's peripatetic pessimism in such films as *L'Avventura* and *The Red Desert* (which was shown in Britain in April 1965, just a few months before Losey started shooting). Seeing what one can do with another artist's favourite model is a particularly appealing challenge, especially if, as in this case, the material can be remoulded into that of a woman who is viewed, as Paul Mayersberg observed, very much as a Losey heroine. Modesty Blaise is seen as a creature who is in conflict with the world, just as *Eve* was, or else disposed to take her feelings out on men, like the fiery heroine in *The Gypsy and the Gentleman*. Modesty Blaise, Mayersberg pointed out, is anti-man as well as anti-Bond.[2] For quite a large part of his career, Losey has gravitated towards actresses who are fiercely independent, jealous of their own power to handle their careers, yet almost welcome the chance to test their strength in vying with an equally

[1] *Monthly Film Bulletin* June, 1966 No. 389, Vol. 33, p. 89.
[2] Paul Mayersberg, *New Society*, 5 May, 1966.

strong-willed director for possession of the part or the film: Mercouri, Moreau, Taylor, eventually Jane Fonda – out of their insistent egotism, at war or in alliance with their directors, something should emerge that will key the film, the role, or the experience to a higher pitch. It was probably with this hope that Losey approached the prospect of directing Vitti. Janni's Italian connections were useful in securing her agreement; but her own wishes were ultimately the decisive factor, and she probably felt the time was propitious, even necessary, to make a change. Her previous film, *The Red Desert*, had been unkindly received at the 1964 Venice Festival and this may have been material to her strongly expressed wish to work with someone like Losey who had a reputation not only for wringing revealing performances out of actresses, but also for recasting a star in a new image as he had done, with Bogarde's help, in *The Servant*. He spent some weeks with her in Rome and later expressed his belief that he had found a lusty, outgoing side to her untouched by Antonioni. The Modesty Blaise role, he believed, would help Vitti redefine herself.

If so, this was not the most striking point the film made. Indeed, Vitti's *dependence* was more in evidence than her independence. Perhaps her unfamiliarity with English sapped her self-confidence: more likely she simply was not temperamentally suited to an action role limned for an Amazon. Instead of pagan, her vitality seemed fey. The very lack of a strong driving force in the film found one's attention even more strongly on the accessories – the whole chic environment, which now looked quite patently the *raison d'être* for making the film. On this level, it worked astonishingly well. It was an advertising age fantasy, an almost plotless series of 'happenings ' – another word in vogue in 1966 – made in the expectation that what is cult property today will be public property tomorrow. It parodied the familiar 'surprise' sequences preceding the credits in the Bond films, when a gent with umbrella and bowler rings the doorbell of a house in Amsterdam, which instantly blows up, and the remainder of the film followed this baroque mood strongly with bravura hints of Dick Lester, like the Arab dagger skimming out of a window in

the Ritz Hotel, where an oil emir is ensconced, and impaling a
London pigeon, thus bringing a barbaric touch to homely Piccadilly. Modesty and Willie Garvin (Terence Stamp) pull up their
speeding Ferrari to croon a mildly ribald duet à la *The Umbrellas
of Cherbourg*. The arch-criminal Gabriel (Dirk Bogarde in a silver
wig which he snatches off when things turn serious, thus illustrating one playtime fantasy wrapped inside another) has his status
denoted by the size of his wine glass whose goblet is big enough
to hold a goldfish (and does). He imprisons Modesty in a cell
decorated with eye-straining designs – and what could be more
apt for a pop art heroine than an op-art dungeon? It borrowed its
glamour gadgetry from Bond's arsenal of machine-tooled
fantasy: Modesty's lipstick-holder elongates into an arrow; her
hat converts into a gas mask. Evan Jones's screenplay is like a
fly-paper that craftily lets a lot of Losey's trademarks stick to it:
the mirrors, the winged figures, even the leather chair used for
a memorable seduction in *The Servant* and now doing duty as a
sheik's throne.

But nothing dominated the film like Richard MacDonald's
production design. He provided his own contemporary titillation
through the multitude of trends he incorporated. The pretty
cassata tints that stained even the fumes of a smoke-bomb recalled
the Jacques Demy film *The Umbrellas of Cherbourg*; Modesty's huge
cone of multicoloured ice-cream was straight out of a pop
painting; her all-white bedroom matched Dick Lester's favourite
bleached-out telly décor; its trick of revolving 360 degrees
incorporated one of the best publicized aspects of the new needle-
thin Post Office Tower, just north of London's Oxford Street,
with its sky-high revolving restaurant. (This addition to the skyline was so regularly featured in 'Swinging London' films from
now on that it came to resemble the maypole round which the
'swinging' acolytes danced themselves to exhaustion point.) The
old archery targets and tailor's dummies cluttering up Willie
Garvin's apartment-lair signified the camp affection attaching to
old junk, but it could also have been the workroom of a photographer who needed kinky props for his models. Modesty's
costumes certainly resembled the bizarre creations which the

glossies feature against some vividly contrasting (often reproach-
ful) local scene or life-style, which thus endows them with an even
more dream-like allure. Willie Garvin's gear came from Carnaby
Street – where else? And the credits carried the season's kinkiest
attribution, 'Miss Vitti's Additional Costumes *and Tattoos* . . .'

20th Century–Fox had involved itself in *Modesty Blaise* as a
direct result of seeing the immense profits that the Bond films
were now making for United Artists throughout the world. It
believed that the 'Swinging London' phenomenon would be
extra additive in the film's tank. While in production, it was
Darryl F. Zanuck's favourite Fox film – and may still be so, for
all one knows – and Losey had an unusually free hand, and a far
more lavish budget than he could ever have dreamed of. The film
is reputed to have cost £1,000,000. The critical reception accorded
to it in Britain was fair-to-indulgent; and much the same was true
of the United States, though the anonymous critic of *Time*
pronounced on it particularly harshly as 'less a spoof than a limp-
wristed kind of fairy tale, utterly cluttered up with homosexual
malice, artsy gift-shop décor and the same old gagging gadgetry
on which the Bondmen have patents pending.'[1] The public
reception was not all that the makers hoped for, considering the
investment, and Losey blamed in part the exploitation publicity
which led people to expect a woman who was 'more dangerous
than the male' – 'a kind of female James Bond (which is) something it isn't.'[2] Well, maybe not, though it sounds ingenuous of
Losey to be protesting on that score when the film fairly insistently
invites parody comparison with the Bonds. More likely it was
the confusing mixture of genres which put some people off it.
The thrills they anticipated did not materialize in the obvious
ways; the comedy was often of a bafflingly 'in' variety. Losey
claimed that the film worked on many levels. But we may doubt
how deeply one needed to dig before the mine was exhausted;
though at least one critic discovered unsuspected ore when he
identified Gabriel's fortress isle, topped by its church tower, as
'a defence of the Christian West against modernism.' One hardly

[1] *Time*, 13 August, 1966.
[2] James Leahy, *op. cit.*, p. 149.

needs to swing one's critical pick into that particular moraine in order to appreciate *Modesty Blaise*.

The likelier truth is that the film is not so much a message for its time as a metaphor of it. Scandal and corruption had made *The Servant* just such a metaphor in its day: but that day was three years earlier, and, instead of austerity of conduct, what had principally been engendered in the interval was cynicism, a detachment of feelings from actions that ultimately freed the mind from responsibility. Instead of 'learning the lesson,' one simply remembered the sensation; and so far from getting to 'the heart of things,' one was seduced away by their imagistic surface appearance. The eye was feasted, excited and gratified, while the conscience was seldom touched except in the most perfunctory manner – and even this was abandoned once the 'swinging' society began to be superseded by the 'permissive' one. All of which suited the film industry perfectly, since it had traditionally purveyed 'novelty' as its come-on, not 'morality.' *The Servant* had appeared at a time when we were all sick with what the social system had revealed; and it acted with the expulsive force of a purgative. By the time *Modesty Blaise* came along, we had begun the slide into unreality and fantasy. Losey's film was just one more distraction provided by the toy-manufacturers.

ALFIE BOY, GEORGY GIRL

If *Modesty Blaise* represented the transient novelty of contemporary fashions in the visual arts, then *Alfie* (24 March, 1967) represented another kind of fantasy whose satisfactions were even more intense and direct – the fantasy of easily and endlessly available sex. *Alfie* was a London cockney boy's dream of a Casanova-like existence which might have been lived out in reality – and in some cases was so – by the self-same cockney boys from South London who had become film stars and fashion photographers. While 'reality' for them often meant taking their dirty washing home to Mum – such avowals of unspoilt stardom quickly became the cliché of a thousand and one interviews – their 'fantasy' remained the showbiz one of easily plucked 'birds.' ('Birds' was a word that came into vogue in the summer and autumn of 1966.)

Alfie was played by Michael Caine, who had been put under contract and into *The Ipcress File* at the end of 1964 by Harry Saltzman, both because he felt he recognised material that could be groomed to stardom and because he wanted a hedge against the innumerable imitations which the James Bond films were now spawning world-wide and which, he feared, might make the public weary of the original. Although Cubby Broccoli asked, 'Why compete with ourselves?', Saltzman believed the time was ripe for an anti-hero of the espionage world, and Len Deighton's nameless character – christened 'Harry Palmer' in the film – fitted the bill. It was a bill deliberately conceived with the feeling of petty cash about it, rather than Ian Fleming's expense account profligacy. Caine fitted the part to perfection, too. Just as Connery's Scots–Irish accent had avoided the 'class' problem with Bond, Caine's East End vowels, which had come ruinously through his otherwise gallant attempt to play an aristocratic English officer in *Zulu* (1963), could adapt themselves precisely to playing a neutral 'meritocrat' who didn't owe his allegiance to a class system, but to his own abilities and to the job he was paid to do. 'Looking after Number One' was Ipcress Man's motto, as it was that of many a native in the near-slum area known as the Elephant and Castle, where Caine had been born as Maurice Micklewhite. The name might have belonged to a friendly milk-man or a cheery barrow-boy who sold his fruit and vegetables by half-flirting with the housewives going by. Local habits and inherited characteristics were used by Caine to erect his career in the way a builder uses scaffolding to mark out the rising structure. The notion of serving oneself first – and only then Queen and Country – was one that touched a responsive nerve in a nation so firmly in the grip of a consumer boom that it had run up an £800 million trade deficit by the end of 1964.

Then, again, Ipcress Man needed to wear spectacles: Bond could not have admitted even to the fractional reality of contact lenses. Caine needed glasses, too, which fitted in perfectly with the low-profile sexiness of Harry Palmer. Other men needed to take off their shirts to be thought 'sexy.' Caine had much the same effect on women simply by taking off his spectacles. Like other actors who are short-sighted, his myopia conveyed the flattering feeling to a woman in his vicinity that she, for him, was the only one who mattered. (The truth usually was that she, for him, was the only one he could see.) Bond's speciality was throw-away quips: Ipcress Man cultivated the dumb insolence, as the Army would call it on the charge sheet, of an Other Ranker – the kind who forgot to say 'Sir,' or left the office door open behind him. These were the traits, too, of cockney independence. Lastly, Caine, though he had been married, gave out the feeling of being an available bachelor; and *The Ipcress File* put deliberate emphasis on those bachelor habits that make a man independent of girls, yet don't interfere with his bedding them down in his pad. Ipcress Man prepared his own meals, whereas Bond invariably ordered them; Ipcress Man shopped at the supermarket, whereas, if Bond shopped at all, it was at Fortnum and Mason's.

The other piece of luck that came Caine's way, as well as finding a role that fitted him like a second skin, was that he came within the star-making power of Saltzman who, with the resources of Bond securely coming in, left no dollar unspent in ensuring that his candidate for Connery's running-mate would be internationally known by the time *The Ipcress File* hit the screen. It was made for distribution by Rank (in Britain) and Paramount (in the United States and other territories), presumably so as to avoid conflict with the Bond films that were a United Artists product. The blueprint of 'ordinariness' was followed sedulously in the look of the film – natural locations instead of superman sets – and the overall colour was restricted to the grey-green-brown hue of London. 'At that time,' said Ken Adam, who brought his drawing-board over from the *Goldfinger* enterprise, '*The Spy who came in from the Cold* was still over the horizon and it was considered quite daring to strip away the glamour of espionage – so that instead of our spymaster sitting in a nest of communications, for example, we made him into an ascetic, with just a camp bed, a trestle table, an ordinary chair.'

Yet the significant thing about *The Ipcress File* when it appeared, apart from confirming Caine's star status, was that much of the careful preparation to make an anti-Bond film went by the board once the action got under way. The pull of fantasy proved just too strong for downbeat reality to resist. For someone suffering from myopia, Harry Palmer wasn't noticeably handicapped in taking aim without his spectacles. The jokey deaths, like the assassination in a traffic jam, could have come from a Bond film (had they not already come from a Fritz Lang film) and though the locations were public ones they reflected Adam's sense of dwarfing design. (One realized how much of London had already been built in the Adam style.) Even the anti-Bondman was a dream hero, impervious to torture, unconfinable by prison cells, though possibly the lineaments that Caine provided made one think that one was seeing Superman perform while still clad in his Clark Kent disguise of cheap suit and spectacles.

At any rate, by the time Michael Caine went into *Alfie*, which was being directed by Lewis Gilbert for Paramount's British production office, he had acquired the valuable inventory of star characteristics. *Alfie* was what got them all together. The very aptness of the billing, 'Michael Caine *IS* Alfie' (instead of simply 'as'), was not lost on the public. His sexuality now invested his whole screen persons with the candid, take-it-or-leave-it attitude of the undomesticated working-class male which, as Isabel Quigly said, was once 'thought totally un-English, but (is) now being fished out of the proletarian pond where Englishness of the traditional kind never flourished. Like the new bright clothes on the new bright boys, he suggests a subterranean national character rising to surprise even the locals (and surely to startle the outsiders).'[1]

This 'proletarian pond' had first been stirred up by *Saturday Night and Sunday Morning*; but whereas Arthur Seaton stayed rooted in the industrial milieu, against whose working-class *mores* he covertly offended, Alfie moved on to flamboyant open conquest of the 'birds,' a recognizable pretender to middle-class status in his flannels and navy blazer with its Services badge on the breast pocket (the perfect notation mark of male solidarity

[1] *The Spectator*, 1 April, 1966.

allied to spivvish vanity). For Alfie, the only real life is sex-life: only then can he kid himself he is living. Sex is not used here as the working-class boy's way to 'the Top.' Executive status has no appeal for Alfie. Nor has class mobility. He is quite content to stay where he is, thank-you, so long as the 'birds' are 'in beautiful condition,' as he assures us they are in one of the candid, over-the-shoulder asides to the camera which the film carried over from *Tom Jones*. Had *Alfie* come out in the 1970s, when Women's Lib was digging its spurs into male flanks, it would have been dubbed a crude propaganda tract for chauvinist male pigs. All women to Alfie are lust-objects: one of his most servile girl-friends is contemptuously and continually referred to as 'it.' The film shows how much of the 'swinging' quality of London life was a male creation and, through the hierarchical dominance of the fashion photographers, a male prerogative. Alfie's eye for a 'bird' is as sharp and pitiless as Bailey's camera lens. With two striking exceptions, such as the married woman played by Vivien Merchant, whose aborted foetus lies on Alfie's kitchen table like a guilt-object, and the mature 'bird' played by Shelley Winters, who betrays Alfie by 'doing it' with a pop singer; all his girls have the rootless pliability of models flitting from appointment to appointment, shutter-click to shutter-click.

Caine's throwaway, ribaldy ironic voice lent Alfie more human-ity than his sexual reflexes warranted. His self-serving badinage, 'looking after Number One,' became on his paradoxically prim-and-pursed lips just the cockney's classic way of chatting up the 'birds' till they fell off the branch. 'He is not overly intense, doesn't display much voice range and seems to eschew flamboy-ance,' Hollis Alpert wrote. 'What he does do is understand his character and parade its enactment with a kind of ironic sympathy . . . (he) might have appeared to be somewhat loathsome other-wise.'[1] On the other hand, the critic of *Time* cried, 'Come off it, lads. A rat is a rat, and hanging a blue ribbon on the beast doesn't turn him into a prize Pomeranian.'[2] These two extreme opinions sum up Alfie's built-in contradiction. His clear-eyed amorality

[1] *Saturday Review*, 27 August, 1966.
[2] *Time*, 2 September, 1966.

('I don't want a bird's respect, wouldn't know what to do with it'), so unflinchingly conveyed by Caine's voice-over narration, is far more convincing than the cautionary moral he extracts from his experiences at the end of the film ('I ain't got my peace of mind and if you ain't got that, you got nothing'). Alfie's honesty is that of the proficient technician. Perhaps there is a point in endless copulation where quantity turns into quality; but it does not so convincingly turn into conscience, too. Alfie's self-engineered comeuppance reminds us of Joe Lampton's in *Room at the Top* and its 1965 sequel, or the heroine's at the end of *Darling*. Alfie is several moves further on into fantasy, but all three figures are consumers in a consumer-orientated society: Lampton laps up wealth, Darling laps up fame, Alfie laps up sex. They recall the characteristic drives attributed by Francis Wyndham to the real-life cult-figures of 'Swinging London' in David Bailey's *Box of Pin-Ups*: '(they) have gone all out for the immediate rewards of success, quick money, quick fame, quick sex.' At least photo-captions are more honest than the codas that the screenwriters feel compelled to devise for their heroes and heroines, which consign them to the modish fates of loneliness and desertion. Egos of their kind can be hurt by various knocks that life inflicts: but being at a loose end is not among them.

But the fantasy dimension of *Alfie* chimed in so well with the hedonistic mood of the era now well publicized and exploited on both sides of the Atlantic that this, plus the variegated sex that was still astonishing for the candour it displayed on the American screen at that date, made it into an enormous box-office success. It remains Michael Caine's most effective film in the way it defines a type who was specific and universal – and above all, human. At the same time its success was such that he had difficulty in persuading producers that he had a future in any other kind of role. The wealth and fame that arrived with *Alfie* did not seem able to supply the acting status he felt in need of – a recognition that playing Alfie *did* involve judgment and finesse – and for the next few years, as far as films went, he quite cynically accepted any part that paid enough. Though extraordinarily frightening in *Get Carter* (1971) as a vengeful racketeer, and hugely comic in

Pulp (1972) as a pulp-thriller writer, he still felt he ought to remove that vestigial cockney cloth cap to his 'betters' in the 'acting profession' till he appeared with Olivier in *Sleuth* (1972) and matched – and sometimes mated – the senior actor move for move. Approached almost immediately afterwards to appear in a sequel to *Alfie* (for a very large fee indeed), he turned the offer down flat. *Alfie Mark II* could have added nothing to what he had achieved with *Sleuth*: a fulfilment of the Cockney boy's curiously dated yet still powerful aspiration to gain the 'respectability' of the class above him.

   Georgy Girl (13 October, 1966) did not even pretend to the recognizable social reality against which Alfie's fantasies were staged. It was a fairy-tale – the one about the Ugly Duckling – that might have been concocted according to *Time* magazine's ingredients for 'Swinging London.' It celebrated the kookiness of Lynn Redgrave, child of the working class but reared in the rich household of her parents' employer (James Mason, self-made tycoon with obligatory north-country accent) who makes her a proposal of marriage in an ending straight out of *Daddy Long Legs*.

   There was a great deal of physical running around town *à la* Godard, dancing in the rain like the bemused people in the telly commercials, and visiting a children's empty playground to frolic on the roundabout like the couple in *A Kind of Loving*. The escalating 'permissiveness' of the era was worked into the *menage à trois* inhabited by Georgy, her extra-cool girl-friend (Charlotte Rampling) and the latter's boy-friend (Alan Bates as a huggable Ur-hippy). Accompanied by a ruthlessly up-beat pop ballad, the film was essentially an extended advertisement, an L.P. commercial, for Georgy's brand of lovableness and London's brand of metropolitan razzmatazz. Nevertheless, it was a shrewdly timed film, save in one respect – it just missed being able to include the first widely publicized evidence of the existence of a British drug scene that came with charges of LSD-taking in Chelsea in the winter of 1966. Otherwise it transmitted all the overladen euphoria of the capital. Directed by Silvio Narizzano and produced by Otto Plaschkes, it proved one of the biggest-grossing films Columbia distributed in the United States in 1967; by 1969 it had grossed $7,000,000 there and $6,000,000 in other countries; and thus another American major was sold on the universal interest, not to say profit, attaching to the life-style of London.

ASYLUM LIFE

Compared with Alfie and Georgy, the central character of *Morgan, A Suitable Case for Treatment* (14 April, 1966) was an even more aggressive and self-admitted dreamer, a fantasist who used his flights of fancy as refuge from external reality, where his unconventional behaviour landed him in a divorce from his wife, trouble with the police and, ultimately, incarceration in a lunatic asylum. Produced by Leon Clore, *Morgan* was directed by Karel Reisz and showed not only the mark of that director's genuine originality, but also how the 'swinging' contagion had afflicted even the most serious film-makers. What the film had to say was highly imaginative; the way it said it, depressingly derivative.

It was probably the first film of social protest to be adopted as their own by the post-Porter generation, the teenagers who had been children in 1959. And in this sense, it was a prophetic film. It was one of the earliest appearances in the commercial cinema of the kid who feels an outcast – the drop-out hippy who doesn't want to stay inside society and bellow with rage, but prefers to take leave of its unnatural restraints by letting himself go – in Morgan's case this is pushed to extremes. He takes his leave of society by taking leave of his senses. It is improbable that David Mercer, who wrote the original television play on which he based his film script, ever intended the film to be propaganda for 'taking off,' which it was swiftly claimed to be by alienated young people in Britain and America, whose presence under the affluent surface of society it helped register like the sweep of a mine-detector over explosive-ridden ground. The play had been inspired by the theories of the psychologist R. D. Laing, who argued that the schizophrenic's view of the world is one that so-called 'normal' people have helped to induce, and that, instead of trying to make a 'sick' person conform to 'ordinary life,' society should exercise a tolerance and understanding towards him and at the same time scrutinize its own values.

'The point Karel Reisz and I were trying to make in our film,' David Mercer wrote in a letter published some months after the London première, 'is that Morgan's predicament becomes increasingly unfunny as soon as his behaviour causes society to intervene in his life – i.e. by sending him to prison . . . We did not assume Morgan to be a paranoiac. How could we, since the main intention of the film is to challenge prevailing assumptions about sanity? . . . Our film is about a human being under stress and about the manner in which he ultimately preserves his integrity against society.'[1] Reisz certainly shared this view. In addition, he had his own very personally cherished interpretation of Morgan's Communist leanings in the film, a heritage from his parents that the character expressed in the hammer-and-sickle symbols he branded into the hearthrug in his wife's chic house. 'The character seemed very relevant to me,' Reisz said, 'since I had had a left-wing youth myself in Czechoslovakia, an allegiance swiftly broken by the Soviet-inspired purges there in 1947–50. Morgan's type has a nursery full of idealistic and ideological toys: it could have been crucifixes, it just happened to be Lenin and Trotsky. In adult life he finds them totally useless. It seems to be extremely germane to the way young people are now.' Reisz denies that Morgan should be regarded as his 'spokesman' any more than Arthur Seaton. 'But I did see in the character a divine spark which provoked the question of who is made and who is sane, analagous to the way our older generation treats today's hippies as freaks, as "cases." The film seemed to me a way to bridge the generations.'

Such a view, however, is not borne out by the film's political emphasis. As Philip French noted in an acute review of *Morgan*, there is an age discrepancy in the very youthfulness of the hero which 'makes nonsense of the socio-political situation of which he is supposed to be the victim . . . Somewhere between people in their sixties (Morgan's mother, the die-hard Stalinist) and those in their early twenties (Morgan himself) there is a missing

[1] *The Guardian*, 22 September, 1966.

generation. It is this generation that is behind the cameras.'[1] The result is that Morgan's Communist antics appear like mere appliqué work. Even in *The Graduate*, a film that has some very close resemblance to *Morgan*, there is a stronger causal connection between the hero and the 'making it' philosophy of his father's generation which he has found obsolete – though *The Graduate* is guilty of the more basic dishonesty in its blanket avowal that it is the young who are beautiful and the middle-aged who are dead.[2]

The part of *Morgan* that works dazzlingly well is David Warner's incarnation of the Divine Fool. His bizarre physique could not be bettered. Gaunt, angular, flint-eyed and feral, he generates the dumb, wounded strength of wild animals which makes people sponsor protection societies. At times he looks like a Saxon warrior who has landed in the modern world through some confusing time-slip; elsewhere he seems to date from an even earlier eon of history and he does not really need to pull on his gorilla suit to convince us that he prefers the fantasy company of the tree-tops to the humans at ground level. Warner generates a prehensile nimbleness, a brute gentleness, an age-old jungle-ness, and gives one of the most bizarre and brilliant performances in the 1960s cinema.

Dissociating himself imaginately from the real world – 'If I'd been planted in the womb of a chimpanzee, none of this would have happened' – he turns society into a jungle. He mates successfully with the rich, debby girl (Vanessa Redgrave), who has married him simply for the very mid-1960-ish thrill of in-security, when he can only visualise her as a graceful zebra. Alain Resnais was the liberating influence that Reisz acknowledged for the way *Morgan* dispenses with linear narrative without becoming chaotic. His intercut fantasies – the shots from safari

[1] Philip French, 'Alphaville of Admass', *Sight and Sound*, (Summer 1966), Vol. 35, No. 3, p. 110.
[2] Reisz's view of *The Graduate* is what one might expect from 'the generation that is behind the cameras'. He disliked its arse-licking dishonesty, 'forever bending backwards to say the young know it all and we are guilty. The ending is wished on the characters: they become what Nichols would like them to be – but haven't been shown to be at all'.

films or old Tarzans – are direct and effective entries into the character's inner life. It is the exterior world that unfortunately betrays Reisz; for how can anything be said about the 'normality' of madness when everyone else, in addition to the hero-victim, acts as nuttily as he does? The whole film appears conceived as one super fantasy, often in thrall to Dick Lester. If Morgan goes ape, then the film itself apes Morgan by rejecting the real world for a wacky one where bombs go off under one's mother-in-law, beds are bugged to eavesdrop on love-making, local policemen play hopscotch when they think no one is looking, and Reisz's technical style compounds the fantasy-feeling with its frenetic pace, frozen frames, accelerated motion, and that pallid trademark of 'with-it' cinema – over-exposed photography. Pictorial effect that sucks up to what people want to *see*, instead of what the film required them to understand, brought from Robert Robinson the comment that it was 'an extraordinary aberration on the part of the director whose access to the authentic (*We are the Lambeth Boys, Saturday Night and Sunday Morning*) had seemed so assured.'[1]

But whether *Morgan* was good or bad, Pauline Kael pointed out, mattered far less than why so many young people responded to it in the way they did – as they did (she might have added), to *Georgy Girl*, to *Alfie*, to all the films that in varying degrees had become virtually indistinguishable from the pop-permissive-fantasy world from which they gathered their elements so eclectically.

Morgan appeared just when the youth audience was hankering for a hero who felt like themselves, a misfit whose self-contained view of the world didn't require one to endure the pains and frustrations of coming to terms with other (and generally older) people's reality, but instead offered a more seductive line of retreat – into oneself. It was the extreme view of the 'Hobbit culture' prevalent on American campuses, in which the miniature universe of Tolkien's folklore could fit in the pants pocket and be a treasured cult-object, a yearning, private world to be shared only with other initiates. Morgan activated this process of opting-out mentally. Even the film's style was like the world seen by

[1] *The Sunday Telegraph*, 17 April, 1966.

someone on a 'high' – out of control, but perfectly happy, 'all furry,' as Morgan puts it, looking down at his strait-jacket and feeling only a comforting animal-skin sensation. It was like a good trip. R. D. Laing had already his commune of disciples in Britain: he was not to enjoy until 1972 the personal canonization that can come from a heady tour of the campuses and lecture circuits in the United States. But *Morgan* was the forerunner of his theory of 'madness.' In the absence of the 'guru' himself, its very popularity gave rise to easy misinterpretations. It was assumed not to be a diagnosis, but actually a recommended remedy for the pain of living. 'Do your own thing and dare others to call you mad' was the lesson many took from it. Psychedelia was still some years away as a popular movement; but *Morgan* was the first push towards the drug culture's more radical effects: it protected the inner world of the self by cutting off the exterior one, where one often had to sell one's 'self' to make a successful living. The product of a cinema that had sold itself on fantasy and of a country that was now the focus for curious youth the world over, *Morgan* contributed a powerful thrust to the total culture of adolescence.

The sensation of fantasy overloading the system was unmistakable when, early in April 1966, Michelangelo Antonioni began shooting in London a film that at first had no name on the clapper-boy's board. It soon acquired a prophetic one: *Blow-Up*.

Chapter Fifteen: Cameraman's Dream

I find this young group the most interesting, but what does it mean? I don't know. I am not a savant. I work with my feelings. Perhaps it is a new morality. Or perhaps it is just an old *civilisation épuisée*. Often I think of the Roman Empire.

Michelangelo Antonioni quoted in *Weekend Telegraph*,
23 September, 1966

Why did Michelangelo Antonioni choose London as the setting for *Blow-Up*? As he himself said, 'It could be set in Paris or New York without losing truth.' One reason put forward was simply the presence of Monica Vitti, who was making *Modesty Blaise* and living in London after the location filming had finished. Antonioni, it was said, wanted to remain close to his *protégée*. David Hemmings, however, believed that the director had a desire to be recognized internationally 'the way Fellini was by this time, and that's why he made the film outside Italy.'[1] To have made it in Rome would have too obviously courted comparison with the subject-matter of *La Dolce Vita*. Then there is Antonioni's own explanation: 'I think London is the best place. Fashion photographers here belong to the moment. And they are without background: one doesn't know where they come from. Like the girl in the film played by Vanessa Redgrave – one never knows anything about her, not even who she is.'[2]

Perhaps all three reasons contributed to the Italian film-maker's arrival in the capital in the early winter of 1965. He had used London once before for a film, a segment of *I Vinti*, in 1952, coincidentally about another murder set in one of the city's windswept open spaces. But the reasons for his choice of location probably matter less than Antonioni's current frame of mind,

---

[1] David Hemmings interviewed by the author, 24 September, 1971. Unless otherwise stated all subsequent quotations from Hemmings come from the same source.
[2] Quoted by Francis Wyndham, *New York Magazine*, 25 December, 1966.

which was one of self-questioning doubt – as he admitted to a few intimates in Rome and London. He had made four major Italian films, all dealing with spiritual desolation; and he felt the theme was exhausted and had, in turn, exhausted him. Now he was assailed by the uncertainty that afflicts many an introspective artist, whether what he had made instinctually ('with my stomach') corresponded to objective reality. Had he captured a spiritual condition that was very real for many people, or had he simply imposed on the subject one of his own devising? In short, how did the way that the artist experienced life relate to the subjects of his art? How did the fact become the fantasy? The most remarkable thing about *Blow-Up* (17 March, 1967) is how, out of all the elements of the 1960s that went into its assembly, Antonioni managed to construct a brilliantly composed puzzle that permitted him to examine his own dilemma of artistic 'truth.' The photographer vainly trying to pry the hidden secret from the frozen moment of camera time was like the film director and his moving picture, which many interpreters would work on with a similar maddening sensation of being always on the brink of understanding something, but never quite succeeding in doing so.

The genesis of *Blow-Up* shows, not for the first time in this book, the wonderfully creative effect of accident. Perhaps things were first set rolling by Francis Wyndham, that unrivalled guide to life on the decade's glossy surface, when he carried out a detailed dissection of the new photographers in an article for the *Sunday Times Magazine* of 10 May, 1964. Entitled 'The Model-makers,' it was based on his intimate knowledge of Bailey, Donovan and Duffy. Now it happens more often than many people would admit that the media's reaction to some trend or phenomenon, particularly one almost next-door to them, does not derive from their separate discoveries of what is going on – but more frequently from an article or enquiry by some single media-man identifying and labelling it for them. Fleet Street and the television networks are quite ready to follow their noses if some-one else first points them in a rewarding direction. To Wyndham's article belongs much of the credit (some would have another word for it) for bringing into prominence that very profession which had been bringing the London scene into focus. (No wonder one begins to have a dizzying sensation of mirrors reflecting other mirrors as the decade enters its last lap.) Wyndham's piece had an air of inside knowingness that certainly wasn't assumed: he was a part of the scene as well as its recorder. He wasn't the only one, of course, but whereas other journalists were swallowed up in the scene, never to be seen again, or else lived it vicariously and enviously in their dispatches, Wyndham preserved the ability to withdraw himself when he came to write of what he observed. His article caught Carlo Ponti's eye; and Ponti proposed to David Bailey the idea of making a short film about his own world called *The Photographer*.

Bailey had closer links with the movies than any of his professional rivals. He had helped 'create' Jean Shrimpton and she was now being sought for film parts; but he had married Catherine Deneuve who was already a film star; and he was eager to turn film director. But for various mundane reasons, mainly to do with schedules and assignments, the moment passed and with it the project – until Ponti, who had a production deal with M.G.M., and his British representative, Pierre Rouve, heard that Antonioni was intensely interested in working in London. To Ponti, this meant the prospect of a much more acceptably 'international' – i.e. English-speaking – film than the director's Italian ones. Like the Hollywood entrepreneurs, with whom he had many dealings, Ponti knew how marketable London was at the moment, especially for the 'youth audience.' Much of London's 'excitement' had derived from Italy in the late 1950s and early 1960s; so there was a certain satisfying sense of closure about an Italian director reporting on the scene that Brioni, Braggi, Gaggia, Vespa, Olivetti, Apicella and others had helped to mould, service and decorate.

But for Antonioni to undertake a film about professional photographers meant devising a much more ambitious concept than Bailey's idea of a 'personal history.' Whether it was Antonioni or his favourite writer-collaborator Tonino Guerra who found the film's inspiration in a short story by the Argentin-

ian writer, Julio Cortazar, is not clear; but the idea in the story
– the ambiguity between the medium which records an event and
the event itself – is one that would certainly have proved very
attractive to the Italian director in his frame of mind at the time.
What is less speculative is the way the two of them accomplished
the metamorphosis of Cortazar's story into the life and times of
'Swinging London.'

The story is not called *Blow-Up*, but *The Devil's Spittle*, a
cumbersome translation of *Las babas del Diablo*, which is how
Spaniards colloquially refer to a 'narrow escape' – i.e. near
enough to calamity to be spat on by the Devil. Nor is the story
about a murder and its witness. It is about an attempted homosexual pick-up which is unintentionally frustrated by the narrator.
The subject which the amateur photographer in Cortazar's story
snaps on a *quai* in Paris one November day is that of a fifteen-
year-old boy and a woman who is old enough to be his mother,
both of them engaged in some intimate conversation. A tree, a
railing, the eleven o'clock sunshine are all present in the narrator's
view-finder as they are in the camera's. An instant after the snap
has been taken, the boy runs off and a strange man, who has been
waiting in a car, makes a short but indecisive protest. Back in his
studio, the blown-up photo is explicitly enlarged to the size of a
movie screen. It then comes to life. And only then does the
photographer realize that the boy was being 'propositioned' by
a female pimp and that he has accidentally saved him – which
makes him happy. In the story it is the photographer who stands
paralysed while the 'film' unreels on the 'blow-up' in front of
him: in Antonioni's film, of course, it is the frozen series of stills
which edit themselves together into a horribly meaningful drama
for the photographer. It is he who provides all the movement;
and David Hemmings is kept so mobile that one commentator,
Karl Miller, actually remarked on his 'vibrant goblin
energy.'

Antonioni's brilliance is to use this central sequence of the
photo-enlargement not only as a detective story in miniature but
also as a metaphor for the whole creative process. On the one
hand the vital clue – the white blur of what may be a corpse and

a gunman – looks always about to come into sight from the mysterious latency of the image, or so it looks to Hemmings as his imagination gives meaning to increasingly abstract interplay of lights and shadows. On the other hand, the very process of the 'blow-up' produces a panic akin to the experience of a movie director who dreads that he may be missing what is essential in his material by 'looking at it the wrong way,' or else fabricating a 'reality' that may not be present in the material at all. What we watch is a dramatized gloss on a particular obsession of Antonioni: a meditation on the nature of creation which recalls what he had said seven years earlier, in an interview in *Positif*, that 'it can happen that films acquire meanings: that is to say, that the meanings appear afterwards.'

At one moment Antonioni had wanted to make the hero of *Blow-Up* into a painter. (Before becoming a film director, he himself had been pulled strongly towards painting and architecture.) The painter remains in the finished film, only now he is the hero's artist friend whose *tachiste* canvases prompt the photographer to look for 'meaning' in his own recorded reality. 'I feel that I am a person who has things that he wants to show, rather than things he wants to say,' Antonioni declared early on in the film-making. 'There are times when the two concepts coincide and then we arrive at a work of art.'[1] London was the place where such concepts met, and from the 'scene' as he experienced it Antonioni drew his work of art.

THE WYNDHAM REPORT

Filming began on 24 April, 1966, the rather grey, overcast weather of the English spring being ideal for a man who disliked the hazy imprecision imposed on his vision of the world whenever sunshine softened its colours. Antonioni had arrived five months earlier in London with a treatment called *The Story of a Man and a Woman on a Beautiful Autumn Morning*, which quickly dropped its seasonable characteristics in favour of a bleakly enigmatic working

---

[1] *Evening Standard*, 10 May, 1966.

title, *The Antonioni Picture*. But he had had his native 'scouts' reconnoitring the unfamiliar scene even earlier. For he realized that this was a film he had to make 'with my head. All my other films were made with my stomach. I had to be lucid with this one because I was in a foreign country.'[1] To help him see the scene 'lucidly,' he recruited none other than the journalist who had first reported on it – Francis Wyndham. Wyndham preserved the lengthy questionnaire he received: which is fortunate in view of the charges later levelled at Antonioni by some critics that he, a foreigner, simply did not know the first thing about the London scene in 1966. The questionnaire which Wyndham had to answer well in advance of shooting was extremely thorough, but then the figure of an English fashion photographer, his life style and his acquaintances, were less familiar to an Italian than one might imagine.

Antonioni asked, 'Are fashion photographers requested to stress the sexual angle or merely to concentrate on the clothes? . . . Private life. Habits. Hobbies. Do they drink? How do they spend their days? Evenings? Week-end? What is really "fun" for them? . . . Some have Rolls-Royces: have they personal drivers? Or do they drive themselves? What is, broadly speaking, their social background? How do they speak? Have they a particular way of expressing themselves, some professional slang, or anything of this kind? . . . Do they eat at home, in their studios, or in restaurants? Do they go to pubs? . . . How do they spend the money they make? Do they think about the future? Do they endeavour to make money outside their profession? . . . Do they worry about themselves, life, death? Are they religious? If not, is it a matter of unconcern about such ethical codes of behaviour, or is it deliberate rejection? . . . What is their relation with their wives? As a rule, are their marriages happy? If not, what is the reason? Have they steady mistresses, or only occasional pick-ups?'

There were many other queries about gambling habits, reading preferences, leisure activities like tennis and squash, political

---

[1] Antonioni interviewed by David Lewin, *Daily Mail*, 16 March, 1967.

make-up, domestic background and décor, professional relations with magazine editors, agents, other photographers . . . The questionnaire covered half-a-dozen closely-typed sheets and Wyndham's replies, based on personal knowledge of the top photographers and taped interviews with Bailey and Duffy, were just as comprehensive. Again a few quotations offer illuminating testimony to the care that went into the preparation of *Blow-Up* – at least inside Antonioni's head, since the finished screenplay selected only those objective facts the director felt he needed, and no others.

'Defiantly,' wrote Wyndham, 'they have made no attempt to become "gentlemen." In this they are like their contemporaries in show business . . . All (of them) sense obscurely that they are artists (although they are reluctant to admit this, for fear of sounding pretentious) . . . They use East End slang effectively and often ironically – self-deprecatingly, lest they be considered putting on airs, they call photography "taking a few snaps" . . . They have a lot of love affairs as well as casual sex . . . Bailey's marriage to Catherine Deneuve was an unusual and significant step to take: usually the photographers' girls are either models or subservient figures . . . They think of themselves as "visual" people and are therefore suspicious of the written word. Bailey shared with Mick Jagger an admiration for the novels of Anthony Burgess.'[1]

Among the transcripts of the recorded interviews with Bailey and Duffy were passages which the film clearly used in re-creating its photographer's professional ambience.

Duffy: '. . . you're so involved in the atmosphere of the studios, and there can be this chemical thing (though I never go to work expecting it) the music on the record . . . and it's going and it's going, and in actual fact one's going through a slightly, a most definitely sexual thing. The only thing between you and the girl is the camera.'

Bailey: 'A three-legged phallus.'

[1] One of Bailey's projects was a film of *A Clockwork Orange* with Mick Jagger in the role ultimately played by Malcolm McDowell in Kubrick's film. The censor turned down the script.

L

Duffy: 'We'd spend an evening in the East End watching Mods and Rockers in their manor. I wouldn't go down there consciously thinking I'm going to observe them and then come back and do a fashion picture from their attitudes of standing, but one finds one does. Last night watching Cilla Black on television, when she walked forward – they sort of walk forward with their elbows slightly bent . . . And you see these things and then all of a sudden you're using them as positions. They're sort of inflections or manners that you see about . . . So you say to a girl, "Stand that way".'

When he got to London, Antonioni did his own leg-work, too. I used to see him at many parties, where his innate shyness and limited English – which is (or was in those days) poor when he did not feel himself among intimates – gave him the excuse for playing the silent observer. There were also reports of him and Tonino Guerra at discotheques and dance-halls in South London and the West End; and the incident in the film which was much criticized for its unlikelihood, when the Yardbirds' guitarist throws down his guitar and stamps on it in a storm of dissatisfaction, was one the director had actually witnessed. For a film that operated at the point where the eye-witness turned into a Doubting Thomas (and 'Thomas' was the hero's name), Antonioni appeared paradoxically determined to ensure that *he* at least saw things as they really were before the cameras started turning. On one of his outings he took in a performance of *Adventures in the Skin Trade*, an adaptation by Andrew Sinclair of the Dylan Thomas book, which the Hampstead Theatre Club was staging with David Hemmings. Hemmings found himself asked to test for the film, which still had no definite title, though, as autumn had come and gone, it was temporarily known now as *A Girl, A Photographer and a Beautiful April Morning* before reverting once again to *The Antonioni Film*.

On their first meeting in Antonioni's suite at the Savoy Hotel, Hemmings was disconcerted to be told that he looked too young. He was then twenty-three. But he assured the director that his hair, which was very blond, could be altered and that this would age him sufficiently. When it came to the screen test, he was asked to do no set piece; so he began doing for the camera scenes from the play he was in till he glimpsed Antonioni's slight tic, a curious sideways 'swallow' like a swan drinking water, which is a sign of incipient rejection. Feeling that a man with poor English would scarcely appreciate the lyricism of a Welsh poet – he had forgotten that Thomas's *Under Milk Wood* had first appeared in the Italian publication *Botteghe Oscure* – he switched to a scene from an early play he had appeared in, Ted Willis's *Woman in a Dressing Gown*. It is uncertain what Antonioni discovered from the test. Perhaps he used it simply to ascertain if Hemmings had any qualities he did *not* want for the film. (This is Hemmings's view.) For a start, he did *not* want an actor who made any attempt to develop an independent reading of the part. If Hemmings knew nothing of the part to begin with, he would not be tempted to improvise on it. Such may have been the convoluted reasoning behind his choice. It is no secret that, at the very time he was testing Hemmings, Antonioni had all but decided on another actor who had been so certain of starring in *Blow-Up*, in what was virtually his own South London background, that he had begun a minute study of Bailey, Donovan and Duffy, even to the extent of imitating their hand movements and improvising the tune he would hum under his breath in the dark-room. Antonioni never explained publicly why he suddenly switched to Hemmings: the likelihood is that he felt an actor who was not an established star would be more amenable to suggestion, even discipline. 'An actor is only one element,' he told Wyndham, 'perhaps sometimes the most important one. But the director is the only person who understands the composition. If an actor thinks he understands, he becomes the director himself, which is a great disaster.'[1]

ADVANTAGE – ANTONIONI

David Hemmings is one of the few actors Antonioni has worked with outside his own country who bears not the smallest degree of resentment at the peculiar constraints and obedience he had imposed on him. 'He directed me like an object,' he recalled,

[1] Francis Wyndham, *op. cit.*

'insisting on my following every instruction precisely and un-waveringly. Sometimes he did not know how a line should be spoken and he would try it in full face, then in profile, till he got the "feeling" he desired – he obviously felt that the outward angle at which the camera caught the actor changed the inner sense of the line. You had to throw away all the crutches you generally used to sustain a role. Not for one minute was I allowed any insight into Antonioni's mind.' Even then, the script was a mere thirty-two pages long and contained no camera directions, just the kind of bare information on which Antonioni could build his direction and – probably more important – none on which Hemmings could construct his character. Hemmings never made suggestions 'unless I felt markedly uncomfortable with something he asked me to do; occasionally he seized on some small gesture of mine, perhaps the way I hunched over a camera tripod, and retained it in each take, but I wasn't allowed to see a single frame of the rushes unless it was a bit of business that had to be repeated a different way in another take. I could never imagine what the film would look like; and when I came out of the screening room in Los Angeles after seeing it for the first time, Antonioni said, "You don't like it, do you?" '

The physical restrictions placed on Hemmings were as severe as the artistic ones. The major interior shooting was done in a studio belonging to the fashion photographer John Cowan, where Hemmings found it difficult ever to relax and even Antonioni had trouble in finding a quiet place for thought. It was 'a relationship of master and servant' between the two, as Hemmings put it, tempered only by the same wry, slightly teasing sense of humour he shared with his director. Antonioni referred fleetingly, and perhaps revealingly, to such a relationship as one of the reasons why he had approved of Monica Vitti's working with Losey, 'who will be able to offer her the personality (to explore) that by temperament I cannot.' Considering the symbiotic closeness of this method of working, and Antonioni's insistence on 'de-dramatizing, even humiliating' Hemmings, it is amazing what spontaneity the latter's performance retains. It is not just Antonioni's unwonted liveliness in the editing of the film that contributes to this impression, though it helps. It is Hemmings's own freshness of instinct which keeps staleness at bay – incidentally, it was his thirty-seventh film role – no matter how many times he was compelled to repeat a take. His slight stature adds lightning to his movements: he is a Puck with a Nikon, spying on Titania and Oberon, and he has the same mercurial flitting movement as he shuttles between developing tank and enlarger, between reality and fantasy. Compared to the somnambulist woman who is usually at the heart of Antonioni's films, he is a virtual Stakhanovite. Considering that Antonioni had been partially attracted to London by the city's well-publicized quality of encapsulating a contemporary mood, it was curious how he insisted on not having a single line of dialogue that might obviously date the film. According to his star, 'this meant getting rid of the "supers" and the "fabs" and phrases of that sort.' Otherwise, the script altered very little, though what there was of it was obviously tailored to be considerably expanded. A direction like 'Thomas gets into his Rolls-Royce and returns to his studio' gave Antonioni the chance for literally scene-painting in which the road surface was coloured a deeper shade of black and the house-fronts that the car passed acquired a poster-like series of hues. Karl Miller pointed out that this is one of the film's strongest links with the colour-supplement world which the photographer serves and in which he is king. In his absurdly capacious car, the symbol of surtax necessity rather than transport convenience, he is an emperor in a chariot whose capital city has painted itself up for his triumphal tour. The whole film has the coloration of high-quality advertising features: even the swift passage of pure green and pure yellow which momentarily fills the screen as the commercial vehicles blot out the shot of the Rolls-Royce sliding through an underpass is like the colour chart a cameraman uses for keying his own more muted effects.

What written changes Antonioni made in the script were nearly all to do with eliminating points that risked dissipating the air of doubt, illusion, and intangible mystery in the finished film. As late as the end of March 1966, less than four weeks before shooting began, the script contained a very early description of Jane (the Vanessa Redgrave character) getting into a car along with a distinguished elderly man (the victim in the park) and driving off, followed at a distance by another car driven by a man of about thirty with what was described as a tense, hard face (presumably the killer in the park). This scene has vanished (if it was ever shot) from the finished film, thus preventing us from expecting what happens, so that Thomas's catching two-thirds of the situation in the park and unwittingly recording the concealed one-third (the killer in the trees behind the paling) is as straight-forward an accident of fact to us as it is to him. Actually, he takes the photograph for the sake of what he interprets as lyrical over-tones, intending it to be the end-piece of his projected book, and by thus effacing the earlier hint of sinister implications Antonioni postpones his (and our) discovery of the terrifying irony latent in the print. Also gone from the completed film is a montage sequence, reminiscent of the 'still-life' shots that ended *The Eclipse*, which would have given us apocalyptic glimpses of contemporary London life: an art school, a student rag, Carnaby Street, polo players belonging to what is called 'the smart set,' people at work in offices, a pop group rehearsing, a closed and silent Stock Exchange 'like a cathedral.' Most of these have been entirely eliminated, the student rag materialising slightly later into the action as the white-faced revellers – more Italianate, surely, than Anglo-Saxon – 'hold up' Thomas for a charity contribution. This early script ends with a shot of Thomas concentrating on something that is not there, whereas the film ends with him, after hearing the 'click' of a tennis-racket on an imaginary ball, simply being subsumed into the grass of the park-land – ceasing to exist in the way that, for him, objective reality has ceased to exist. A totally disintegrated being.

What is not generally known is that Antonioni shot two ver-sions of the ending. The one that exists in the film shows Thomas picking up a non-existent tennis-ball and returning it to the players: the other one showed a real tennis-ball landing on the grass near him, although the players had not been using one in their mimed match. This ball Thomas threw back to them – and we hear the noise of the rackets striking it as before. The implication here was that objective reality (like a ball or a corpse) can materialize if one wishes hard enough for it to do so. But this would have rendered the ending of the film needlessly complicated, as well as thrown more doubt than mystery on to the existence of the dead body. For if Thomas can hallucinate a tennis ball adequately enough to grasp it, it needs only a little more cerebral effort to hallucinate a corpse. Antonioni was right to reject this alternative ending.

But *Blow-Up* is not simply about a man ultimately unable to tell illusion from reality. It is about a society paralysed by its own distractions. The people in it never attain the ends they seek. They are forever being interrupted in the middle of what they are doing, distracted from their quest or impelled to seek distraction, in the purely entertainment sense of the word, when they should be engaged on more serious things. Thus the photographer distracts the couple in the park; he is distracted from his search for the 'truth' in the photograph by the arrival of the nymphet models; Jane distracts him from resuming his scrutiny of the blown-up images; the delivery of the propeller he has bought in a junk shop (whose owner has confessed her need to seek distraction in a trip to Nepal or Morocco) diverts him from the *avventura* his visitor promises; and the drugs party at his agent's home distracts him from following up the evidence of a corpse. The click of the camera is the only finite element in this world whose inhabitants' mode of life appears outwardly so glamorous, lucrative and successful but actually encapsulates a repetitive incompleteness and purposelessness. It makes us understand why Hemmings throughout the shooting had the conviction that it was a film about despair – the despair at the heart of the artist's soul as he finds reality is so treacherous for those who interpret it – also the despair at the heart of society which prevents itself from dwelling on anything except the magical moment by the sheer non-stop, hustle-bustle of the swirling scene, a churning *status quo*. Except that the tempo is faster, *Blow-Up* is not all that much different in feeling from *La Notte* and *The Eclipse*. All three are films about the ultimate emptiness of living.

BLOW-UP'S LONDON

If Antonioni in his Italian films had been given over-much to
meditation, the brisker life-style of London might be said to have
inspired a sermon in him. But if so, it was one whose text was
dauntingly misconstrued by a remarkable number of people. The
two surprising qualities in most of the English reviews of the film
are their bafflement and their indignation. It was as if Antonioni
had tried to present the vacuum at the 'swinging' centre of
London and had then found himself arraigned in the dock on a
charge of lending a false impression of reality to the glamour.
Even Nina Hibbin, the critic on the Communist morning paper,
while getting the point of the picture with Marxist approval,
somehow contrived to mix resentment with her praise. 'There's
no one to identify with, nothing to follow through; only the
harsh, bleak show images of "swinging" London, which don't
intrigue, but baffle.'[1] Most of the early notices, however, roundly
condemned Antonioni for letting himself be taken in by the whole
deluding set-up, in the way the photographer in the film had been
taken in by *his* set-up. If ever Antonioni feared he might have
been looking in the wrong direction, 'missing the essential,' as
Francis Wyndham put it, he must have felt the charge brought
home to him as he read the British Press.

'A precious film version of *Time* magazine's celebrated clanger
recently about swinging London,' wrote Penelope Gilliatt,
accusing him of showing off the same grainy nihilism as the glossy
magazines. 'They (the characters) exist to maintain the ruthlessness and superficiality of a with-it system, yet they are themselves
fabricated with little generosity or depth of insight.'[2] 'Antonioni's
swinging London is the fantasy of the popular Press worked over
by an outsider of willing gullibility,' wrote David Robinson.
'Apart from the down-and-outs of a Salvation Army hostel, and
an occasional red-coated Guardsman, all life in London has given
way to the weirdies and junkies and swingers . . . And the clubs
and drug parties are as . . . laughably absurd as they might have

[1] *Morning Star*, 18 March, 1967.
[2] *The Observer*, 19 March, 1967.

been in some socio-sensational second feature.'[1] 'There is enough evidence to suggest that Antonioni has fallen unreasoningly for the ad-man's tawdry, swinging city,' wrote Penelope Houston.[2] 'Perhaps his dream of London wasn't matched by the reality . . . The place sits tentatively at the periphery of the film, not entering in,' declared Robert Robinson.[3] 'The sad thing is that the film comes out looking far too much like the colour supplements . . . He should have heeded his hero's advice to his model, "Go against the beat",' wrote Richard Roud, adding, "If you make a film about essentially shallow people, you risk making a shallow film. This is reflected in the swinging London bit."[4] And Richard Gilbert writing in *Peace News*, but not at all swayed by the nuclear apocalypse which some thought the film's title suggested, declared, 'The film panders to the desperately unoriginal images of colour-supplement London . . . This is a London overpopulated by nuns, queers, poodles, Africans in robes and discotheque dollies.'[5] (Just as well Antonioni hadn't, after all, put in the 'mauve garbage bags in front of Belgravia houses' which the draft script mentioned.)

All this sounds precisely the sort of review that might have been meted out to that album of arty 'London' photographs which Thomas is assembling for publication in the film. Such a strong dissent from the picture of London life that *Blow-Up* represents, mingled with backhanded slaps at *Time* magazine for encouraging a deception practised on the natives and the tourists, appears to argue a chauvinistic distaste for the whole commercial preening and grooming to which this section of mid-1960 Britain was gaily submitting. Coupled with this is a very real confusion as to the film's motives: one prominent critic felt it set out to condemn the empty life of a fashion photographer, which at least is plausible, and to indicate how all his time is spent photographing crimes!

[1] *The Financial Times*, 17 March, 1967.
[2] *The Spectator*, 24 March, 1967.
[3] *The Sunday Telegraph*, 19 March, 1967.
[4] *The Guardian*, 17 March, 1967.
[5] *Peace News*, 4 April, 1967.

But the central issue in much of the criticism – as in the film itself – is the nature of reality. How far did Antonioni wish his film to be a 'real' picture of a life-style whose nature was visible to both those who lived it and those who simply observed it? Ane how far was the director compromised by the contagious 'unreality' of what many people had more or less consciously rejected once they had been made aware of its proliferation in the 'Swinging London' syndrome? The number of times I heard *Blow-Up* put down as a totally false view of the capital because of some passing detail, like the coloured nun, argues a xenophobic resentment of the suspected tourist inside the distinguished visitor. London must, after all, be capable of producing one black nun in white vestments – if *that* constitutes evidence of a city's 'reality.' Anyhow, as Robin Wood remarked, the accusation that Antonioni falls short of documentary verisimilitude 'need bother us no more than complaints that *King Lear* has its shortcomings if judged as a documentary portrait of prehistoric Britain.'[1] To capture a tone and transcribe a style, whether of an advertising supplement or of a way of life that it services, need imply no capitulation to its values. On the contrary, projecting them on to a different plane of reality in a motion picture can isolate the fantasy element in them. At the heart of every bit of shallow, superficial existence, observed by Antonioni from his own first-hand experience, or remitted to him by a detached observer like Francis Wyndham, lies a bleak evaluation of its essential melancholy which is totally at variance with the smart, hip, relentlessly up-beat 'scenarios' of the London scene published in *Time*. '*Blow-Up* enhances and exaggerates in a spirit of celebration or display which reminds you of supplements and photographers,' Karl Miller conceded; yet he added, 'But this is a true London of the time such as no other film has shown.'[2] Though much is selected from the 'swinging' scene, Antonioni is not infatuated with it: nothing is wished on to it in the consciously mod style of *Darling*, or *Morgan* or *Alfie*: unlike these films, it is not packaged

[1] Ian Cameron and Robin Wood, *Antonioni* (Studio Vista, 1968), p. 125.
[2] Karl Miller, 'A Sunday Dilemma: Getaway People and Ghetto People', *Sunday Times Magazine*, 14 December, 1969.

to be consumed the minute it is opened. Instead of being dated by the fashionable ethos, the film will date *it*.

By chance I met Antonioni on the morning when most of the bewildering London reviews had broken; and as if someone were trying to pin a crime on him, he could only repeat his account of the immense pains he had taken to get the scene 'right,' and laugh sadly at the irony of being berated by critics for getting 'wrong' a reality which the whole film was designed to show as essentially subjective.

Blow-Up came at the end of a series of movies that had made everyone over-familiar with even the phrase 'Swinging London' and heartily sick of it. *Blow-Up* was about this surrender to fantasy which the mid-1960s cinema, and an influential sector of metropolitan life, had made. It abstracted what it wanted from it, and framed it in a separate reality. It wasn't easy for anyone whose eye was jaded, as if from a hangover, to experience the freshness of the scene when an artist's eye viewed it. But if David Bailey's *Pin-Ups* are the world of an insider creating his own fantasy, then Antonioni's *Blow-Up* is just as surely that of an outsider finding his own reality and showing up the perilous irrelevance of the other.

Chapter Sixteen: Problems, Local and Universal

The last statement we got was September, when it had only been showing in America about six months and it hadn't gone into profit there, and there was an odd item, I remember. 'Australia,' it said, '13 dollars.' Four people on a very rainy night in Brisbane stayed out for the late-night show. It must have opened on the last day in August.

Albert Finney, after a screening of *Charlie Bubbles*,

8 February, 1969

One hardly knew whether to laugh or cry – probably both – when the Monopolies Commission published its long-awaited report at the end of October 1966, 'on the supply of films for exhibition in cinemas' in Britain. To those independent film-makers who looked for a redress of their grievances, the report spoke with the forked tongue that wily palefaces were traditionally supposed to employ on the ignorant Redskins. It was a masterpiece of double-think.

Yes, it said, things were certainly unsatisfactory when two giant cinema circuits controlled the outlets for film-makers. Rank and A.B.C., it stated, 'so conduct their affairs as to restrict competition . . . The experience of other countries shows that a successful film production industry is possible without such a tightly organized market. The evidence put to us by other producers revealed a marked lack of confidence arising from the policies of the circuits. Such producers were convinced that if they had free access to the market for films and did not have to rely on acceptance by one of the two major circuits, they would be able to produce films which would appeal to the public and have a reasonable chance of success. In the light of this we find it hard to reject entirely the view that the dominance of the two major circuits does not to some extent discourage production, at least of certain kinds of films.'[1] In spite of that premonitory word

---

[1] *The Monopolies Commision. FILMS: A Report on the Supply of Films for Exhibition in Cinemas* (H.M.S.O., Cmnd. 31242, 28 October, 1966), pp. 68-9.

'entirely,' this must have made the hearts of independent companies like British Lion soar with expectation, especially when
the report went on, 'The two-release system (on A.B.C. and
Rank) is remarkably rigid – uniquely so, since there is nothing
resembling it in any other country. Such a rigidly organized
market seems peculiarly inappropriate in view of the nature of
the product . . . it is desirable that any producer who has a good
idea should be free to compete for the public's support, and that
the market should therefore be organized on more competitive
lines as in other European countries. Whether the films produced
under such a system would be either better or more numerous
than those produced at present is unpredictable. But at least the
consumer would have a better chance to show his preference and
producers' ideas could be put to the test of the public without
first having to surmount the obstacle of acceptance by one or
other of the two major circuits.'[1]

Now this was exactly what British Lion and the other independents – i.e. those producers not tied to Rank or A.B.C. and
not dependent on financing from the British subsidiaries of
Hollywood production companies – had been demanding.[2] But
it became distressingly clear before many subsequent paragraphs
had been scanned that, in saying as much, the Monopolies
Commission was stating an ideal, not recommending a policy.

A note of hesitation was sounded when the report continued
with a perceptible sigh of regret, 'If we were starting with a
clean slate we should prefer to see some looser and more competitive structure in the film industry. But given the situation as it
now exists we are impressed by the formidable and probably
expensive, practical problems in the way of adopting any of the
proposals.'[3] Then came the crunch. In a brief and cheerless passage, the report said, 'On balance, therefore, we think that,
although the present system is undesirable, the suggested alterna-

[1] Ibid. p. 69
[2] The report named the suppliers tied to Rank as Disney Columbia, 20th
Century-Fox and United Artists: those to A.B.C. as Warner M.G.M. and
Paramount.
[3] Ibid,. p. 80.

tives involving the dismantling or re-arrangement of the two
major circuits offer insufficient assurance of benefit to justify the
difficulty and upheaval that they would entail and we do not think
that they should be considered unless other, less drastic, expedients prove ineffective.'[1] Even while admitting that competition
for films was desirable, as opposed to the 'tied' system, the report
'would not recommend introducing it between the circuits as
they stand.'[2]

Finally came a paltry and nugatory suggestion that Rank and
A.B.C. cinemas should give trial runs, 'limited or partial circuit
bookings,' to 'films of limited appeal' – and even this timid idea
was opposed by a Commissioner who expressed the dissenting
opinion that the circuits 'should not be under pressure (sic) to go
beyond the limits of their good commercial judgment.'[3] No
wonder John Boulting, of British Lion, declared upon reading the
report, 'If one didn't have a high regard for the members of the
Commission, one might describe their proposals as idiotic.'[4]

The result was wholly predictable. Both circuits were allowed
to consolidate what they already controlled, with only relatively
minor changes in programming constituting those 'other, less
drastic, expedients' referred to in the report: i.e. Rank phased out
its own series of *Look at Life* shorts which it had booked into its
own cinemas, and some minority interest-films were given 'trial
runs.' But complacency was now backed by the legitimacy
reluctantly conferred on the situation by the Monopolies Commission. The *status quo* had been sanctioned, the monopolistic
interests safeguarded.

On British Lion, a company already hesitant about financing
films while their future on the cinema circuits remained uncertain,
the impact of the report was equally predictable. 'We still hoped
that after the Monopolies Commission had reported,' said David
Kingsley, British Lion's managing director, 'the Government
would do something. In fact, it did nothing. Though we had gone

[1] Ibid., p. 81.
[2] Ibid., p. 82.
[3] Ibid., p. 89.
[4] *The Times*, 29 October, 1966.

into British Lion to produce a production programme, I and others felt we could not stick our necks out to make films with the odds stacked against us if the Government did not want to reduce the odds. The report's attitude was one of "live and let die" – it was certainly not us who were encouraged to live, but the cinema circuits.' British Lion had not been entirely inactive while awaiting the report. It had in fact produced three extremely profitable films: *The Family Way*, *The Great St Trinian's Train Robbery* and *Morgan*. None of these had experienced any fatal difficulty in getting shown widely on the circuits. *Morgan*, the doubtful starter by reason of its material, got off to a flying start and maintained its pace at the box-office almost everywhere: a case of a film striking a hidden public nerve at the right time. The other films, being safer situation-comedies, also did outstanding business. But two of the films had been made by members of the British Lion board: the Boultings, who had most confidence in movies when they themselves were making them, and the Launder-Gilliat axis which liked the comfort of the successful St Trinian's formula. *Morgan* had been one of the few movies brought to British Lion for financing by 'outsiders' at a time when most of the latter were crowding the anterooms of the American majors. In a way this confirmed the difficulty, alluded to by Kingsley and others, of getting the Board's autonomous members to agree on financing a film programme; and when the Monopolies Commission declined to alter the rules of the circuit game in their favour, the divisions between the Board members opened even more widely.

Balcon, in fact, had taken his leave of the chairman's job early in 1966, extremely disenchanted with the whole situation and at odds with his principal colleagues. He believed that the company was playing things too safe: it was sitting on assets that it ought to have been using: in short 'it had become too much like the other two big groups' (A.B.C. and Rank).

British Lion's reluctance to commit itself fully to the risks of film-making could not have been more ironically illustrated than by a proposal which the National Film Finance Corporation made to it shortly after the Balcon group had won control in March 1964.

The N.F.F.C. had decided to filter out the risk it always took in supplying the so-called 'end money' in financing any movie-maker who had already got, say, 75 per cent of his cash from a distributor and wanted the rest from public money. This arrangement had simply left the N.F.F.C. last in line for any pay-back from profits, often holding an empty hand out for an unconscionably long time while others took their cut first. To avoid this, the N.F.F.C. had taken a leaf from the Hollywood companies' book and planned 100 per cent financing from one source. The scheme was for the N.F.F.C. and a major British distributor each to commit a sum and arrange for a bank to provide a larger amount than the joint facility – the producers' share of revenues from the films financed constituted the bank's main security. Thus the N.F.F.C. would be in a *pari passu* relationship to the revenues – i.e. it would share in the first pound sterling earned. An approach was accordingly made to work the plan in association with British Lion. Agreement was never reached. So in June 1964 a plan was concluded with the Rank Organization which agreed to participate in the joint financing up to a minimum aggregate of £1,500,000. Choice of films was left to the N.F.F.C. Thus, in default of securing agreement with the chief independent outfit in the country, the N.F.F.C., it could be argued, was lending public money to support production by one of the very film groups that would come under the Monopolies Commission's investigation before the year was out.

Sad to relate, the Rank–N.F.F.C. consortium did not produce the envisaged happiness for both partners. Of eighty scripts submitted in the first place, three were selected and four more added over the next year. Only one, *They're a Weird Mob*, was described as 'a smash hit,' and that in Australia, 'but has not done well in the rest of the world.' Paramount purchased another, *Maroc Seven*, for the western hemisphere, paying an advance of about half the production cost; revenues on a ballet film were predictably slow to come in; losses were feared on *The Sandwich Man* and *I was Happy Here*; *Two Weeks in September* ended the co-financing, and the N.F.F.C. report for the year ending 31 March, 1967, concluded impassively, 'It is unlikely that further films will

Crusader: Lindsay Anderson surrounded by the school cadet corps, prepares to turn the public school into the battlefield where youth will win its liberation in *If . . .* (*Paramount*)

Expatriate: Joseph Losey, who survived Hollywood blacklisting to explore some of the equally vicious traps of English society, leads Mia Farrow through a scene in *Secret Ceremony.* (*Universal*)

Pop Star: Dick Lester (above), caught in a rare moment when not running or jumping, found the style to fit the idols of the age of *Yeah! Yeah! Yeah!* (*Thames TV*)

Tycoon: Bryan Forbes (bottom), multi-talented writer, actor-producer-director-studio boss, photographed on his last day as head of Elstree studios. (*Evening Standard*)

Both these men and the two below are producers. All are wearing black ties because producers mostly get photographed at the premières of their pictures. It is popularly – but wrongly – assumed that most of the work producers do is attending premières. These men did much more: they backed (and sometimes found) directors, subjects, stars and writers and helped shape the films of the 1960s. George H. Ornstein (above left), when production chief of United Artists in Britain, backed *Tom Jones*, the Beatles and the Bond movies; Nat Cohen (above right), as head of Anglo-Amalgamated, backed such films as *A Kind of Loving*, *Darling* and *Family Life*.

Joseph Janni (left), long-time associate of John Schlesinger, produced among others *Billy Liar*, *Far From the Madding Crowd* and *Poor Cow*. Walter Shenson (right) producer of the two Beatles films, *A Hard Day's Night* and *Help!*

Bond's Men: Harry Saltzman (above) and Cubby Broccoli (below), eight Bonds and a multimillion-dollar fortune behind them. By accident, they struck a responsive nerve in the 1960s: by inventiveness and extravagance, they created the one entertainment formula to endure successfully into the 1970s. (*Tim Graham*)

Fantasies of the Era: Sex. 'Michael Caine IS Alfie', cried the posters; and for millions of filmgoers he certainly WAS. It was the cockney boy's daydream of endlessly available 'birds' personified by one of the authentic cockney boys who crossed 'the River' to success in the West End. (*Paramount*)

Fantasies of the Era: Class. If sex was the great leveller in the 1960s films, class was the great escalator. Like so much that depended on 'appearances' in an era when 'taste' was, as *Queen* described it, simply 'a way of looking', you only needed to acquire the right exterior habits of the class above to be accepted as one of them. Alan Bates did it in *Nothing but the Best*. (*Anglo Film Distributors*)

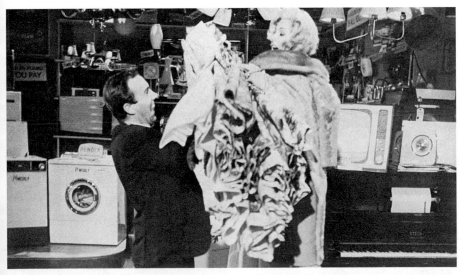

Fantasies of the Era: Affluence. *Live Now – Pay Later* not only anticipated the film industry's own mode of life, but summed up the consumer gluttony of the 'never had it so good' society in a scene like that in the supermarket where Ian Hendry's smooth salesman heaped June Ritchie with armfuls of goodies. (*British Lion/Columbia*)

Pop and Op: surrealism amidst the high snows with four Beatles and one grand piano in Dick Lester's *Help!* (above). Pop gradually assumed psychedelic dimensions as it was absorbed into the perceptual revolution on screen and off, and the Beatles' last appearance together, to date anyhow, was appropriately enough as cartooned figures in George Dunning's *Yellow Submarine* (below), an animated guide to the mind-expanding side of the 1960s. (*United Artists*)

Op and Pop: Monica Vitti in *Modesty Blaise* descends into the 'op' art dungeon designed to hold a comic-strip 'pop' heroine like her (above). The neural jag of Bridget Riley's paintings was one of many imagistic influences that penetrated films from the mid-1960s on. The comic-strip's popularity was evidenced by the revival of the *Batman and Robin* serials; and pop visual style, as far as the cinema was concerned, reached its height when Alan Aldridge applied his fantasy airbrush and glowing colours to designing the poster for the most commercially lucrative fantasy of the era, the 'swinging' London phenomenon that *Smashing Time* set out to guy to death (below). There was no need: it was already dead, but its imagery lingered on. (*Twentieth Century-Fox and Paramount*)

The 1960s cinema kept pace with 1960s permissiveness. Until about 1967, the British cinema explored hitherto 'forbidden' areas of image and experience more candidly than the reviving new American cinema; and even when the latter caught up with it in films like *Bonnie and Clyde* or *The Graduate*, the British screen, not to mention the British censor, still held a lead in matters of sex and nudity – for a short time, anyhow. *Women in Love* first revealed male nudity in the wrestling scene between Oliver Reed and Alan Bates. (*United Artists*)

In *Performance* (above right), a *bain à trois* was a feature of the *ménage à trois* shared by a Pop idol, his junkie mistress and her girl friend, played by Mick Jagger, Anita Pallenberg and Michele Breton. And Malcolm McDowell's nude encounter with Christine Noonan in *If. . .* (below) had the raw animality that, as one critic said, forged the regenerative links of revolution. (*Warner, Paramount*)

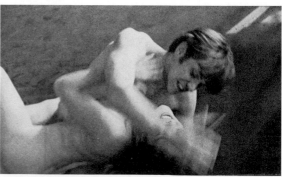

be selected for filming under the scheme until further revenues have been received from the five films already in distribution.' So another attempt to sustain the pure-bred British film faded away. Perhaps it was British Lion that ended up with a smile on its face.

But *which* British Lion? For at this very moment – March 1967 – something resembling a 'palace revolution' was attempted in the boardroom when J. Walter Reade, the American distributor-exhibitor, Sir Michael Balcon, and a mysterious 'Mr X,' whose identity had never been made public (or confirmed to me), attempted to buy out other stockholders. Reade expressed himself increasingly dissatisfied with the way things had been going. 'In film-making, you have to gamble,' he said, recollecting the episode some years later, 'and we just were not ready to put our money down. I found an English passivity I could never accommodate myself to accepting. I really felt I had to get control – or get out.'[1] The Boultings, as well as Tony Richardson and John Osborne, refused to sell their holdings, the former explaining, with a cool assurance that Reade found particularly irritating, that the Government would not have been happy had they accepted a bid which meant passing over control to a group that had predominantly American interests. So Reade got out. He sold his one-fifth interest to Mr (later Sir) Max Rayne, the financier, who became deputy chairman. Shortly afterwards, the one-eighth holding of Tiberius Film (John Schlesinger, Joseph Janni and David Kingsley) was also acquired. 'Our management board is now far more compact,' John Boulting, the group's new managing director, said in October 1967. It was, indeed: five-sixths of the equity was controlled by Lord Goodman, Max Rayne, the Boultings and Launder and Gilliat: with the exception of the first two individuals and David Kingsley, who resigned from the board in 1962, it was virtually the same team as had run British Lion before the Balcon group bought it in 1964. In or around September 1968 the holdings of Long Distance Films (Woodfall, Brian Epstein and Border Television) were purchased; and when capital reconstruction was completed at the end of

[1] Walter Reade interviewed by author, 25 June, 1972.

1968, British Lion was valued at £3 million. Balcon wrote in a dry footnote to his memoirs, 'It will be recalled that the purchase price in 1964 was £1,600,000.'

He added, 'If I had known how the whole adventure into British Lion was going to turn out there would have been no justification, except on principle, for my interfering over the original Sydney Box deal for control of the company. I would have saved myself a great deal of work and worry, and in the end severe disappointment.'[1]

OUR AMERICAN FRIENDS

The Monopolies Commission had not been instructed to look into the American dominance of the British film market; but of course it could not ignore it completely, and a section of the report entitled 'United States Participation in British Film Production' relayed some familiar misgivings. It found the proportion of 'wholly British financed films' had fallen from 67 per cent in 1960 to 46 per cent in 1965; but it absolved Rank and A.B.C. from any blame for this and, characteristically, accepted the circuits' preference for 'the large and costly films, which, for the most part, the wholly British distributors could not finance (partly because they cannot normally get their films shown widely in the United States).'[2] It also accepted Rank's explanation that the smaller investment in British features was due to the drain on its investment resources in financing co-productions with United States companies. (How fortuitous it was that during the enquiry Rank was co-financing 'purely British' pictures under the N.F.F.C. consortium agreement!) While the report correctly found the right reasons why film-making in Britain was so attractive to the Americans – lower costs, subsidy money – the reasons it advanced to explain why the American financing of 'British' films was 'very welcome' were themselves rather naïve. It believed, for example, that the profits accruing to the American distributors from the exhibition of

[1] Michael Balcon, *op. cit.*, p. 209.
[2] Monopolies Commission, *op. cit.*, p. 72.

films they had financed in Britain were in general retained there for financing future films. This simplistic view failed to make allowance for the frequency with which films that were bound to *lose* money tended to go into release about the time that their distributors were trying to count the money pouring in from some box-office hit. The fiscal advantage of this was attractive. Even more so was the difficulty that 'outside parties' may have had in tracing the passage of the receipts back from the box-office to the source. Film companies were ideally organized to make any hardy explorer of this financial territory feel that the origins of the Nile were by comparison easy to locate. In the very lush period of American production in Britain, huge bills run up in London (or abroad) by film-company executives could be set against the revenues from the British box-office. (A jaundiced British producer, who had had no luck in getting his script financed by American companies in London, looked around a supper-party after a film première and complained to me, 'They are eating the budget of my next movie.' It was a slight exaggeration.)

The Monopolies Commission did not accept the view that films made for the British subsidiaries of the Hollywood majors were not entirely British in content, and it quoted the National Film Finance Corporation as saying, 'Many of the most talented British producers are now working with U.S. finance, but none of them is under the yoke of the organizations providing it. On the contrary, such producers are still emphatically free-lance, even though they may regularly make use of the attractive facilities available to them and may have certain contractual arrangements with the organizations concerned.'[1]

But was too much American finance being provided? In the very year the report was published, 1966, American finance accounted for 75 per cent of 'British' first features or co-features given a circuit release, and the figure was to rise to 90 per cent in the years 1967 and 1968. A slight note of apprehension was sounded in the report, though as usual it did its best to stifle it

[1] National Film Finance Corporation Report for year ended 31 March, 1965, H.M.S.O. Cmnd. 2770.

almost at once. 'We were warned of the serious consequences for British film production if United States financing were ever to be withdrawn.' However, the reason the report gave for this alarm was extremely odd: ' . . . not so much because there would be difficulty in finding alternative sources of finance, as because much of the talent required for film production would be likely to follow the United States companies and would be very difficult to replace here.' This was only half-true. When the crunch did come at the end of the decade, the money supply dried up first and the talent stayed grounded in Britain until, early in the 1970s, some of the major directors went to work in America.

The report continued, 'We are not in a position to assess the degree of risk of such a withdrawal, but a question of public interest could (sic) arise if it should happen.' Then came an astonishingly pious expression of hope. 'No doubt the Board of Trade . . . are considering the effect of such an event on the British film industry and, if at the time this were thought to be in the national interest, what steps if any should be taken to support the industry?'[1] The guarded nature of this extraordinary statement revealed – if it needed revealing – how little natural affection there was between the Government and the film industry: but its very reticence was an accurate foreshadowing of the official attitude towards the film industry's troubles a few years later. The number of careful qualifications, the frequency of the 'ifs' and 'buts,' and that ominous little disclaimer, 'if any,' in the last sentence, were proof to a large and well-informed number of observers that the Board of Trade no more had a contingency plan in its pigeon-hole to save the film industry than its principal spokesman, Edward Heath, had a proposal of marriage from Greta Garbo lying unanswered on his desk.

Yet why indeed should the Government have worried, for wasn't there evidence everywhere of an unparalleled boom-time in the film industry? One had only to look at the escalating fees paid to the film-makers, never mind the artists who appeared in the films: they were sky-high in the one case, out of sight in the other. A producer with a good track record could expect to get between £5,000 and £7,500 from an independent British distributor before the Americans arrived in force: but when they did he might eventually be able to get between £45,000 and £100,000 from a Hollywood major, particularly if he owned a property that the American company hankered after. A British company preferred a small fee with a percentage deal, but even here the American companies gave larger percentages. On *The Knack*, for example, the producer got £7,500 and the director £12,500, which may seem small – though the total budget was only £125,000 – but the production company got 50 per cent of the net profits, which were very large just because of the small negative cost. Most of the American companies were working on the scale of 10 per cent of the budget as the director's fee, before the boom started: when it got really under way from 1965–6 onwards, and available pools of proven talent were being frantically mopped up, the price was the one that the man in demand wrote on his own ticket. Terence Young reputedly got over £200,000 for directing one of the Bond films, Tony Richardson an estimated £150,000 for *The Charge of the Light Brigade*.

By mid-1965 there began an ever-increasing flow of American producers and directors into Britain to swell the numbers of the old-established residents like Kubrick, Lester, Losey, Foreman, Shenson and Stanley Donen. Donen had already used the opportunities open to Americans in Britain with notable success – by making films whose production values and general polish were conspicuously American. *Charade*, in 1964, with Cary Grant and Audrey Hepburn, had cost $3 million and grossed many times that sum; and he had followed it up, in 1965, with *Arabesque*, starring Sophia Loren and Gregory Peck, at $4,800,000. 'The big cost,' he said, throwing an interesting sidelight on what a Hollywood company now expected a 'British' picture to have, 'came from making it dazzling to look at. I had worked on the script for eighteen months and was so dissatisfied with it that I implored Universal to let me out of doing the film. But Peck and Loren wanted to work together, which was good enough reason for doing it, they thought. We spent $400,000 on the script alone; but the interest it might not otherwise have had came from the photography.'[1] This was conceived in the visually baroque style emphasizing treacherous focus-changes and restless re-angling of the camera. The same photographer, Christopher Challis, conjured up much the same visual modishness for the well-named *Kaleidoscope*, which the American director Jack Smight came to England to make for Warners in 1966. 'A groovie movie' was how it was advertised; and this was what Hollywood companies back home now expected their British-made movies to do – 'to groove.' This was what 'swinging' meant, wasn't it? This was the label the customers would buy, wouldn't they?

Christopher Challis also photographed Donen's next picture, *Two for the Road* (1967), from a Frederic Raphael script, with Albert Finney and Audrey Hepburn as perfect examples of the sort of 'getaway people' to whom the weekly colour supplements paid homage. Underneath the lives they led of rush and consumption, Raphael suggested, lay confusion and impermanence: the perfect example of the phrase Kingsley Amis was to popularize, that 'More is worse.' It was *Darling*'s lesson all over again, showing that it's possible to be 'goodtime people' without actually having a good time. The disenchantment of Antonioni had now definitely replaced the rebarbative Godard as the heavy influence from across the Channel. Even so, the main appeal in *Two for the Road* came from the external look of colourfully jigsaw lives reflected – often too literally – in wax-polished photography. 'Foreign film-makers,' said Donen, who had been a Londoner so long that he was fully entitled to view his countrymen with a certain detachment, 'felt they had only to get to England, start making a film and somehow the excitement of life here would rub off on it. For a time it did, too. The British film people learned that instead of fighting the Americans, they could make money with them. And for a time they did, too. Later on, everybody learned better.'

It was in very much this mood that American production offices began putting their shingles up all over London in 1966. One of

[1] Stanley Donen interviewed by the author, 16 February, 1972. Unless stated otherwise all subsequent quotations from Donen come from the same source.

the most ambitious, certainly the smartest-looking, outfit was
Universal Pictures. And because its production programme was
so ambitious, so costly, so deliberately designed to take advantage
of all the contemporary ingredients and talents that made
'British' films saleable and successful internationally, and especially in America, it merits deserved attention. There is another
reason for a close scrutiny. It turned out to be a failure of unanticipated and unparalleled proportions.

JAY KANTER MOVES IN

Universal Pictures' London office wasn't lodged in Wardour
Street, but in a Piccadilly mansion a few doors down from one
that had been owned by a former Royal Duke who became King,
and was just a stone's throw from Buckingham Palace. The style
of furnishing also reflected the fairly regal tastes of Dr Jules
Stein, founder of the Music Corporation of America, which
controlled Universal. No other film staffers worked amidst such
lovely antiques which were periodically changed for others, like
exhibits in a museum, presumably as one lot was shipped off to
Dr Stein and replaced with fresh and rare pieces he had chosen on
his London visits. Knowing how spartan by comparison were the
executive offices in the fourteen-storey black tower that rose
above Universal's home lot in California, some observers
wondered whether the sheer affluence of the London set-up was
responsible for generating the sarcasm, tinged with envy, whenever the Hollywood people referred to it towards the end of Jay
Kanter's days as its boss. Kanter had been an agent before
becoming a vice-president of M.C.A.; and he arrived in London
just at the time the ex-agents were moving into strong positions
– or as strong as the New York or Hollywood companies would
permit – as production chiefs with responsibility for making or
co-ordinating film activity in Britain and Europe. As agents, they
had been accustomed to reading and deciding on scripts quickly,
handling clients, working with writers, making contracts – and
finding good reasons for breaking them, as well – all abilities that

supposedly transferred well to producing pictures. Kanter was a trusted intimate of Lew Wasserman, M.C.A.'s austere and powerful president, a man who delegated authority either totally or not at all. Kanter came to Britain with an enviable freedom probably not matched by the European production chief of any other comparable Hollywood company. For instance, he claimed that he was not obliged to consult with the home studio 'unless the budget for a film we were making was over two million dollars, which I'd do, anyhow.'[1] For Universal to be actually making films in Britain was a considerable departure from established policy. Though the product that M.C.A. handled was film, its main interest did not lie in motion pictures, but in providing material for television. In 1972, M.C.A.'s Universal TV accounted for 25 per cent of all networked television in the United States. Television took care of the overheads and expanded the budgets for big films; it is not overstating the case to say that M.C.A. thought of motion pictures largely as leaders for television programmes on the networks, to which they would speedily be sold after they had established themselves in the prestige slot of theatrical release. In its fairly short existence as a major film producer, M.C.A. had made an impressive number of money-making movies, some of them, like *The Chalk Garden* and *Charade*, produced abroad. But these overseas films were under the supervision of the home studio. Kanter's production office was the first to dispense with the Hollywood apron strings.

Universal provided 100 per cent financing for the British films – it was all Hollywood money, not funds that were already in Britain – and no limit, according to Kanter, was ever fixed for any of the films or indeed for the total amount of money to be invested. As it happened, none of the films ever 'went wild' where money was concerned and all of them are said to have come in on budget, or even under it, though this is not to say that they were therefore necessarily good investments. (As we shall see, some were risky even at their price.) The British box-office subsidy for which all the films were eligible never played any

[1] Jay Kanter interviewed by the author, 24 June, 1971. Unless stated otherwise all subsequent quotations from Kanter come from the same source.

decisive part in attracting Universal to Britain. Much more important was the then current charisma that British films possessed. M.C.A. particularly noted the appeal they had for younger audiences in America: the things that were happening in Britain were of more interest to 'the kids' at that time than those in their own country, though a shrewd observer of the American scene in 1967 would have detected signs that the quiescence or apathy of the native youth about their own backyard was drawing to a close. Another attraction was the pool of acting talent in the British theatre and television which could be easily dipped into. British television, in particular, struck the American producers as a vast casting office, maintained by British licence-holders and advertisers, where new talent was nightly tried out for them which they could then snap up at attractively low prices. (This was a view repeated to me endlessly by American producers in Britain.) Lastly, cheapness counted in Universal's move into Britain: three films could be made at Pinewood, Shepperton, or Elstree for every two in Universal City. (Even as late as 1973 it was still an attractive enough factor for Paramount to shoot the exteriors of *The Great Gatsby* in the United States locations, then move the production across the Atlantic to Britain for the more economically-budgeted interior scenes!)

In just under three years Universal financed more than a dozen films in Britain. The total cost is estimated to be in the region of $30 million, which includes the running costs of Universal's London office and its staff's salaries. Figures for each production have never been officially made known, but people well placed to judge have estimated the budgets of the major films; and the sincerity of Universal's financial investment, as well as the astonishing range of subjects that Jay Kanter spread it over, is obvious in the following list:

Privilege (1967: $700,000); *A Countess from Hong Kong* (1967: $3,500,000); *Fahrenheit 451* (1967: $1,500,000); *Charlie Bubbles* (1968: $1,000,000); *Work is a Four-Letter Word* (1968: $800,000); *Boom!* (1968: $3,900,000); *Secret Ceremony* (1968: $2,450,000– $3,120,000); *Three into Two won't Go* (1968: $1,500,000); *Isadora* (1968: $1,700,000); *The Bofors Gun* (1968: $800,000); *The Night of the Following Day* (1968: $1,500,000); *Can Heironymus Merkin ever forget Mercy Humppe and find True Happiness?* (1969: $500,000); and *The Adding Machine* (1969: $500,000).

No one could deny that such a list represents an impressive investment – and not merely of money, but also of stars (Brando, Loren, Taylor, Burton, Finney, Redgrave, Christie); of fledgling but highly promising directors (Watkins, Hall, Gold) combined with others of distinction and stature (Chaplin, Reisz, Losey, Truffaut); of high-risk subjects off-laid against safe-seeming ones – in short (and on paper) a production roster that deserved the fortune said to attend the brave. It did not get it. Several years later a regretful but unrepentant Jay Kanter spoke with baffled resignation of the fact that 'amongst the whole bunch there was not a single runaway success that might have made the difference – not one.' From start to finish, he claimed, Universal stood by him and never over him; they put no pressures on him. 'They simply kept hoping – and spending the production money – and trusting that the next one from Britain would turn out the winner. In such a project, "Pushing on to the next" must be your slogan always.'

Why did the programme fall so utterly flat? In some cases the answer is painfully easy to see, at least with the facility of hindsight. *A Countess from Hong Kong*, for example, was lamentably old-fashioned. It showed its years without grace. Chaplin had tinkered with the novelettish story for decades and could not graft his clowning style on to Brando or Loren, while the latter's technical dexterity grew cold and stiff at the Nth re-take he autocratically forced on them. 'High hopes were placed on *Fahrenheit 451*,' said Kanter, 'perhaps too high.' Based on Ray Bradbury's allegory of a totalitarian State where books are burned, not read, and preserved only in the minds of a *maquis* of secret *litterateurs*, it relied heavily on the vogue of François Truffaut (who was off-form, perhaps because he was working in a language he didn't understand or speak readily) and even more on Julie Christie, who had just won an Oscar for *Darling* and was reputed to have 'mystique.' 'Everyone expected her to work wonders for the film,' said Kanter, 'and was disappointed when the magic failed. The New York reviews also proved hurtful to the film's chance of a wider screening.'

Three into Two won't Go proved a more inexplicable disappointment. Directed by Peter Hall, its theme was that of the revenge which a footloose teenage girl takes on the domestic set-up of a middle-ageing couple whose marriage is based on a lie – the man had casually picked her up, then found she was not so easily laid – or laid aside. Judy Geeson precisely incarnated the ruthless girl, her sexual candour contrasting sharply with Rod Steiger's flagging potency and Claire Bloom's menopausal resignation. Set in a new, bright, rootless housing estate for the executive class, it pinned down a generational conflict in English society with unusual truth and lack of compromise. It should have had an instant appeal to youth, if only for its honesty and apart from the fact that the teenager was a winner all the way on her own terms. Instead, it flopped. Even Steiger's recent award of an Oscar for *In the Heat of the Night* conferred on it no 'mystique.' 'I feel its failure was an omen for us,' said Kanter. 'It ran into the disenchantment with English films then becoming apparent at the American box-office.' Fitting his production roster to this imperative, without prejudicing its native qualities, was his biggest problem. Some films like *Work is a Four-Letter Word* or Anthony Newley's sexy extravaganza-cum-morality-play, *Heironymus Merkin*, had of course no strong national traits: neither did they have an appeal to any specific territory where they had to be sold. They were films set in limbo, which is where they perished.

Work is a Four-Letter Word, also directed by Peter Hall, relied on David Warner's previous success in *Morgan*, for he was playing another fantasticated drop-out – indeed it had seemed to many who saw his *Morgan* that it was based on the character he had originally played in Henry Livings's play *Eh?* which had been re-titled *Work is a Four-Letter Word*! It simply proved one should not try to compete with oneself.

The Bofors Gun, on the other hand, was a film so essentially British that its meaning, never mind its appeal, was hard to transfer successfully overseas. It introduced one of the Royal Court Theatre's heirs-apparent to Scofield and Olivier in the person of Nicol Williamson as the intransigent Irish soldier whose self-destructive urge shatters the promotional hopes of a 'class turncoat.' (It was a *Long-Distance Runner* theme.) Williamson had every capacity except that of finding any element in himself or the role which an audience might think attractive. Heavy, sour, uncompromisingly introverted, he would probably spit on the element of 'charm' if it were offered him as an artificial sweetener for a rancorous disposition. But it was its absence which made the film more of a depressant than an intoxicant. *The Night of the Following Day* did not cost much to make, despite having Brando as the star, since Kanter made use of an old Universal contract he had negotiated 'at a very favourable price' (perhaps around $500,000) when he had been Brando's agent. Yet this film failed, too.

Kanter's critics asserted that the 'wrong values' had been attached to such subjects in order to make them attractive propositions for financing. They were devised to be sold to film-financiers, they said, not to film-goers. Instead of going for popular elements, the emphasis was put on qualities that might be expected to appeal to a man of sensibility and taste, like Kanter, who, as an agent, had had no hurtful contact with the crude realities of the box-office. Too often, his critics said, he saw films as 'interesting chemistry,' but was not equipped by experience to follow through and see whether they were also profitable business. The subjects he picked from the ones he initiated, or had brought to him by other producers, were 'intellectual' or 'pseudo-intellectual.' In a word, 'pretentious.' 'It gave one a great deal of pleasure to make pictures for him,' said one such critic, who had also gained a not inconsiderable insight into the agent side of the film business before he turned producer, 'but when it came to giving other people pleasure when they saw them, such films were useless.'

There is something in this view: but nothing that, given just one hit in the production programme on the scale of *Tom Jones*, would not have been deemed worth the risk of self-indulgence.

What the films did make apparent was that the British label and the 'swinging' look were not the wonder-ingredients that had been supposed. What *Time* magazine had once promoted on its front cover, time in the strictly temporal sense was now exiling to the back row of fashion. There could be no better example of what should have been a profitable union between pop culture and the *avant garde* than one of Universal's early productions, *Privilege*, the story of a British teenage idol who is manipulated by a right-wing government, first as a release mechanism for youth's violent emotions, then as a conformity symbol for youth's enslavement. Paul Jones, the pop singer, played the idol, and David Bailey's own protegée, Jean Shrimpton, had her first featured role. The film was based on a story by Johnny Speight, later the creator of the television series *Till Death us do Part*, known as *All in the Family* when it reached American screens, which in turn was based on an idea by Terence Stamp. The origins were impeccably 'swinging.' Moreover, it set out to be 'a picture of Britain in the near future,' where money is the only viable relationship, the Church has sold out of the media men, public spectacles have become sado-masochistic orgies, and showbiz-capitalism rules the opinion makers. In a Britain where, in August 1967, Mick Jagger had been flown in a helicopter by a television company almost directly from the Appeal Court, where a three-months' jail sentence passed on him for a drugs offence in June had been reduced to a conditional discharge, to a secret country rendezvous and there solemnly interviewed by a group that included Malcolm Muggeridge, the Bishop of Woolwich, a leading Jesuit priest, an ex-Home Secretary and the Editor of *The Times, Privilege's* vision of the near future was perhaps not so fantastic after all.

The director was Peter Watkins, well-known and even notorious for his television documentary *The War Game* which BBC TV commissioned in 1965 and had then refused to show on the grounds that its 'vision' of the horrors that thermo-nuclear war would unleash was too terrifying. The film, subsequently shown in some British cinemas, contained the bud of *Privilege*, since Watkins applied the techniques of the television news enquiry to both themes, with interviews, commentary and the sense of 'life' seized apparently when it wasn't looking or stuttering out the concealed truth among the official platitudes. Watkin's great technical gifts had their disquieting side, too, when one realized how expertly he wielded the selective quotation, the high-visibility stereotype, the hypothesis-as-fact, and the propaganda bias. Fortunately, he had – and has – an apparently invincible habit of protesting too much and too shrilly; instead of insinuating his case, he asserts it and thus makes it easier to decry and some-times reject. His passion verges on the neurotic, the obsessed. But the subject and his name caught Kanter's imagination – and got Universal's backing – when John Heyman, another agent turned producer, brought him the 'package' of *Privilege*. Heyman said later, 'The main fault was that we flailed away at too many targets all at once: we wanted to hit everything we knew or suspected was wrong with Britain.'[1]

Kanter saw its failure much more in terms of not packing in the American teenage audience which he had hoped would buy the universal idea of exploited youth. Curiously enough, a short time afterwards, American International Pictures produced *Wild in the Streets*, about a pop idol who inflames teenage youth and is elected President of the U.S.A. – and this did excellent business. Inevitably the fact that *Privilege* had had a British slant was blamed for its relative failure. But even in its native land, it had a rough ride. The Rank circuit, to whom Universal were 'tied,' gave it only hesitant exposure. A spokesman said, 'This is an unusual film, interesting and problematic (*sic*). We are not sure how to sell it. We want to try it out with all kinds of audiences and be guided by public acceptability. But we would not offer it for normal general release yet.'[2] Privately, the film was regarded, by a film industry chief with the power to determine its exhibition, as an immoral and un-Christian picture which mocked the Church, defied authority and encouraged youth in lewd practices. (It must be said in fairness to Rank, that it subsequently modified the moral stand it sometimes took against playing such films

[1] John Heyman interviewed by the author, 13 January 1973. Unless stated otherwise all subsequent quotations from Heyman come from the same source.
[2] *Daily Express*, 19 April, 1967.

widely, or at all, as public preference showed itself at the box-office. Unfortunately, this came too late to help *Privilege*.) The film's failure to get a wide screening even in its country of origin was an embarrassment to Kanter – and an omen for his production programme.

His bad experience with *Privilege* had one ironic side-effect. He turned down a project brought to him by Albert Finney's production company, Memorial Enterprises, which the actor had set up with his continuing percentage from *Tom Jones*.[1] The subject was about a revolution in an English public school: 'An interesting theme,' said Kanter, 'but after *Privilege*, I felt it might present difficulties for an American audience.' The film was of course *If . . .*, which caught the imagination of youth everywhere, irrespective of nationality, when Paramount backed it a year or so later. However, Kanter did finance another project of Finney's that looked quite a *coup* at the time: the first film with Finney as director and star – *Charlie Bubbles*.

THE BALLOON GOES UP

Charlie Bubbles persists in raising the question of how much of it was rooted in Albert Finney's own experience. It was a success story gone sour. When Shelagh Delaney's script began, Charlie Bubbles was a best-selling writer whose success has brought him no happiness. 'What does it all mean?' is the question he asks himself, as agents chatter away around him, deciding his future. At the end of the film, when he is floating away in an aerial balloon, literally suspended between decisions, the question has clearly become, 'Is this all there is?' Agents, friends, servants, his estranged wife and child, are all used as the means to reflect Charlie's disillusionment. The film replaces a narrative theme with an emotional one. There is Charlie's disenchantment with success that, like Finney's, came quickly – perhaps too quickly.

[1] Called facetiously after the monument to the Prince Consort in Hyde Park, the Albert Memorial.

There is the hesitation of the creative will, the aridity that comes over an artist when his inspiration has ceased to flow – which recalled for some the protracted identity-crisis that Finney had suffered after *Tom Jones*.

Some time after *Charlie Bubbles*, he conceded that 'it was a highly magnified expression of a certain mood I had, a certain distrust, a certain worry about the way I might develop as a man, as an artist in my profession.'[1] He pointed out that Shelagh Delaney had gone through the same phase when she had written *A Taste of Honey* at the age of nineteen and then been overwhelmed by success and acclaim. 'The kind of identity crisis she went through,' said Finney, 'was quite considerable. Much more, I think, *much* more than mine.' Not surprisingly, therefore, there was a tight emotional bond between Finney and Delaney, both of whom came from the same Midlands town. More than anything it was this that influenced Finney to turn film director. 'I received from Shelagh Delaney a thirty-two-page outline . . . and I responded to it. It was about this man, slightly different in feel, but the character was there, the emotional state of the man was the same, and I felt an immediate recognition and wanted to record it, wanted to be involved in it, in the development of it *myself* – at that time, originally, just as an actor. Then I thought, well, if I'm going to set up the production, I know what I want to do with it. I understand what should be done with it. I would then have to hire a director who would do it *my* way, which isn't right. So I thought I should do the two – act and direct.' Finney's services as star and director probably accounted for £200,000 out of the film's £450,000 budget. (In retrospect he conceded that the cost was 'a bit inflated . . . due to what at that time was my market price. I've gone down a bit since.')

The trouble with Charlie Bubbles is that the character is an extremely passive type. All the other people in the film are seen or felt through him. While this basic simplicity made Finney's début as a director easier than if he had landed himself with a more complex characterization requiring to be viewed from many

[1] Albert Finney in discussion with an audience at the Essoldo Cinema, Chelsea, 8 February, 1969.

points, there was an up-tightness about his playing of the part, a refusal to 'give,' to be more wryly involved in Charlie's fate, which stemmed directly from the responsibilities he had undertaken. 'I think,' he said, 'my performance spoils the picture.' This is arguable. But it certainly offered a public no attractive means of access to a film already carrying a heavy load of introspection and pessimism. This had been even more emphasised in the original script, where Charlie died at the end. 'The next morning,' said Finney referring to this, 'Charlie gets in his car and drives off (from his estranged wife's). The Press follow him – not a kind of chase, they just want to see where he's going, and they come round a bend and his car's gone off the cliff edge. And they run down and there's Charlie, obviously getting paler and dying. But it seemed (to me) very brutal. The comedy in the film we tried to keep gently ironic, and this seemed rather a stab in the back after the audience, we hoped, would have been patient with us. So we tried softening it. The Press run down and there's Charlie, obviously dying. The camera goes in on Charlie. He looks up wryly into the lens and says, "Leave me alone, I'm busy." That, I thought, was a way of handling death that was quite nice, but it still seemed basically something that left no possibility of any future whatsoever. The fact that (in the ending eventually filmed) he goes away in the balloon could mean anything; but I wanted it really to be an emotional expression – after this intense study of him – of a sense of freedom, a hopeful possibility in some way. A friend of mine saw that as (meaning) his death: well, that's what it seems to *him*. The fact is that if Shelagh Delaney hadn't somehow come out of that mood, she wouldn't ever have been objective in seeing a phase she once went through; and I wouldn't have been able to direct it because I wouldn't have seen a phase that *I* went through. That's why we thought it worth recording.'

It was on this painfully personal aspect of the film, clear to the participants, but confusing to others and communicable to a smaller audience than might have been attracted by the name of Albert Finney, that the blame was later laid for the film's commercial disappointment. Even Finney acknowledged that this was the price he had to pay for 'a sense of creativity, more power-

M

ful than any experience as an actor that I've had.' But it was an unpalatable fact that, in its low-keyed, open-ended way, the film 'knocked' success. It drew bleak reviews in New York in 1968, where it opened almost a year before its London première. After a short run at one of Rank's West End cinemas, it failed to get a circuit release and simply made the occasional appearance wherever it was hoped there might be an audience for it. When a Rank executive claimed that such a 'staggered' release was all part of a well-thought-out policy, Finney answered him in a letter that overflowed with sarcasm and bitterness. 'The imagination and thought behind such an original scheme for the distribution of a film is staggering – to the ingenious and inventive minds that conceived this novel "slow burn" distribution pattern, I take off all my hats, including my Sherlock Holmes deerstalker, for they certainly managed to keep any suggestion of their genius a secret from me during the last twenty months.'[1]

The two films Jay Kanter made with Elizabeth Taylor – *Boom!* and *Secret Ceremony* – did not lessen the growing problems of a man whose production policy was disastrously failing to yield results. At the end of 1968 his Hollywood boss, Lew Wasserman, forecasting that the company's earnings for the current year would be significantly below those of 1967, singled out *Boom!* as one of the films that had particularly disappointed him. John Heyman, who had 'packaged' it for Kanter since the Burtons were his clients, and also acted as producer, took a somewhat cooler view of it in retrospect. 'A piece of sheer opportunism,' he called it, though he remembered a Universal executive viewing the final print and crying out deliriously, 'We've got *Virginia Woolf* in colour!' Kanter, equally candid, later acknowledged that he hadn't liked the Tennessee Williams material it was based on, 'but when the Burtons were involved, a lot of my judgment was coloured by the magnitude of the star she was considered to be. She made the material more viable, since a younger woman in the role was more attractive at the box-office than Tennessee's ageing heroine.' Even if it had been so, the casting of Richard Burton as the 'young' poet, the angel of death who helps Mrs

[1] *Today's Cinema*, 27 June, 1969.

Goforth into the next world, would have made the film's resemblance to the original theme at best a wishful one, for in some scenes he actually looked older than the Taylor character. Kanter would obviously have done better to stick to his sound judgment as a producer and not let it be coloured by the 'possibilities' that might suggest themselves to him as an agent. Despite its stars – who cost an estimated $2,000,000 just to sign up – the film disappointed Universal once again.

Immediately after it came *Secret Ceremony*, again with Elizabeth Taylor and Joseph Losey as star and director respectively. 'We were regarded as whizz-kids,' said Heyman, who again produced, 'just for making two consecutive films with Elizabeth Taylor and bringing them in under budget.' About a million dollars is reported to have been spent afterwards on publicising *Secret Ceremony* in the United States: it did quite well, but not on anything like the scale anticipated. It failed at the British box-office. 'A cold picture,' Heyman called it. A modern version of the Cencii story, it was set in one of those magnificently baroque mansions beloved by Losey (the music-boxes recalled the ones he used to hear tinkling away in the great mansions that stood along the river banks in his Mississippi childhood) where Elizabeth Taylor, an 'outsider' and freelance prostitute, is fatally involved with a friendless rich girl who 'adopts' her. Together they act out an equivocal 'mother and child' relationship, their fantasies about each other completing their separate needs, until the eruption of the girl's stepfather (Mia Farrow and Robert Mitchum played the roles) into the relationship contributes to their mutual destruction. 'It should have been the story of two people who need and trust each other until one leans on the other a little bit more than she should,' said Heyman. 'Unfortunately the kind of sympathy which Losey shows for people in real life was absent from the relationship, which is what I think made it unacceptable.'

The dissatisfaction that Universal's home office must have been feeling with their British programme – the office in London was referred to snidely by Hollywood staffers as 'the country club' – may be apparent in the sequel to *Secret Ceremony*'s box-office performance. Universal went about recovering their investment in it in a severely practical way. It was one which they were perfectly legally entitled to take. In late 1970 they did a deal with a major U.S. television network for two screenings of the film – for which they were to be paid $1,250,000 – a very welcome sum – one in which Joseph Losey could also expect to participate. But the subject of the deal was by no means the same film that Losey had shot in England. It was a radically revised, specially prepared version of *Secret Ceremony* which, Losey claimed, 'exactly reversed the meaning and intention of my film.' While it is sadly commonplace for production companies to cut films in order to prepare a television version of them, Universal were much more 'creative' and the alterations they proposed extended to shooting new material, completely new scenes, and creating new characters. This entailed a running commentary by these characters, a London barrister and an American psychiatrist who is trying to persuade him to undertake the Taylor character's legal defence, which, at major points in the film, attempted to 'clarify' for the mass television audience in the United States, in the most banal terms, the human motivations whose very ambiguities Losey had dwelt on with subtlety and success. Into the oblique and atmospheric story were inserted scenes – Losey was not informed who had scripted or directed them – which spelled out the story with the simple-mindedness of alphabet blocks. The proposed alterations detailed in a script on which Losey was not consulted – Universal later put this down to the pressure of time, and in any case they were under no legal obligation to consult him – ran to nineteen pages and nearly 300 lines of additional dialogue. They effectively turned Losey's film into an extended flashback, which now ended with the English barrister agreeing to defend the Taylor character on a murder charge and indicating that his plea would be, 'Not guilty by reason of insanity.' No such plea exists in English law!

Losey asked for his name to be removed from the 'new' film. He acknowledged he had suffered no material damage; but he was widely known for having directed the original version – 'and which parts are mine and which are the work of new hands may not be distinguishable by people who have not viewed the original film.'[1]

Similar treatment was given Peter Hall's film *Three into Two won't Go*, which Hall claimed had twenty minutes of new scenes (a fifth of the picture) added to the cut and re-edited film, turning it from the study of a marriage being broken up into a probation officer's search for a girl who has broken her parole. 'Three weeks ago,' Hall wrote later, 'Universal shipped me a copy and asked for my "response." I asked to have my name removed, and the title changed. I also have to report that I was bored. I would not have made this script in the first place.'[2]

By the time Universal had Karel Reisz's *Isadora* ready for its American première something akin to a curse had settled upon American-financed films that were being made in Britain. The euphoria had turned into apprehensiveness. People in other film companies along Wardour Street kept their fingers crossed and hoped that 'the next one' would prove a blockbuster on the scale once achieved – did it really seem so long ago? – by the Beatles, the Bonds, *Alfie*, *Morgan* and *Georgy Girl*. *Isadora* confirmed their fears rather than alleviated them. The initial audience response was lukewarm and Universal insisted, again with full legal rights, on the film being cut and re-edited. If these alterations made appreciable improvements to the film – and its reticent director doubts it – they were hardly manifest at the box-office. Part of the blame was attached to American public opinion, sections of which were antipathetic towards Vanessa Redgrave for her vigorous work in various protest movements and her criticism of the Vietnam War: in 1969 the war still commanded a majority following in 'Middle America.'

After the disappointment of *Isadora*, Kanter's production programme teetered to a halt like a hoop that has spent its momentum. One of the last films to be released, having been kept on the shelf because of exhibition difficulties, was *The Adding Machine*. It produced the inevitable wry quip that it would come in useful for adding up the losses.

[1] *Evening Standard*, 17 November, 1970.
[2] *The Times*, 27 October, 1970.

Kanter resigned at the end of February 1969, and shortly afterwards joined an independent production company based in London and headed by three Americans, Jerry Gershwin, Elliot Kastner and Alan Ladd Jr. Early in the 1970s he was able to look back and view his efforts in a mellow frame of mind – a slightly-built man still showing traits of that 1960s modishness that was supposedly part of the recipe for success in those days, and talking in a low equitone voice that handled large figures and small in the same even-tempered, regretful flow. It was at times almost drowned by the Mayfair traffic passing outside the high-ceilinged room with the heavy doors, moulded cornices and 'good' furniture that recalled the other elegantly furnished private house which had been the old Universal offices in Piccadilly.

'If I had it to do all over again,' he said, 'the one area I'd be more cautious about would be financing. I'd be making the pictures on much, much lower budgets. Everyone is working along that line now. But in those days stars still expected to be paid hundreds of thousands of dollars before the cameras turned – and they were. And properties were further inflated by the belief that there were "magic" ingredients that would sell them internationally. It was a feeling of the times. I guess we just forget how quickly times change.'

Taking the long view, Universal's losses may be few enough. Careful programming, sales to television, exposure via hotels and in-flight projection will probably bring most of the British films into profit. Some are already there. But no amount of slow and steady income ever compensates a movie company for the loss of expectations that the initial receipts will be multi-million-dollar ones. 'Universal were the perfect money source,' said John Heyman, 'clean to work for, unbelievably honest, offering no arguments of a mean or frustrating nature to the people they signed.' A lesser company might have come out of it shouting that they had been 'screwed.' Universal simply and honourably called a halt. They abandoned some projects they had been working on – a film about Biggles, the pilot adventurer, which was to star James Fox, and had had $400,000 spent on its script already was among them. They called production back to

Universal City and for the next couple of years Hal Wallis and Alfred Hitchcock were the only producers who worked under the Universal banner in Britain. But the spectacular failure of their British production hopes had knocked on the head and left for dead the belief that films, any films, made in Britain with the right polish and mix were just what the world wanted to see. Should expectations ever have been pitched so high? Maybe not. But film-making is a business where hopes race ahead of realities and confidence is often indistinguishable from delusions. As Jay Kanter said, I guess we just forgot how quickly times change.

Chapter Seventeen: Old Hands, New Boys

It's wrong to say we were a carbon copy of the cinema: we were
a copy but better.

Richard Cawston, Head of Documentaries, B.B.C. TV[1]

It is in the years 1967–8 that one hears the unmistakable sound in
the British cinema of a 'New Wave' hesitating as it crawls up the
beach it had hitherto foamed over, and starting to ebb back, while
another crest of talent coming up behind it prepares to break and
scatter . . . Save for Lester and Schlesinger, the first major
arrivals of the 1960s had come out of stage-directing or the movie
studios: the second wave of directors came out of television. And
this is not all that distinguishes them from the older group.
Though they have made 'names' for themselves in the cinema,
they have retained a loyalty to their first love that the earlier group
either never had or wished to acquire. They have never cut
themselves off decisively from the smaller screen; but where the
opportunity exists they have gone back to work for it, some
sustained by a social purpose they feel beats more strongly in
television than in the cinema, others by the relative ease of
realizing their vision of things. And the cinema films they have
made have frequently been influenced by the functions of entertainment and information, and particularly the social responsibilities, which they developed as makers of documentaries or arts
programmes on television. Their sense of purpose contrasts
strongly at this time with the sense of repetition and hesitancy one
feels about the careers of the earlier group of film-makers.

For most of these, the year 1967 was a disenchanting one.
Nearly all of them were now working for American companies,
or making films as co-productions with a Hollywood major. But
they were conscious of how the taste of the public, as well as the
expectations of their backers, had been altered by the very success

[1] Quoted in Joan Bakewell and Nicholas Garnham, *The New Priesthood,
British Television Today* (Allen Lane, Penguin Press, 1970), p. 180.

of some of their earlier movies – and what these tastes and expectations now were had to be discovered anew. John Schlesinger and Joseph Janni were developing 'a small film' for Julie Christie after the international success of *Darling*; and they proposed an embryonic idea to M.G.M., only to be told, 'We are not interested in a small movie: we want a roadshow film.' Janni admitted later, 'I yielded to pride. I will be the first to say I was "corrupted" by ambition. I gave in to the desire to make a "big important picture," to say to Nat Cohen [whose company, Anglo-Amalgamated, had Julie Christie under contract and who would participate in financing the film with M.G.M.] in the very best Hollywood tradition of carving up the world market, "Nat, you and I and John and Fred [Frederic Raphael, who was to write the screenplay] will take England." It was a heady prospect and I capitulated.' Schlesinger may have had *Far from the Madding Crowd* (19 October, 1967) in mind – though M.G.M. had proposed a remake of *Tess of the D'Urbervilles*, which they had filmed in 1924 – but he very definitely had Vanessa Redgrave in mind for Hardy's heroine. 'But we've got Julie under contract,' Janni protested. ('Oh, I was totally corrupted,' he added, years later, with a Latin shiver.) The choice of this particular Hardy novel had an irony possibly not appreciated till afterwards. It was in essence the same story as *Darling*, relocated in the nineteenth-century countryside instead of the twentieth-century metropolis, with the elemental quality of Nature replacing the endless flux of the consumer society. Hardy's 'Darling,' one Bathsheba Everdene, reproduces the same feminine dissatisfactions as she seeks fulfil-ment with three men: Alan Bates, as her devoted herdsman nursing his love with dumb-ox loyalty, is the Dirk Bogarde character of the other film; Terence Stamp, as truculent Sergeant Troy, is strikingly like the sexual swaggerer played by Laurence Harvey in *Darling*; Peter Finch, the bachelor landowner who is said to lack 'passionate parts,' duplicates the impotent Italian prince whom 'Darling' married. Once Julie Christie had been cast, the dice was, too: try as the film-makers might, it was impossible to keep the one film from recalling the other – to its detriment.

The trouble was, Julie Christie had personified so vividly the restless, uninhibited 1960s 'swinger,' soothing her frustration by perpetual movement, that she failed to stretch herself to encompass the larger passions of life against the backdrop of Nature and its elemental rhythms. To portray so vigorously endowed a woman as Bathsheba, boss of man and beast in an age when well-bred women barely lifted anything heavier than an embroidery needle, required an actress beyond the ordinary with some oddness of feature, reserve of mystery or unpredictable temperament – at the very least a Vanessa Redgrave. Christie revealed a painfully restricted emotional repertoire for such a tumultuous heroine; and no amount of inner radiance – she sang radiantly, paid her workers radiantly, even milked the cows radiantly – could lift the curse that made Bathsheba look and sound like a 1960s girl. A Hardy film without a Hardy heroine was like a fine watch without a spring – all craftsmanship, but no tick. The film was far more successful in re-creating Hardy's perspective of man's littleness measured, physically and spiritually, against God's scheme. The pessimistic acceptance of one's condition is what had appealed to Schlesinger.

The romantic aspect of Hardy, on the other hand, seldom sprang out of the screen as it did off the page. It was a moment-to-moment flare-up, most imaginatively realized in the sequence where Sergeant Troy lays siege to his beloved in a cut-and-come-again series of mock charges and lunges with his sword and then, in a wonderfully lucky conjunction of light and drifting shadows, pressing the seduction home till the sabre stands planted in the turf, winking out its owner's victory. This bizarre courtship was the film's imaginative highlight. But it needed more than that to make it a success. *Far from the Madding Crowd* cost $2,750,000 and did well in England despite mixed notices. In America it got a disappointing reaction, neither an artistic nor a commercial success. Janni vowed he would never again make a film based on such a period novel or at such excessive length: it ran to 169 minutes. Schlesinger had to wait till *Midnight Cowboy* to repair and enhance his reputation in America.

Jack Clayton was also working for M.G.M., filming a curious

blend of elements from his previous films: the Gothic horror story of *The Innocents* cross-bred with the swarming presence of children out of *The Pumpkin Eater*. The result, *Our Mother's House* (14 September, 1967), was the sort of black fairy-tale that adults make up about children, but tend to tell to other adults. The mainspring of inspiration is guilt. Look, it says, how our sins, vices and superstitions pervert the innocence of childhood. The evil in *Our Mother's House* was a more insidious one than the struggle for possession of infant souls in *The Innocents*, for this time it was a Christian perversion, not an infernal visitation. Mother had lived a loose life, but raised her brood in the hellfire-and-damnation atmosphere of a suburban London home plastered with Biblical texts, and she ultimately died a penitent; whereupon her God-fearing children gave her a decent Christian burial in the back garden and, to save themselves from the orphanage, went on living in the house, while spiritual discipline crumbled into élitist intolerance – until their long-lost father walks in, in the shape of Dirk Bogarde, and for a time the profane world lifts the curse off the sacred one.

It was a craftsman's film, but unfortunately little else. Its Dickensian terrors fitted awkwardly into Welfare State England. The children were gratifyingly – and predictably – Clayton's 'signature' on the film and he gave interesting testimony to the pleasures and pains of the film, and where they lay *for him*, when he said, 'You've got to give (children) absolutely total direction, including the emphasis of the words and every single moment. You've got to use every trick, including a semi-hypnotic approach.'[1] But the film failed to evoke any comparable response from the box-office; and it was unhappily one of those films that could be used as evidence in the corporate tensions still disrupting M.G.M.'s production policies and about to erupt in a protracted and bitterly fought battle for control of the Hollywood company.

For Dick Lester, too, the year 1967 produced a sense of dis-appointment, though he had already had advance notice served on him by the hostile reviews generated by *A Funny Thing happened on the Way to the Forum*. 'That's the first time, I think,

[1] *Variety*, 11 October, 1967.

when critics really began to attack what they called my style, my technique,' he said later.[1] For the first time, audiences didn't react to his manipulation of them as he had intended. *How I won the War* (19 October, 1967) was meant to correct this. It was conceived as a 'self-alienating' war comedy which would turn audiences off the heroics and jingoism associated with 'the two-a-year Mirisch films that just grind it out and make it cheap entertainment.'[2] Made for United Artists (to whom the Mirisch film-making brothers were major suppliers), Lester's film set out to make the audience ashamed of having fun at the expense of men dying. Their happy identification with a cast of well-loved Goons would, he hoped, be frustrated by the way he aimed to reduce his platoon members to two-dimensional figures, so that 'whenever any person was killed or attacked, he would turn and talk to the audience and remind (them) that they were only watching a film.' One can only say in answer to this pious aim, 'Alas for those who try to apply Brecht to the cinema.'

As a parody of war films, the movie succeeded very well, gagging and jesting about their clichés and stereotypes. It ran absolutely no risk of engaging its audiences' jingoist emotions so long as its shower of surrealistic misfits were the exemplars of military zeal. At the same time I doubt if it turned a single person who saw it into a pacifist. It is all right to take on the Mirisches, but one should not attempt Von Clauswitz in the same day's march. The surrealistic squibs exploded on the dot: the generals swapping bubble-gum cards of famous victories (in British terms this meant famous defeats); the wife materializing beside her husband, whose legs have been shot away, with the advice, 'Run them under the cold tap, dear.' But it was impossible to feel any moral responsibility for these farcical tragedies: they belonged in an absurd film, not a film about war's criminal absurdity. For all his sincerity, Lester's whimsicality betrayed him. His comment that all men are indistinguishable cannon-fodder, made with the artful combination on the screen of his 'awkward squad' men and tinted soldiers from real war-time newsreels, was not as trenchant

[1] *Movie*, No. 16. Lester interviewed by Ian Cameron and Mark Shivas, p. 19.
[2] Ibid., p. 23.

as the gag itself; and the belief that war is an immoral business had already gained such general acceptance that to seek to shock by showing the bloody uselessness of it all was like preaching to the converted. Lester also discovered that the public did not like clowns to turn preachers. 'The word of mouth killed us,' he said afterwards. 'At the London Pavilion, it did enormous business the first week . . . and that was it, finished . . . On Memorial Day (Armistice Day in Britain) the Rank circuit refused to show the film on its first Sunday in release, but *The Dirty Dozen* was playing on the A.B.C. circuit . . . Everybody went and saw *The Dirty Dozen* and thought it a fitting tribute to the people who died.'[1]

Bryan Forbes was now working for United Artists, after directing two films for Columbia: one, *King Rat* (1965), he had done in Columbia's West Coast studios, largely in response to Mike Frankovich's desire to keep the studios operative, though its English-in-captivity theme might have been done as easily, and for less cost, at home; the other film, *The Wrong Box* (1966), had employed a long list of comedy stars, in which the professional actors like Caine, Richardson and Sellers exposed the glibness of the telly satirists like Peter Cook and Dudley Moore. But given the inventiveness of the original R. L. Stevenson–Lloyd Osbourne story, the last thing the film needed was the heaped-on inventiveness of professional zanies and the decorative paraphernalia which recalled 'Swinging Britain's' camp flirtation with Victoriana and the era of imperial junk.

Forbes found compensation in directing what is possibly his best film, *The Whisperers* (24 August, 1967). It is rooted from start to finish, like a suspension bridge, in the performance of Edith Evans, as a near-derelict old woman, the subject of the self-declared 'study of solitude,' whose assumed gentility in her fanciful impostures on the Welfare State embodies the necessity of dreams to keep the soul intact even while the body is being state-fed and maintained. The plight of the old, the handicapped, the distressed, above all the stoic, revealed more of Forbes than any earlier film; and with Edith Evans he entered into so tight a partnership that it was impossible to say where one left off and

1 Ibid., p. 24.

the other began. With her 'dot-and-carry-one' hobble; ears like radar dishes picking up imaginary whisperings in her cluttered room; a nose like a bayonet to challenge strangers, Dame Edith created a woman who was poor but not pitiable, filling her day with enough self-busying eccentricities to make the Queen of England footsore, inviting chuckles of sympathy but fending off premature pathos by giving the old woman a wintry haughtiness from the fantasies lingering on after her days 'in service' to the aristocracy.

Possibly there was something deeply conservative in the film's thesis – that the world's wickedness is not as fatal as the world's charity – which appealed to Forbes's own political Conservatism. The reproach could be made – and was – that the film underwrote individual endeavour at the expense of state-subsidized welfare. Yet it is the director's skill and his sympathy which convert the raw material of a party manifesto into a humanist approach to the plight of one individual, rendered with such fairness that it fits flush into life and not just the cinema screen. United Artists production chief, David Picker, intimated the company's pride in having made the film, but also his belief that it might not have an easy life commercially. Forbes observed that had Edith Evans given such a performance in a London theatre, the house would have been kept filled by the reviews for six months. As it turned out, the film opened long before the day had arrived for 'twinning' or 'tripling' the large cinemas in London and elsewhere, and when it went out on circuit release, it predictably died – not even recovering the cost of its prints and advertising.

United Artists was certainly not feeling the pinch, although, in common with other American majors at this time, it was spending more money on making more films than was prudent. Success had made the company 'fat.' And the influx of new cash supplies from the conglomerate, Transamerica Corp., which would take over United Artists in 1968 (as Gulf and Western was to with Paramount and Kinney National with Warners), would be a temptation to indulge in even bigger spending. The company was to post a loss for 1970 of $45 million, only the second in its history as a public corporation but almost unbelievably large considering its phenomenal run of sucesses.[1]

But great expectations, and considerable finance, were invested in what was hoped would be the company's 'block-buster' for 1968 from the man who had given them *Tom Jones*. Tony Richardson's *The Charge of the Light Brigade* (10 April, 1968) was backed by $6,500,000 of United Artists money.

It was a film that artistically lived up to everything except the title. Unfortunately for everyone concerned, that was what people wanted to see it for. Richardson had arranged to shoot the Charge first, so as to be at his freshest. It was felt to be the film's *raison d'être*: but it wasn't. Right up to the moment of the Charge, the film was a savagely illuminating period reconstruction with an excoriating running commentary on the class system and military castes which combined to produce one of Victorian England's greatest blunders. But those who expected the film's social criticism – and this meant the popular audiences – to be climaxed by a memorable spectacle in the Valley of Death had to go away disappointed by an anti-climactic cavalry charge over almost before it was begun. The 'epic' consisted entirely of 'reasons why': the Charge was only the tailpiece. This was the 'blunder' that cost the film dear at the box-office. There were other flaws, but they were mere hairline cracks in Richardson's imposing social panorama, filling every half-minute with a telling hit at the 'two nations' of rich and poor reproduced in scenes from military life: the raw and naked recruits swabbed down under the barracks pump; the officers' mess which serves champagne only; the awful humility of the lower classes and the military fervour spilling over together in the nation's war fever. Richardson forced one to look through his eyes and see the Crimean expedition as slowly dawning nightmare, dust washing the colour out of the screen as cholera washed the health out of the army.

Far better than he had done for Dick Lester in *How I won the War*, Charles Wood in his script (which might have been called

---

[1] United Artists, a listed corporation from 1950, had posted its first loss in 1963: it was $800,000. Two years later, largely owing to receipts from its British films, its profits were $12,800,000.

How I lost the War) captured the murderous insanity of running a military campaign on Alice-in-Wonderland logic. The casting proved Richardson unrivalled at matching a performer to a role. All that was lacking to complete the film was the audience in the 'epic' numbers budgeted for.

Joseph Losey was one of the few directors in the old wave not working for the American companies in 1966. He made *Accident* (19 February, 1967) for an independent group of financiers called London Independent Producers. Its chief was ironically the same Sydney Box who had tried to acquire British Lion three years earlier. Among its members was at least one Greek shipowner. The budget was around $1 million and the N.F.F.C. contributed its share. From such familiar 'improvization' emerged one of Losey's finest films. It is not just the presence of Harold Pinter as screenwriter, which recalls *The Servant*: for the closed world of a Chelsea house, Losey and Pinter substituted the cloistered one of Oxford dons; and as Bogarde had been the revelation of the earlier film and was predictably flawless as he writhes in guilt inside the skin of an average sensual don in *Accident*, Stanley Baker was the revelation this time. Losey drew out of him, and at the same time refined, his aggressiveness, turning it into the prickly ambiguities of a man whose nature it is to hurt others, manifesting in jokey but jealous ways a myriad mean flicks of animosity.

Accident is about treachery: the way people's acts betray their moral assumptions. It is about the destructive emotional jealousies of so-called civilized men in love with the same woman – and the fact that their society is privileged and outwardly placid adds to the indecencies of their moral, sexual and social misconduct. 'It is really about responsibility to other people,' Losey said later, 'to what degree you indulge yourself at their expense and to what degree you deny yourself and to what degree you can make your accommodation with them without finding you can't live with yourself.'[1] The Losey–Pinter axis had never worked in such perfect complicity: one has only to recall the long sequence in which the usual lazy English Sunday lunch-party in the country

[1] Joseph Losey interviewed by the author, Thames Television, 22 October, 1969.

turns into a hundred horrid little acts of murder round the table, or the way that the indolent postures of people on a daisy-covered lawn suggest that each one is a radar station of suspicious watchfulness. The film confirmed an interdependence of ends and means between its makers in even more refined form than *The Servant*. One hardly needs to add that, as far as its commercial chances went, it got nowhere. No one associated with it made money out of it; the group financing it no longer exists; the monolithic solidarity of the cinema circuits defeated it. In fact it has all the embattled appearance of a 'hold-out' film in its acceptance of the hard life and hazards of independence at a time when American money was sustaining the industry. As most of the directors who came to the fore in the 1960s moved into the orbit of the American majors, there was a feeling of disintegration setting in where hitherto the artistic momentum had carried them forward. Bidding for talent in the 1968 period was increasing to wild proportions as competition between the various companies pushed up the budgets and the proffered profit percentages. 'You weren't alone any more,' David Picker said. 'Now it was a question of aggravated bidding. The Hollywood syndrome was starting to take place – not what is the movie I'm going to make, but what is *the deal*. And from just being "aggravated," it soon became hysterical.'[1]

Fortunately there was that other 'wave' of new talents on the way in . . .

PROPAGANDISTS: GOLD, LOACH, GARNETT

Television was not so rigidly structured as the film industry, nor (then) so union bound: young men with talents could get into it and work there without the heartbreaking wait for a union card and the time-serving erosion while waiting for promotion in the film studios. Television's vast output was liberating: where programmes were short, quick and cheap, failure was pardonable

[1] David Picker interviewed by the author, 17 July, 1971. Unless otherwise stated, all subsequent quotations from Picker come from the same source.

– as Schlesinger had found. (Later, however, the sheer logistics of feature-film-making daunted some of the neophytes, who thankfully faded back into the relative simplicity of television: but they were few.) Another bonus was the vast 'training-school' of television, a kind of 'National Film School' more expansive than any film studio could maintain. Its students were kept in touch with life as it was being lived hourly: they took their cameras where the action was, seized its essence quickly, and transmitted it with the minimum delay. There were also the sheltered areas: the so-called 'arts features' where tele-journalism gave place to the tele-essayist and more private, personal, 'engaged' attitudes were fostered.

But on the news and current affairs side of the medium a social outlook was nurtured in a totally contrary way to the escapist outlook fundamental to the commercial cinema. The BBC had a built-in public conscience: its charter. The ITV companies had a Parliamentary obligation imposed on them to show a minimum of social seriousness: for example, the 'Tuesday Documentary' programme was mandatory showing for all the ITV networks in Britain, unless they had some very good reason for opting out. Young men who were committed socially or politically and who would once have naturally turned to journalism, now were drawn to television. Again, there was a sudden flowering of television dramatists in the 1960s, the equivalent on the box of the stage playwrights of the 1950s; and directors and writers found social and political reinforcement from working closely and often continuously with each other in a way impossible in the movie industry.

Jack Gold learned 'to do things in six months which the film unions would have kept me from doing for six years.'[1] In the six years he was with BBC TV he made between 300 and 400 short pieces for the news-interpretation programme *Tonight*, plus 30 documentaries and fictional pieces. He had taken a degree in law and economics at London University, which probably

---

[1] Jack Gold interviewed by the author, 11 September, 1971. Unless otherwise stated, all subsequent quotations from Gold come from the same source.

contributed to his Marxist outlook, and *Tonight* reinforced this by bringing him into direct, painful contact with people in every class and job who were often under stress, or involved in sudden tragedies, or simply victims of their own limited attempts to adjust to life. Not surprisingly, Gold prefers conflicts to be inside the characters of his documentaries or fiction films, rather than incorporated in the action. His attitude to violence, as he showed in *The Bofors Gun*, which has already been referred to, is ambivalent – and he is aware of it. On the one hand he condemns and detests it, on the other he admits one can be fascinated by it; and this he attributes to 'the Jewish thing of wondering how one can measure up to the challenge.' To work through character, especially if it has a redeeming humanity, is safer than to be tempted into portraying violent action for its own sake. His social attitudes were also shaped by his technical means. The more mobile Arriflex cameras with transistorized sound-synchronization came into use in BBC TV just when he was aching to achieve even closer contact with his subjects. 'Up to then one had to ask people to repeat things for the cameras: now they could "behave" more normally because they were less aware of me and asked to do less.' This attitude gave Gold's early television films a self-effacement very different from the attention-grabbing style of cinema directors who had borrowed techniques from television commercials. In 1958 he shot a short film for the British Film Institute Experimental Film Board called *The Visit*, a study of an ageing single woman visited by her nephew and niece. 'Most films have peaks, climaxes,' he says about it; 'this one was all valley. I put my faith in the revealing human gestures, not in the drama – for there wasn't any.' His television subjects reveal the same sympathies, though now with an occasional excursion into peak-land. There was a documentary on a labour strike using *ciné-verité* techniques, with the agreement of the strike-locked management and union, to record the immediate, unpredictable way things happened; a workers' outing to the sea which he caught in all its uninhibited zest with hand-held cameras (he claims this was the first time they were used on BBC TV); a study of the horrifying confinement of flesh and spirit under the detention laws in South

Africa; a film on the famine in Bihar, which he characteristically hesitated to make because it would have meant living in a good hotel and eating well while all around people starved; an indictment of fox-hunting in Britain, and a study of a black campus in the United States, both of which enlisted his sympathies against authority and on the side of the oppressed whether on four legs or two.

Gold has what he calls 'this Puritan thing' about swerving aside from painful social realities, which is why he so long resisted the blandishments of the fantasy-oriented film world. But he was brought to television drama by the desire to control his material even further and found kindred material in a play called *The Lump* (1 November, 1967), written by an angry and impassioned Marxist, Jim Allen, which centred around an arrogant revolutionist on a building-site, and was 'one of the earliest television plays to show that political motivations can be as important as sexual or financial ones in influencing people's actions.'

It was a dry run for his first feature film a year later in 1968; *The Bofors Gun* contained a similar bloody-minded revolutionist whose anger turns against the class 'quisling' in a group of conscripts ordered to guard an eminently futile piece of artillery in a peace-time Army camp. Its link with Gold's earlier work is clear. 'It aimed to show what happens in an extreme situation; it might have been a labour strike, or a civil riot, it just happened to be a barracks-room dispute in which a "type" is forced to behave like an individual. To get out, not to "get on" – this is what made it a film of protest. The man who betrays the rest must perish, even if the weapon that destroys him is the sacrifice of another man's life.' After the critical success and commercial failure of the film, Gold returned to the cinema to direct *The Reckoning* for Columbia in 1969. Scripted again by John McGrath, with Williamson again the star, Gold describes it as 'rather a cynical piece about a hero of our time.' It ricocheted between the London world of ruthless big business and the Liverpool slums where the hero, an Irish Catholic who has made good as an industry trouble-shooter, is called back to his roots to avenge the death of his father in a pub brawl – *Room at the Top* put violently into reverse. The tribal battles of the boardroom differ only in sophistication from the tribal obligations of the slum boy. It was a portrait of British society from both sides of the class barrier – or *should* have been. But the nervousness now evident among American majors in Britain about the reception awaiting their movies back home in the States resulted in a coarsened approach to the subject that drove points home with sledge-hammer force; the big-business scenes in particular resonated with the ringing of a referee's bell for 'seconds out,' and only in the Liverpool scenes, the packed pubs, the sweating wrestling halls (all created in the studio, but faultlessly life-like) did Gold extract any depth of feeling. But it was the film's split-mindedness that persisted. It failed to reach either kind of audience, and Gold returned to television.

It's important to stress that such a return in no way connotes a failure for him, or for most of these directors like him; for it is his commitment to the audience in the widest social sense which is best fulfilled by the little screen: it reaches a population of stupendous numbers. The wear and tear involved in always having to fight the cinema industry in order to reach 'the people' with a committed work can breed in film directors a debilitating cynicism and weary resignation to compromise. On the other hand, the relative ease and immediacy of access to the television-viewing audience continually revive creativeness, and invigorate political convictions.

The 'Free Cinema' directors, with whom this study began, had involved themselves sympathetically with the working-class milieux; they showed compassion and understanding and looked as unpatronizingly as they could at this under-explored section of society. What they did *not* commit themselves to do was – to change it. They operated from a middle-class attitude, not a revolutionary one; they accepted that the work was there and had to be done – and done by the workers. It was from television towards the end of the 1960s that the much more critical attack on ingrained class assumptions was mounted. Where Jack Gold prised the gap open, the producer–director team of Tony Garnett and Ken Loach really breached it. 'Roundheads,' someone aptly described them, 'using the Cavaliers' entertainments for their own propaganda weapons.' Garnett, a psychology graduate, a passionate Marxist, an actor who had tried the theatre and television, and finally became a producer, joined the BBC TV team who were launching a new series called the *Wednesday Play* in 1965 – and there he linked up with Ken Loach. Both men believed the series was slanted towards the problems of the middle-classes, whereas as good Marxists they were bound to reserve *their* compassion for the mass of the people, not the favoured individuals. Behind the outwardly quiet and clerkly disposition of Loach bristles fierce indignation manifested, for instance, over a film like *The Angry Silence* having the temerity to attack the only thing the workers have to offer besides their labour for the capitalist system – which is their solidarity. 'Maybe if you had made twenty films about the workers you could afford the luxury of making one about a casualty of their political solidarity,' says Loach. 'If you are going to make only one film, you must select your viewpoint to sustain the aspirations of the mass, not the selfish conscience of the individual.[1] A tough-minded tone like this had not been heard on the cinema screen, nor on the television one, much before the mid-1960s, when everything tended towards the 'balanced' approach. Typical of this was what had happened when Garnett and Loach did a programme on a labour dispute at a glass-works and ran into trouble when they ended it with a shot of one of the workers speaking a passage from Marx. The BBC executives insisted on a typical compromise: the worker could be heard, but must not be seen. Loach and Garnett devised a typical strategem. They filmed the scene both ways, then simply switched reels an hour before transmission. 'No one complained, no one probably even noticed,' said Loach, 'but the insistence on the disembodied voice of the proletariat was a characteristic class weapon of the Establishment.'

Television, both men believed, had a great natural advantage for propagandists seeking to reach the people: by and large, the

---

[1] Ken Loach interviewed by the author, 21 October, 1971. Unless otherwise stated, all subsequent quotations from Loach come from the same source.

working class watches television, goes to the cinema less and less, and almost never goes to the theatre in any numbers. 'Therefore television is where we have to be,' Garnett says, 'if we want to address ourselves to that class which is politically interesting to us.'[1] 'Interesting' in the sense that it is the only one, they claim, which could make a revolution in England. So, in spite of the visual impoverishment both felt inherent in the television image, they believed a *Wednesday Play* was a chance to proselytize and they consciously set out to redefine the content of the material which was customarily slotted into either 'drama' or 'documentary feature.' They ended by forging a dazzling weapon of persuasion by simply effacing the traditional separation between these categories so that it was difficult to be sure which it was that one was viewing. They manufactured a dramatic structure so skilfully that it appeared to generate the beat of real life better than any obviously fictional reconstruction. 'He (Loach) claims to catch contemporary life on the very wing, as it were,' wrote the television critic, T. C. Worsley, 'so that you can hardly tell what is observation and what is fiction.'[2] For a start, in their early documentaries they made the conventional commentator redundant and replaced him with the voices of 'the people,' often recorded on tape with no camera present and then mixed into the image according to the concept, be it artistic or political. This device produced a new feeling of 'reality' as well as shielding Loach and Garnett from the charge of editorializing. 'Our concept of reality is subjective, anyhow,' says Loach, 'and any reporting of actual events tends to dispense different values and interpretations.' The way he and Garnett worked simply gave this truism a structural shape and when they extended it into fiction, and not simply investigative journalism, they created the political tool they wanted. Ideally, they wanted their programmes to be indistinguishable from the items on the television news which preceded them: hence the importance they attached to the right time-slot. Their programmes would then resemble actuality

---

[1] Paul Bream, 'Spreading Wings at Kestrel' *Films and Filming*, March 1972, p. 38.
[2] T. C. Worsley, *Television, The Ephemeral Art*, (Alan Ross, 1970), p. 64.

material, now used for propaganda and not balanced reporting. In a phrase they were fond of using, they wanted to 'stretch reality' – not remove it, as they felt the conventional television plays were doing. (The fiercest opposition to them came from colleagues in the BBC's drama department who resented these documentary trespassers on their territory who were blurring the line between fact and fiction: Loach said in defence that all the conversation he ever heard inside the BBC was about aesthetics, not politics!)

Their technique really registered with a *Wednesday Play* called *Up the Junction* (3 November, 1965) an acutely observed story of three girls in the working-class neighbourhood of Clapham Junction in which the writer, Nell Dunn, pleaded that an inimical environment was to blame for their stunted life-chances. The same accusation was contained in *Cathy Come Home* (16 November, 1966), a documentary-style fiction seen by six million viewers which created the most clamorous 'morning after' furore in British television history. 'Its pinpointing of an ugly social problem,' wrote T. C. Worsley about its examination of the plight of the homeless in South London, 'set tongues wagging and protesters protesting and councillors scurrying . . . It was in fact the combination of the message with the particularly pungent technique adopted which combined to make the impact; and the producer and director, Tony Garnett and Ken Loach, if they didn't become household names, did begin to impinge on the public consciousness.'[1]

Just this kind of instantaneous reverberation is what makes Loach and Garnett value the television medium: it is not an experience that the contemporary cinema, however successful, can often bestow on its creators. As Garnett says, 'The fact that so many people are watching (television) at the same moment and might go to work the next morning having experienced the same thing – the quality of that is something you'd never get in the cinema, however many prints you'd be making in however many cinemas.'[2] But though the response was exhilarating, did it have

[1] Ibid., p. 63.
[2] Paul Bream, *op. cit.*, p. 38.

any practical effect on social conditions? Did it change them? Ideally, Loach and Garnett wanted *Cathy Come Home*, which was written by Nell Dunn's husband, Jeremy Sandford, to lead to the nationalizing of the building industry and home ownership; in fact the passionate national indignation it created remained diffuse and unchannelled into action. The implication that only direct action could change the outlook for the masses was missed by the majority of viewers, who offered genuine sympathy to the homeless girl but, to the producers' mortification, refused to draw a general political lesson out of the play. People reacted to what they believed to be a genuine hard-luck story, not a generalized social condition: the old pull of fiction refused to be broken; and the persistence of bourgeois tradition tempered the practitioners' satisfaction with their propaganda technique.

It was Anglo-Amalgamated who gave Loach, as they had given Schlesinger, his first chance to work in the film industry. For them he made *Poor Cow* (7 December, 1967), which Joseph Janni produced as part of his vow to make amends for the *hubris* of making 'a big important picture' like *Far from the Madding Crowd*. *Poor Cow* certainly wasn't in that class! Based on a Nell Dunn novel, it was about a South London mother who sets up temporary home with a young criminal while her husband is in jail. Her lover himself ends up there for robbery with violence. Nat Cohen had his doubts about the film: he felt there was not much humour in such people. 'Trust me' Janni told him, 'back the director, not the subject.' Cohen did, for £210,000, including some N.F.F.C. money; and on the strength of a cutting-copy screening, *Poor Cow* was later sold to American distributors for more than its negative-cost. It did spectacularly well in Italy, and in Britain was judged 'the outstanding success of the year' by the N.F.F.C. in its 1968 report – at least by the amount of money it returned to the N.F.F.C.'s coffers. Loach's own view of it was, in retrospect anyhow, a cooler one. 'There wasn't enough self-criticism as I went along: I didn't organize it rigorously enough.' Perhaps not, but its social realism was mixed with enough raw language, that caught the authentic tone of the street corner, and randy attitudes to sex to insure it the profitable shock of recognition where the popular audience was concerned. Carol White, who played the girl, grafted her own warmth on to a determinedly downbeat picture of someone who was feckless, disloyal, mendacious and downright shrewish. In keeping with Loach's political bias, she wasn't blamed for what she was: it was her inability (some said 'unwillingness') to escape from a society she had had no part in creating which had doomed her. The cinema revealed the sentimental fallacy in this much more heartlessly than the television screen, where the audience took Loach's programmes (and politics) on trust. The cinema audience, lacking the lulling effects of the contiguous realities of the world news, insisted on identifying emotionally with the sentimental clichés of *Poor Cow*, in spite of Loach's insistence on importing into the film the brief, disjunctive episodes, subjective monologues, Brechtian titles and *ciné-verité* discussions between the heroine and an unseen interviewer. The frenzied technique itself betrayed the director's doubts. As Penelope Houston noted, 'in spite of style, its content is *Room at the Top* realism.'[1] (One 'New Wave's discovery' quickly becomes the next 'New Wave's' driftwood!)

The next film Loach made, and his first in partnership with Garnett, showed a great advance. At least *Kes* resolved the conflict between aesthetics and propaganda revealed in *Poor Cow*. *Kes* had originally been backed, early in 1968, by National General Corporation, one of the new American conglomerates anxious to buy into the British film boom. The budget stood at £187,500 when another £10,400 was prudently added on to it by a completion guarantor company, one of whose functions is to vet film budgets before insuring productions and guaranteeing their completion either by the makers or, if they go over budget, by the guarantors putting their own crew in – in effect, a form of disaster insurance. At the new price, National General withdrew, and ironically the film went to one of the founder-members of the film boom, United Artists, owing to a nick-of-time intervention by Tony Richardson's Woodfall Films, who talked Ornstein's successor at United Artists, David Chasman, into backing the film if it could be shot in eight weeks on a £157,000 budget. It was.

[1] *The Spectator*, 15 December, 1967.

'At that price, it obviously wasn't a major risk,' said David Picker later. True: but it had features that might have appeared scarcely saleable. *Kes* attacked the function of the modern educational system which it saw as simply reflecting the ruling class's need to produce docile workers who would accept the battery-hen discipline of the factory floor once they had been moulded into obedience by the assembly-line techniques of the classroom. 'The present educational system,' Garnett said, 'is concerned with exchange values, not use values – with commodity production.'[1] Even the title *Kes*, which came from a book called *A Kestrel for a Knave*, signified the makers' preoccupation with class, as it referred to the feudal ranking of hunting-birds. A kestrel was the only one that the knaves, the lowest social order, were permitted to possess. Loach and Garnett characteristically called their production company Kestrel. But in making *Kes* they managed to transfer their Marxist ideology – for whose driving force Garnett is probably the responsible partner – to the screen in a totally non-didactic way. Gone was the glum self-consciousness of *Poor Cow*, replaced by a relaxed humanity. The nervous style of the earlier film now had the confidence of the story's direct simplicity. The quality of compassion wasn't forced into the story against the social grain, but sprang naturally from the dilemma of a small boy, a sturdy weed despite the poor soil he is doomed to grow in, who springs up after everyone's uncaring feet have passed over him. School has modern window-walls enclosing teachers with blankly unimaginative minds; the headmaster is an automatic martinet; the careers officer defines the dead-endedness of society by slotting people into jobs for life – the coal mines, perhaps? – at a time when life for most of them has just begun. The film had the grace to leave it an open question whether the flicker of fulfilment that the boy briefly finds in training a kestrel will feed on its own energy, or be snuffed out in a life imposed on him by others. Like that of Bresson and Milos Forman, directors he admires, Loach's austere approach is offset by his warmth of principle.

By a fluke the film became a box-office success in England,

[1] Paul Bream, *op. cit.*, p. 40.

after hanging fire for months while the circuits dickered with it and Rank confessed itself not exactly ecstatic with its chances. By 1969 the first thaw in the hitherto virtually locked-in relationships between film companies and cinema chains was apparent and permitted United Artists (a company 'tied' to Rank) to try A.B.C. Tentatively released in the north-country towns familiar with the strong local accents of the kids in *Kes,* and then discreetly post-synchronised in places to clarify the vowels for southern audiences, the film gradually asserted itself through judiciously chosen television clips and word-of-mouth publicity, till it took off nationally and, considering its cost, turned a satisfactory profit in Britain alone. 'In America,' David Picker confessed sadly, 'you couldn't buy it an audience.' It was another film for United Artists to write down to good-will and the encouragement of talent. But its carefully nursed release pattern did show up well against the rigid system operating in Britain up to then: it proved in a small but noteworthy way that the structure must accommodate itself to the films, not the other way round, if originality and independence were to survive and thrive.[1]

Garnett's next production was *The Body* (5 November, 1970) with Roy Battersby directing, and remarkable micro-photography by Tony Imi of the body's internal organs. Virtually a life cycle of the human condition, the film managed to give it a Socialist emphasis, in keeping with Kestrel's outlook, by illustrating how society wears people out. Life was a long assembly line along which the camera passed like a dispassionate factory inspector showing the obsolescence taking place in the human product. The aim was to teach people a better understanding of their bodes and of the society they live in 'so that they will be better able to change it.' The affluent intake of a lifetime's consumption in the West was contrasted with the meagre stockpile of food for an Asian; but this black mark on the capitalist score-card was not nearly so effective a means of propaganda as the funny, often perceptive, comments on their own condition contributed by the film's patient band of human guinea-pigs in the regional 'British'

[1] See John Russell Taylor, 'The Kes Dossier', *Sight and Sound* (Summer 1970), Vol. 39. No. 3. pp. 130-1, for a full account of this affair.

accents of Welsh, north country, cockney, even Carribean. The un-solemn and vernacular accents of democracy were now the Kestrel trademark.

The most successful film Loach and Garnett have made to date is *Family Life* (13 January, 1972). It has all their aesthetic strength, if also a few of their ideological blindspots. It was the only subject they were able to have two goes at, since they had done the original television play, *In Two Minds* (1 March, 1967), written by David Mercer, the author of *Morgan*. It was based on R. D. Laing's theory of mental illness which had inspired *Morgan*, namely that the patient's 'illness' is often in itself a criticism of the 'normal' conditions he or she is forced to adapt to in the name of 'sanity.' The television play drew its lifelike feeling from its documentary construction as a series of interviews, in which visuals and voices did not necessarily coincide; but the whole effect was a lifelike indictment of the conventional hospital treatment of 'insanity.' Mercer's film-script took this conclusion as its starting point, dispensed with the interview structure, and put the emphasis on the plight of a girl whose family shows itself little by little to be the disturbed element in her life. Mental illness was viewed as a family-induced ailment. If society is to be changed – as the film urged it must be – then the family unit, the preparation for conformist and passive serfs in the wider world of school and work, must be abolished.

The film confirmed Loach and Garnett as the most skilful film-makers working with non-professionals in Britain. They used a group of Liverpool people whom they got to know well during filming – 'like a family,' they said with unconscious irony. Loach again used *Kes*'s deceptively simple approach. With the same television cameraman who had made some of his documentary programmes, notably the glass-makers' strike, he used to shoot as much as three hours of material a day. Film-stock ran to a major item on the £180,000 budget. The approach was quite plain and unadorned. Since he was intent on improvising, he could not do elaborate shots. He needed simple set-ups so that people could feel free to behave as they wanted to, which meant that the camera must be free to follow the intuitive human response and capable of being altered quickly, so that the players could preserve the momentum of the experiences they were living through. The situations were kept open-ended: which is to say that the structure of the film was settled in advance with Mercer, but the details of a scene were intentionally left to the players to devise. 'Give people their heads,' Loach says. 'A film is a dialectic between the script and the characters in the picture. What is true of the people in the script must be true of the people in the film.' Out of the huge amount of exposed film – one day Loach shot so much that the Arriflex burned out – he edited the moments he wanted so that *Family Life*, better than any earlier film of his or Garnett's, gives the most uncanny impression of capturing life as it is happening to people.

'Editing' he once defined as 'a tension between the script's stated intention and the possibilities and people involved in putting it on film.' It is this tension that *Family Life* holds structually, like the tensile strength of the 'skin' on a drop of water.

The film's major fault lay in its habit of pushing its thesis to extremes, suggesting that a particular case like the one it featured, with Sandy Ratcliff as the girl winning a lot of compassion in spite of being treated throughout as not much more than a mute object, was true of what happened to the patient in societies not sympathetic to Laingian techniques. Such societies, they implied, were prone to the insensitive, mechanistic, conveyor-belt treatment of mental illness administered by a state machine riddled by status conflicts and containing a potential for the Fascist-like compulsion of defenceless people, in contrast to the humanitarian, democratically-run 'commune' of the film's Laingian doctor. Like all proficient polemicists, Loach and Garnett simplified situations to suit their arguments. The brutalism of electro-shock treatment in the traditional hospital; the soulless arrangement of rows of beds like a conveyor-belt set-up; the Gestapo-like dispositions of medical attendants who come to cart the girl back to the wards at the end . . . It is a pity that people otherwise so humane and sophisticated still feel the need to allow an audience no choice but to see things their way. The polemical distortion looks what it is in contrast with the far more disturbing success in showing the actual dynamics of a family that is 'sick' and doesn't know it – in a scene like the one at high tea, where the neuroses are handed round the table like the plates of fresh-cut bread and butter, from parents to children.

But as Loach and Garnett enter the 1970s they look to be among the cinema's best hopes of sustaining the traditional humane involvement of the Left with a changing society. The irony is that their involvement continues to be with only a section of society, and not the one they are bound to by political sympathies. Very much the reverse. They prick the conscience of the middle classes, the 'responsible centre' whom in general they mistrust and despise, while still failing to elicit practical responses from the working class whom they seek to reach and politicize. Their success has been achieved as humanists, not propagandists.

FANTASISTS: BOORMAN, RUSSELL

John Boorman is a much more private film-maker and Ken Russell a much more public one than Gold, Loach or Garnett. Neither involves himself in social reality so much as in personal fantasy: inside his head is where each of them makes his film; and they work inside 'the system,' not actively against it. But their resemblances end there: it is impossible to think of either finding himself at home in the other's concepts or conceits.

Boorman is the more interesting of the two, with a surer sense of development and a finer – much finer – sensibility. Though a Protestant, he was educated by Jesuits, and the Catholic idea of the Grail quest, the endlessly receding vision, has inspired several of his films. His family originally came from the Netherlands and he is second-generation English, though he belongs by temperament to northern Europe, in particular to Germany and Scandinavia. Jung attracts him, rather than Freud, and Jungian archetypes figure in his films, especially the warrior types like the modern 'samurai' in *Hell in the Pacific* and the hunters in *Deliverance* and *Point Blank*. His interest in astrology is strong and not insignificant in his movie-making; he is a Capricorn and believes it is in his nature to beat his way up towards the top of the mountain, though he may be destined never to arrive there. Altogether, he is an odd, complex man to find in the British film scene. Television was his first school and he might have followed Gold's footsteps into the area where fact meets fiction had he not made a detour out of Independent Television News and ITV documentaries to settle in Bristol and work for the BBC in the west country, on the borderland of that south-west peninsula of Celtic myth and Arthurian legend. One of Boorman's closest associates, the artist and writer Bill Stair, has spoken of Bristol as a 'culture pulse' – 'one of those cultural nuclei where creative people congregate and inspire each other.'[1] Besides Stair and Boorman, Bristol in the early 1960s held Charles Wood, Tom Stoppard and Peter Nichols, all of whom would soon arrive with the second wave of British dramatists. Nichols was even then writing *A Day in the Death of Joe Egg*, in which Stair caught echoes of his own pessimistic feelings about his future as an art teacher. Charles Wood was just starting to stake out military life as his dramatic territory, and meanwhile collaborated with Boorman on an ambitious television series called *The Newcomers*, tracing in documentary fashion the friends, marriages, daily life and eventual births among a group of young married people: the series ended with an Antonioni-esque flourish in which twelve cameras filmed what went on in Bristol in the last half-hour as the birth of twins took place. But even more significant was a programme he made called *The Quarry* about a sculptor with an artistic block who can't force himself to begin work on a slab of marble. 'Quarry' not only stood for the source of the marble, but was a pun on the word's meaning as an object of a quest, like the Grail; while the artist's name, Arthur King, was of course 'King Arthur' in reverse. Boorman felt that the legend of Camelot and King Arthur was a Mithraic theme which the Roman Catholic Church had 'Christianized' into the Grail quest. This interest of his might seem like a side issue, except that it profoundly influenced a most decidedly un-Arthurian subject which was the first one Boorman

[1] Bill Stair interviewed by the author, 17 February, 1973. Unless otherwise stated, all subsequent quotations from Stair come from the same source.

was asked to direct for the cinema, *Catch Us if You Can* (1966. U.S. title: *Having a Wild Weekend*). It was about a pop group called the Dave Clark Five.

Anglo-Amalgamated had observed that the success of the Beatles' first film could stand imitating and Boorman was therefore engaged to turn out what might have been another pop musical in the surrealistic vein of Dick Lester. This is not what happened at all. Boorman has described himself frequently as 'a disappointed romantic,' which any man must be who is obsessed by the Arthurian legend and the dashing of all the grand hopes enshrined in Camelot. A feeling of betrayal sticks to his films, and *Catch Us if You Can* showed the early traces of this, as the story veered away from all the usual teenage sign-posts and took a quirky cross-country journey with a runaway pop idol and accompanying model girl – not exactly Tristan and Iseult, perhaps, but certainly cult figures of *their* time – who fled through a wintry landscape expressive of youthful disenchantment at every turn. The pop songs simply became music *en route*. Eventually they finished up on an island that looked like a drop-outs' oasis – until at low tide it turned out not to be an island at all. So the fantasy fades into the light of common day. It is better to travel imaginatively in search of the Grail than hope to seize it at the end of the journey. Boorman resisted pressures to let the boy and girl walk off together – *he* goes off, *she* is left to face the publicity cameras – since this would betray the disenchantment he felt must impregnate his films' endings, an aim he has followed with remarkable consistency. Not surprisingly, the fans who expected something simpler and more to the pop beat were disappointed, and the film did poor business. But it launched Boorman.

From an expedition to Los Angeles, to gather material for a television film on D. W. Griffith, came a meeting with Lee Marvin, another Catholic-educated kindred spirit, who fell in with Boorman's vision of *Point Blank* (1967) as a 'quest' through the bleak modernity of Los Angeles – San Francisco was rejected as too pretty – where the gangster hero in search of his missing 'cut' of the loot submits to tests of endurance before the ultimate

N

disillusionment. *Deliverance* (1972) was also to emphasise the 'tests,' the endurance, the disappointment, and both films even repeat the vivid metaphor of an age-old burial ground being mechanically flattened by soulless progress. After *Point Blank*, Boorman made *Hell in the Pacific* (1968), reviving the island theme in the story of two American and Japanese combatants washed up on the same atoll, unable to communicate but discovering through trial, torture and error that men can co-exist peacefully until the final irony, when their few shared words drive them apart. It almost realized the ambition Boorman had contracted from his viewing of the old Griffith films: to make a completely silent picture.

If the more dynamic side of Boorman's career belongs to a study of the new American film, his return to Britain in 1968 was marked by a movie that revealed the disenchantment that had begun settling over the scene there. United Artists backed *Leo the Last* on their principle of getting the most interesting talent to work for them. They had to move more quickly than in earlier years, because there were now more companies in London with the same idea. More time might have dictated more prudence. *Leo the Last* was written by Boorman and Stair, though dialogue is possibly neither's forte. Stair's great contribution lies in production design and colour consultancy, and it was his uncredited contribution to *Point Blank* which gave this film its peculiarly arid and waste-land look. He also advised on the colour values of *Leo the Last*, which was set in a black ghetto in London whose only 'island' of affluence was the mansion residence of Marcello Mastroianni's eccentric expatriate prince, the Fisher King of the Grail legend, who lived surrounded by gourmandising subjects and plotting revolutionaries and who, in the film, is condemned by his own atrophied sensibilities to view his black subjects from afar. As far as the aesthetic of the colour was concerned, the film was remarkable: the prevailing black and white was fragmented into a dozen in-between tones in a way a British film seldom attempted much less achieved. But at the centre of the film there was confusion and – worse – sentimentality. It felt like a throwback to Ealing comedy, a *Passport to Pimlico* with colour consciousness. The attempt to ingest the American experience of racial strife and bring it forth again as a benignly well-meaning *Mr Deeds goes to the Ghetto*, where white and black march together against the heartless property speculators, all grated against the painful first-hand experience of the 'year of violence' which preceded the film's appearance. The very artifice of the settings outraged any radicals whose sympathies might have been enlisted. 'The film was worth making,' David Picker said in retrospect, 'but not at the price it cost, which was over £400,000. By the time it came out, the majors were in a terrible financial crisis through overspending. No one had any money to lavish on creating an audience for a picture if there was the slightest doubt it wouldn't find one lining up to see it. A film either made it – or it died. There was nothing in between. And *Leo the Last* didn't make it. We were sorry, all of us, and we certainly want to make more films with John Boorman, but this one in the prevailing circumstances of 1968–9 was a mistake.' It contributed to the far too common feeling – that British films had lost their market.

Boorman fortunately made a swift and brilliant recovery with *Deliverance*, directed in America for Warners. It was demonstrably a commercial success. And in the skill with which it fused allegory and adventure, unbearably harsh violation of the civilised order and echoes of the raw tribalism of earlier primitive society, it showed this director, like Schlesinger, to be enviably free of the shackles of English insularity. He is able to hear echoes of his themes anywhere in the world. He does not need to feel the soil of national tradition securely round his roots – for his art is rooted in the interior landscape of the imagination.

Ken Russell is the rogue talent among the directors who emerged from television in the 1960s. One had better try to enumerate his considerable gifts when they are most in evidence in his early work; later on, they are harder to discern so confidently, as he lets his temperament ride roughshod over his talent. Russell shares with Boorman a very rare quality for an English director – great visual flair. He can hardly help making pictures interesting: the pity is, he so obviously does not know when to leave off, and contrives to make them overwrought, too.

Historical styles, places, and people fall easily and dazzlingly within his visual imagination. He knows how to make a detail of architecture, costume, even movement, suggest a distant country or bygone era, and he is quite simply the British screen's best positioner of figures in a landscape, particularly when he wants to convey some baroque sentiment or event. Unfortunately such qualities of *mise-en-scène* swiftly wear out their welcome when the content is shallow and the concept banal or vulgar. With Russell, the effect is everything: the result, too often, is excess. It was working for the BBC's prestige arts programme, *Monitor*, that apparently got him into the habit of hitting the public over the head – a method he has been known to use physically on at least one critic – to keep their attention or make his point. 'On *Monitor* we had to follow a cinema film,' he once explained, showing interestingly enough how his style, like Loach's, was to some degree influenced by television's time schedules, 'so I just thought I'd rather clout them over the head than lose them. Art to the mass audience isn't a dirty word. It's a bloody boring word.'[1] A protégé of Huw Wheldon, another almost messianic populariser of 'art,' but without his pupil's assault-and-battery approach to the *Monitor* audience, Russell made about thirty BBC documentaries, quite a number of them biographies of musicians, but he is remembered by the ones expressing a bull-headed kind of bohemianism. By overturning the conventional barriers or notions about form, style or taste, he seems to believe that he himself comes nearest to the liberating vision of the artists or composers to whom he is so strongly drawn.

Russell's curiously naïve longing to be the rebel at odds with the system yet indulged by it – to be the free spirit operating inside his own empire – was best expressed when he said to an interviewer, 'What I'd really like to do would be to get my own little film unit together . . . And we could all go down to the New Forest and maybe I'd film a story about a composer, or a Dostoievsky story, and all the unit would bring down their families and I'd put them up in caravans or a hotel, and if it was fine we'd work, but if it rained, well we'd just go off and have a

[1] Interview by Ray Connolly, *Evening Standard*, 25 February, 1971.

party.'[1] The *déjeuner sur l'herbe* aspect of film-making, the Renoiresque aspirations, the commune conviviality are all aspects of a popular and usually unfounded conception of how the Great Artists work. Like some of the artists he interprets in his films, Russell lives in the constant din of his own invective. Just as he has seemingly set himself few limits in the desire and pursuit of the whole experience, he has few inhibitions about the way he presents the nature of artistic creation when it comes to Elgar, Delius, Rossetti, Debussy, Richard Strauss, and Isadora Duncan on television, or Tchaikovsky and Gaudier-Brzeska in the cinema. Believing that the public has a fixed delusion that such artists did not labour and sweat over their compositions – the Hollywood syndrome, in which all comes in a flash of banally inspired inspiration – he has gone to extremes in order to emphasize the opposite. But it is precisely the efforts which artists make to control and shape their inspiration which Russell's films omit in favour of the far more graphic illustrations of mental and moral turmoil experienced in the gestation period. 'All art is hard work,' was the 'revelation' promulgated on the posters for his Gaudier-Brzeska film; when the public appeal of that pronunciamento had been tested and found somewhat lacking in box-office bite, it was revamped by the publicists to 'All art is sex.' Hard work of an exhibitionist kind and sex of a pathological sort are frequently found together inside a Russell film: he is a master of the *Kulturkampf*, the psychodrama of the artistic soul, the porno-biography which is not quite pornography but is far from being biography, which his visual virtuosity and compulsion to shock strive to make over into a different kind of film from the old-fashioned Hollywood 'biopic' of the unruly creative genius.

Russell, in contrast, has been at his best when the quiet tenor of the artist's life, like that of Delius or Elgar, has enjoined on him a muted psychological interpretation. The cultural pretensions of the historical Isadora Duncan and the natural inclination of the 1920s towards 'doing your own thing' were also fed rewardingly into Russell's film about her. Like some Busby Berkeley set-up, its tableau-esque hyperbole was all of a piece with

[1] Ibid.

its subject, and his casting of Vivian Pickles as Isadora was the shrewdest stroke, immensely more effective than Vanessa Redgrave's Isadora in the Karel Reisz film. 'At least my Isadora was Mae West, not a hockey captain,' is one of Russell's most perceptive comments on his own work.

He certainly made a splash in the culturally pure waters of BBC TV's arts features because the 'art film,' as it was then understood, was such a dull, respectable and respectful affair. Russell's corrective emphasis on the personal involvement of the artist, the secret springs that released genius, was refreshing – so was his understanding that people living in the past naturally thought of themselves as part of the present, which swept away the cloistral cobwebs hanging round many an academic tribute to the artist.

His first film is one that sometimes does not figure in those he recalls for interviewers. *French Dressing* (21 May, 1964) was made for Associated British-Pathé who had been attracted to the free-and-easy breeziness of Joan Littlewood's *Sparrows can't Sing* and possibly wished to have another film in that line of proletarian grotesquerie. Both films had the same producer: Kenneth Harper. *French Dressing* was very nearly all top-dressing. It was a series of comic turns in an English sea-front resort where every character was valued for the freakishness of his or her outline, like those on the bawdy comic postcards. It anticipated *The Boy Friend* (1972), another seaside-set comedy of camp attitudes. Scene after scene was highly stylized. The mayor and councillors were deployed like a *corps de ballet*, and some of the sight gags worked well – in particular the brawl at the world première of a sexy film, where a running punch-up ends with combatants getting knocked bodily through the sixty-foot-wide mouth of the star on the screen and her tongue comes out to lick lasciviously along the frieze of fighting figures.

But it was an affair of moments and in its Tati-esque moments it made one aware of Russell's hankering after better models to parody. This was even more obvious in *Billion Dollar Brain* (1967), the third of the Ipcress Man thrillers which he made for Harry Saltzman while waiting for the latter to set up a film biography of Nijinsky. It had more pictorial sense than dramatic tensions, and the ending, with the American fascist leader disappearing through the ice and taking his army with him, was a wild borrowing from *Alexander Nevsky*. (He would have used the Prokofiev music, too, had he been able to obtain permission.) The effect was unpleasantly debasing to the Russian original: which was the main feeling about *The Boy Friend* as well, and characteristic of *The Devils* (1971) in the employment of material better treated in Huxley's novel and John Whiting's play to cater to Russell's own fixation in the film with physical pain and debauchery. The approach of the latter film was not dissimilar from that of the Inquisition: both tried to reach the soul through the mortification of the flesh.

The one exceptional film which Russell can sign with pride is *Women in Love* (13 November, 1969), an immensely complex but perfectly controlled film which displayed his talent for matching landscape with the emotional affinities of the people in it and infusing both with Lawrence's argument for love in the widest, freest sense. Shot at the very earliest moment when permissiveness on the screen made it possible to do Lawrence justice, the film's fidelity to the novel suggests that Russell had at last found a model to overawe his own tempestuousness. He found the perfect visual translation for the passions of Lawrence's characters which the novelist had prudently dissolved into the prose that was permissible in the more restrictive era when the book was published. Russell rendered them solid again in vivid, fleshly encounters in forest and undergrowth which soaked into the quartet of lovers like a pagan aphrodisiac. Better than a chapter of words, his images carried the silent implication of what the institutions of marriage and society could do to lovers – in the shots, for instance, that duplicated the postures of the copulating lovers in the woods with the death-lock of the drowned newly-weds in the drained lake. The philosophical wrangling over love versus friendship found its un-didactic correlation in the male wrestling scene – an audacious advance in the nudity which the censor then permitted in the case of women on the screen, though he still restricted it in the case of males to the rear view. The scene allowed marvellous access into the consciousness of the two totally naked men straining and flexing against each other in the *chiaroscuro* of the firelight. The period re-creation seldom lapsed into the merely pretty or fanciful. The enormously privileged life led by the English county families in the post-Edwardian era gave Russell's predilection for the baroque a firm purchase on social reality. And a perfect cast knew how to trim the sails of Lawrence's overblown romanticism.

The later Russell was to go on to other subjects, all certified in the original as major or minor masterpieces, whether a composer's music, a playwright's version of satanic possession, a parody period musical, or a neglected sculptor of now acknowledged mastery; but his instinct for the look and feel of a film have never been so admirably in touch with the inspiration of a great artist as they were in *Women in Love*. His talent to appal and abuse is what remains, but even that may lose its impact by sheer repetitiveness. It would be a pity if what began as impassioned iconoclasm threatened to end as simply boorish megalomania.

People began to make pictures for trends.   David Picker

George H. Ornstein at the end of 1966 had been made an offer that he had refused – to join Paramount as the new European production chief based in London. He was then with the Saltzman–Broccoli company. But the offer was repeated by Robert Evans, who was in charge of all Paramount's production and based at the West Coast studios, and backed up by Charles Bluhdorn, president of Gulf and Western, the giant conglomerate which had just acquired Paramount as a wholly-owned subsidiary. Ornstein searched his conscience, consulted his then bosses, finally yielded, and took the job. Privately, he knew that Saltzman was negotiating with Paramount to make *The Battle of Britain* and assumed that Bluhdorn wanted someone on the Paramount strength who got on well with such a powerful independent producer as Saltzman. But, as it happened, Saltzman took his film to United Artists . . . So Ornstein in 1967 started once again building up a programme of British films which he hoped would repeat the success of those he initiated and supervised for United Artists. But things were very different this time.

Bluhdorn had acquired a somewhat atrophied company. Paramount was run by a much older set of executives than the relative youngsters who replaced them. They had built up solid property investments, though such things as a film studio were now more of a liability than an asset in film-making. The company needed the dust shaken out of its thinking and Bluhdorn appeared aggressively imaginative, a mogul whose conglomerate zeal was fired by the acquisition of a famous film trademark, and something of a fan, too, who revelled in the glamorous proximity of film stars. Although he had built one of the largest fortunes in America on company amalgamations, he soon found that the daily running of a company, particularly a film company, was a very different operation from the overall high-command of a conglomerate. His very enthusiasm for mingling personally in the dream-making side of the industry exposed him to other people's dreams as well as his own, some of which turned out costly when converted into motion pictures. However, he was an exhilarating influence, and Ornstein approached his job buoyed up by the cash which Gulf and Western was pumping into Paramount, and by his president's impatience to get things rolling. He was assailed by a flood of projects, some of which had already been begun before he moved into his job. One of his first acts was to approve an extra $800,000 in the budget of *Half-a-Sixpence*, a $2,500,000 musical initiated by Paramount's previous production chief in Hollywood, and being shot in England by George Sidney. Based on H. G. Wells's *Kipps*, and starring Tommy Steele, it was meant to be an invigorating return to the engine-roaring musicals with big set-pieces; the early money supplies had certainly been expended to impressive effect on sequences such as the Henley Regatta, springing to life on the actual banks of the Thames populated by a hundred-and-one other fringe activities, as in a painting by Frith. (Sidney is probably the director with the most 'painterly' eye in America.) Steele's performance was charged with a robust professionalism that stood fair and square on its own two cockney feet. It was meant to possess an American energy that would commend it interntaionally and a family appeal that would hopefully repeat the success of *The Sound of Music*. In spite of its virtues, it signally failed to achieve these aims.

Ornstein always considered the fault lay in its length (146 minutes); but it also had the misfortune to look and sound English enough to attract more than faint damns then being meted out to other English-looking, though officially American, musicals which opened around the same time, with calamitous box-office results. One was *Star!* and the other *Doctor Dolittle*, both of which contributed to 20th Century-Fox's economic troubles since they had been made at huge cost, locked up vast sums of money, and apparently defied all the efforts of the publicity departments to sell them. The relative disappointment of *Half-a-Sixpence*, another English subject starring another hyper-English

artiste, contributed to the American majors' doubt about investment in Britain. 'There was no validity for the view that any film
from Britain would be a blockbuster in America,' said Ornstein,
'but until the money began to vanish, no one believed it.'

Ornstein was now having to deal with the American side of
Paramount on a very different basis from that of his United
Artists days. Though it sounds a paradox, the men at the top of
United Artists were not film-makers: they did not directly engage
in film production. They were financiers and lawyers: they simply
put up the money. But the head of Paramount's production was
also head of a studio and it was towards the studio, in planning
terms, anyhow, if not in physical production, that Ornstein had
to orientate his thinking. Robert Evans was an ex-actor who had
played important roles in several films, notably as Irving Thalberg
in the Jimmy Cagney tribute to Lon Chaney Sr, *The Man of a
Thousand Faces*, in 1957, and some believed that the experience of
the early role had carried over into the aspirations of his current
post. Whether they wished it or not, he and Ornstein were in
competition. Ornstein never approved a film without checking
with Bluhdorn in New York, for there was a real danger that
'the others' might be making the same kind of picture out in
Hollywood. But communications with New York were not so
easy or constant as they had been in the days of dealing with
David Picker at United Artists. 'I was unreasonable many times,'
Ornstein commented, 'so was Bob Evans many times. It was not
good for film production.' Moreover, the Irving Thalberg mode
of operations was no longer viable: films were now so expensive
(or could become so in spectacularly swift fashion) that the nitty
gritty of each one had to be argued out well in advance of production and could not be juggled as one went along to make the
winners and losers even out. 'If you get pictures approved that
you don't want to make,' Ornstein said, 'you still want to get
films approved that you do want to make. You end up having
too many pictures and a not very well-balanced programme.'

Trends were harder than ever to avoid over-exploiting and
Ornstein's programme picked up several of them without much
advantage to itself. One was *The Penthouse* (28 September, 1967),

a film that had been independently produced by Michael Klinger and bought by Paramount largely to prime the pumps of its British operation, and because the subject matter seemed fashionable. It was – all too fashionable. Its trouble was that Harold Pinter had been there first with the theme of the menacing outsider who insinuates himself into the bourgeois consciousness of a couple spending a night in an untenanted penthouse; hard on the imprints of Pinter's carpet-slippers came the heavy boots of Joe Orton with the kinky novelty of immobilising the male occupant in fancy ribbons while the intruder rapes his mistress. The second Paramount film by the same director, Peter Collinson, next penetrated the territory of the television drama-documentary which Ken Loach and Tony Garnett had made their own. *Up the Junction* (25 January, 1968), which Loach and Garnett had first done on the box, from Nell Dunn's script, revealed how swiftly social reality turns into social cliché, unless there is insight and sympathy to refresh it, with a story of a deb girl in search of Life who sheds her trouser suit for a miniskirt, gets an unbecoming proletarian hair-do, takes a chocolate-packer's job, and settles into a sleazy room to taste the uncorrupted sweetness of slum life – inevitably finding she has just gone 'slumming' and is using other people's squalid lives to sustain her own class rebellion. It was all too pat in its parade of slumland London.

Nor was Ornstein more fortunate in trying to extend the lifetime of 'Swinging London' in *The Bliss of Mrs Blossom* (19 November, 1968). Its director, Joseph McGrath, came from television – he should not be confused with the script-writer John McGrath – and had already made a Dudley Moore comedy, *Thirty is a Dangerous Age, Cynthia*, produced by Walter Shenson for Columbia, a hangover from the telly-satire shows, in which the antics of a familiar cast of showbiz folk were run through a frenetic series of wipes, pans, jump-cuts and montages. *The Bliss of Mrs Blossom* hit trouble before shooting began, when the actress set to star in it declined to play her role; would not be budged by cajolery or stronger persuasion; and had to be replaced by Shirley MacLaine, whose fee was reputedly $750,000. The film's budget had been set at not many thousands of dollars more. It was a nervous augury and may have accounted for the impression that everyone in the film was working in overdrive on excess adrenalin. It is possibly the most frantically modish film to come out of the late 1960s: one can find in it nearly any reference to the style and content, and even the décor, of earlier movies that had pioneered their effects with wit, élan and novelty. The story of the neglected wife of a brassière tycoon taking on a living-in lover in the shape of an orphaned sewing-machine mechanic in need of mothering was unashamedly Pinterish. The jokey *art nouveau* décor in glorious hippy-colour inside a conventionally 'straight' suburban house expressed the 'knowingness' of film-makers who, as John Russell Taylor put it, 'throw in a bit of everything which is on the scene . . . or seems likely to be . . . [trying] to keep us guessing with a constant dazzle of stylistic reference, half straight, half ironic, full of get-out clauses if anyone asks awkward questions.'[1] The film's fantasy-inserts, paying homage to the screen's great lovers, demonstrated the same nostalgic hankering after the past now tossed away on the transient imagery of the present. Since most television commercials for confectionery, detergents, gasoline, or disinfectants take the form of fantasy, there was no reason why a fantasy comedy about adultery should not take the form of a commercial, except that on the box the experience lasted an average of fifty seconds whereas in *The Bliss of Mrs Blossom* it ran to an endless ninety-three minutes confected with such frenetic sock-it-to-em style that it seemed the director feared to lose a sale by letting his audience relax for a second, and kept moving his star cast around like so many glossy products to be displayed to the best advantage in the shortest time with the fullest impact.

ROMEO AND JULIET

Ornstein sometimes felt that he was presiding over the frenzied disintegration of the very trends he had helped to initiate in the early 1960s. But the cinema's habit of imitating its last success is

[1] John Russell Taylor, 'Larking Back', *Sight and Sound* (Spring 1968), Vol. 37, No. 2, p. 70.

producer's viewpoint, it would also provide the film with a stop date that must be kept! It was. The final budget was $1,300,000.

Where *Romeo and Juliet* is concerned, youth *is* realism. Zeffirelli succeeded in emphasizing both qualities in an exhilarating fashion. His audacious casting of relative beginners provides a couple who are neither too young to be able to make love convincingly, nor too old to make us doubt they are doing it for the first time. It is easy – and just, too – to criticize the verse-speaking on the ground that it doesn't make the most of Shakespeare; but when the verse-speaking is infused with such physical passion, then the poetry of love is a glorious bonus to the experience. The sizeable sacrifice, in commercial terms, of not having stars in the title roles is more than made up for by the natural contemporaneity of the unknown youngsters, he with the solitariness of a boy who maybe sees his parents only at mealtimes, she with a shy, awkward obedience to parental discipline, and both of them discovering how love gives release and purpose to young lives. The duels have the rare quality of making one feel the sharpness of the blades as the dust hangs like a premature funeral pall between the sweating combatants; and though there are omissions and changes galore in the text, they are made good by Zeffirelli's brilliant touches of intuition – like the transformation of the balcony which is only a sprinter's hurdle to Romeo in love, but becomes a Berlin Wall to the lovers when he is banished. Launched with total honesty on the 'youth market,' the film rode it at full tide. *Variety* at the end of 1972 listed it as having grossed $14,500,000 in North America alone – one could probably add between $8–10,000,000 more for the rest of the world.

IFS AND BUTS

The tensions between London and Hollywood were ever present in the Paramount production programme, and they revealed themselves in the production history of Lindsay Anderson's film *If . . .* (19 December, 1968). Ornstein always had a strong regard for Anderson, and while he was still with United Artists had tried to set up a production of *Wuthering Heights* for him to direct, with Richard Harris as Heathcliff. Once at Paramount, he tried contacting the director 'to see if he had any good ideas,' but Anderson was in Poland shooting *The Singing Lesson* at the Warsaw documentary studios, and immersed in his own work. Actually, *If . . .* had been brought to Anderson's notice in September 1966 by the producer Seth Holt, and its origins dated back eight years earlier when two ex-public schoolboys, David Sherwin and John Howlett, had begun work on a story called *Crusaders* when they went up to Oxford, finished a screenplay by 1960, and finally interested Holt in it. Such facts are useful if only to scotch the rumours that *If . . .* grew directly out of the year of the youth revolt in Europe and America, namely 1968. Given the conditions of the English public schools, the revolt could have happened in any year: it was just the film's beautiful luck to coincide with the international unrest. Anderson was instantly stirred by the original title, *Crusaders*, 'with its overtones of idealism, struggle and the world well lost . . . he was always attracted towards the kind of heroism that ends in defeat but is not defeatist.'[1] During most of 1967 the script was developed and refined by Anderson and Sherwin, but when Holt found that another film was going to keep him in Rome, he agreed to Anderson taking the project to Albert Finney's production company, Memorial Enterprises. Memorial approached Jay Kanter, then at Universal, but he decided against financing it. Then Ornstein heard that Finney had set up a deal with C.B.S., the American television network which had just established a films division, was in search of subjects, and hadn't yet caught a whiff of the Anglophobe attitude beginning to drift through the Hollywood distribution companies – or so it seemed. However, for reasons still undisclosed, C.B.S. suddenly cooled on the project within six weeks of the date set for shooting to start. At this critical juncture, Finney personally telephoned Charles Bluhdorn. Bluhdorn was flattered by the star's appeal for finance; others, however, knowing that Paramount had just committed itself to making the British anti-war musical *Oh! What a Lovely War*, believed that Bluhdorn might have been shrewdly hoping

[1] Elizabeth Sussex, *op. cit.*, p. 68.

that Finney would do him a favour in return and accept a star part in it. Anyhow, Bluhdorn expressed himself willing, even impatient, to make *If . . .* , grasping that it was about an armed revolt in a boys' school. Back in London, where he would have to carry the can for his boss's decisions, Ornstein was more cautious. But after being given a 'sketchy idea' of the film at a hastily convened Sunday morning conference, he felt obliged to 'commit' to the subject. 'Faced with men like Anderson, Kubrick and a few others,' he said, 'you are obliged to go with them – the whole way. *They* are in large part the film that emerges; and there's no way of determining the end result in advance since in many cases they don't know it themselves. What's in their minds may be viewable later, but often it can't be written down, or even satisfactorily explained, at the time the money is required.' He added, 'In any case, *If . . .* hadn't a ruinous budget, between $450,000 and $500,000.'

Shot in what Anderson would call, in one of his favourite expressions, a 'bourgeoningly simple' style, *If . . .* was not only a blessed relief from the frenetic trendiness of so much contemporary British production, it also pushed to logical conclusions the director's own reaction against the stifling effect of British institutions, traditions and social classes on the individual's capacity to develop his potential to the full. Anderson viewed the public school, where Mick Travis and his companion guerrillas make their rebellion, as a metaphor for society. It may have been intended as specifically British society, though Anderson would probably deny this now, but, owing to the perfect timing of the film's release, it fired the half-articulated aims of youth in a multitude of countries. It was a film of emotional anarchy: the deed was its own justification. Anyone foolish enough to ask a redundant question, such as just what kind of society Mick and the others visualised after they had Sten-gunned down the school's Old Boys, masters, governors, and reactionary prefects, was sure of a tart response from Anderson implying incomprehension of the true centre of rebellion. The belief in service to God, man and society, on which the English public-school system rested, was denounced as a giant lie in a story that cross-sectioned the power-structure of the school, displaying its in-grained self-service, self-perpetuation and self-protection. The flogging inflicted on the non-conformists gave the film its sense of pain and outrage, and provided the monstrous injustice that made anarchy a plausible moral response. Anderson correctly anticipated that there would be those to whom the film was evidence of how savagely he was denying his own public-school past; yet there are scenes in the film, glowing softly in Miroslav Ondricek's pearly black-and-white tones or luminous colours, which convey a hankering for that pristine sense of community which is a public-schoolboy's most lingering memory – even when he carries away a hatred of such life-enhancing feelings being imprisoned within a life-denying system. *If . . .* has this ambivalence, too, which saves it from being pure spleen.

Constructed in eight chapters, whose titles provided the thematic links to the events, the Brechtian schema is gradually infused with the film's most controversial aspect – the surrealistic tinge that events take on in the later sections. Opinions differ about the point where *If . . .* parts company with reality, and leaves it dropping away, below and behind, like a landscape as an aircraft gains height into a new realm. But Anderson, who detests the very word 'surrealism' and prefers the phrase 'heightened reality' or 'poetic naturalism,' might pinpoint the moment when the rebel leaders, played by Malcolm McDowell and Richard Warwick, break bounds on a stolen motor-bike to enjoy the primitive sense of communion (sexual this time) with a girl in a motorway café. McDowell's raw lovemaking has the ambiguous encounter of animals beyond the pale of civilization: no rules are recognized beyond instinctive reflexes. As Gavin Millar wrote, 'The regenerative links are forged. Nothing remains but the provocation that will spark the revolutionaries into the necessary brutal action.'[1]

But to film people, uncertain anyhow of what they were going to see on the screen, the poetic significance of the everyday was confusing. Particularly disquieting was the blurring of the line between fantasy and reality – what *was* one to make of the nude

[1] *Sight and Sound* (Winter 1968–9), Vol. 28, No. 1, p. 43.

housemaster's wife drifting through the dormitories fetichistically touching the boys' clothing and bed-linen? Or the school padre being pulled out of the drawer in a bureau in the head's study? 'When I saw the film, it was half-assembled,' said Ornstein, 'and I'd be less than honest to say I hadn't grave doubts. I asked Lindsay, "Would it be possible to define by music or photography, say, the moments when we go from reality to fantasy?" Lindsay's answer was, "Well, perhaps you should wait till we've finished it and that may clear up all your doubts." Well, as I said, with people like Lindsay, you just have to go along with them . . .'

Of this period, whose omens he could read as well as anyone, Anderson later said, 'You nearly always have such difficulties when the film is finished. The important thing then is not to lose your head. It's vital to keep your cool and say to them, "Ah, now do you think so? I don't really think it'll work, but we'll try it *your* way." With *This Sporting Life*, we actually cut out all the flashbacks in the first five reels, projected the film and said to them, "Look, it doesn't really work, does it?" That way, you've much more chance of their saying "Yes, you're quite right" than if you meet them head on and say "Look, you cretins, what do you know about art?" For then you create a situation that's impossible to move.'

Once the film was finished, it was viewed in London by top Paramount executives from New York and the Coast, without its producer or director being present. The verdict was highly unfavourable, according to Anderson. It was deemed virtually unshowable. Quite apart from the difficulties they obviously had in accepting the reality-fantasy shifts, another reason for their apprehension may be guessed at: it was the fact that Robert Kennedy's assassination had taken place not long before and there was still deep concern about a possible armed conspiracy and the role of the gun in American society. There is some reason for believing that the 'campus' insurrection at the end of *If . . .* weighed on Paramount's official conscience. Ornstein was considerably thrown by the negative response. 'I certainly hadn't been thinking in disaster terms,' he said, 'and tried to smooth things over. But Lindsay wasn't rolling with the punches any more and was bitterly offended. The ghastly meeting finished at last and the only thing that raised my spirits was a word from Peter King, then head of Paramount's distribution company in Britain, who said, "I must tell you I like the film".' This was the first intimation of support for the film within the company and it was important; for there is little doubt that had *If . . .* not attracted enough adherents in the London and New York offices, who saw good in it and, even more to the point, possible profit, then its fate would have been sealed. As it was, an art-house release was suggested in London – in a cinema Paramount did not own. Anderson vetoed this, dryly observing that the art-house management might well be entitled to ask why *they* should show it if Paramount's two West End cinemas would not take the risk. Such a dialogue is probably more frequent in the film business than outsiders imagine, but it crystallizes the dilemma produced by off-beat films and the obstacle course that separates many of them from a screening with a decent chance of success. Eventually enough intramural support was mustered to justify opening *If . . .* at the smaller of Paramount's two West End 'showcase' cinemas exactly a week before Christmas 1968, a time generally considered to be the worst in the calendar for the box-office. 'Fortunately we had given the film saturation coverage in advance, with previews for critics and opinion-makers practically every night in the week and some afternoons as well,' said Ornstein. In short, the London office was going all out to beat the odds laid against the film across the Atlantic. 'The critics proved invaluable,' said Anderson, who up to then hadn't been known to hold such views. 'Every word they wrote was Telexed to New York – movie companies had so little confidence in their own judgment. And the reviews were followed by phenomenal business.'

In New York, too, the reviews were generally excellent, though Anderson later complained that the film had been given its 'play-off' on the neighbourhood circuits too soon. Later on Stanley Jaffé, the independent producer who had joined Paramount and was an enthusiast for *If . . .* ('A genuine one, I think,' Anderson said dourly) had the film re-released: it sometimes played in a double bill with *Goodbye, Columbus*, which was Jaffe's last production before joining Paramount. On the occasion of its New York première, one of the cooler reviewers, Pauline Kael, had written, '*If* . . . may have a potential appeal for young people, but I rather doubt whether it would reach much of an audience without a brilliant selling job.'[1] She then referred to a *Variety* report about a 'new scientific group' inside the distribution company who prided themselves on the way they had 'sold' *If* . . . to opinion-makers before the British première. One may merely observe that not all the 'opinion-makers' who have to be 'sold' on such a film exist outside the production company.

The disquiet which Ornstein sensed in Paramount's home office over *If* . . . became absolute displeasure over two other films on his British roster. One was called *Negatives*, the other *Two Gentlemen Sharing*. Both represented a considerable switch of policy by the National Film Finance Corporation. The N.F.F.C.'s plan to co-finance films with the Rank Organization had petered out while awaiting the delivery of profits from the pictures they had made together. Further, the N.F.F.C. had had to suspend normal lending activities in October 1966, at the very moment the American boom was building up; for owing to economic uncertainties in Britain and a savage credit squeeze, it could not borrow more than £750,000 of the £2 million it was entitled to obtain from non-Governmental – i.e. private – sources. The reason for the reluctance of the private money market to under-write film production was quite simple: the British Treasury simply would not guarantee repayment! For almost half the year until 31 March, 1969, lending facilities remained suspended. And thus the N.F.F.C., which had been specifically founded to assist *British* films, was forced to enter into co-financing arrangements with Hollywood companies. It undertook to contribute to the production by Paramount of two films on a *pari passu* basis of profit-sharing from world-wide revenues, one of which was *Two Gentlemen Sharing*, produced by Barry Kulick and directed by Ted Kotcheff, the other *Negatives*, produced by Judd Bernard and directed by Peter Medak. John Terry, the N.F.F.C.'s managing

[1] Pauline Kael, *Going Steady* (Temple Smith, 1970), p. 281.

director, believed that American backing was essential to get the films widely shown in the North American market.

Two Gentlemen Sharing, written by Evan Jones, the West Indian screen-writer who had worked with Losey, was about a confrontation between the races when the 'two gentlemen,' one white and English, the other a black immigrant, share a London bed-sitter, but discover at the end of the film how little they have in common. The Negro is trying to gain a foothold in the same middle class which the white boy is dropping out of; while the latter comes to see that all he is doing is borrowing sexuality from his contact with the blacks. The black man's disillusionment is bitter: so is the white boy's disgust at the degree of self-knowledge he has gained. This, anyhow, is how things appeared in the finished film, which cost £315,000 according to Kulick, or £380,000 according to John Terry. (Some necessary re-recording expenses as well as deferred payments may account for the difference.) Not a cheap film; and even a 'risk' one because of the attitude it took to its subject. Differences of opinion began almost as soon as it was finished, with Paramount insisting that the makers had not delivered the film 'as scripted,' and the latter asserting that it was essentially the same, allowing for the 'inevitable' changes in shooting due to second and presumably better thoughts, or the reshaping of scenes that did not work in front of the camera. It had supporters inside Paramount, but none in the top echelons. Jones and Kotcheff supposed the down-beat treatment was the cause of the distributor's dislike. 'I suppose they wanted another *Guess Who's Coming to Dinner*,' Jones said, 'a film where white and black go off together into the sunset. The suggestion that white and black couldn't make it together was thought to be offensive to the Negroes. They may have feared it was inflammatory: there was a scene where the white boy projects his self-disgust on to the black and cries, "Throw them all out".'[1] But he added that some blacks who had seen the film considered it equally anti-white. It should be remembered that at this time, 1967–8, race films were a rarity on the screen, black consciousness was still in white liberal hands when it came to film-making, and

[1] Evan Jones interviewed by the author, 17 April, 1969.

the rise of the militantly black movie had not even begun. But nervousness was apparently expressed on other scores, too – on the story's latent homosexuality. 'Most race films are about equality or justice,' said Kulick, 'and ask questions like "Are all men equal?" "Is life fair to them?" "Can white and black co-exist?" and they inevitably give impeccably liberal answers. We tried to show there were liberal myths which approximate as little to reality as racial prejudices. It's this new frame of reference which was received with intense dislike.'[1] Paramount maintained – and maintain – that their objections were solely on the grounds that the film as delivered simply did not correspond to the film script as financed. Executives at M.G.M. viewed the film; but they had recently been disappointed by the reception accorded Jules Dassin's *Up-Tight*, a remake of *The Informer* with an all-black cast, and felt that there could be no deal at the price asked. And so on 9 April, 1969, *Variety* carried the news that '*Two Gentlemen Sharing* is up for sale. The film's co-producer, the National Film Finance Corporation, is seeking a distributor . . . Paramount Pictures, co-producer of the film, declares it cannot find room in its distribution schedule for (it).' Thus the N.F.F.C., which had banked on an American distributor to carry it into the U.S. market, found it had to go a-hunting for a new partner, or else jeopardize the £200,000 it had put up as its share of the budget. Ultimately a deal was done with American International Pictures, who had a reputation for being in first (and frequently profitably) on any new trend; but the film's success in America was limited and it has not been shown in Britain to date.

The other Paramount–N.F.F.C. film, *Negatives*, was about the games people play, and whatever its defects – which were con-siderable – it had the important merit of reflecting a social feature of a time when the 'Swinging London' scene had degenerated into a huge morass of make-believe and mock role-playing. Playtime had been overtaken by the search for new experience, particularly the drug experience, among the 'in' groups. Fantasy had escalated to the point where it subsumed the individual

---

[1] Barry Kulick interviewed by the author, 18 April, 1969.

identity of the fantasist. It was hard to tell the haberdashers' boutiques in the King's Road or Carnaby Street from theatrical costumiers'. *Bonnie and Clyde*'s success in Britain, for example, had been reflected with a swiftness unparalleled by previous trend-setting movies, in the craze for wide-striped, broad-brimmed gangster outfits (for him) and maxi-skirts and gangster-moll beanies (for her), and this added impetus to the craze not just to be 'with it,' but to escape 'from it.' The hippie culture had arrived in Britain direct from San Francisco at the end of 1966, killing or gravely weakening the attraction of pop. As Nik Cohn recorded, for a time 'there was a sense of a completely fresh start, all sensation created anew . . . Clothes came from all over the place.'[1] Though the fancy-dress boom was taken up, exploited and ultimately exploded by the media in the 1967–8 period, and then the hippies moved into the softer lures of psychedelia and the Flower Children, the craze for role-playing in fancy dress reached the screen sometime later in the 'wish I were' theme of a film like *Negatives*.

Peter McEnery and Glenda Jackson starred in it as a couple living above an antique shop – the craze for campy junk again – and continuously re-enacting the tragic relationship of Dr Crippen, the mild-tempered wife-killer, and his mistress Ethel Le Neuve, both of them in full Edwardian costume. Their fantasy relationship is brutally short-circuited with the arrival of an interloper, a female German photographer played by Diane Cilento, who switches the man on to playing one of *her* fantasies, Manfred von Richthofen, the World War One air ace, complete with a full-size scarlet biplane anchored on the roof. An imaginary bullet from a machine-gun in a fantasy dog-fight draws real blood from the pilot behind the controls – just as the photographer in *Blow-Up* heard real tennis sounds when he returned the imaginary ball. What the film showed was how strong the temptation is to repeat a formula – and how treacherous it becomes if imitation isn't matched by fresh inspiration. Its indiscriminate mix of fantasy and

---

[1] Nik Cohn, *Today There Are No Gentlemen* (Weidenfeld and Nicolson, 1971), p. 121.

reality, coupled with extremely familiar elements from other films, made *Negatives* an essentially negative exercise. So Paramount thought, and with the N.F.F.C.'s consent (and doubtless relief) the film was sold to Walter Reade, Jr, who bought out the Paramount interest at the end of 1969. The N.F.F.C.'s report for the year ending 31 Mrach, 1970, made no mention of further co-productions with American majors.

The strains and stresses within Paramount became public knowledge in an announcement made on 13 July, 1968, which stated that henceforth the company would put more emphasis on the Hollywood studio under Robert Evans, vice-president in charge of world production. George H. Ornstein would remain vice-president in charge of foreign production, based in London and co-ordinating his activities more closely with Hollywood. To insiders, the meaning seemed clear enough: the West Coast side of the movie company was asserting its dominance, the British end being correspondingly demoted. 'We now feel that by co-ordinating and controlling our production activities in Hollywood,' the statement went on, 'we can effectively control a programme that will continue to draw from a talent pool found all over the world. We expect to have our Hollywood studio operating at peak activity during the coming year.' This was judged bleak comfort for the Paramount programme in Britain.

At the start of 1969 it was announced that George H. Ornstein was resigning his post with Paramount and turning independent producer. Further, it was not intended to fill his post. Robert Evans said he would keep control of all Hollywood pictures throughout the world, and Michael Flint, an English lawyer who had been Ornstein's deputy, would continue in charge of foreign production administration, based in London, and supervise the setting up of films in Britain. Eventually Michael Flint, too, moved into independent production elsewhere. And in January 1970, Max Setton, who had been with Columbia, was appointed Paramount production chief in Europe. Exactly a twelvemonth later he was quoted as referring to the company's recent 'orgy of over-production.' Belts, it was indicated, would be worn tighter, much tighter, in future.

NO SYMPATHY FOR THE DEVIL

Ornstein was not long without a function, however. Enough was still happening in 1969 – mergers, take-overs, new groups – to make experience like his valuable and sought after. But before examining the extraordinary situation he next found himself in, it is necessary to trace the history of a film that is not only a key one in the late 1960s, but also a cult one and something of a *cause célèbre*. The film is *Performance* – perhaps the last genuinely exotic fruit produced by the bizarre mutations of British society in this decade.

Prior to 1968, its producer, Sanford Lieberson, possessed a high-powered job, a corresponding salary and a roster of talented clients at Creative Management Associates (C.M.A.), a leading agency which represented stars, writers, producers, directors, photographers and others. Like similar outfits at this time, it was intent on switching from merely representing clients to 'packaging' complete deals involving them. In short, it wanted to move 'into production': the very phrase had a glamorous nimbus that for a brief eighteen months or so appeared to burn round the brows of every second person one met on the British film scene. Towards the end of 1967, therefore, Lieberson was assigned the task of creating a vehicle for Marlon Brando and Mick Jagger. C.M.A. represented Jagger – but, not surprisingly, it proved impossible to satisfy two such exacting artists at one and the same time; so Lieberson instead invited Donald Cammell, a writer C.M.A. also represented, to create an original subject for Jagger. As the ideas took shape, James Fox was approached to play opposite him. Fox had starred in the last film whose story Cammel had written, a 'campy' comedy called *Duffy*; and the writer at that time had discerned an aspect of his personality, a part of him that appeared vulnerable to sudden changes of mind or attitude, which he now thought appropriate for *Performance*, as the new script was called. Its theme was the interchange of identities.

'Right from the beginning,' Lieberson said later, 'the concept was heavily influenced by the times in which the film was made –

the political, social, psychological mood of the country as it appeared to all of us preparing the film.'[1]

When Jagger quoted Nietzsche in the film and said, 'Nothing is true, everything is permitted,' he was summing up and scarcely overstating the prevailing feeling behind 'permissiveness,' as the media had begun terming the mood of the country round about 1967. It was an atmosphere reaching into all aspects of popular culture, in which it appeared that all things, all manner of sensate experiences and erotic experiments were discussed, practised, advertised, promoted and above all 'permitted.' The running together of fantasy and reality, till no one could tell which was which, has been noted as the marked characteristic of films in the middle years of the decade. 'Permissiveness' was a much more intense, proselytizing emphasis on fantasy. Where its source could be located at all – the term's very vagueness was a great part of its spell – it was among small groups of large reach and influence whose behaviour and outlook were fed back into society by the media and reinforced by their own capacity for magnification and dramatization. The pop culture had begun to change after 1967 and to assume the characteristics of 'drug culture' as the use of the soft hallucinogenic drugs became written about and practised. Trendiness turned ever more inwards as the exterior look of things went stale on the very people who had done most to decorate the social and cultural scene a year or so earlier. It could not compete with the bright exciting experience of being 'turned on.' Very swiftly what _Queen_ magazine in 1964 had defined as 'a way of looking,' and thus had given pop culture its sanction and impetus, became a way of feeling. The pleasures of the inward eye took over from those of the external scene, so that the things seen now grew corespondingly vivid in their attempt to induce the same feelings of release and euphoria in those who hadn't yet been 'turned on.' George Melly noted that, from 1967 onwards, shapes and colours began to figure far more prominently than ever before in the lyrics of pop music and in

[1] Sanford Lieberson interviewed by the author, 2 April, 1973. Unless stated otherwise, all subsequent quotations from Lieberson come from the same source.

street posters which now aped the style of the Underground advertisements that had emerged during the summer of 1966, with their peculiar phosphorescent use of Day-Glo paints and dyes designed to convey the effects of mind-blowing drugs. In 1967, the same year as Jagger and Robert Fraser were arrested on drugs charges, Richard Neville, an Australian journalist and Underground propagandist resident in London, wrote his manual for all 'turned-on' souls entitled *Play Power*, in which he gave a graphic description of central London at the time. 'Every Friday night until dawn shimmering Flower Children, splashed with Day-Glo, spotted with marcasite, clad in diaphanous re-vamped négligés, tarted-up Grenadier Guards jackets, in tat and glitter from the markets of Asia and the stalls of the Portobello Road, in anything as long as it was beautiful, tripped inside the mushrooming numbers of psychedelic venues whose membership constituted a hippy Mafia all over Inner London.[1] The London hippy movement, which had arrived in Britain trailing the glamour of illegality from the outlawing of LSD in the United States in 1966, had come fully into fashion above ground by the winter of 1966-7 and was given even wider advertisement with the arrival of 'Flower Power' in the summer of 1967. 'Flower Power' made the hippy culture vastly more commercial. Ethnic garments could be pushed over the counter more safely than hallucenogenic drugs; the media could palm off the shimmering transcendentalism as a viable life-style without incurring (as yet) any charges of debauching those who were hooked on it; when the Beatles adopted the Maharishi as their personal guru in August 1967, the trappings of hippiedom assumed an even more beatific radiance – 'a prettily tinted jelly-fish' was how George Melly described the pop world in mid-1967 – which suffused the worshipful ranks of faddists, addicts, hermits, meditative acolytes and acid-dropping communicants; and the cartoon film *Yellow Submarine* (1968) provided a brilliantly designed lexicon that summed up the 'experience' by translating the Beatles into the landscape of Psychedelia and including enough 'code' words, or what were taken to be such by initiates, to seem like an animated gospel for everyone who

[1] Richard Neville, *Play Power*, (Cape, 1970), p. 30.

viewed it, sober or stoned. To those who 'turned on' to the experience, everything was interchangeable, melting indeterminate, ambiguous, preparing the way for the reign of bi-sex and ultimately unisex.

This was the psycho-social environment that Donald Cammell absorbed into the *mise-en-scène* of *Performance*. But it was not all he did. He made a connection between this transient sensate environment and a much older and more enduring London, namely the criminal underworld whose power base had been the East End but which, like many more reputable and talented East Enders, had 'crossed the river' to exploit the new social and cultural flux in the West End and to put the frighteners on the profitable new businesses from pop discotheques to gambling clubs. To know a criminal was fashionable; to be one was acceptable – acceptable enough, anyhow, to be included in the Bailey collection of *Pin-Ups*. *Performance* had the originality of bringing together these two worlds, the hippy-permissive world and the criminal underworld, and to demonstrate elliptically, making use of current moods and artefacts, how much they had in common and how one could draw from the other the elements it needed for its own feeling of spiritual well-being, artistic completeness and ultimate self-fulfilment – or, as it turned out, self-destruction.

Jagger played a retired superstar, a pop singer who one day had caught a glimpse of his 'daemon' in a mirror – whereupon it had deserted him, leaving him stricken and appalled by recognition of the evil from which he drew his potency as a celebrity. As Michael Goodwin noted perceptively in *Rolling Stone*, the movie was a weirdly accurate anticipation of the moment at the Altamont concert when Jagger glimpsed the satanic forces unleashed in mounting tensions among the audience by the Rolling Stones, which resulted in at least one violent killing not many feet from himself. 'The Maysles aside,' Goodwin wrote, referring to the directors of *Gimme Shelter* (1972), '*this* [*Performance*] is the Altamont movie' shot two years before the event.[1]

James Fox, shorn of his languid upper-class English manner-

[1] *Rolling Stone*, 3 September, 1970

isms as well as his fairly lengthy locks, played a cockney thug who, in underworld slang, is another kind of 'performer' – a bully boy whose 'performance' is terrorizing the victims of an extortion racket. On the run from his own bosses, who are bent on teaching him a lesson for exceeding orders, he shelters in the basement of the house which the pop star has turned into a mystic hermitage for himself and two androgynous girl-friends who share bed and bath with him in an ambience of sensuous experience. The adviser on the house's furnishings, material as well as mystical, was Christopher Gibbs, one of the most conspicuously successful cult-riders, dandies and fashion-setters of the mid-1950s and 1960s. Nik Cohn described him once as 'sitting at home propped up on his Marrakesh cushions (which he had brought back from Morocco as well as vast quantities of Arab robes and slippers) and making one of the first English attempts at what later became the hippie life-style.'[1] It sounds like Jagger in the film.

The pop star, sensing the atavism of his unexpected visitor, detains him as a house-guest in order to siphon off his predatory persona, like Dracula drawing in the life-giving plasma, and so refresh himself for his return to the world. With his East End puritanism badly unsettled by the atmosphere of exotica, irridescent colours, intangible reflections, free love, drugs and gratification of every kind for body and soul, male and female and the sex in between, the gangster has his will sapped, his self-respect eroded and his personality prised from its anchorage in the real world and shuffled like the wild card in a pack through excess after excess until his identity is interchangeable with his host's. His fate proves to be, too.

The script underwent what Lieberson called 'only superficial changes, the ones usually necessitated by the casting and the budget and the occasional objection from the stars.' (Among the latter, he claimed, was Fox's unwillingness about doing a scene in bed with Jagger.) The project was approved by Kenneth Hyman, a personal friend of Lieberson's and an independent producer with such commercial successes as *The Dirty Dozen* to

[1] Nik Cohn, *op. cit.*, p. 91.

his credit, who had recently become production chief of Warner–
Seven Arts in California. Seven Arts, the company previously in
partnership with Bryanston, had bought control of Warner
Brothers in July 1967. Now C.M.A. already represented Warners
in the field of television in the United States, and the *Performance*
deal was an attempt to establish it as an agent for Warner–Seven
Arts in other fields – notably the 'packaging' of film productions.
Mick Jagger had previously been approached by Warners with an
offer, reputed to be $250,000, to act as the company's 'youth
adviser' – since the 'youth audience' was now the one that the
Hollywood majors were gearing up to service. Consequently, if
Jagger wanted to do a subject like *Performance*, it couldn't be bad,
could it? At this point the only difference of opinion was about
having two directors for the film. One was Donald Cammell, its
script-writer, the other was Nicolas Roeg, a brilliantly atmospheric
photographer who had worked on films like *The Caretaker*,
Fahrenheit 451, *Far from the Madding Crowd* and *Petulia*. But
Liberson said the deal depended on the pact made by these two
to co-direct the film, so it went ahead. It was to be the start of
Warner–Seven Arts's British production programme.

It was not necessarily odd that, according to Lieberson,
shooting got under way without a production and distribution
agreement being signed. Agreements that a layman might think
essential where large amounts of capital are being spent have a
way in the film business of being left to one side; a partner in the
deal, usually the one advancing the money, generally considers
this is a strong lien on the other and looks to custom and
traditional practice as well as to his own power-base in the
industry to protect his interest; and certainly no one was anything
but honest in this relationship. The film was made with a loan
advanced by the distributor, again the normal practice, which the
'P. and D.' agreement would discharge upon signature at the end
of shooting. Filming began in the autumn of 1968 with a budget
then fixed at £400,000 and an eleven-week schedule – it went one
week over – and all the scenes were done on location. It is always
hard to discover precisely when differences of opinion begin over
a film that ultimately proved highly controversial, though

Lieberson believes that Warners–Seven Arts began to be upset when some of the more 'permissive' rushes, showing James Fox and one of the girls, or both, were screened. 'We switched to more normal things,' said Lieberson. Only five or six weeks' preparation had been allowed, and it is one of the best indications of how thoroughly the then booming American production in Britain had mopped up the available technical talent – for the Paramount and Universal programmes were going full blast, and Columbia, United Artists, Fox, even M.G.M. and newcomers like Embassy and Filmways were stepping up their schedules – that fully experienced technicians other than Roeg's camera crew were almost impossible to come by for the film. Consequently, when the distributors requested a screening of 'prepared material' in the third week of shooting, no one was familiar with presenting such an assembly. Instead of selected takes and rough sequences, 'we screened everything we had shot,' said Lieberson, 'and they saw hours of it. We were giving them an education in our ignorance.' Immediately the lights went up, strong objections were voiced. And the producers got their first inkling of the extreme reactions that the finished film would later arouse. Remember that the Seven-Arts men, shrewd and sophisticated film-makers, were viewing the film as distributors, too, calculating its probable impact on American film-goers, even on American censors. Though the Production Code had been revised after 1965 to permit things once held to be totally unshowable on American screens, there was still at this time, around 1968–9, great apprehension among the Hollywood majors about any stigma they might incur, particularly a dreaded X. rating from the Code Administration, and even Antonioni's *Blow-Up* had caused M.G.M. anxiety on account of shots like Vanessa Redgrave's exposed bosom or the photographer's frolic with the nude model girls in a sea of blue posing paper, and was released without the M.G.M. trademark. The Americans, viewing *Performance* and having it hammered home in repeated takes, saw a representation of British decadence coming into full flower. And they liked it not.

What did they especially object to? It was really hard for

o

anyone to say. For the film's air of decadent behaviour was
unlocalized: it was everywhere, dissolute things being obliquely
cogitated and elliptically put into effect, no story-line clearly
visible or being hewed to, no sense of moral equation worked
out, attitudes as unanchored in recognizable reality as air currents,
and shocks delivered to the senses as much as to the body and
equally without conscience . . . The characters possibly came as
an unpleasant shock, even in their partially realized state. A
'youth film' was one thing: but to which 'youth audience' was
this addressed? Why, the film didn't even get to Mick Jagger till
half-an-hour had gone by. The main concern, however, was
confided to the producers when they were asked whether the
characters in the film – the boys, that is – were 'bi.' 'Bi what?'
Cammell and Roeg asked, unfamiliar with the familiar American
term for 'bi-sexual.' 'I knew we were in trouble then,' Lieberson
recalled. But since production was technically excellent, the filming continued and cheer was soon brought by a Warner Brothers
representative, a former aide to Jack L. Warner, who viewed
some footage and said he thought it looked 'interesting.' Three-
quarters way through, the distributors again viewed the material.
It confirmed their dislike; and they particularly hated the Mick
Jagger character. 'The film was finished and locked up,' said
Lieberson, 'and I felt terribly depressed. I knew Seven Arts were
angry that their production plans in Britain should have had what
was considered a disgraceful start.' More baffled than anyone
perhaps was Mick Jagger, once a potential 'youth adviser' and
now unharkened to. 'It was clear that this film, for whatever the
reasons, was having a tremendous emotional effect on people
intimately concerned with it which couldn't be countered or
contained by rational argument,' said Lieberson. 'It was to have
the same effect on nearly everyone who saw it. It changed people
from relatively reasonable individuals into impassioned denounc-
ers of the evil they claimed it represented. We really began to
wonder had we made such a corrupt film? It was a nightmare.'
Various well-meaning attempts to resolve the deadlock were
unsuccessful, since the release of the film was complicated by the
position of the 'P. and D.' agreement. Respite came, however, in

the spring of 1969. Warner–Seven Arts had rejected a bid to purchase them from Commonwealth United, one of the so-called 'instant majors' and a company that was shortly to founder in the débâcle following the collapse of Bernard Cornfeld and his Investors Overseas Services. But a bid was accepted soon afterwards from Kinney National Services, whose corporate fortunes had come mainly from car-parks. They now wanted to diversify into the film industry. In August 1969, Warner-Kinney, as it then became called, announced their vice-president in charge of foreign production. He was George H. Ornstein.

Warner-Kinney's new board was headed by Ted Ashley, chairman, and John Calley, executive vice-president in charge of production, and it was on behalf of this team that Ornstein ordered *Performance* to be screened for him. He thought it a really original film with considerable potential in the 'youth market,' that magic phrase breathed like a spell in all film companies at the time. 'Calley liked it, too,' Lieberson recalled; 'doors started opening and money to flow again.' Not for long, though. Whenever a film company has produced, acquired or otherwise inherited a controversial film, one so way-out that it fits no previously recognized production pattern, or one with ingredients in it that actively work against the accepted context of the company product and policy, the effect can be very divisive and the film itself can become the focus for competing, if not actually conflicting, opinions about how best the company's fortunes can be furthered. Individual heads are laid on the block unless their owners are exceptionally wary. And the desire not to be proved wrong can become entrenched, hardening previous attitudes or causing new initiatives to flag and languish. Though Warner's ownership had changed, many of the same middle-echelon people remained, and *Performance*, really without conscious intention on anyone's part, tended to become the touchstone or anathema of official or unofficial thinking. The pattern of *If . . .* was in fact being repeated. Fred Weintraub, a newly appointed executive with special responsibility for youth affairs – he had started a successful chain of campus coffee-shops and affected the dress and life-style of hippy youth to a spectacular degree – was one of the enthusiasts for the film, and a screening he arranged for 'hip' people in New York endorsed his view. But a subsequent preview at a Santa Monica second-run cinema brought out the over-forty ex-urbanites to view it in the company of Warner executives and the British film-makers – and a small but vociferous section of the audience began complaining soon after the start. It left the film-chiefs huddled in groups whose conversation, Lieberson recalled, fell off when he approached and picked up when he moved away.

The preview appeared to confirm the way *Performance* was dividing the company into the 'Woodstock' adherents, who were hip on the youth revolution and related excesses, and the far more conservative elements who disliked the film or mistrusted the consequences of showing it widely. The United States was then undergoing the traumas of a year of marches, demonstrations and rock-pop festivals, one of which at Newport, a suburban community in the Los Angles area, had blown up in the face of its organizers with rioting kids, hundreds of injured (though none fatally), and scores of teenagers being busted for possession of pot or acid. Though Warners were later to distribute with most successful (and peaceable) results the film of the Woodstock music–and art-fair under the slogan 'Three Days of Peace, Love and Music,' it was, after all, a record of an event staged with Warner's patronage – a very different matter from putting out a film under the Warner trademark that could be interpreted by some as a conscienceless exploitation of drugs in a very 'un-American' ambience and an illustration of debauchery possibly injurious to law, order and religion – never mind peace, love and music. In the event, the advice tendered was considerably broad-minded and less penalizing than had been feared: it was principally a request to cut the film so as to bring Jagger onscreen much earlier. It was clear to the makers that if they did not do the re-cutting themselves, Warners would exercise their legal right to do so; but, in the event, the experience was nothing like so harsh. Cammell stayed in Burbank for several weeks, working closely and agreeably with a Warner editor, becoming quite absorbed by the business and able to report a 'strongly positive' reaction from the San Francisco campus and film-buff preview audience which viewed the re-cut movie. Even so, Lieberson felt a solid supporter was lost when Ornstein, for reasons of internal policy, resigned from his London post in 1970.

Performance eventually opened at a Manhattan cinema to capacity business. Outside the sophisticated neighbourhoods, it was a different story. It did not reach London till 7 January, 1971, nearly two years after it had been finished and ready for screening, though part of the delay was due to Warners wanting to open their new West End 'showcase' theatre with it. It got a mixed reception, some critics going all out to praise and succour it – for its 'martyr' status was by then a matter of knowledge and gossip, some of it highly inaccurate in the film industry – while others experienced its baleful power but were left unpurged by any detectable element of humanity or conscience. The critic of *Rolling Stone* gave the presumably *ex cathedra* judgment when he wrote, 'This is a weird movie, friends . . . Use Only As Directed. One of the attributes of evil is ugliness and on one level *Performance* is a very ugly film. Hallucinating though it may be, I would not recommend viewing it while tripping.'[1]

'Evil,' in fact, was the most frequently recurring word in the reviews on both sides of the Atlantic. Some reviewers even intimated that not only had the vivid imagery of the hippy sub-culture been brilliantly distilled into the film, but also certain passages were those of an 'acid film' fabricated to reproduce the dislocation of reality experienced on a trip – while other items in the film were barely disguised symbols of sorcery rituals!

The style was jagged and violent – possibly rendered more so by the enforced re-editing – until the more tranquilized habitat of the pop singer's home was penetrated. At the start, the film did indeed flicker into being in acid flashes like mercury-strip lighting coming on, or a television picture looming up on a faulty tube – at times it vanished like a blown light-bulb. It was composed entirely for the eye and senses in a way that recalled LSD to those who had sampled it. Colours swam. Perspectives abruptly altered. Reality proved a treacherous illusion. The rapid-fire editing was

Rolling Stone, *op. cit.,*

a series of narcotic blinks. A bullet hole in a head opened up to absorb the camera on a trajectory through the cortex and brain-cells towards the bottomless pit of the wound, where the image of Jorge Luis Borges, patron of the revels and inspiration for the theme of interchangeable identity, was ultimately plumbed. The violence, even with several minutes pared away from it by the British censor, set new (though soon surpassed) limits – the chauffeur being shaved to his scalp while his Rolls-Royce is bathed in corroding acid, Fox being whipped, or a room being vandalized so that the very furnishings seem to be gutted or flayed alive. Some of the excesses were as silly, however, as anything in *The Picture of Dorian Gray*. Flashing amethyst rings or rubbing baby powder into one's tender parts, or even taking a bath *à trois* and sticking five-pound notes on wet rumps, looked more camp than corrupt. But a quite different sort of intensity was evoked by the scene where Jagger, with his snake-like Medusa locks scraped into a gleaming skull-cap of brilliantined hair and his mouth writhing out a menacing song, *Memo from Turner*, imagined himself a modern Scarface and put his obese henchmen through a strip routine that left the screen as raw-looking as a Bacon painting of sub-human nudes. Both male stars were used powerfully for physical appearance and personality. Fox was an astonishing mutation. With his tubular body and cropped, bullet-like head, he was no more the well-bred playboy, but rather the progeny of a Frankenstein monster. And Jagger in frock, smock, sari, kaftan or whatever ectoplasmic wrapping he wore, resembled the survivor of an Indian famine. He fastened on his victim like a piranha fish wearing Day-Glo make-up. It was the most disturbing evocation of, yes, evil the whole decade produced.

Performance remains a *film maudit*. It did indeed seem to have a curse set on it early in its conception and it fully lived up to all the disquieting rumours about it one heard over the years. *The years!* That in itself shows it was a victim of the system of film production and exhibition – without possibly anyone wishing it to be so. It was off-beat to an aggressive degree, a film so personal in the insight it gave into the disintegrating section of society that had produced so many marketable trends and viable fashions that it perplexed and shocked its sponsors. Wherever it is shown, it still draws young audiences who want to taste the dregs of an experience that the 1970s are making recede ever more quickly, so that one asks oneself if it really all happened, or if one helped to invent it.

On the stars of *Performance*, the effects were felt, too. And they were bizarre and to some extent still inexplicable. About the time the film was screened in Britain, America was having the première of *Gimme Shelter*, the record of that ill-omened Altamont concert that put the curse on the pop-rock scene in the United States. In his review of it, Richard Schickel described Jagger, confronted by the mutinous crowd and later by the action re-play of the murder in front of the concert platform, as a scared boy riding a tiger and hanging on for dear life. 'Finally, one imagines, he will withdraw physically, as he already has psychologically, from his public – just as the character he played in *Performance* did.'[1] This forecast has proved correct – at least up to recent months. But considering that the theme of *Performance* was the interchange of identities, and how the pop idol at the end takes the mobster's place in the car containing his executioners, even though he has apparently had his life extinguished earlier by his guest, then the aftermath of *Performance* was even stranger in the case of James Fox. He also retired from the world that had made him a star. Barely a year after its screening, and despite lucrative offers from film producers, he abruptly gave up the world of movie-making and announced his conversion to evangelical good works as a member of a sect called the Navigators. At the time of writing he is still actively engaged in this vocational work, preaching the Gospel and seeking converts for Christ in the midlands of England. It is, he insists, far more fulfilling than any 'performance' could be. The film's playing on 'illusion' and 'reality' had entered more deeply into Fox than he had thought at the time, though his dissatisfaction with acting had actually begun earlier, when he was playing Edward Gordon Craig, the theatrical designer and lover of Isadora Duncan in Reisz's film *Isadora*. It was the first

[1] *Life*, 29 January, 1971.

time he had had to play a character who actually existed. 'I began to think of [him] as . . . being a real live person. And I thought I wasn't really alive . . . I was doing an acting job . . . I have missed certain things through choosing success as my goal and one of them is just expressing life and who I am. I began to search for some reality.'[1] He tried to do this by making an expedition up the River Amazon, encountering hardship, isolation, and a certain degree of risk. But it was *Performance* which precipitated the crisis. 'At that time I thought that if you showed something true, then it was valid. But subsequently I've thought dramatists and actors and writers have an obligation to their audience. I think there should be restrictions on things which, just because they are true, need not necessarily be valid.'

Such doubts, though, were kept at bay during the film, which was in essence a test for the kind of faith that Fox was seeking – a confident dependence on certainties that would give a sense of purpose and fulfilment to his life. He sought it in the film's directors and said later, 'I think one can give oneself whole-heartedly to whatever one does and to me at that [time] acting involved a wholehearted commitment. I remember you [Nicolas Roeg] saying, "Look, I want you to get your hair cut and I don't really want to see you for at least a week, while you really begin to live, walk and breathe the character." And because at that time I trusted you and Donald [Cammell], as the directors of it, and believed in what we were doing, I was able to say to myself, "I'm wholeheartedly going to do this . . .".' But the film brought no such certainty and only appears to have deepened doubts already strongly present. 'After I made *Performance*, for about a year and a half I started to try and reform my life . . . I thought it was a mess. I did start going back to church and I started to read the New Testament.' Encountering an evangelist at this decisive moment, a long conversation that began at lunch and lasted till the dinner-things were being laid, prepared Fox for his new vocation: it is one of the most extraordinary turns of fate that any actor in the 1960s took; and there can be little doubt that the

[1] James Fox quoted from and interviewed by the author in *Escape to Fulfilment*, directed by David Gerrard for BBC TV, 23 September, 1971.

powerful catalyst of *Performance* contributed to Fox's discovering Christ and the screen losing, to date anyhow, one of its most finely constructed talents.

The British film industry also lost a man who had helped put a lot of it together in the early years of the decade. George H. Ornstein gradually withdrew from active production after he left Warners and fulfilled a desire of his own by settling with his wife in Spain, from there watching with a certain detached cynicism the run-down of the American investment in Britain. All in all, *Performance* was a natural chapter ending – though there was an appendix, a British attempt to put the situation to rights by embarking on a home-built film programme of its own.

Chapter Nineteen: The Last Tycoon

> I knew I was there to be shot at, but somehow I never found
> time to be fitted for a bullet-proof vest.   Bryan Forbes

Bryan Forbes, who had started his screen life as actor and part-time script-doctor, gone on through frustration to be a screen-writer and producer, turned director next, and then incorporated himself into a hyphenated animal called a producer-writer-director, was to add one more rank to his promotion at the very end of the 1960s. He was the decade's last tycoon.

The chain of events that were to install him as production chief of one of the (then) 'Big Four' film studios in Britain was forged early and circumspectly. In a way, it duplicated what was happening in the United States. There, the big business conglomerates had bought their way into show business; in Britain, the show-business conglomerates were bought up and promoted into even bigger business. Electrical and Musical Industries (E.M.I.) was one of the country's biggest conglomerates, a complex of recording and electric equipment interests, headed by a quiet but approachable millionaire, Sir Joseph Lockwood, and a grayish and rather unapproachable managing director, John Read. Its entry into the film industry was a natural extension of its show-business hardwear. It had been preparing for it as early as March 1967, when E.M.I. acquired control of the Grade Organization, which has already been mentioned in another chapter. This production and talent agency was headed by Leslie Grade and Bernard Delfont (brothers, despite the name Bernard had taken on as more in keeping with an impresario). They and other shareholders held 40 per cent of the equity, and Bernard Delfont moved on to the E.M.I. board. The intention was to set up a 'third force' chain of cinemas, rivals to Rank and A.B.C., based on the existing Shipman and King circuit. There was a strong feeling of strings being drawn ever tighter in the controlling pattern of British film exhibition. Soon production, too, would be part of the new pattern.

Early in February 1968 E.M.I. bought the 25 per cent stake that Warner–Seven Arts owned in the Associated British Picture Corporation for a price of £9,500,000 and said they intended to make an offer for the remaining 75 per cent at a total price of £38,000,000. At this time A.B.P.C. owned 270 A.B.C. cinemas in Britain, a half-share of Thames Television (the independent company operating in the London area from Monday to Friday evening), and 74 per cent of Anglo-Amalgamated, the production and distribution company headed by Nat Cohen. But negotiations fell through in April 1968 after the Independent Television Authority, the statutory watchdog of the networks, had frowned on the proposals to take over Thames Television, and rejected E.M.I.'s counter-proposals. Still, E.M.I. was a persistent wooer and announced that it hoped to co-operate with A.B.P.C. on future 'entertainment ventures.' At the start of 1969 a further declaration of love was made, totalling £34,000,000, later improved to £40,000,000, but rejected by the A.B.P.C. board on 11 January, 1969. The strength of E.M.I.'s determination to cut itself in on the expanding leisure-market was now revealed. All protestations of mutual happiness were thrown aside and a short, fierce battle for control ensued. On 1 February, E.M.I. was declared the winner with 53 per cent of A.B.P.C.'s shares. E.M.I. had already got into the A.B.P.C. nest through the Grade Organization's part-ownership of Elstree film studios, and it now proceeded to occupy the whole of the nest. This time the I.T.A. allowed E.M.I. to keep its interest in Thames Television, provided it sold off its agency interests. It complied; the largest part of them went to a group whose directors included Leslie Grade's son. In March 1969, Nat Cohen joined the board of A.B.P.C. and the alphabet soup of company titles was stirred once more, as Anglo-Amalgamated eventually became known as Anglo-E.M.I., and A.B.P.C. gradually fell into disuse as people spoke of E.M.I.-Elstree when referring to the film studio.

One of the first actions of Bernard Delfont was to sign Albert Finney's production company to make a north-country comedy, *Spring and Port Wine*, as the opening film of the new order. Some people took a look at the project and asked, '*New* order?' It

looked exactly the type of folksy human-situation comedy that
the 'old' one had sponsored year after year.

At this time the American production boom in Britain had
passed its peak and the gnawing realization of hard times ahead
was sinking into all grades of talent and competence as they
apprehensively anticipated the withdrawal of Hollywood money
back to the United States. Consequently, much, much more than
usual seemed to depend on E.M.I.'s entry into film production.
The promises made were scrutinized anxiously by the British and
sceptically by those American production chiefs in London who
had hit trouble with their own praiseworthy intentions when they
tried to turn them into profitable realities. Now it was up to the
British. Had they learnt from the success of others? More
important, had they learnt from the mistakes of others?

Now Bernard Delfont was not anxious to be the man to make
mistakes. Though he was one of the most successful theatrical
impresarios in Britain, he was shrewd enough to appreciate that
he knew much less about the film business. Sums of money were
tossed about casually there that would have been handled more
nervously or respectfully in theatre-land. Accordingly he looked
about him for a production chief to take charge at Elstree, and
early in March 1969, meeting Bryan Forbes at a Mayfair dining-
club called the White Elephant, he asked him if he would take on
the job. He wanted someone who knew the film business intimately, he said, someone with whom he could have a completely
candid relationship. Forbes took the first requirement for granted
and entered on the second almost at once. 'What's in it for you?'
was his first question to Delfont.

For Forbes, there was considerable attraction in the post. He
had made a suspense thriller for 20th Century Fox, *Deadfall* (1968),
which had turned out as good as, but no better than, it could be:
it was a project his agents had signed him to a few years earlier
and enthusiasm had to be rekindled with much technical polish
and a guitar concerto counterpointing a twenty-three-minute
burglary sequence: elsewhere enthusiasm had flagged. He had
also directed *The Madwoman of Chaillot* (1969) for Commonwealth
United, stepping into John Huston's shoes after seventeen days'

shooting, and at least he had given elegance and a redeeming fantastication to Giraudoux's simple-minded fable which the producers, who visualized it as a multi-million dollar block buster, had absurdly if dazzlingly 'over' cast. Not fulfilling expectations based on a primitive head-count of the number of stars in it, the film had proved a disappointment. In this depressing aftermath – not that the chance of directing Katharine Hepburn, Charles Boyer, and others from one's star-struck adolescence was to be regretted – Delfont's offer promised a fresh stimulus. The general economic outlook was bleak and getting bleaker. To be offered the post of production chief and assured of a free hand (within agreed budgetary limits) in picking one's projects was tempting and timely. Money, power and patronage were extended – and accepted. And on 9 April, 1969, Forbes, who had begun his directing career barely nine years before and had once been refused admittance to this very same film studio when he was an unknown actor in search of work, was officially appointed head of production at E.M.I.-Elstree. (Actually, it soon became known as E.M.I.-M.G.M. when the Hollywood company came in on the deal by agreeing to co-finance some of the films made at Elstree and to distribute their own American-made films in Britain through the A.B.C. cinema chain now owned by E.M.I.)

By an ironic mishap Forbes's appointment was announced on the same day as Paramount were giving a Press reception for the first film to be directed by Richard Attenborough. It took place at the same hotel, too. Forbes's old partner had finished *Oh! What a Lovely War*, and some of those who were present at both functions didn't fail to observe that their coincidence was an omen for a rather bellicose phase of film-production history. So it proved. On Forbes's first day at Elstree blows were exchanged between a member of the craft unions and one of his new production team. Morale at the studio was at an all-time low: a long period of what they felt to be stagnating production policy had inculcated a cynicism into the management at all levels. 'I expected a disaster area,' Forbes said, 'but I hadn't been prepared for a Hiroshima.' Ripping out the time-clocks and letting it be known that he was running a studio, not a factory, Forbes successfully appealed for a truce in stormy labour relations and got new agreement for an industry-wide productivity deal by going directly to the Ministry of Labour; and, knowing at first hand the fears of fellow film-makers, he gave an undertaking that there would be no redundancy. It was a humane approach, but perhaps an unwise one. It was a promise that haunted E.M.I. in the next year or so, when the cost of running a film studio at full strength became crippling, and Elstree was not by any means the most up-to-date or efficient of the 'Big Four' studios. They in fact became the 'Big Three' (Pinewood, Shepperton, Elstree) in 1970 when M.G.M. closed their British studio at Borehamwood, almost across the road from Elstree, in pursuance of the new policy put into effect by James T. Aubrey, who had been appointed M.G.M.'s president in October 1969. Aubrey was determined to raise cash on any asset that M.G.M. was able to spare. Nothing at this time looked so 'spare' as a vast movie studio abroad: they already had to keep one open at home in Culver City. So the British set-up was sold in a profitable property deal and its costly technical equipment transported swiftly, in one week-end, to Elstree's lot, where M.G.M., thanks to the links between the companies, proposed concentrating any future production in Britain. Knowing the relative modernity of the studios, many felt the move should have been the other way round. But it was made at probably the last feasible moment when it could pass off without industrial resistance from the film unions. Within months unemployment in some craft sections would rise to 90 per cent and, with it, the will to oppose almost any deal that seemed to be to the profit of employers, whether or not there were side benefits for the workers.

Thus at the very moment when flexibility was needed to adapt to the new poverty that struck the film industry as financial investment fell, the unions were encouraged to adopt the most obdurate policies in protection of a standard of living and continuity of employment that had only been made possible by American finance – and its subsequent inflationary effect.

Such was the slack apparent in British film-making at this period that, the day after Forbes's appointment was announced, scripts began to arrive by mail or hand delivery, several hundred of them, all gasping for finance like stranded fish for water after the dollar tide had turned so cruelly on them. Too many of the scripts had been turned down elsewhere for good reasons. But Forbes selected fourteen subjects and announced them. This was his first mistake, his critics said later. By committing himself to make projects, he lost the flexibility vital in a market more than ever before at the mercy of fickle public taste. It was a programme influenced by the old Thalberg idea of balancing the whole output: Forbes constantly appealed for it to be viewed 'as a whole.' Unfortunately, finance was bought at dearer rates of interest than in the days of the Hollywood conveyor-belt system; and no one could any longer reckon on the losses incurred on one or several films being made good by the others. The first three projects appeared dismayingly 'square,' but safe in their audience-appeal. 'Square' they were: safe they were not. *And Soon the Darkness* (1970) was a modestly conceived suspense thriller about girl cyclists in France running into the local rapist: it was shot with the precision, and limited impact, of a television drama. *Hoffmann* (1970) looked like a middle-aged edition of *The Collector*, as Peter Sellers engineered the kidnapping of the office-girl. *The Man who haunted Himself* (1970), a quasi-science fiction melodrama, provided Roger Moore with a moustache and a *doppelganger*. They were all films obviously rushed into production to get the studio ship-shape again: Forbes couldn't afford the luxury of waiting for the off-beat, or chancing an untested project. But it might have been better if he had. The three films were released 'back to back' (i.e. following each other in consecutive weeks) across the country – as E.M.I. had then no West End 'showcase' cinema – and coincided with the World Cup football play-offs, a heat wave, and a general election.

Forbes had also incurred the suspicions of some board members. They disliked the 'exposure' he was being given in the media, and attributed it to an ex-actor's penchant for the limelight. He pleaded justification, and said it was vital to re-establish the studio as a recognizable going concern. They then transferred their dislikes to his habit of coming direct to board meetings from the studios, dressed in a manner that wouldn't have gone amiss in Burbank or Culver City, or even Haight-Ashbury, but struck the conventionally suited Wardour Street and City men as a sign that he was almost aggressively dissociating himself from them.

'THE BOSS'S FILM'

The first calculated risks that paid off had to be taken over the opposition of men with a very different, more aggressively lower-middle-class outlook than his. A 'class' thing was certainly linked with the fight he had to get *The Railway Children* (1970) and *Tales of Beatrix Potter* (1971) past board members to whom the books they were based on represented secure-to-cosy, middle-class childhoods which they had not shared and which, more to the point, they suspected the majority of film-goers no longer recognized. The box-office proved them wrong. Both films were commercial successes, the former getting its cost back in Britain alone, and each represented an 'annuity' film for every future generation of children reaching cinema-going age. Disney would have seen what good bets they were: Disney had tried to get hold of the Beatrix Potter stories for years, and had failed. But perhaps the main error Forbes made in the eyes of board members was not finding a bread-and-butter genre of film which could be guaranteed to pay the studio rent. A horror series such as Hammer Films specialized in, or a *Carry On* type of comedy cycle, would have kept the cash flowing. But of course such series need time, luck and, above all, public familiarity with a company product or a team of comics if they are to repay their makers continuously. Forbes didn't have the time – and his luck was running out.

He put into production *The Breaking of Bumbo*, Andrew Sinclair's satirical attack on military caste and social class, entrusting its direction to the author – he had promised to give new talent a chance, remembering his own hard struggle to succeed against apathy and active antagonism. Woodfall Films had made one attempt to film the 1959 novel, which had been inspired 'by the same disenchantment with élitist attitudes that also produced

Look Back in Anger and *Room at the Top*,'[1] but it had come to nothing, because there was not sufficient intervening time to allow the 'youthful follies' of the Suez War generation to have turned into the 'camp amusements' of the 'Swinging Britain' one. It was neither 'period' nor modern. Whether Sinclair found a viable solution when he filmed it has yet to be discovered, for after one or two sneak previews the film was put back in the cans and has not to date been theatrically released in Britain. (Sinclair went on to make the film version of *Under Milk Wood* with relief and obvious relish; it was for an independent company part-financed by the N.F.F.C., not part of the Elstree programme, and he shot it all on location, as he would have preferred to do *The Breaking of Bumbo* if the need to keep the studio operating hadn't taken priority.) Another film, a period romance called *A Fine and Private Place*, got mired down by excessively bad weather on location in Cornwall and Forbes abandoned it after a gallant but financially taxing rescue-operation with a second film unit. Then there was the affair of *Forbush and the Penguins* (1971) . . .

The National Film Finance Corporation had had its financial life extended till the end of 1980 by Parliamentary legislation announced in August 1969 (and enacted in May 1970), and was thus able to resume advancing loans to film-makers from a replenished purse of £5,000,000. Its report for the year ending 31 March, 1971,[2] stated that since it became known in the industry that the N.F.F.C. was 'back in business' it had received 'approximately 200 projects – in various stages of development – for consideration,' a startling contrast to the dribble of subjects that had trickled in seeking assistance in the years of dollar plenty. It was stark evidence of how ruthlessly selective the Americans had now become in deciding which British films to finance with their companies' hard-pressed (and in some cases pawned) assets after their own experience with ruinously expensive pictures and clogged inventories. Of the forty-five British first or co-features

[1] Andrew Sinclair, *The Breaking of Bumbo* (Penguin Books, 1970), p. 3.
[2] N.F.F.C.: Annual Report for the year ending 31 March, 1970. (H.M.S.O. Cmnd. 4402).

shown on the two main circuits in 1969, the Americans financed wholly or partly 78 per cent – the N.F.F.C. 2 per cent – and though this was still high, it showed a decrease on the previous year and 'the proportion will diminish still further in respect of the calendar year 1970,' added the Report. It concluded with some words of pious justification. 'In its report for the year to March 1966, the (N.F.F.C.) pointed out that there was no assurance that the U.S. distributors would continue to finance British films on the large scale then obtaining; the events of the past months have shown this warning to have been justified.'

The N.F.F.C. then singled out for special mention one British project which it had viewed favourably enough to back with £200,000. This was *Forbush and the Penguins*, a comedy scripted by Anthony Shaffer, set partly in Antarctica and dealing with a young naturalist's devotion to the penguins there and to his girl-friend back home. The film was also financed by the E.M.I. set-up and by British Lion in shares believed equal to the N.F.F.C.'s – 'a departure from the traditional trade practices, under which the principal distributors do not normally finance each other's films . . . the (N.F.F.C.) is pleased to be participating in it.' This satisfaction scarcely lasted long. The film ran into difficulties that might have furnished material for an Ealing comedy. Part of the trouble was that the footage on the habits of the Antarctic penguins, shot by the Swedish director Arne Sucksdorff, simply did not cut smoothly into the human situation involving John Hurt and a young actress from whom much – too much, perhaps – was expected. Eventually Roy Boulting had to come to the rescue, and sequences directed by an American, Al Viola, were replaced not only by fresh material but also by a new leading lady, Hayley Mills. The film was not released till the end of 1971, when its box-office results were discouraging. Its final cost was considerable.

But the heaviest blow which Forbes suffered was in some ways the most personal. No film incurred so much criticism as 'the boss's own.' This was *The Raging Moon* (1970: U.S. title, *Long Ago Tomorrow*), a love story about a pair of wheelchair cripples played by Malcolm McDowell and Nanette Newman. The stoic response of the handicapped was what appealed to Forbes, as it had done in *The Whisperers* – could the relationship be made true and realistic without being sentimentalized? The practical advantages were that the studio labour force could be kept employed more cheaply than on any other film production, since neither Forbes nor Bruce Cohn Curtis, his producer, took a fee, and locations were picked to be as close as possible to his studio office.

All the same, it was asked how the 'boss' of a studio could afford to take the time off to make a film of his own. Inside the E.M.I. organization it was asked with a bitterness that reflected a growing discontent – or, rather, confusion – over what kind of films they should really be making. *The Raging Moon* only dramatized the split, already seen in some of the American companies, between the creative and financial sides of a film company. Remember, too, this was a situation that had conflict locked into it much more tightly than could ever have happened in America, where production, distribution and exhibition were specifically divorced from each other, or at least from forming an inseparable trinity as was the case in E.M.I. The battle ground was shrewdly picked by Forbes's critics, for any defence he made of the film, whose leading actress was his second wife, would be interpreted as sheer self-interest. (The reviews of Nanette Newman's performance subsequently showed how groundless was any snide insinuation of favouritism.) The strain was such that the film eventually had to be run in a private viewing-theatre in the presence of E.M.I.'s chairman, Sir Joseph Lockwood, and an invited audience of mostly young people. The reaction was overwhelmingly good. Dutiful words of praise now came forth from the E.M.I. offices, though some felt they were like the words of a man who congratulates a Channel swimmer on his efforts while holding his head under water.

In spite of this, the film received no official première and to this date has obtained no full circuit distribution. Even after the huge commercial success of Malcolm McDowell's next film, *A Clockwork Orange*, Forbes's film was not relaunched, in spite of an above-average number of excellent reviews and box-office returns in the small number of cinemas where it had been shown.

Nor was any attempt made to take advantage of the romantic taste that young film-goers were showing at the time of its release for the American-made *Love Story*: *The Raging Moon* anticipated this mood by several months. Forbes tried to make up for this by making 'personal appearances' and doing 'talk-ins' with cinema audiences, but he remained profoundly depressed by his inability to alter the traditional pattern of showing films which had defeated many a film-maker before him. Even inside the company he felt he had no leverage on the situation. Among the board members another contrast was making itself felt. This was the film programme being backed by Anglo-E.M.I., the wholly-owned subsidiary controlled by Nat Cohen, which had financed proven commercial hits like *Percy* (a penis-transplant comedy), *Get Carter* (a very brutal *Point Blank*-type story of a gangster's revenge), and the first of a farcical series starring the comedian Frankie Howerd. Though such films as these, with their emphasis on sex, violence and blue gags, ran counter to the intention of Forbes and Delfont to make 'family entertainment,' and in the case of *Get Carter* actually seemed to mock an early and much misconstrued statement Forbes had made about 'the pornography of violence,' their box-office success at the A.B.C. cinemas was noted enviably by executives who were finding that the 'official' production roster at Elstree was eating up the available funds and being slow to disgorge the expected profits.

THE GO-BETWEEN

Early in May 1970, with rumours sweeping through the industry that Forbes's departure was 'imminent,' he was asked if it was true that he had cancelled the film Joseph Losey was scheduled to direct – *The Go-Between*. 'Totally untrue,' he replied. 'We have simply had to be awfully careful about when we start shooting it. There's a sequence in the middle of the film where crops are harvested; and we have had to rent land in our location area and sow our own crops which, hopefully, we shall bring in with the picture this summer.' Actually, there was more faith at the time in the crops coming up than in the film getting made – or so at least the makers thought. But Forbes's firm declaration of intention had the effect of settling the issue – the picture went ahead. And if Forbes's programme had enabled only this film to be made it would have been accounted effort well spent.

The Go-Between (23 September, 1971) is to date probably Joseph Losey's best and most popular film. Popular in the sense of being readily understood: yielding its story directly, without confusion, yet incorporating a most subtle series of 'time changes' into its chronology of an Edwardian scandal in 1901 and its consequences fifty years later. Only a director totally confident of what he was doing would have risked introducing a 'flash forward' technique into a story otherwise so well furnished with temptations to tell it in an orthodox way. The scandal, naturally enough in a Losey film scripted by Harold Pinter, has its roots in class: the offence committed by the young, unmarried daughter of the manor who has an affair with a man 'beneath her,' aided by a small messenger boy – the 'go-between.' The present-day scenes of the 'go-between,' now a grown-up man returning to what is the scene of a moral crime he helped commit and himself suffered from, are at first cut like eye-blinks into the Edwardian story, then increased in number and duration until at the climax, when we see what the girl has become years after her lover's suicide, the present seems to rush forward and throw itself into the arms of the past. This superbly tempered moral refinement on Losey's previous use of temporal re-arrangement in *Accident* adds ironic intensity to a tale that might otherwise have moved in too measured a mood – though Losey, with Forbes's encouragement, used not Elgar but a traumatically strident orchestral score by Michel Legrand to set up the tragic dissonances of wasted lives.

The sense of superiority and privilege that Losey is politically opposed to once again supports and guides him unerringly; and in the guilty setting of deceitfulness, where the scandal going on in the woods and barns must remain unmentioned by the girl's suspicious parents, Pinter once again displays his uncanny skill at depicting people who use words to avoid commitment and conceal meaning. The story suits the talents of both men to convey an atmosphere of smothered anxiety. The lovers never once meet passionately in our sight, much less carnally, till the thunderous *flagrante delicto* scene at the end, but we read the indictment of their affair in the countenances of others, in pursed lips, hardening glances, discreet avoidances, chilly silences . . . Having to gauge the strength of disapproval in the reserve or resentment of people only indirectly involved gives the situation the force of an implosion.

The thematic connections with Losey's early work in England make it satisfying, too. For it is hypocrisy that *The Go-Between* explores through something as enjoyably commercial on the surface as a period love story. The county family pay lip service to ideals of love, marriage and responsibility which they do not hold intellectually at all, but only use emotionally to cling to their privileges. The deceit infects everyone and, as in *Accident*, people never learn their lesson till it is too late – and sometimes not then. Patterns repeat themselves, post-mortems are never held into the true reasons, but only to provide veiled excuses. The Losey-Pinter universe holds out no indulgence to its trapped characters, only sad inevitability.

With one sizeable reservation, the acting is flawless and some of it a revelation – particularly Edward Fox, brother of James, who was Losey's 'discovery' in *The Servant*, giving the girl's titled suitor a blend of that charm and breeding which seems to attract Losey and certainly explains why the English aristocracy exercise such a fatal spell in history. The exception is Julie Christie – a fatal shade too old for the role of the girl. Instead of the convincingly hot-blooded young lady who cannot be bent to her family's will, she sometimes suggests an ageing daughter who has to be married off – a very different kind of family problem. She draws the character well enough to carry the story, but one regrets that the girl in the film isn't quite enough of a well-born Lady to make a passion for an unpedigreed lover feel like an unspeakable transgression.

If *Accident* goes as deep into human motive as *The Go-Between*, the latter covers a broader area of human conduct, a wider social scene. 'More even than in his previous films,' Richard Roud wrote, 'Losey here achieves an almost palpable sense of reality which gives the moral force of the film a greater intensity because of the heightened contradiction between apparent surface and true object. You can feel the clothes, you can smell the heat; and because all these sensual details are so physically realized you end up hearing the unsaid, seeing the unseen.'[1]

Half the film's production cost of £500,000 was coming from M.G.M.; but Forbes and others felt a lack of enthusiasm for the film at Culver City, which strengthened when M.G.M. proposed opening it at cinemas in the Mid West and on the Coast. Losey and Forbes preferred the film to have its first exposure at the 1971 Cannes Film Festival, where they felt it would be well received and reap reviews of world-wide usefulness. To their astonishment a reply came from M.G.M. that *they* had not much faith in film festivals as launching-platforms, and in any case doubted if Losey's name would have more effect there than in Chicago or Los Angeles! It was intimated to Forbes that if E.M.I. were unhappy, it was quite possible to do a deal that would let the British company handle the film themselves. Shortly before Cannes, therefore, Columbia Pictures acquired M.G.M.'s participation interest in *The Go-Between*. The film went on to win the Festival's main prize. Everyone agreed that M.G.M. had behaved very correctly in not seeking to sell their share in a film they didn't want for more than they had been prepared to invest in it. The old-time movie moguls of Hollywood might not have been so liberally disposed – but then they might have waited till after the prize-giving before divesting themselves of the movie.

Forbes was no longer head of Elstree when the film won. Early in February 1971, addressing an industry banquet, he quoted Samuel Johnson's remark that 'when a man knows he is to be hanged in a fortnight, it concentrates his mind wonderfully.' As a forecast of the time left to him, it was not far out. He resigned on 25 March, 1971. It was announced that he would not be replaced, but E.M.I. planned to make its film-making programme at Elstree the responsibility of Nat Cohen. Cohen had been the name mentioned for the job a year earlier, when it was clear to

[1] Richard Roud, 'Going Between', *Sight and Sound* (Summer 1971), Vol. 40, No. 3, p. 159.

some observers that E.M.I. would have to stick to a production programme with which some important executives were out of sympathy, or suspend production and have a radical re-think about the kind of films it wanted to make and show.

Forbes had attempted much during his two years – too much, said some people, who would have counselled fewer films more adroitly aimed at contemporary tastes. But the system inside which he had agreed to work was against this. He was obliged to keep a studio open, working, and profitable at a time when hardly any studio in the world was achieving this by film-making alone. He had launched a programme on a market which was falling, when confidence and finance were hard to come by – and audiences were even harder. He had introduced some new talent, backed a lot of good talent, made some successful films and one very fine one – and he had kept faith with studio employees and with himself. But such virtues did not ensure success any longer. What did, it was hard for anyone to say – even people better placed than Forbes were finding that out. Moreover, to have 'the system' against him at the same time meant fighting on a second front in the board-room with energy that was needed on the home front. More spectacular film programmes had been launched by the Americans in Britain: earlier chapters have examined them and recorded the spectacular losses some of them made, too. By their standards, Forbes's programme bears the marks of cautious insularity; but then by their international standards his budget was parochial and had to be frugally spread out. If he needed anything, it was above all luck – the kind of luck that had helped to make United Artists a rich and powerful company in Britain early in the 1960s. He did not get it. But then luck was a commodity in desperately short supply for the whole British film industry as it faced the grim prospect of the 1970s.

Chapter Twenty: *Why did it happen? Where did it go?*

Films can't live in a vacuum: they relate to the tempo of the times, the postures of today.
Jack Valenti, President of the Motion Picture Association
of America

The British film industry entered the 1970s not looking nearly so bankrupt, on paper, as the Hollywood film industry did – yet feeling altogether sorrier for itself. This is perhaps a characteristic of kept women everywhere: they resent the sudden impoverishment of their benefactor as a personal slur on their own worthiness. Calamity brought with it a sense of betrayal: it was a time for reproaches as well as regrets.

Yet it should have been obvious to anyone – and indeed it was to many, who are on record as saying so – that the Americans would not go on indefinitely doling out the money for film-making in a foreign country once they started getting poor value for it in return. It shows the extent to which the majority of British film-makers were so protected from reality that, when the crisis came, they behaved as if it was the last event they expected to see in their crystals. The hurt sounds coming from Hollywood should have alerted them to the fact that even at home the Americans had scarcely enough money in the bank to pay their bills and continue in business. For the truth is that just as their British-made films were, for the most part, being spectacularly unsuccessful in the United States, the American film companies, through their own profligacy, were running into serious economic difficulties that threatened to engulf them. In 1969–70 it really looked as if Hollywood would go corporately bust, so vast was the debt that the 'majors' had piled up in the last year or two of the 1960s, when they had indulged in an orgy of over-production and over-spending.

It was estimated in 1969 that the American film industry had an inventory of movies awaiting release – and meanwhile piling up huge bank-charges that could outrun their projected rentals even before they were released – which totalled an investment value of $1,250,000,000. Virtually every company was affected, save Disney and Universal. In 1969 M.G.M. had a loss of $35 million; Fox, a loss of $36,800,000 in 1969 and $77,400,000 in 1970; Warners, a loss of $52 million in 1969; and even United Artists, a loss of $45 million in 1970.[1] Paramount, whose company accounts for 1966–9 have not been made available, still had an operating loss of $22 million in 1971, the very year when the company actually had the huge grosses of *Love Story*, pulling in $19,300,000, to replenish the kitty – so the extent of its losses can only be guessed at. It was widely reported that Paramount alone in 1969 had $120 million tied up in unreleased films and Fox over $200 million. With such frightening sums to do at home, it was small wonder that Hollywood did not harken to the cries of pain from Britons feeling the squeeze in the industry that had once been humming. Part of Hollywood's conspicuous expenditure at home had been encouraged by the presence of the very conglomerates which had bought control of some of the old companies, like Warners, United Artists and Paramount. They fed in too rich a supply of new cash too quickly. In attempting to enter the so-called 'leisure-time field,' the conglomerates miscalculated disastrously. They purchased some two cents' worth in the 'leisure-time dollar' and proceeded to over-invest capital by making immensely expensive films. Traditionally, the American film industry counted itself fortunate if it got a 20 per cent return on its risk money and prudently expected to get only 15 per cent; but in 1968–9, with the willing approval of their conglomerate owners, they borrowed lavishly to create profits through some of the most expensive motion pictures that have ever been made – and then found that the profits showed no sign of materializing. Even companies with no conglomerate overlords to open their bank accounts to them were lured into the trap by a belief that a film like *The Sound of Music*, which was producing receipts of nearly $100 million in 1968–9, had located a new mother lode in film-going audiences; and they sank fortunes into creating

[1] Figures supplied by *The Economist*.

conspicuous 'blockbusters': *Hello, Dolly!, Doctor Dolittle, Star!, Catch-22, Ryan's Daughter, Darling Lili*. Not one of these was budgeted at less than $10 million; at least two rose to around the $15 million mark; and three went over the $20 million. Most films enter into profit when their box-office gross reaches two-and-a-half times their negative cost: for blockbusters like the above, the multiplier is slightly less. Even so, it can be appreciated what huge grosses were essential if everyone was to come out of it smiling with at least the fare home.

While most of these expensive items were American made, a clutch of films that the American majors had financed in Britain contributed their share to the costly roster. Among them were: *The Battle of Britain* (United Artists: 1969), estimated to have cost a reported $12 million, which failed to make any commensurate impact in America despite a skilful and extensive publicity build-up; *Goodbye, Mr Chips* (M.G.M.: 1969), an inflated musical re-make of the 1939 film, which was eventually drastically shortened in its American play-off to try to restore its box-office fortunes; *Cromwell* (Columbia: 1970), which cost over $8 million and proved a very hang-fire spectacular; *Alfred the Great* (M.G.M.: 1970), intended as a 'youth epic,' but ultimately failing to appeal to any audience on a sufficiently epic scale: a wit said that omitting the burning of the cakes hadn't stopped the film-makers burning their fingers. The smell of burnt fingers was predominant in 1970.

All these films, and more, had been vastly more expensive than they had any warrant to be; but they had been caught up on the production escalator, operating in Britain in the last few years of the 1960s boom, which dragged films up to and past the floor where their makers should have prudently called a halt or got off.

David Picker, speaking shortly after the crisis had peaked, forcing one Hollywood company after another into savage economy cut-backs, write-downs, write-offs, asset-sales and budgetary resolutions of draconian grimness, analysed the situation in Britain in a way which suggested that the Americans had transferred their vices there as well as their virtues. 'United Artists got there first and got ahead,' recalled Picker, who, in the late 1960s, had become president of United Artists. 'But after a while everybody else finds out what you're doing – what you're making. The other companies realize they're missing a good thing. As competition starts, the profit percentages paid to film-makers rise, so does the price of the picture. There was a slow escalation at first of the rising price-scale: we simply weren't alone any more. Then it gets to be a case of aggravated bidding between companies for properties, directors, stars, writers, photographers, designers . . . The Hollywood syndrome starts to take place: not "What is the movie I'm making," but "What is the *deal* I'm doing?" From being just aggravated, it becomes hysterical . . . That's when the cost kills you.' Hollywood, in short, had exported its own inflationary drives to Britain and now found itself going horrifyingly deep into debt at home and abroad. With awesome suddenness, there was no more production coin available for spending at home, so the first move was to reduce the flow of cash abroad. If it was not possible to increase one's profits, then one cut out one's risks. The British pictures had become risks – they were cut out.

'SWINGING AMERICA'

But it might be objected that the American-made movies, some of which have been named, constituted risks, too – and even bigger risks at the price they cost. Unfortunately, charity is not the only thing that begins at home. Salvation starts there, too, slightly earlier. Hollywood saved herself by her own energies, ruthless and autocratic though they were, but her very example doomed Britain. The American film industry emerged from the crisis determined not to repeat some of the mistakes that had been made in producing films in Britain. Shortage of cash at a crucial moment is not the only reason why the Americans pulled out of Britain. The longer-term answer lies deeper. The economic crisis only dramatically precipitated a change that was already in the making, not only in the film industry, but also in society.

What we find if we look at the social history of the United States in the last half of the 1960s is the enormous acceleration in change of every description, producing a society that, in the extremes and variety of phenomena it threw up, seemed far more revolutionary and all-involving than anywhere else outside America. From 1964 onwards, the U.S.A. began moving into what sociology would term 'a late sensate period' with an ever-increasing emphasis on the release of feeling and the tasting of experience: the same sense of 'unleashing' was perceptible there as Britain had already been experiencing from the beginning of the 1960s. It took the same form, too: a revolution in *mores* and a slow and then accelerating erosion of morals. The demise of puritanism began to be hailed as within sight in America from the mid-1960s, as the legal guide-lines for what was tasteless or obscene were rendered ever more arguable and vague by court decisions or community practices. Pleasure became something regarded as a right, not a rarity – and never as a taboo, as the proselytizers for the 'new freedoms' claimed that they would humanize and improve life, not degrade and debase it. It was undoubtedly something of this pent-up excitement that the new films from Britain released or at least answered, especially among the young – Tom Jones, the Bonds, the Beatles, the whole 'Swinging Britain' phenomenon – and they managed to do so because at this very same time the American cinema, which still meant largely the Hollywood-based cinema, could not begin to compete with them in candour of thought, speech, deed, or even technical novelty. The Hollywood cinema, up to the end of 1965, was still clamped rigidly between the hypocrisies of the Production Code and the ratings administration on the one hand and, on the other, the pressure-groups, secular and religious, who were still trying to impose a consensus attitude on a society that was everywhere disintegrating into a sensation-seeking culture.

The changing mood of America was visible everywhere except in the home-produced movies. Anyone studying the film-industry periodical *Variety* in, say, 1964–5 will be amazed by the swelling civic indignation – sometimes genuine, sometimes fomented – engendered by American films that dared deviate from a restrictive set of thou-shalt-nots that the Production Code represented. Films like *The Carpetbaggers*, whose only sin lay in its verbal vulgarities, and Billy Wilder's *Kiss Me, Stupid*, an inept sex comedy, were blasted as patently indecent, if not nearly obscene, and sometimes branded by the Legion of Decency with a C. for Condemned for Roman Catholic eyes. Foreign – i.e. imported – films were less subject to this; even so, some Hollywood majors released dubious imports without their familiar company trade-mark on them. The thinking was that, as the films were of minority appeal, the moralists gave a grudging, 'All right, but keep your hands off the masses' to their distributors. The success of the British-made movies from *Tom Jones* on would probably have changed this perilous tolerance, for, though technically 'foreign,' they offered none of the barriers to widespread distri-bution, such as a foreign language, and they presented American film-goers with the novelties of randy dialogue, uninhibited behaviour, permissive themes and visually 'with-it' experience. But before these imports could rouse the local vigilantes, the latter took a knock, from which they never recovered, over a film called *The Pawnbroker* (1965), directed by Sidney Lumet for United Artists, but distributed for reasons of commercial prudence by the latter's releasing company headed by Ilya Lopert, in which a black prostitute momentarily exposed her bare breasts. This scene, entirely innocent in intention, provoked a major clash between the Code Administration, which had approved it, and the Legion of Decency, which declared it would 'open the gates to a host of unscrupulous operators.'[1] In the long run the Legion was probably right: in the short run, which was what mattered, it unwisely forced a showdown at a moment when the permissive temper of the times was against it. Since the Production Code had failed to protect Hollywood from moral censorship, and even commercial boycott, and since the Courts were now handing down emboldening liberal verdicts, Hollywood embarked on a rewrite of the Code to bring it into line with present-day social realities. This took place in 1965. The new freedoms won for film-makers were rapidly confirmed by the salty dialogue of *Who's Afraid of Virginia Woolf?* directed by Mike Nichols for Warners in 1966. But this film simply transferred the New York

[1] *Variety*, 4 April, 1965.

stage's freedom of speech on to the screen: not till the late summer of 1967 did *Bonnie and Clyde* serve notice of a new kind of cinema in the making – one that deserved to be called 'American,' not merely 'Hollywood.'

'The most important fact about the screen in 1967,' said *Time*, 'is that Hollywood has at long last become part of what the French film journal, *Cahiers du Cinema*, calls "the furious spring-time of world cinema" and is producing a new kind of movie.'[1] *Bonnie and Clyde* was directed by Arthur Penn from a screenplay by Benton and Newman, two writers who had offered it first to Truffaut, and harkened to his advice, and subsequently to Godard. It thus derived from the same source as had refreshed the British cinema; and it had nothing in common with the orthodoxly constructed, moralizing Hollywood movies of the earlier years of the decade. By linking the violence of its characters to the present day, even as *Tom Jones* had done in the matter of sex and licence, and by telling its story with the same fluency and disregard of time and sequence as the British and French films had done, it gave American film-goers the sensation of seeing a home-produced film picture their society in an exciting, modern, morally ambiguous but emotionally involving way. The camera turned an eye on life and heightened it. The film had a feeling of youth, novelty and iconoclasm. And it would scarcely be overstating it to say that, from this moment on, their own cinema became a more fascinating experience for the American film-goers because it began to mirror (and sometimes to distort) a more immediate and all-involving society than the British one. Up to then the British cinema had been selling the sensations of its own social revolution to America: from then on, the American film-goers had the experience of their own social revolution to contend with, as well as their native cinema to encapsulate and sometimes encourage it. From 1967 we feel 'the New American Cinema,' as it was dubbed, regaining its international role, showing the world what was happening inside America and doing so now with the sophisticated and permissive grammar of world cinema, not Hollywood's old enforced euphemisms. And it was at this very

[1] *Time*, 8 December 1967.

moment, 1966–7, when the constraints on their own screen were loosening, that the Hollywood majors chose to invest most heavily in film production in Britain. They sent their money abroad just when their own audiences were discovering the excitements of home.

With the exception of such international subjects as the Bond adventures, John Woolf's production of the hit musical *Oliver!* and Stanley Kubrick's *2001: A Space Odyssey*, hardly any film made in Britain from 1967 till the decade's end appealed to American audiences on the same scale as such indigenous successes as, say, *In the Heat of the Night* (1967), or *The Graduate* (1968), or *Easy Rider* (1969).[1] From then on the Americans found their own social phenomena more engrossing. Racial tensions, black militancy, the sex fantasies of adolescents on and off campus, or middle-ageing swingers in the exurban belts, drug experience, the search for self through nomadic hippiedom, revolution in the universities, violence in the big cities, the counter-culture's epiphenomena, the 'nationhood' of rock concerts: to all these indigenous themes the American cinema now gave emphasis and interest. It was a market it knew – or thought it did – and there was dramatic proof of how lucrative it could be if 'sold' the right product. *Easy Rider* cost $500,000 and made $50 million. *The Graduate* cost under $2,500,000 and made over $40 million. *Woodstock* cost Warners $100,000 to film the rock concert, another $900,000 to produce a film from 120 hours of footage, and a final million dollars to purchase music rights: within a year the film had grossed $14 million.[2] The industry was right when it believed that huge grosses could still be made from movies: where it made its error was in forgetting that such figures are even more massive because the initial outlay was so small – it was when the films' budgets ran off to the moon a year or so later that the crisis came.

[1] One exception was the Sidney Poitier vehicle *To Sir With Love*, a black teacher's experiences in London slumland, which did so unexpectedly well in America that Columbia did market research to find out why people had gone to it.

[2] Source: *Variety*. All figures are North American grosses.

In 1967, moreover, production at three American majors, at least, was in the hands of men in their thirties: David Picker (thirty-six) at United Artists, Robert Evans (thirty-seven) at Paramount, Richard Zanuck (thirty-four) at 20th Century-Fox. Besides the attraction they must have felt of playing the old-time Hollywood mogul in a new-style industry, such men were naturally turned on by what the largest part of their own mass audience – the kids – found engrossing. This was definitely not films from Britain: such was plain as one picture after another, from the Universal production programme in Britain, or the Paramount one, or the United Artists one, failed to do the expected business in the United States. All this pushed them even more resolutely towards indigenously American themes. Of course, mistakes were made. Scarcely any of the 'trends' the American companies latched on to produced more than one or two box-office fortunes – but one fortune was often enough! They were aimed at the audience whose attention span was short and fickle and whose sense of being exploited was often naggingly sharp and instinctive. Fifteen so-called 'youth revolt' movies were released in 1969: only *Woodstock* and *Getting Straight* pulled through the casualties. The 'road' films, the 'now' films, the 'under $2 million' films were all quickly abandoned recipes for success; and the only trend, it was concluded, was no trend at all. Yet there was a demonstrably giant audience for explicitly American movies; and one must not forget such 'straight' productions as *Airport, Patton: Lust for Glory, Butch Cassidy and the Sundance Kid, Love Story*, all with strong American themes or overlay, and with just enough chauvinism or permissiveness (*Patton*'s flag-waving, *Love Story*'s semi-permissiveness) to give middle-aged 'squares' a taste of novelty without turning off the kids. Compared with such movies, the British product now arriving in the United States seemed inbred, effete, remote. It was also – much of it – skilful, well-crafted, meaningful. But these considerations weren't inside the heads of its potential audience. What *was* there, on the contrary, was the American experience which their own films now represented – and not just their films. New directors emerged swiftly, and established ones caught up

P

quickly with the new subjects: Penn, Altman, Peckinpah, Nichols, Coppola. And new stars to fit the subjects: Gould, Nicholson, Sutherland, Hoffman, Voight, Dunaway, Redford, Benjamin. They appeared almost as promptly on the American scene as their British counterparts had done in the early 1960s on *their* screen; and they helped transfuse through the films what was happening in the heads of millions of Americans. And so long as American film companies believed in the vitality of their home market, their old love back in Britain would take second place – in fact it soon did not occupy even that ranking. By 1973 the American companies were tending to invest their money in Italy or France. These two countries represented about 27 per cent of all European revenues to the major American distributors in 1972: Britain represented only 8 per cent.[1] Both Italy and France had a home market capable of showing a decent and sometimes spectacular return on 'domestic' pictures underwritten by the Americans, which was an assurance that Britain's home market continued to give less and less, and it was figured that, in return for some additional production coin, the 'domestic' picture could be made internationally acceptable, too. So long as all these factors were uppermost in Hollywood's thinking – and much of the 'New American Cinema's' thinking gravitated back to Hollywood despite their films being made elsewhere – then the British could whistle 'Do not desert me, O my darling' for as long as they had breath . . .

VICES AND TEMPTATIONS

The feelings of many of the American film-makers still resident in Britain in the early 1970s were summed up by one who had been among the most successful in the mid-1960s. 'It is a low profile country now,' Walter Shenson said. 'Still a lovely place to live, no longer any place for a film-maker to work. For an American, it is impossible to make a film reflecting the British scene – there just *is* no scene today. This place no longer makes

[1] Source: Motion Picture Export Association report for the first quarter of 1973.

news that is of interest to the world. When society is under stress or going through change, the outlines of what's happening are unfamiliar and exciting and the artists are under pressure to react to it all. When we are over-familiar with what has been happening, all that is left is a hangover.'

Christopher Booker expressed much the same disenchantment at the end of *The Neophiliacs*, blaming it on 'the power of fantasy to lead men away from reality' and seeing in the 'climate of aftermath, disillusionment, exhaustion, even of reaction,' which was characteristic of Britain as the 1960s passed into the 1970s, all the stigmata of a society that was stunned by the amount of experience it had been through and which was now striving to adjust to a new kind of reality. The film industry was in poor shape to help formulate what kind of reality this should be. Judged by output, the sheer number of films produced in Britain in the early 1970s did not noticeably diminish: the quantity remained about seventy a year – what it had been at the height of the boom. But the volume of finance this represented fell off disastrously: by 1972 it was estimated that financial investment in the production side of the industry was down to 65 per cent of what it had been in 1968, the peak year of the previous decade. In some cases the American majors simply stopped making films for a year or two: in others, they limited output to two or three movies a year, smaller and rather more carefully budgeted than the previous spendthrift climate had accustomed them or their British talent to accepting. The slack was taken up by smaller companies doing formula pictures; by industrial corporations, like General Electric, Brut, Quaker Oats, which had decided to invest, sometimes for fiscal advantage, in film-making; by organizations run by producer-packagers which pre-sold the idea of a film, its director and stars, throughout some sixty to seventy territories in the world, obtained advance guarantees from distributors or exhibitors in each territory, discounted these with a bank and used the money to produce the picture: an edge-of-the-seat operation, at least one of which foundered badly, leaving bankers even more wary. By 1971–2, the native British film industry was grasping at television to save it, ripping off the serials so popular on the small box and turning them into pallid, stereotyped pop entertainment on the large screen; a few made surprisingly large amounts of domestic cash, then the public got tired, and this paltry parasitic sub-industry withered away.

The retreat of American confidence and capital hit the established talents hard. With the withdrawal of Richard Burton from the cast of *Laughter in the Dark* (1969) – he was replaced by Nicol Williamson – Tony Richardson had to surrender his percentage share in *Tom Jones* in order to be re-financed by United Artists: after splitting his share with partners and associates, he had ended up with 'about 10 per cent.' The film, already expensive because of money laid out by the previous owners of the Nabokov property, failed to make money. *Ned Kelly* (1970) was hardly more successful, though it cost very little money – 'United Artists were nervous of me,' Richardson said later, 'and quite rightly' – and its director gallantly accepted the blame for Mick Jagger's poor showing as an almost puny outback bandit. 'I didn't breathe life into him,' said Richardson. From this débâcle, Richardson picked himself up in one unexpectedly vital effort and made a version of *Hamlet* (1970) inside two weeks by shooting it in the inky cavern of the Round House, a former locomotive shed turned theatre, for only $350,000, with the actors' faces manoeuvring for a place in the lens of Gerry Fisher's colour camera and conveying the sense of currents and eddies in the charged atmosphere of the otherwise black void in which they were marooned. It was a *tour de force* – but not the work to restore box-office confidence in its author, who tried and failed to find backing for *I, Claudius*. Dick Lester's last United Artists film in the 1960s was *The Bed-Sitting-Room* (1970), a rather dated critique of 'civilized' society whose fragmented elements go on repeating their demented antics in a post-nuclear wasteland. But the goonery no longer seemed fresh or even pertinent: and the film's American sales slogan, 'We've got a bomb on our hands,' proved sadly apt.[1] Lester tried unsuccessfully to set up several projects – a film about race tensions in a British Cabinet, a version of the first of the *Flashman* novels – but could not get backing. Early in 1971 he commented, 'One of

---

[1] 'Bomb' is American show-business slang for a disaster.

the pictures I should have been doing started out at $2 million and I was told by the distributor – this was about two years ago – that, "All right, If you want to keep making these low-budget pictures we'll accept it for a while, but it isn't the kind of thing we want." By the time I'd got it prepared and cast, they were saying, "Look, I'm sorry, we just don't have the money any-more".' Even directors with an international success to their credit found it difficult to get financed. John Schlesinger, after the profit and acclaim of *Midnight Cowboy*, managed with difficulty to beat the squeeze and set up *Sunday, Bloody Sunday* (1971) for United Artists. Scripted by Penelope Gilliatt, produced by Joseph Janni, this above all other turn-of the decade films evoked the 'state of change' in the London sliding from its 'swinging' euphoria into its 'hang-over' period – from 'What's it all about?' to 'What will you settle for?' It caught the insecure, self-questioning essence of the 1970s just as *Darling* had embodied the mood of aggressive self-advancement of the 1960s. But caught in that vice of distri-bution, where a film must make it big or not at all, it had one successful London exposure, then tended to drop out of sight. Schlesinger could not raise the money for his next project, *Hadrian VII.* 'Success,' he said, 'in itself makes problems. You have to keep up, or try to keep up, to the standards you have established, or value. This on its own is a problem and on top of that you still have the money difficulty . . . The only weapons you have are your own persistence and passion.' Joseph Janni had spent the time Schlesinger was in America directing *Midnight Cowboy*, by making an Anglo-Italian co-production, *In Search of Gregory* (1970), with Julie Christie, which turned out a vacuum-packed fantasy suffering the worst vices of 'international' movies – i.e. little discernible nationality. Janni, with the rueful candour which distinguishes him from most producers, admitted that he had been seduced by the new Anglo-Italian co-production treaty into showing that he could do as well at home, in his native Italy, as he had done abroad. After *Sunday, Bloody Sunday*, he returned to the scenes of his South London success in *Poor Cow* with the film *Made*, and with the same star, Carol White, tried to mate the social problems of an unmarried mother with the new phenomenon of a Jesus Freak pop star who uses reality for source-material. But there was a sense of two themes uneasily meeting across a decade that had made us over-familiar with the one and already weary of the other. The film was poorly received.

Joseph Losey's next two films, *The Assassination of Trotsky* (1972) and *A Doll's House* (1973) were international co-productions made outside Britain: in 1973 he was still trying to raise money for Pinter's screenplay of *A la recherche du temps perdu*. Bryan Forbes, since leaving Elstree, had made two television programmes, one of them a masterly and loving study of Dame Edith Evans, but he had not found a film he wanted to direct. Four years went by between Karel Reisz's *Isadora* and his going to New York in 1973 to direct *The Gambler*; and seven years elapsed between Jack Clayton's last film and his starting to shoot *The Great Gatsby* in 1973.

Such lengthy gaps underline one of the worst vices of British film-makers: their relative paucity of output. By temperament, as well as the proximity of the London theatre, British directors have means of waiting until the right film comes along that are denied to their Hollywood counterparts: it may help them keep their artistic integrity, but I doubt if it has benefited the film industry. A Michael Winner will always be working, but more fastidious talents have been simply too choosy about what they did – even allowing for an artist's preferences and unforeseen reverses in setting up subjects. Richardson has his critics: but say what one likes about the varying quality of his films, in terms of quantity he used his 'blank cheque' to the limits of credit (and over the limits in the end), and the result is an *oeuvre* whose interest will increase when time adds its perspective and subtracts the parochialism of native detractors. As for Woodfall Films, it lent its name and backing to many other talents besides its partners. British film-makers work in an industry bereft of the traditions and machinery – even of the restlessness – that spur their American counterparts to sustained output. Pressures build up on American directors – particularly successful ones – to commit themselves to their next film even before their last one is finished. A man who is not working, or at least making deals, is felt to be somehow going against the grain of the industry. In England, on the other hand, it is too easy to sit back and be choosy in a gentlemanly way. The pressures in America can be terrifyingly destructive: but the sheer concentration of the film-making apparatus, financial and technical, and the existence of the resilient *genre* films, have sustained more talents than they have destroyed. Here in Britain we lack both concentration of means of production and tradition in the end-products. Instead of setting firmly in a production alloy, the British talent has dispersed itself into the efforts of individual craftsmen. Fine craftsmanship is something the Americans know the best British film-makers will always be prepared to give them – but what else? Craftsmanship by itself can become a vice. The temptation is to reduce output and go for the masterpiece, instead of the standard article. Fine, if the aim is achieved: but the cost may be high in the contribution made to a resilient industry and even to a creative artist. 'Bracing up to the anguish of committing oneself to a subject before the greater anguish of making it,' as David Robinson wrote of one of the directors in this book, 'can lead to an extruded artistry that is meagre in quantity and not always flawless in quality.'[1]

What one feels throughout the middle years of the decade under review is the sheer hustle of the Americans, who put their dollars so lavishly, and often so profitably, into British pictures. They brought with them something of the ethos they lived, breathed and worked in at home: a vital, brash, extravagant, riskier style than the more cautious, not to say lethargic, mood that prevails in Britain. Of course, they also brought with them the confidence that comes from having a world market as well as full purses. The British have traditionally started off cutting corners when it came to fitting films to markets – or else, as the Rank Organization did when it embarked on an imperialist programme to sell British films to the world, allowed far too much cloth for the customer's needs, and cut it in a style he won't wear.

The central weakness of the British film industry was the fact that the home market simply would not support a film industry. It was not big enough to give producers the reassurance of seeing

[1] *The Financial Times*, 17 October, 1967.

their money back with a profit, unless they were exceptionally cautious or lucky. And with the current return on a film inside Britain down to an average £100,000 – *if the film does well* – small wonder that British film-makers could rarely muster the reserve of nerve or capital that came naturally to American distributors well entrenched throughout the world markets. What the Americans did in the 1960s was to open those markets to the so-called British films in which they had invested. And for a time they did well – very well.

But if the Americans put financial muscle into their production in Britain, they did not hesitate to pull it – at precisely the time when the British independents were weak and growing weaker. The production crisis of 1963–4 – which was really an exhibition crisis – dealt a blow to the confidence of independent British film-makers from which they never recovered. The inability to get the films they had made shown, or to raise cash to make new films, sapped their financial resources as well as their nerve. It was easier afterwards to sit on one's assets, assuming one had any, than to deploy them with the odds so heavily against success. The American majors, with their tied relationships to the cinema circuits, had no such worries, or, in the case of individual films they financed that suffered from lack of exhibition outlets, they were well able to write them off. During the same part of the decade a large part of the exhibition side of the industry was physically dismantled by shutting down cinemas no longer deemed profitable. Probably there were sound economic reasons for the closures: but the result was that, while talk continued of setting up a 'third circuit' of cinemas available to independent film-makers, there simply was not capacity left in terms of bricks and mortar to bring this about after 1965 – without dispossessing the major circuits of their own profitable cinemas. This recommendation the Monopolies Commission report conspicuously failed to make in 1966. The circuits were left in possession of their cinemas; and beyond making minimal adjustments, they did nothing to break the rigid pattern of exhibition until relatively recent years, when the continued decline in the size of the audience that still went to the movies compelled them to physically remodel their cinemas, twinning and tripling them as catchment areas for the dwindling number of patrons, and at the same time fragmenting the monolithic national play-off of only a couple of new films weekly so as to give much greater variety to programmes. This 'floating release,' as it was called, came too late to help the independent film-makers with films that were hard to market – or American majors with similar movies, for that matter.

The major blot on the era is that the wealthy cinema-owners in Britain, left in charge of production, distribution and exhibition, did relatively little except serve their own interests and their shareholders. The Rank Organization made the attempt, in consortiums with the A.F.M. group and the N.F.F.C. co-financing deal, but their enthusiasm waned. The E.M.I. take-over of Associated British Picture Corporation and the A.B.C. cinemas raised hopes: but the production programme embarked on was not accompanied by any timely reorganization of the profitable exhibition outlets and seemed, in any case, undertaken mainly to keep the studios open. Though admissions fell in Britain from nearly 900 million a year in 1961 to just under 215 million in 1969 and the numbers of cinemas fell from 2,711 to 1,581 over the same period, the average price of a cinema seat precisely doubled in those nine years. Whoever had to suffer, it was not the exhibitors.

'ART FOR ART'S SAKE,
MONEY FOR GAWD'S SAKE'

What other sources of finance, besides dollars, were open to British film-makers? Precious little private capital. London merchant banks had no traditional ties with the film industry. City bankers generally did not comprehend why films should cost so much: and they had no means of knowing what films were worth when they did get made. They had no means, even, of telling honest men from crooks. (One merchant bank during this period actually tried to recruit a film critic to sit on a sub-committee dealing with film investment and advise on the

'character' of independent producers, as well as their films: it was
thought the critic would be knowledgeable, but independent.
The critic declined.) Bankers wanted evidence of collateral, which
was just what independent film-makers did not have, save in rare
instances when they owned their backlog of movies. Producers
like the Woolf brothers who carried the expense of making *Room
at the Top* themselves – as John Woolf did later to the extent of
Oliver!'s first £250,000 – until they got a distributor's backing –
were, and are, rare birds in the movie industry. In part, the
Bryanston consortium was an attempt to seek in numbers a
financial bargaining power that the banks did not find impressive
when presented singly. Had Bryanston made *Tom Jones*, then, as
Max Setton said, the group would have been 'set for life.' As it
was, the Americans not only reaped the harvest of talent others
had sown, but saw what crops the soil could produce. After that,
American finance of the 100 per cent kind was a magnet that
inevitably drew British talent away from the weaker British
deal-makers. Allied Film Makers illustrated how perilously
balanced a group of producer-directors was: a single expensive
flop by one or more could turn them into another sort of hyphen-
ate – producer-bankrupts.

As for British Lion, its reconstituted state after 1964 showed
that, however films are made, it is not by committee. Individual
board-members did make successful films: they tended to be the
older, more cautious directors settling for safe subjects geared to
domestic tastes. *Morgan* is one of the few exceptions – a British-
Lion-financed film that found a wide market and struck a new
response from an international audience. But the men who ran
British Lion were well placed to know what assets were worth,
and how quickly they could be dissipated by a few poor judgments. In any case, they were stuck with keeping Shepperton
Studios open – and not being able to realize their potential for
property development so long as the National Film Finance
Corporation, the State's watchdog, refused to agree that the
studios could only be operated 'at a critical loss' or that there
were 'satisfactory alternative facilities' available. This the N.F.F.C.
refused to do – and respite did not come till November 1972,

when the N.F.F.C. agreed that a 'compromise' had to be found 'if the spirit of Mr Heath's assurance to Parliament (back in 1964) was to be preserved.'[1] At the time of writing, this 'compromise' takes the form of reducing the size of the studio and concentrating production on the remaining acreage. Meanwhile, British Lion itself has passed successively through the hands of two groups of financiers (in 1972 and 1973), neither of which has a previous history as film-makers.

The withdrawal of American finance occurred at the very worst time for the N.F.F.C. itself. For at the end of the 1960s it was operating production agreements on a *pari passu* basis – sharing in the first cash earnings – and the Film Act, 1970, had increased its borrowing powers to £5 million. Then came the crunch – the Government refused to pay more than £1 million from the State purse and the N.F.F.C. was required to raise £3 million from private investors. In short, it was the State's way of intimating its withdrawal from film financing. The City bankers had not been eager to invest in the film industry's boom years: it was like asking for a miracle now to beg cash for an industry that was giving up the ghost. By 1973 the consortium that John Terry had gallantly set up to facilitate this had raised only £750,000 – and it had required no fewer than ten groups in the private sector to dig into their pockets for that sum – a sum, moreover, that Hollywood, even in its own period of crisis five years earlier, had deemed to be a meagre budget *for one picture*. With £1,750,000 as its resources, the N.F.F.C. was now forced to go for what looked like commercial certainties: and if they failed, then it would have to close its doors, making private investors even more nervous of footing the bill for films 'for a very considerable time.'

During what the N.F.F.C. regarded as 'the good years' of the 1960s, it was used to investing between £1,500,000 and £2 million a year: in the year since March 1972 its investment totalled a frugal £350,000 spread over four films.

Despite the losses it incurred since 1949, it would have left the industry worse off if it had not existed. Up to 1970 it had made

[1] N.F.F.C. Report for the year ending 31 March, 1973, Cmnd. 5422.

loans totalling £27,500,000 to keep production going. But the odds were always stacked against it. It was an investment group, not a production company: hence it could not tie the talents that did make money for it to a multi-picture deal, or option their services, or hire them out to other companies. One good reason was that it might not have had the financial resources to put them to use again. And once the talents that the N.F.F.C. backed had made their breakthrough, they tended to gravitate away from it – to the Hollywood majors. And the N.F.F.C. might, or more usually might not, have the chance to invest in their success again.

The biggest set-back the N.F.F.C. suffered was in trying to control film-making costs – the fees paid to producers, directors, stars, etc. These were inflated as more and more American companies invested in the British film industry. The escalating effect helped to discourage private capital even more. At the height of the boom the average fee of £10,000 which a first-rate director or producer could have obtained a few years earlier from a film company had shot up to £50,000 – in some cases to over £100,000, or higher still with percentages. The N.F.F.C. could not possibly compete and was aware that any producers who came to it for finance were probably American 'rejects.' In short, the Americans encouraged financial unreality.

How important the box-office subsidy, the Eady Levy, was to American film-makers in Britain varied according to the type of films they made. To George H. Ornstein, of United Artists, it was not all that important. But then United Artists was a company with major international hits – the British box-office levy was nice to have, but not vital. John Van Eyssen, when he was Columbia's head of production in Britain, reckoned it mattered a lot in his company's decisions. A film made for 'local' appeal would be dependent on the British box-office almost 100 per cent – in which case the levy was life-blood, as it returned money direct to the producers at an early stage in the game. Of course, one had to be successful to qualify. If one was, one didn't need it. If one wasn't, one didn't get it. In this lay a 'Catch-22' situation for the independent British film-makers. What the levy did was make the rich man richer still. Successful American companies with tied relationships to the cinema circuits were in better shape to profit from the levy than their wholly British counterparts. So not only was the home market inadequate to give milk to keep the local producers happy, but also its very cream went to keep the foreigners fat.

Had the levy been apportioned on a less brutal basis than box-office success – and had the circuits agreed to give a wider play-off to risky subjects that needed special nursing – something might have been done to improve the independents' position. Nothing was.

But when considerations of art and cash have been reconciled with each other, the fact is inescapable that to operate film-making successfully as an industry one needs a temperament of a certain kind – a combination of experience and intuition that might be more prosaically called 'gambling.' One need not be a reckless gambler: more often than not, that way bankruptcy lies. But the willingness to risk putting one's money down after one has assessed the risks is perhaps the best *modus operandi* in a business that no sane economist would underwrite, in which only the prospect of colossal profit continues to tempt others. Many of the successful people in this study have this gambling streak in them, but they are more likely to have been American than British. Part of the satisfaction mentioned by directors who worked for American companies came from the lack of inter-ference they reported – at least while the film was in the making. Part of the frustration they experienced working for British distributors came from just the opposite experience. One out-standing exception was Anglo-Amalgamated, a British company not tied to the Americans, and significantly a one-man operation, which gambled on new talents and fresh subjects – and, more often than not, won. Where only two films out of seven are expected to make money, two to break even, and three to lose money, it is an industry for gamblers. It is not surprising if the Americans excelled in this, backed as they were by Hollywood tradition, financial skills, and a certain Jewish faith in the favourable disposition of providence.

TALENTS AND TRENDS

The nationality of a film industry, considered in its narrowest definition, does not really matter: 'nationality' is, in any case, something that gets harder to establish annually as multi-national talents combine to make movies. Thus xenophobia should not make us condemn the American investment in our films throughout the 1960s – though it certainly encouraged us in the vice of remittance-men everywhere, which is 'dependence.' The positive aspect is that American confidence lent the British industry drive and impetus and gave its film-makers a far wider creative horizon than anyone thought available in the previous decade. The fact that this horizon has once again contracted does not invalidate the promise and achievement it fostered. The really sad feature is that the artistic virtues which the commercial confidence of the Americans called into being should not have developed – or not yet, anyhow – into talents as sophisticated, individual, and free of social constrictions as the best European talents.

Where in the period under review does one look for the British equivalent of Bergman, or Forman, or Rohmer, or Antonioni, or Truffaut, or even Godard? The answer is, nowhere. Style is attitude, Lindsay Anderson has said: yes, but it is also aesthetic. And it is the inability, or disinclination of even established-name directors in Britain to articulate a view of life and society in freshly conceived and individual terms, and to translate these aesthetically to the screen with an unmistakable signature, that which one most feels the absence of during the 1960s. In part, this was due to the industry set-up; in greater part, probably, it was due to the 'literary' bias of the cinema. So many of the directors were dependent on the novels, plays and television programmes that had already been seen, read and acclaimed that their work was inevitably one of transplanting the creative talents of people other than themselves – doing so with consummate craftsmanship, admittedly, but without the temperament of a true *auteur*. It is hard to think of half-a-dozen films which were created *as films* during the era, and not simply re-created as the screen versions of other tried and proven works: *A Hard Day's Night, If . . .*

certainly, and shall we admit *Blow-Up* and stretch the limits of the 1960s to include *Performance*? At least there are four films that seize the essence of the 1960s and express it in concepts that have an authentic aesthetic freshness that hasn't been drained off from the theatrical production or the printed word. They are also four of the most sheerly 'visual' films the decade produced.

The decade began with a great gain for realism. The films that followed *Room at the Top* at least freed the cinema from a lot of its clichés and stereotypes, opened up a far greater area of geography than we had been permitted to see before, and took us into social territory that for a time was individual human territory, too, before it turned into 'sociology.' The trouble was that what was 'unique' tended so quickly to turn into what was 'representative' – so that instead of reacting to what was extraordinary about the characters in the films, one found oneself anticipating what it was they had in common with those of other films. The trend kills the innovation; and what was so depressing in the early years of the 1960s was to realize how quickly it did so – so that the retreat from social realism, which began with the exploration of the characters' fantasies and memories, was embraced with relief by the very critics who had been calling out for a 'look at life' that was real and earnest. It is round about 1963, as has already been mentioned, that one senses the cinema pulling back geographically from the provinces to the metropolis and reflecting or being infected by the excitements of a society in the grip of what Christopher Booker diagnosed – for the most part accurately, I think – as a vast vitality fantasy. Once the cinema began relaying the sensations of the market-place, where youth and affluence were the predominant values, it became subject itself to market pressures. It could be manipulated, exploited, promoted – everything could be encapsulated in a trend and packaged for home consumption or export. The phenomenon of 'Swinging Britain' lent international fascination to what was happening in the country – or at least what many believed was happening, which was almost the same thing. Before one crows too cynically at the gullibility of readers of *Time*'s view of 'London Life' as a series of movie scenarios, in continuous dissolve, one should remember there were plenty of native Britons who willingly exchanged the 'reality' for the 'fantasy' and, like the photographer in Antonioni's film, soon heard the sounds of 'playtime' where there had only been silence before.

At least the British cinema, encouraged by the much more merchandise-conscious reach of Hollywood, grasped the dominant life-styles of these years as they succeeded each other in bewildering acceleration. One could write a social history of the country simply by analysing the content of the movies – and, sometimes, not even the content, but just the style. At its worst, it seemed the cinema was a continuous commercial whose dimensions were those of 'sheer fantasy' – the uninhibited sex, the progressive nudity, the frivolous dress, the rhythm of pop music, the visual intensity, the affluent hedonism of all descriptions. Everything was marketable, being sold back to the public who inspired it, or remade in an even newer trend when they had sickened of it. So strong was the drive to promote novelty that art rarely had the time to seek a pattern in the phenomena – and when it did, as in *Morgan* or *Performance*, it took the disquieting form of a withdrawal into insanity or some separate reality. How swiftly the artists lent themselves to selling-trends in the cinema: exploiting the milieu for its exoticism! Small wonder, either, that when the rest of the world ceased to be interested in the trends, or developed a greater fascination with their own phenomena, there was a sense of exhaustion and bankruptcy in Britain.

To retrieve a sense of momentum, it is probable that film-makers will have to focus once more on the milieu – not on the saleable items of short-lived sensation, but on the social realities whose measure is not simply material pleasure. It may be harder to find the way back than it was to find the way forward a decade or so ago; it will certainly be harder to find what is unique and individual in society, which is where art has to begin, since individualism is sinking itself more and more into the identity of the group. The cry one hears now is one for meaning, not sensation. 'I was seen to be successful very quickly and I was disenchanted by it very quickly,' said Albert Finney, early in the 1970s, in words that contained an echo of the industry's wider disenchantment. 'You tend to forget the things that spurred you on to success, the cause of the revolution. There is the illusion that, because some of us achieved success and affluence, things may be a bit better – but the change is not nearly big enough. We've still got a long way to go before we change Britain.' Just as long a way, he might have added, before we change Britain's film industry.

1959   Year opened with air of despondency. Total admissions to the 3,400-odd cinemas in Britain were down during 1958 by 17%, to just over 600 million. Discontent voiced in House of Commons over Board of Trade allowing the new directors of British Lion, appointed in 1958, to obtain what was alleged to be a 'tax-free fortune' in return for minimal investment stake. British Lion answered by reference to the talent, commitment, etc., involved, and pointed out it was having to make TV series at Shepperton in order to keep studios open. Concern voiced by British Lion's chief, David Kingsley, about lengthening time between *premières* of their films and country-wide release which slowed up the cash flow on which future projects depended. In February, British MPs were urged to abolish war-time Entertainments Tax still being levied on cinemas: but the April Budget left it in place. Film unions, concerned about unemployment, urged the N.F.F.C. to invest in more films; but Pinewood Studios had to take in three major TV series to keep in good financial shape. Solace for tough economic position sought in boosting the box-office levy for second features, which now collected double the subsidy on first features. This was condemned as a retrograde step by some who pointed to public preference developing for bigger-scale films. At the end of March, Rank announced that its American film distributing division was shutting down: it had started two years earlier and was now running at a loss. In April, Bryanston was set up, a consortium of 16 independent producers headed by Balcon, tied in with British Lion, aiming to muster collective strength behind film-makers by offering distribution guarantee, freedom to directors, etc. N.F.F.C. reported a loss for year ending March, 1959, of £222,567 compared with £116,443 for 1958, which left only about £352,777 in the kitty for financing future British production. N.F.F.C's managing director, John Terry, called for more discriminating film-backing, recommended that stars should take smaller down-fees and shares of the net profits. Federation of British Film Makers, the chief grouping of independents, called 1959 'a very difficult year for independent producers,' but production began to pick up in mid-1959, chiefly through new independent groups like Beaver Films, making *The Angry Silence*, and Woodfall, producing *The Entertainer*; and in October, the expectation of things improving was boosted with announcement that Walter Wanger's *Cleopatra* would be filmed in England. In November, new production-distribution group of

Allied Film Makers (Forbes-Attenborough-Green, Dearden-Relph, Jack Hawkins) was set up. Year closed with *Kinematograph Weekly* declaring it to have been 'a significant one,' because of the unexpected increase in volume of production, 'from 76 to 86 first features, a new-found awareness that pictures can be adult and entertaining' – this was caused by successful release of the X.-rated *Room at the Top* – 'and the emergence of a new pattern of production and distribution in which creative individuals have as much say as impersonal mammoth corporation' – which referred to Bryanston and Allied Film Makers. British films premièred during year included: *Room at the Top*,[1] *The Horse's Mouth, Operation Amsterdam*,[1] *The Lady is a Square*,[1] *The Thirty-Nine Steps, The Doctor's Dilemma, Tiger Bay*,[1] *Sapphire*,[1] *The Mouse that Roared, The Scapegoat, Ferry to Hong Kong*,[1] *Blind Date*,[1] *Yesterday's Enemy, I'm All Right, Jack*,[1] *The Siege of Pinchgut*,[1] *Libel, North-West Frontier*,[1] *S.O.S. Pacific*,[1] *Expresso Bongo*,[1] *Our Man in Havana.*

1960 Cinema admission for the year 1959 went on declining, to below 600 million. Production in the studios encouragingly high at the start of year, but expectations of expansion not maintained: not even TV series could fill the gap as American networks were still undecided about whether the format should be full hour or half-hour. Relief came with April Budget, abolishing Entertainment Tax paid on admissions: it pleased exhibitors most of all, left producers dubious about whether benefit would be passed on to them. Federation of British Film Makers, in May, demanded increased production levy on box-office takings to yield yearly maximum of £5 million. It stayed the same. But by June production was rising, thanks partly to success in stimulating second-features. In July, 20th Century-Fox announced £7 million line-up of British productions, including *The Innocents* and *Cleopatra*. N.F.F.C's loss for year ending March, 1960, declared to be £194,095: John Terry stressed there must be wider acceptance of *pari-passu* recovery of investments, rather than N.F.F.C. finishing up last in line for profits as provider of the 'end' or 'risk' money. Industry view was that this would take a long time to gain acceptance. (It did – almost ten years.) British Lion showed a profit of £126,771, attributed to 'new blood' directors on the board who were also film-makers, plus outstanding success of *I'm All Right, Jack*. Bryanston given timely fillip by huge success of *Saturday Night and Sunday Morning* in Novem-

---

[1] Film made for a British, or preponderantly British production company and distributor. Films unmarked indicate existence of American interests.

ber. Dimensions of *Cleopatra* fiasco – attempt to film sunny Egypt in wintry England – became clear when filming was suspended in November and 1,000 jobs were threatened: it would later resume in Italy. Catastrophe involved cut-back in Fox's immediate British production plans. At end of December a Parliamentary Question to President of Board of Trade revealed that since 1954 about 24% of cinemas in Britain had closed permanently. Supplementary Question on monopolistic tendencies by remaining cinema circuits elicited no reply from Minister. British films premièred during year included: *The Battle of the Sexes*,[1] *Sink the Bismarck*, *Never Take Sweets from a Stranger*,[1] *Conspiracy of Hearts*,[1] *The Angry Silence*,[1] *The League of Gentlemen*,[1] *Peeping Tom*,[1] *Cone of Silence*,[1] *The Day They Robbed the Bank of England*, *Oscar Wilde*, *The Trials of Oscar Wilde*, *Never Let Go*,[1] *Sons and Lovers*, *Light Up the Sky*,[1] *The Millionairess*, *Saturday Night and Sunday Morning*,[1] *The Criminal*,[1] *Tunes of Glory*, *The World of Suzy Wong*.

1961   Outlook far from cheerful. Cinema admissions in decline at 520 million; 350 fewer cinemas. BBC TV begin screening 'X'. Certificate old movies, blamed for the falling box-office. 'National' cinema circuit abolished at the start of the year, depriving independent producers of outlets for films and strengthening duopoly position of Rank and A.B.C. circuits. Despite steady amount of work in the studios, a feeling that production steam generated by formation of new groups was falling off: Bryanston slipping back into pop formula films, though *Saturday Night and Sunday Morning* was the brightest thing in new cinema, taking over £100,000 in first three weeks on London A.B.C. cinema circuit. At end of July, Osborne and Richardson joined Bryanston. In August, British Lion announced landmark profit of £576,800 net up to 31 March, 1961. On 2 November, Woodfall announced million-pound programme to include *Loneliness of Long-Distance Runner*, *Tom Jones*, with Bryanston participation promised. On 30 November, Bryanston merged with Seven Arts (U.K.) Ltd, to finance 'five or six' big-budget features with 100% backing: first to be *Sammy Going South*, *Tome Jones*. British films premièred during year included: *No Love for Johnnie*,[1] *Whistle Down the Wind*,[1] *Victim*,[1] *A Taste of Honey*,[1] *The Innocents*, *The Full Treatment*, *The Long and the Short and the Tall*,[1] *The Rebel*,[1] *Very Important Person*,[1] *Mr. Topaze*, *The Greengage Summer*, *Flame in the Streets*,[1] *The Kitchen*,[1] *The Young Ones*.[1]

[1] See footnote page 468.

1962   Rank Organization began year with complaint that there was not enough good product to support a 'Third Circuit' of cinemas for independent releases. Admissions fell by 11% in 1961, to just over 449 million. Proposal to reform Eady Levy subsidy so as to assist art rather than simply reward success rejected by producer bodies: 'any limit would penalise success.' In May it was announced, *Tom Jones* was to be made by Woodfall for United Artists. British Lion again announced excellent profit for year ending 31 March, 1962, of £310,162. National Film Finance Corporation announced best-ever profit for same year of £49,564, as against previous year's profit of £18,441, but added: 'This does not mean that British films are generally profitable.' John Terry, N.F.F.C. managing director, commented that profitable opportunities were lost by not being able to option successful talents for future productions: he added, ominously, that N.F.F.C. contributed only quarter of British features on circuits – less than any previous year. Stricter selectivity essential. In July, producers' body asked Government to appoint committee to enquire into monopolistic practices in film industry. Request rejected. In July, provincial cinemas asked if they would play programmes, mostly independents' films, recommended by industry trade bodies. Proposal rejected. After tasting success in America with *A Kind of Loving*, Anglo-Amalgamated announced doubled budgets for future films. 'New Wave' features now passed into trade parlance – sure sign of an ending trend. E.g. *The Wild and the Willing*, 'a University story of the "new wave" category,' and *Live Now – Pay Later*, 'a kind of comic equivalent of *Saturday Night and Sunday Morning*.' Bryanston announced programme of modest-budgeted films for 1963. British films premiered during year included: *It's Trad, Dad! A Kind of Loving*,[1] *Term of Trial*, *Lolita, The Loneliness of the Long Distance Runner*,[1] *Billy Budd*,[1] *Dr No, Live Now – Pay Later*,[1] *The L-shaped Room, Lawrence of Arabia, Only Two Can Play*,[1] *The Waltz of the Toreadors*,[1] *Some People*,[1] *Life for Ruth*,[1] *The Dock Brief*,[1] *The Wild and the Willing*.[1]

1963   Cinema admissions for 1962 declined by 54 million; 240 fewer cinemas than in 1961. In February, Woodfall announced new film programme to be made for United Artists. Bryanston demoted some announced first-features to supporting-feature status. In March, Government hinted that N.F.F.C. could use option early in 1964 to buy out directors of British Lion: hint generally overlooked in industry. In July, Bryanston, entering fifth year with 18 first features,

[1] See footnote page 468.

announced three new modestly budgeted movies completed and hoped it would find early release for them. In September, trade bodies reported insufficient independent cinemas available to form 'Third Circuit' nucleus, would need to be augmented by more important circuit cinemas, and concluded this did not seem to be 'sufficiently attractive'. In October, independent producers' concern at being 'excluded' from early circuit release now manifested openly. Trade reaction unsympathetic. Rank Organization alleged small-budget movies lacked competitive edge: N.F.F.C. urged independent companies to 'pool or perish.' Producers' body urged Government to raise quota for British films from 30% to 50%, to assist independents, and bring 'economic sanity' into industry. In November, head of Rank Organization theatre division said public indifferent to origins of films, current trading conditions made 'Third Circuit' unrealistic, increased quota no solution. Rank and A.B.C. declared they already played more British movies than quota required. Redundancies at film studios. Bombshell dropped at end of December: N.F.F.C. to buy out share capital of British Lion. Independents in total disarray. British films premiered during year included: *This Sporting Life*,[1] *Sparrows Can't Sing*,[1] *Billy Liar*,[1] *Tom Jones*, *The V.I.P's*, *From Russia with Love*, *The Victors*, *The Servant*,[1] *Summer Holiday*,[1] *The Mind Benders*,[1] *I Could Go On Singing*, *The Wrong Arm of the Law*,[1] *Sammy Going South*, *Call Me Bwana*, *The Punch and Judy Man*,[1] *The Small World of Sammy Lee*, *The Mouse on the Moon*, *Heavens Above*,[1] *The World Ten Times Over*.

1964   Cinema admissions slumped in 1963 by 37,800,000: 240 fewer cinemas. Strong protests voiced over sale of British Lion to the Sydney Box group: likelihood of rival bidders. In January, Board of Trade came out against proposal to forcibly split off one-third of the country's cinemas and form a Third Circuit for independent productions: it also opposed raising quota for British films to 50%. David Kingsley, managing director of British Lion, claimed that 'In a short time in private ownership British Lion will have to come to terms with Rank and A.B.C. (cinema circuits), as all the American companies have done.' In that event 'the last competitive distributing company would disappear.' Promise given in early January that no deal of any kind would be concluded before Parliament reassembled in mid-month. Subsequently other bids were invited. Potential bidders multiplied, but numbers greatly diminished again after Government announcement that the successful buyer would

---

[1] See footnote page 468.

not benefit from £2 million tax loss, nor be able to dispose of Shepperton film studios without N.F.F.C. permission. Industry stimulated by overseas receipts of *Tom Jones* which had grossed nearly $1,500,000 in only 18 theatres in twelve U.S. cities. Further good news came from M.G.M. announcement of nine films to be made in British studios at Borehamwood, and Paramount's plans for 17 movies, budgeted at £9 million, to be made in next year, some of them in Britain. Improvement in production scene called 'dramatic.' By mid-March, Balcon group won control of British Lion – expectation of 12 films a year. By June, British Lion announced list of projected films and B.F.P.A. urged release of money to get production going again by independent film-makers. Growing realization that there were now insufficient areas in Britain with cinemas located in them to enable a Third Circuit to be set up, even if exhibitors agreed. British Lion report for year ending March, 1964, showed effect of production hiatus: profit slumped from £418, 181 in 1962 to £240,694. N.F.F.C. announced that in future it would switch loans to the 'more profitable, bigger budget type of production' – less dependence on 'chancy' films in the £100,000– £120,000 range. Excitement in August when Government, under pressure, decided to refer the question of supply of films for exhibition in British cinemas to the Monopolies Commission. In September, Anglo-Amalgamated announced £3 million production programme of British films, beginning in 1965 with *Darling*. In October, F.B.F.M. warned that Monopolies Commission report might be a lengthy time in coming. In December, George H. Ornstein, head of United Artists production in Britain, announced resignation – effective from spring, 1965 in order to turn to 'packaging' films in association with Brian Epstein's company. British films premiered during year included: *Ladies Who Do*,[1] *Zulu*, *The Leather Boys*,[1] *Charade*, *Carry On, Jack*, *Dr Strangelove, or How I Learned to Stop Worrying and Love the Bomb*, *Nothing But the Best*,[1] *The Caretaker*,[1] *Becket*, *A Jolly Bad Fellow*,[1] *Woman of Straw*, *The Pumpkin Eater*, *The Girl With Green Eyes*,[1] *French Dressing*,[1] *Night Must Fall*, *Seance on a Wet Afternoon*,[1] *Wonderful Life*,[1] *A Hard Day's Night*, *Lord of the Flies*, *Goldfinger*, *Guns of Batasi*, *It Happened Here*,[1] *The Comedy Man*.[1]

1965 Cinema admissions dropped by 14,427,000 in 1964: 124 fewer cinemas. In February, N.F.F.C. and Rank announced joint production venture with £1,500,000 revolving fund: choice of subjects

[1] See footnote page 468.

left to N.F.F.C. which revealed British Lion had turned down similar proposal a year earlier. Rediffusion TV ended up possessing 30-odd features made by Bryanston: thus ended consortium venture. Balcon called TV's deal 'a wonderful bargain.' All the signs of industry boom. In February, Anglo-Amalgamated announced £3 million programme. British Lion, not to be outdone, announced £2 million one for 'about a dozen features over the next year or two' – but few of films listed made by British Lion. In March, United Artists declared record profits, £4 million of which was due to British productions. Having urged British film quota be raised to 50% in 1963 as protectionist policy, producers' body now urged it be kept at 30%, lest higher figure harm British film exports. Shepperton Studios showed increased profit on last year; but British Lion, studios' owner, hung fire over anticipated production increase – Balcon blaming American majors for attracting away best film-makers with more lavish deals. British Lion group profit shrank to £194,741 in 1964. Balcon resigned as chairman, disenchanted with prospect. N.F.F.C. lost £265,555 on year ended 31 March, 1965, and spoke of American financial domination 'if allowed to expand unchecked,' posing 'threat to the continuation of a truly British film production industry.' Bigger plans afoot by end of year for American production in Britain. In November, Universal announced massive film-making programme for 1966 in Britain headed by Jay Kanter. Expanded British production offices in M.G.M., 20th Century-Fox, Columbia, Embassy, Filmways, and other American independents, establish British bases. Shortage of film labour in the industry. British films premiered during year included: *One Way Pendulum,*[1] *Young Cassidy, The Ipcress File, The Knack, The Hill, Repulsion,*[1] *Catch Us If You Can,*[1] *Help! Darling,*[1] *Lord Jim, The Yellow Rolls-Royce, Joey Boy,*[1] *Two Left Feet,*[1] *Masquerade, Rotten to the Core,*[1] *You Must Be Joking, The Bedford Incident, The Collector, The Nanny,*[1] *The Wild Affair,*[1] *The Amorous Adventures of Moll Flanders, Those Magnificent Men in their Flying Machines.*

1966 Further fall in cinema admissions – down by 16,200,000 in 1965. But production rose: 61 feature films in 1965 as against 58 in 1964. Year got off to good start with nine new American-financed productions, and announcements for future movies from Universal, Columbia, Warner-Seven Arts. The 'new wave' was officially pronounced 'dead' by several production chiefs: 'escapism' was declared to be the 'new mood' – general air of thankfulness that

[1] See footnote page 468.

cinema was at last back to something it understood, that lent itself
to trad. methods of promotion and wasn't at the whim of *auteur*
directors. United Artists announced record profits – British-financed
films again heavy contributors to them. In mid-April Paramount
announced they were stepping up production in Britain, beginning
with *Half-a-Sixpence* musical. Warners announced at end of April
expanded production programme in Europe, including films to be
co-financed with Rank. By mid-June British Pay TV had been five
months in operation without adversely affecting cinema takings and
now wanted to expand: permission not given by Government.
Peak reached in the 'Anything British' euphoria. Returning Rank
executive spoke, in July, of American acceptance: 'Anything you
like to name as British is going out there.' New American group,
National General, moved into British production in July, announcing
plans for six movies a year. National Film Finance Corporation, in
report for year ending March, 1966, welcomed 'a livelier industry,'
but announced a loss of £292,245. Monopolies Commission sent its
report to Board of Trade in August: industry interests awaited its
publication apprehensively or hopefully. British financial crisis resulted in sudden imposition of severe credit squeeze on all sections
of economy from mid-1966. N.F.F.C. forced to totally suspend its
loans from September as its credit had been limited to £750,000
and all of this sum was already committed. Selective Employment
Tax further increased sudden descent of woes on film industry:
Andrew Filson, director of Federation of British Film Makers,
warned: 'Once you create any disincentives, people will cease to
think of Britain as *the* production centre.' Monopolies Commission
report published at end of October. Bitter disappointment experienced by independent producers and distributors at lack of teeth
and refusal to interfere in more than minor ways with duopoly of
cinema circuits, notably outright rejection of 'Third Circuit' hope.
Corresponding righteous concordance expressed by Rank and
A.B.P.C. Executive of latter group called report 'a vindication of
the part played by A.B.P.C. in the British film industry.' In November, Seven Arts acquired one-third of Warners, George H. Ornstein
took up functions as Paramount's new production chief in Europe,
announced intention to supply half the company's product and
make some 15 films in Europe, mainly Britain, in months ahead.
Rift in British Lion, with Balcon and J. Walter Reade bidding to
acquire control, backed by an unnamed financier 'Mr. X'. Industry
ended year still on the crest of rolling, almost wholly American wave
of film production. British films premiered during year included:

[1] See footnote page 468.

Life at the Top,[1] *The Spy who came in from the Cold, Thunderball, Bunny Lake is Missing, Where the Spies Are, Alfie, Morgan, A Suitable Case for Treatment,*[1] *Modesty Blaise, Othello,*[1] *Cul de Sac,*[1] *Khartoum, The Wrong Box, Arabesque, I Was Happy Here,*[1] *Kaleidoscope, Georgy Girl, The Blue Max.*

1967　Estimated British first features for 1966 number 65, compared with 61 in 1965. Trade press writers noted full-spate trend in 'ambitious international films with "Made in Britain" label.' Universal programme at its peak. In January, Paramount announced biggest world production programme for 20 years, with British features bulking large. Industry euphoric, experienced technicians at a premium. Monopolies Commission's recommendations, including more flexible film bookings and trial runs of minority-interest movies, accepted as whole by producers' body not disposed to argue for more at time of full production. No fewer than 15 movies shooting in Britain at end of February. British Lion rift continued: in March, J. Walter Reade reported wishing to sell his holdings after unsuccessful bid, along with Balcon and 'Mr. X,' to secure control of British Lion last year. In March, E.M.I. took over Grade Organization: first move into production-distribution-exhibition industry. In May, United Artists with 15 British films already completed announced more to be made in Britain. In July, Seven Arts completed acquisition of Warner Brothers, prepared to start British film-making programme. 20th Century-Fox had biggest-ever British film roster shooting by mid-summer. N.F.F.C. loss for year ending 31 March, 1967, was £369,699; announced suspension of Rank-N.F.F.C. consortium film-making programme till further revenues came in, and declared financial support of U.S. companies welcome – 'Without it, indeed, there would scarcely be a film industry here.' N.F.F.C's own lending activities, suspended due to continuing credit freeze, allowed to resume in August on limited scale. Cinema admissions in 1966 estimated 289 millions, a decrease of 37 million on previous year: 111 fewer cinemas. British films premiered during year included: *A Countess from Hong Kong, Mademoiselle, The Family Way,*[1] *Accident,*[1] *The Deadly Affair, Funeral in Berlin, A Man for All Seasons, Marat/Sade,*[1] *Blow-Up, Casino Royale, Privilege, You Only Live Twice, The Jokers, The Sailor from Gibraltar, Two for the Road, Ulysses,*[1] *The Naked Runner, Our Mother's House, To Sir, with Love, The Whisperers, The Dirty Dozen, How I Won the War, The Penthouse, Far from the Madding Crowd, Bedazzled, Billion Dollar Brain, Dutchman,*[1]

[1] See footnote page 468.

I'll Never Forget What's-'is-Name,[1] *Night of the Generals, Drop Dead, Darling, The Double Man, The Shuttered Room, Robbery, Pretty Polly, Dr. Faustus.*

1968 Renewed despondency over continuing drop in admissions, down by 24,000,000 in 1967. Year also got off to a shiver of apprehension about the pull-out of American finance. Film Production Association of Great Britain made immediate approach to Board of Trade following President Johnson's announcement of the curtailment of U.S. investment in Europe in order to assist country's balance of payments. Hopes expressed it would not affect local production level. Feature films produced in Britain in 1967 numbered 76, compared with 63 in 1966: of those 76, over 60 were wholly or partly financed by U.S. money. Paramount announced biggest-ever world production roster, including some films destined to run up biggest ever budgets in inflationary spiral ahead. (In United States, Jack Valenti announced at end of January that eight members of M.P.A.A. were committed to no fewer than 117 U.S.-based films in 1968, at cost of $306 million – highest commitment for five years.) At start of February, E.M.I. bought Warner-Seven Arts stake of 25% in Associated British Picture Corp. for £9,500,000 – intended to make offer for remaining 75%, making total of £38 million. Production boom continued to reach new levels: 12 first features by mid-February, compared with seven at same time in 1967: by mid-March, 19 features before the cameras. In April negotiations for E.M.I. to buy rest of A.B.P.C. fell through following failure to agree on acquisition of latter's TV interests. Smaller U.S. companies continuing to move into Britain. In July, Commons expressed concern about investment level of U.S. in British film industry: level of 'overseas' investment in British films estimated to be £15 million in 1965, £18 million in 1966, nearly £21 million in 1967. Strains inside Paramount reflected in mid-July announcement of more power being concentrated in Hollywood studio, as distinct from British operation. N.F.F.C. report for year ending 31 March, 1967, announced corporation had come near to breaking even – loss of £199,000 compared with £369,699 in 1966. *The Family Way* and *Poor Cow* had been two films making 'massive contribution' to N.F.F.C. funds, proving still need for N.F.F.C. services despite immense U.S. investment – nevertheless N.F.F.C. announced it would be entering into co-financing arrangements with Paramount for two features. Boom conditions producing their own backlash of apprehension. By mid-August the F.P.A. asked Government to re-finance the N.F.F.C. against the possibility of American withdrawal: Andrew Filson, now F.P.A. director, said, 'It is in the national interest as well as the industry's for British production to have a significant section of British finance.' At end of August, leader in *Kinematograph Weekly* asked: 'Have the Americans overreached themselves in their investment in British film production?' Bad news of box-office for American-financed British-made films in U.S. kindled fears further. 'It is certain,' continued *Kinematograph Weekly*, 'that too much artistic freedom has been allowed to young talents with not enough experience of, or regard for, popular boxoffice . . . The situation, too, is affected by American pressures to boost feature film production in Hollywood.' But still the Americans came to Britain – Commonwealth United established London base in August. Much whistling to keep courage up by those who (correctly) felt it was too good to last: a count made in September indicated 16 films being shot in Britain or elsewhere, either of British nationality or using British crews and stars, by American majors. All of them, later, flopped at the box-office, some disastrously so (M.G.M's *Alfred the Great*); none was a big money-maker, several were not released till years later (*The Adventures of Brigadier Gerard*) and some were never released but sold direct to television (*The Picasso Summer*). Every week brought black predictions of American finance being reduced from flood to trickle. High profits being made in U.S. by indigenously American films (*Bonnie and Clyde, The Odd Couple, The Graduate, Rosemary's Baby, In the Heat of the Night*) blamed for this. Pay Television in Britain, begun with high hopes by limited area coverage in January, 1966, ended abruptly in November, 1968, company blaming Government fixed ceiling of 150,000 subscribers till end of 1976 as non-viable. Year ended with prayers going up that Hollywood would not desert Britain – less strong was the actual belief that U.S. cash would remain. British films premiered during year included: *Here We Go Round the Mulberry Bush, The Anniversary,*[1] *Up the Junction, Romeo and Juliet, Sebastian, Eye of the Devil, 2001: A Space Odyssey, The Charge of the Light Brigade, Work is a Four-Letter Word, Oedipus the King, Petulia, Yellow Submarine, Prudence and the Pill, The Bofors Gun, Charlie Bubbles, The Strange Affair, The Decline and Fall . . . of a Birdwatcher!, Interlude, Oliver!, The White Bus, Duffy, Thirty is a Dangerous Age, Cynthia, The Long Day's Dying, The Bliss of Mrs. Blossom, Till Death Us Do Part,*[1] *If . . ., Deadfall, Only When I Larf, Witchfinder General.*[1]

1969   Cinema attendances down nearly 28 million in 1968. Industry's sense of flux increased by bid in early January of £34 million from

[1] See footnote page 468.

E.M.I. conglomerate for Associated British Picture Corporation. Rejected, even when sweetened to £40 million. George H. Ornstein decided in mid-January to resign as Paramount's production chief in Europe: it was announced from Hollywood he would not be replaced – which was taken as omen of declining American interest in British film scene. *The Times*'s Business Review predicted on 11 February that American investment in U.K. would slacken and *Kinematograph Weekly* was moved to hope smaller U.S. film companies would take up the slack. One of these, Commonwealth United, announced a Eurobond fund raising plan to stimulate U.K. production: but it was shortly to be involved in the collapse of Bernard Cornfeld's I.O.S. empire. At start of February, E.M.I. announced it had gained controlling interest in A.B.P.C. At end of the month Jay Kanter resigned as Universal's head of production in Britain. (He would go into independent production, later return to Hollywood to head the First Artists consortium of producer-stars.) Warner-Seven Arts rejected overtures from Commonwealth United in March, preferring to accept one from Kinney National and George H. Ornstein was made chief of Warner-Kinney's (later Warner Communications) foreign production in mid-1969. Show-business impresario Bernard Delfont moved into film production at A.B.P.C's Elstree studios. Bryan Forbes appointed head of production at Elstree in May and in August it was announced E.M.I. would make 15 features for the world market there. This cheered up industry, as it suggested the gap left by the vanishing Americans would be filled by home-made product. In June it was estimated there had been no drop in British production in the first six months of the year compared with same period in 1968 – 24 films in the studios or on location. But not to be ignored was the fact that some of these were much smaller-budgeted or less ambitious films and that some of the American majors had no films shooting or scheduled. Dimitri de Grunwald had a roster of British independent productions under way, financed by merchant bank in City of London and pre-sold to territories round the world. News from N.F.F.C. was brighter: it made its second-biggest profit, nearly £300,000, for year ending 31 March, 1969, a substantial part of it coming from *Poor Cow*, *The Family Way* and *Ulysses*: but it pointed to a 10% cut in British films financed wholly or partly by U.S. money. Year ended on an extremely jittery note, much hanging on Elstree's film production programme, on non-major American companies, and on the self-help efforts of few remaining British independent producers or groups. Final wave of depression occasioned in December by rumours (soon substantiated) of M.G.M. cancelling work on films due to start shooting at their Borehamwood British studios. British films premiered during year included: *Dance of the Vampires*, *Boom!*, *Twisted Nerve*,[1] *Shalako*, *Joanna*, *Play Dirty*, *The Lion in Winter*, *A Midsummer Night's Dream*, *Isadora*, *The Prime of Miss Jean Brodie*, *Where's Jack? Lock Up Your Daughters*, *Oh! What a Lovely War*, *All Neat in Black Stockings*,[1] *The Assassination Bureau*, *Hannibal Brooks*, *Ring of Bright Water*, *Sinful Davey*, *Inadmissible Evidence*, *Otley*, *Secret Ceremony*, *The Italian Job*, *Can Heironymus Merkin ever forget Mercy Humppe and find True Happiness?*, *Alfred the Great*, *The Dance of Death*, *Laughter in the Dark*, *Three into Two Won't Go*, *The Best House in London*, *Battle of Britain*, *The Madwoman of Chaillot*, *A Touch of Love*, *The Royal Hunt of the Sun*, *The Virgin Soldiers*, *Women in Love*, *The Magus*, *Goodbye, Mr. Chips*.

1970   Admissions went on falling in 1969 by over 22 million, a drop of 9%: but increase in box-office prices resulted in high gross takings, up from £57,677,000 in 1968 to £57,695,000. Approximately 1,558 cinemas open in Britain – 1,942 fewer than in 1959. In early January, Max Setton was appointed Paramount's head of European production. M.G.M. announced it would make between 10 and 12 films a year from its London base; this did nothing to allay rumours of imminent M.G.M. studio closure, which was again denied. In late February, George H. Ornstein resigned as head of Warner's foreign production. (He would soon retire to live in Spain.) Smaller American companies in Britain began slowing down production in response to 'ever changing market.' In late April, closure of M.G.M.'s British studio announced; M.G.M. would link up with E.M.I. to operate latter's Elstree Studios almost opposite its own lot, which was declared 'no longer economically viable.' Calls followed for N.F.F.C. to step in and acquire M.G.M. studio. In July M.G.M.-E.M.I. announced co-production deal for four films. Part of agreement was that M.G.M. would guarantee annual subsidy of £175,000 to re-named E.M.I.-M.G.M. Studios, Elstree. (In 1973, when M.G.M. was pulling out of all but major feature production worldwide, and assigning distribution rights in M.G.M. films to United Artists (U.S. releasing) and C.I.C. (elsewhere), M.G.M. was to give notice terminating subsidy to Elstree, which would contribute to bringing Elstree's by then depressed economic state near to one of closure.) At end of July it was stated in House of Commons that N.F.F.C. had no power to acquire M.G.M. studios, film unions were resigned to closure. British Lion studios at Shepperton hit by American cut-back, made profit of £46,848 in year ending March,

[1] See footnote page 468.

1970, compared with £65,534 for previous twelve months. (British Lion would be taken over by two City finance groups in quick succession in 1971–72: its Shepperton studios space would be reduced from 60 acres to 20 acres, to make it economically viable and save studios from possible complete closure.) In August, N.F.F.C. proposed forming a consortium of investors for financing films on a *pari-passu* basis. 'Several merchant bankers are at the edge of the water, but haven't got their feet wet,' said John Terry. N.F.F.C. had its functions extended to 1980 and £5 million to refresh its kitty as loans to film-makers. Omens seemed favourable for more sensible financing arrangements. (But in June 1971, Government would announce its intention to withdraw from financing film production and allow N.F.F.C. only £1 million on condition private finance sources put up £3 for every £1 from public funds. N.F.F.C. would obtain commitments from 11 private groups of only £750,000 to float its consortium. Government would relent slightly, contribute £1 million to National Film Finance Consortium which would be formed in May, 1972, with working capital of £1,750,000 – and no more cash to come from Government.) In November, Dimitri de Grunwald resigned from his independent production venture, London Screenplays, which, after a promising start, had hit troubles which led to disagreements with his City backers. In December, Sir Joseph Lockwood, E.M.I. chairman, spoke at annual meeting about company's film interests: 'I think we have got the situation under control. It's a little more risky than ordinary business. But we shall not allow ourselves to lose lots of money in film production.' Film-making continued at E.M.I.-M.G.M. Elstree Studios under Bryan Forbes, but disagreements appeared over type and profitability of films produced. (Forbes would resign as production chief in March, 1971.) Despondency was thick as the year ended. Although about 70 films, around the average yearly number in the 1960s, were in production in 1970, their budgets were smaller, their shooting time was shorter: most were made on location, leaving studios groaning under continuing heavy overheads. Industry hoped E.M.I. with 12 films and Rank with seven, plus independents, would fill the gap left by the Americans: but as some of the independents got into difficulties, the hopes were tenuous. In 1970 Columbia was the only American major to maintain its production in Britain, with six films. United Artists had only two M.G.M. three, Paramount two, and Universal and 20th Century-Fox had no British pictures in production. But for some people things were not so black: the Rank Organization announced an all-time high in profits, £15,060,000 in year ending June, 1970, an increase of 31% on the previous year. British films premiered during year included:

David Copperfield, The Looking Glass War, The Reckoning, Twinky, The Birthday Party, Spring and Port Wine,[1] Anne of the Thousand Days, The Last Grenade, The Magic Christian, The Sea Gull, On Her Majesty's Secret Service, The Bed Sitting Room, Entertaining Mr. Sloane, Kes, Hamlet, The Walking Stick, Julius Caesar, The Adding Machine, The Executioner, Hoffman,[1] Leo the Last, Ned Kelly, The Virgin and the Gypsy,[1] And Soon the Darkness,[1] The Games, The Man Who Haunted Himself,[1] Cromwell, Fragment of Fear, The Buttercup Chain, Bronco Bullfrog,[1] Three Sisters,[1] The Body,[1] Figures in a Landscape, Scrooge, The Private Life of Sherlock Holmes, Ryan's Daughter, The Railway Children,[1] There's a Girl in my Soup, Perfect Friday,[1] Loot.[1]

[1] See footnote page 468.

Index

Secombe, Harry, 223
Secret Ceremony (1968), 200, 345, 354–7
Sellers, Peter, 98, 223, 226, 229–30, 365, 431
Sequence, 27
Serpell, R. D., 259
Servant, The (1963), 205–18, 246, 288, 290, 300, 303, 368–9
Setton, Maxwell, 72, 73–4, 133–5, 138, 151, 288, 410, 458
Seven Arts Productions, U.K., 124, 134, 256. *See also* Warner-Seven Arts
Shaffer, Anthony, 434
Shapiro, Helen, 233
Shaw, Artie, 247
Shenson, Walter, 228–35, 237–8, 239, 241n., 267, 271, 396, 450–1
Shepperton Studios, 256, 257
Sherrin, Ned, 274
Sherwin, David, 401
Shipman, Gerald and Kenneth, 73
Shiralee, The (1956), 71
Shrimpton, Jean, 293, 294, 317, 349
Sidney, George, 394
Siege of Pinchgut, The (1959), 1971
Sight and Sound, 26, 53, 81, 156, 251
Signoret, Simone, 47, 51, 52, 91, 160
Sillitoe, Alan, 43, 80–5, 86, 109–10, 125–6, 127
Sinclair, Andrew, 432–3
Sleeping Tiger, The (1954), 200, 202
Sleuth (1972), 309
Slocombe, Douglas, 213–14
Smashing Time (1967), 262
Smight, Jack, 342
Smith, Constance, 92
Sons and Lovers (1960), 77
S.O.S. Pacific (1959), 98
Spare the Rod (1961), 74–5
Sparrows can't Sing (1963), 390
Speight, Johnny, 349
Spiegel, Sam, 87, 256
Spring and Port Wine (1970), 427
Spy who came in from the Cold, The (1966), 305

Stair, Bill, 384, 386
Stamp, Terence, 161, 290, 301, 349, 361
Stanley, Kim, 246–7
Star! (1968), 394, 443
Starr, Ringo, 238, 240. *See also* Beatles, The
Steele, Tommy, 231, 237, 394
Steiger, Rod, 347
Stein, Dr Jules, 343
Steinberg, Saul, 107
Stevens, Jocelyn, 40
Stockwell, Dean, 77
Stoppard, Tom, 384
Storey, David, 146, 171–2
Story, Jack Trevor, 168
Subotsky, Milton, 227
Sucksdorff, Arne, 434
Summer Holiday (1963), 262
Sunday, Bloody Sunday (1971), 453
Sunday Dispatch, 49
Sunday Times, 49
Sussex, Elizabeth, 29, 172

Tales of Beatrix Potter (1971), 432
Taste of Honey, A (play), 54; (film 1961), 65, 91, 120–3, 290, 352
Taylor, Elizabeth, 354–5
Taylor, Gilbert, 240–1
Taylor, John Russell, 76, 123, 217, 397
Tennant, Cecil, 136, 137
Tenser, Tony, 256
Terminus (1961), 115–16
Term of Trial (1962), 160–1, 209, 290
Terry, John, 256, 406–7
That was the Week That Was (TV programme), 274
They're a Weird Mob (1966), 336
Thirty is a Dangerous Age, Cynthia (1968), 396
This Sporting Life (1963), 146, 170–7, 404
Three into Two won't Go (1968), 345, 347, 357
Thunderball (1966), 186, 192
Thursday's Children (1953), 25